AF775148

Coercion

Coercion

The Power to Hurt in International Politics

Edited by KELLY M. GREENHILL

PETER KRAUSE

OXFORD
UNIVERSITY PRESS

OXFORD
UNIVERSITY PRESS

Oxford University Press is a department of the University of Oxford. It furthers the University's objective of excellence in research, scholarship, and education by publishing worldwide. Oxford is a registered trade mark of Oxford University Press in the UK and certain other countries.

Published in the United States of America by Oxford University Press
198 Madison Avenue, New York, NY 10016, United States of America.

© Oxford University Press 2018

All rights reserved. No part of this publication may be reproduced, stored in a retrieval system, or transmitted, in any form or by any means, without the prior permission in writing of Oxford University Press, or as expressly permitted by law, by license, or under terms agreed with the appropriate reproduction rights organization. Inquiries concerning reproduction outside the scope of the above should be sent to the Rights Department, Oxford University Press, at the address above.

You must not circulate this work in any other form
and you must impose this same condition on any acquirer.

CIP data is on file at the Library of Congress
ISBN 978–0–19–0–84634–3 (pbk.); 978–0–19–0–84633–6 (hbk.)

CONTENTS

ACKNOWLEDGMENTS

This book grew from a shared realization that the foundational scholarship on coercion that we regularly read, taught, and utilized was no longer adequate to explain much of the behavior we observed in the world around us. From forced migration in the Middle East and North Africa to cyber threats from Russia (and targeted sanctions on Russia), and from drone strikes in South Asia to terrorist attacks across the globe, understanding contemporary coercive dynamics clearly requires an expansion of our analytical toolbox to include new concepts, theories, and analyses. We are enormously gratified to be joined in this endeavor by a diverse array of experts who offer innovative and penetrating contributions on a diverse array of coercive tools, actors, and environments. Our editor, David McBride of Oxford University Press, offered enthusiastic encouragement from the outset, and his and the external reviewers' sharp insights helped shape the final product into a more cohesive and powerful book.

We thank the faculty and researchers of the MIT Security Studies Program, where we first rigorously studied coercion and learned to appreciate its myriad shades and manifestations. Kelly M. Greenhill further thanks Tufts University and the International Security Program (ISP) at Harvard University's Belfer Center for their intellectual and financial support of her research and, in the case of ISP, for its support of the Conflict, Security and Public Policy Working Group, out of which a number of contributions to this volume grew. She also thanks her *besheryt* for providing inimitable daily reminders that effective persuasion and influence also come in noncoercive packages. Peter Krause would like to thank all members of his research team, the Project on National Movements and Political Violence, especially Eleanor Hildebrandt. He also thanks his colleagues and administrators at Boston College, who provided academic and financial support for this volume. Finally, he thanks his parents and sisters who, in addition to a great deal of love, gave him his very first lessons in the causes, strategies, and effectiveness of coercion.

CONTRIBUTORS

Robert J. Art is Christian A. Herter Professor of International Relations at Brandeis University.

Jasen J. Castillo is Associate Professor in the Bush School of Government and Public Service at Texas A&M University.

Timothy W. Crawford is Associate Professor of Political Science at Boston College.

Alexander B. Downes is Associate Professor of Political Science and International Affairs at the George Washington University.

Daniel W. Drezner is Professor of International Politics at Tufts University's Fletcher School of Law and Diplomacy.

Keren E. Fraiman is a member of the faculty at the Spertus Institute.

Erik Gartzke is Professor of Political Science and Director of the Center for Peace and Security Studies at the University of California, San Diego.

Kelly M. Greenhill is Associate Professor and Director of the International Relations Program at Tufts University and Research Fellow at Harvard University's Kennedy School of Government.

Phil M. Haun is Professor and Dean of Academics at the US Naval War College.

Peter Krause is Assistant Professor of Political Science at Boston College and Research Affiliate at the MIT Security Studies Program.

Jon R. Lindsay is Assistant Professor of Digital Media and Global Affairs at the University of Toronto's Munk School of Global Affairs.

Austin Long is Senior Political Scientist at the RAND Corporation.

Jonathan N. Markowitz is Assistant Professor in the School of International Relations at the University of Southern California.

Todd S. Sechser is Associate Professor of Politics at the University of Virginia.

Tristan Volpe is Assistant Professor of Defense Analysis at the Naval Postgraduate School and Nonresident Fellow at the Carnegie Endowment for International Peace.

James Igoe Walsh is Professor of Political Science at the University of North Carolina.

INTRODUCTION

KELLY M. GREENHILL AND PETER KRAUSE

From the rising significance of nonstate actors to the increasing influence of regional powers, the nature and conduct of international politics has arguably changed dramatically since the height of the Cold War. Yet much of the existing literature on deterrence and compellence continues to draw, whether implicitly or explicitly, upon assumptions and precepts formulated in a state-centric, bipolar world. Although contemporary coercion frequently features multiple coercers targeting state and nonstate adversaries with nonmilitary instruments of persuasion, most literature on coercion focuses primarily on cases wherein a single state is trying to coerce another single state via traditional military means.

This volume moves beyond these traditional premises and examines the critical issue of coercion in the twenty-first century, capturing fresh theoretical and policy-relevant developments and drawing upon data and cases from across time and around the globe. The contributions examine intrastate, interstate, and transnational deterrence and compellence, as well as both military and nonmilitary instruments of persuasion. Specifically, chapters focus on *tools* (e.g., terrorism, sanctions, drones, cyber warfare, intelligence, and forced migration), *actors* (e.g., insurgents, social movements, and nongovernmental organizations), and *mechanisms* (e.g., triadic coercion, diplomatic and economic isolation, foreign-imposed regime change, coercion of nuclear proliferators, and two-level games) that have become more prominent in recent years but have yet to be extensively or systematically addressed in either academic or policy literature.

At the same time, there is also significant continuity in how states wield power and exercise influence. Strategic and crisis deterrence, threats backed with military force, and exercises of state-on-state coercive diplomacy are enduring features of international politics. Consequently, there remains a great deal of relevant wisdom in existing scholarship on coercion. Therefore, this volume also features chapters that proffer novel and innovative theoretical approaches to historical exercises in coercion and highlight the contemporary implications of historical cases. An introductory chapter offers an overview of the state of our knowledge about the theory and practice of coercion and analyzes the extent to which previous theories and arguments apply to current and future coercion challenges.

The chapters in this volume employ a variety of analytical tools and methods, including rational choice modeling, deductive theory building and extension, historical case study analysis, and large- and medium-N statistical analysis to shed new light on an old issue. The authors are equally diverse in their paradigmatic viewpoints, and several of the contributions wholly defy ready categorization in this regard. Power and its distribution, institutions, norms, ideas, and information all play analytically important roles, and several of the chapters combine these well-known variables in novel ways. In a similar vein, some commonly recognized theoretical concepts are deployed in as yet underappreciated yet analytically quite profitable ways. In sum, while no single volume of several hundred pages can be truly comprehensive, this book offers readers a hearty and edifying brew of old and new, of continuity and change, and of the theory and practice of coercion.

The volume is organized into five sections that speak to our focus on increasingly relevant actors, tools, and mechanisms in the study of coercion. Taken as a whole, the contributors approach the topic of coercion with three key questions in mind: What have we long known and still know to be true about coercion? What did we once think we knew, but now know needs to be revised or reconsidered? What did we simply not think about before now? The next section offers a brief description of each of the chapters within the five sections and their initial answers, grouped by relevant themes. The final section offers some ideas for instructors and others seeking to use this book to get smart about the power to hurt in today's world.

A Preview of the Chapters in This Volume

Coercion: A Primer

The volume opens with an introductory essay by Robert J. Art and Kelly M. Greenhill that lays the groundwork for the chapters that follow by offering an analytical overview of the state of the art in the study of coercion. Their chapter is loosely organized around the three key questions that motivate this volume. Art and Greenhill systematically interrogate the premises that undergird our assumptions about coercion and explore issues of continuity, change, and innovation in our understanding of coercion in the twenty-first century. In addition to identifying foundational insights from the traditional (state-to-state, Cold War–focused) coercion literature, the authors also highlight more recent, post–Cold War contributions as well as particular questions and heretofore underexplored topics examined by the contributors to this volume.

In chapter 2, Austin Long extends Art and Greenhill's discussion of coercion by analyzing its understudied yet integral connections with intelligence. Drawing upon evidence from Iraq to illustrate his key propositions, Long identifies three central ways in which intelligence and coercion are inextricably linked. First, intelligence provides a coercer with an understanding of a target's values, resolve, and capabilities, and thus the capacity to evaluate whether coercion is feasible. Second, intelligence effectively directs the tools of coercion—whether military force or economic sanctions—at specific elements of a target's political, economic, or military assets. Third, intelligence provides a discrete mechanism of influence—covert action—that lies between the overt use of military force and other nonviolent mechanisms of coercion. In addition to highlighting the underappreciated role of intelligence, Long sets the stage for subsequent contributions that focus on the importance of information in effecting successful coercion.

Coercion in an Asymmetric World

Coercion is often not a confrontation among equals. Instead, stronger states regularly employ threats and the limited use of force against weaker ones. As the chapters in this section demonstrate, however, superior strength is insufficient to guarantee coercive success and, in some cases, can even be an obstacle to success. The authors in this section reveal that the coercer's selection of target and specific policy demands—often made amid significant uncertainty—drive the initiation, dynamics, and outcomes of coercion.

In chapter 3, Todd S. Sechser employs rational choice theory to delve into the dynamic, iterative processes that characterize the bargaining game that is coercive diplomacy. Sechser develops a model of crisis bargaining to evaluate the strategic choices faced by coercers. He explores how coercers weigh their desire for gains against the risk of war that inevitably rises when they make threats and demand concessions of targets, as well as how power and (often imperfect) information play into these calculations. Sechser's analysis generates two counterintuitive hypotheses that challenge conventional wisdom about coercion. First, greater military power emboldens coercers to make riskier demands, increasing the likelihood of coercion failure. Second, coercers are motivated to attenuate their demands when target resolve is high, thereby making coercion success against resolved adversaries more likely. Both insights underscore the importance of the magnitude of coercers' demands in analyses of coercive bargaining.

Focusing on the employment of coercion using both military and nonmilitary instruments of influence, in chapter 4, Phil M. Haun makes a broadly generalizable argument about how powerful states can squander their multidimensional coercive advantages over weaker adversaries by treating coercion as an exercise in brute force rather than as a bargaining game. Using the case study of the 1994 Kuwaiti border crisis between the United States and Iraq as a illustrative example, Haun demonstrates how, by failing to modify their own behavior in response to target concessions, strong states provide (weaker) targets no incentive to sustainably modify their behavior, leading to coercion failure, even by the most powerful of states. In such cases, states may accept coercion failure as the price for an ongoing, successful containment strategy.

In chapter 5, Alexander B. Downes explores the puzzle of why compellent threats that demand foreign leaders concede power seem to succeed so often. Drawing upon data from the Militarized Compellent Threat (MCT) data set, Downes argues that demands for regime change succeed so often (about 80 percent of the time) because, historically, such threats have largely been made against highly vulnerable targets, namely when the coercer possesses crushing material superiority, is geographically proximate to the target, and the target is diplomatically isolated. However, Downes cautions that before one concludes that regime change is easy, one should keep in mind that the conditions that made regime change successful in the past are not features of most recent attempts to persuade foreign leaders to step down. Thus in an era in which leaders have grown more willing to issue such demands, they have grown correspondingly less likely to engender the desired response and coercive success.

Coercion and Nonstate Actors

Since the end of the Cold War, ongoing civil wars have outnumbered interstate wars by about 10 to 1. More people died in terrorist attacks in 2014 than ever before, and Americans regularly identify terrorism as the most critical threat to the nation. Nonetheless, we lack critical tools to understand and address issues associated with the violence perpetrated by nonstate and substate actors because the vast majority of existing studies still focus on states coercing other states. The chapters in this section help address this lacuna by exploring how states can coerce terrorists and insurgents via drones and state sponsors, as well as how insurgents themselves effectively coerce governments.

In chapter 6, Keren Fraiman explores "transitive compellence," a method of coercion whereby states that seek to affect the behavior of violent nonstate actors (VNSAs) do so by targeting the states that host them. The expectation is that the real and threatened costs imposed by the coercer on the base state will then persuade the coercee to crack down on the VNSAs, leading to their containment within, or forceful eviction from, the base state. Fraiman argues that this trilateral brand of coercion is both more common and more effective than is generally recognized. This is because the conventional wisdom regarding base state capabilities and motivations—that they are both too weak and too reluctant to take effective action against VNSAs—is wrong. Rather, many base states *are* in fact both capable and willing to effectively coerce VNSAs residing within their territory.

Nonstate actors are themselves often practitioners of coercion, rather than simply its targets. In chapter 7, Peter Krause explores the question of what makes nonstate coercion by national movements and insurgencies succeed or fail. The balance of power within a movement drives its outcome, Krause contends, and groups' positions within that balance of power drive their behavior. Although all groups prioritize their organizational strength and survival, hegemonic groups that dominate their movements are more likely to pursue the shared strategic objective of regime change and statehood because victory moves them from the head of a movement to the head of a new state. The hegemonic group's dominance enables its movement to successfully coerce the enemy regime by delivering a single clear, credible message about its objective, threats, and guarantees that is backed by a cohesive strategy. Krause demonstrates the viability of his generalizable argument with a longitudinal analysis of the Eritrean national movement and its decades-long insurgency against the Ethiopian government from 1960 to Eritrean independence in 1993.

In chapter 8, James Igoe Walsh evaluates the efficacy of drones as instruments of deterrence and compellence, especially in the context of counterinsurgency operations. Drawing upon evidence from a variety of theaters, including Pakistan, Afghanistan, and Iraq, Walsh argues that the use of drones can be a double-edged sword. On one hand, they offer noteworthy technological, force-protection-related, and collateral-damage-limiting advantages. On the other hand, the employment of drones often also catalyzes retaliatory and signaling counterattacks by insurgents and other VNSAs, which can in turn exercise deleterious effects on counterintelligence campaigns and undermine efforts at coercion.

Domains and Instruments Other than Force

State-to-state coercion still dominates the headlines, but it has increasingly taken on new forms and is transpiring in new domains. The United States is actively sanctioning Russia and China in response to increasing cyber attacks. The European Union (EU) and many Middle Eastern states are struggling, even teetering, under the political and economic weight of an unprecedentedly large influx of migrants and of refugees forced from their homes. At the same time, regional powers are scrambling to coercively compete over natural resources in the Arctic and the South China Sea. The chapters in this section provide powerful new theories and frameworks to explain how states coerce others using often effective, but understudied, instruments other than force.

In Chapter 9, Jon R. Lindsay and Erik Gartzke analyze the relationship between cyber means and political ends, an issue that was long neglected in the popular focus on technological threats. The authors present typologies of potential cyber harms in terms of costs and benefits and of political applications of these harms for deterrence and compellence. They then use the latter to explain why the distribution of the former is highly skewed, with rampant cyber frictions but very few attacks of any consequence. Specifically, they propose that a variant of the classic stability-instability paradox operates to constrain cyber conflict: ubiquitous dependence on cyberspace and heightened potential for deception expand opportunities to inflict minor harms, even as the prospect of retaliation and imperatives to maintain future connectivity limit the political attractiveness of major harms.

In chapter 10, Kelly M. Greenhill explains how, why, and under what conditions (the threat of) unleashing large-scale movements of people can be used as an effective instrument of state-level coercion. This unconventional yet relatively common coercion-by-punishment strategy has been used by both state and nonstate actors as a tool of both deterrence and compellence. After outlining the precepts of the theory, Greenhill illustrates this unconventional instrument in action with a longitudinal study of its serial use by the former Libyan dictator Muammar Gaddafi against the EU, from 2004 until his deposition in 2011. The chapter concludes with a discussion of theoretical and policy implications, observations about how this tool appears to be used increasingly as an alternative to or complement of military force, and what such developments might portend both for the future and for its real victims, the displaced themselves.

Timothy W. Crawford further expands our understanding of the dynamics of coercion in chapter 11 with the introduction of the concept of "coercive isolation." Coercive isolation refers to an oft employed but undertheorized nonmilitary instrument of coercive diplomacy that relies on manipulation and exploitation of shifts in a target state's alignments and alliances to influence its cost-benefit calculations and, by extension, the probability of coercive success. After presenting the theory of coercive isolation and the logic that undergirds it, Crawford offers a plausibility probe of six historical cases, from before World War I through the end of the Cold War, that illustrate the logic of the model and its key propositions. The chapter concludes with a discussion of contemporary theoretical and policy implications of the role played by coercive isolation in diplomacy in the post-post–Cold War world.

In chapter 12, Daniel W. Drezner examines the state of the literature on the coercive power of economic sanctions, with a particular emphasis on the use of targeted sanctions. Drezner argues that the development of smart sanctions has solved many of the political problems that prior efforts at comprehensive trade sanctions created. In many ways, these sanctions are, as advertised, "smarter," but there is no systematic evidence that smart sanctions yield better policy results vis-à-vis the targeted country. When smart sanctions work, they work because they impose significant costs on the target economy. It would behoove policymakers and scholars to look beyond the targeted sanctions framework to examine the conditions under which different kinds of economic statecraft should be deployed.

In chapter 13, Jonathan N. Markowitz asks why some states coercively compete militarily over the governance and distribution of natural resources, while others favor reliance on market mechanisms. In this hypothesis-generating contribution, Markowitz argues that the choices states make lie in their domestic political institutions and economic interests, which in turn determine their foreign policy interests. Specifically, he posits that the more economically dependent on resource rents states are and the more autocratic their political institutions, the stronger their preference to seek direct control over stocks of resources. Conversely, the less economically dependent on resource rents states are and the more democratic their political institutions, the weaker their preference to directly control stocks of resources. He presents and demonstrates the viability of his argument using a combination of deductive theorizing and historical analysis of recent jockeying over control of maritime seabed resources in the East and South China Sea, Arctic, and Eastern Mediterranean.

Nuclear Coercion: Regional Powers and Nuclear Proliferation

The field of coercion studies was founded on the analysis of nuclear weapons in the Cold War, and yet a number of related dynamics remain unexplained as a consequence of the field's traditional focus on strong states that already possess nuclear weapons. The chapters in this section focus on two types of significant coercive threats by relatively weaker states: the threat of nuclear weapon use to resist demands and ensure regime survival, and the threat of acquiring nuclear weapons to compel concessions.

In chapter 14, Jasen J. Castillo examines how the acquisition and threatened use of nuclear weapons can be utilized by weaker states to resist the demands of their more powerful counterparts. The uniquely destructive power of these weapons allows conventionally weak states a method of guaranteeing their survival and, due to the dangers of escalation, a potentially potent countercoercive tool. Employing an explicitly neorealist perspective, Castillo explores not only how regional powers may use such weapons as a powerful deterrent but also how they might theoretically employ them in war should deterrence fail.

In chapter 15, Tristan Volpe explores how states can use the threat of nuclear proliferation as an instrument of coercion. He argues that while the conventional wisdom suggests states reap deterrence benefits from nuclear program hedging, many use the prospect of proliferation not to deter aggression but as a means of compelling concessions from the United States. Some challengers are more successful than others at this unique type of coercive diplomacy, however. When it comes to cutting a deal, Volpe argues, there is an optimal amount of nuclear technology: with too little, the threat to proliferate is not credible, but if a country moves too close to acquiring a bomb, a deal may be impossible to reach since proliferators cannot credibly commit not to sneak their way to a bomb. Volpe draws upon the cases of Libya and North Korea to demonstrate the power of his theory in action.

Conclusion

The concluding chapter by Greenhill and Krause underscores the volume's key findings and their theoretical import, identifies policy implications and prescriptions highlighted by the contributions to the volume, and points to unanswered questions and directions for further research.

Suggested Ways to Use This Volume

The contributions to *Coercion: The Power to Hurt in International Politics* were solicited with a number of theoretical and pedagogical goals and approaches in mind.

First, the chapters were selected to provide both historical and theoretical perspectives on contemporary exercises of coercion from around the globe. While many chapters unsurprisingly offer evidence from North Africa and the Middle East, given recent history, the book also includes potent illustrations from East Asia, Southeast Asia, sub-Saharan Africa, Europe, and North and South America.

Second, a number of the chapters are designed to speak to ongoing policy debates. These include the efficacy of sanctions (Drezner and Haun) and other nonmilitary instruments of influence (Crawford, Lindsay and Gartzke, and Greenhill); the costs and benefits of using drones (Walsh); conflict over natural resources (Markowitz); the significance of failed and failing states in our understanding of the twenty-first-century security environment (Fraiman and Walsh); the virtues and vices of foreign-imposed regime change (Downes and Greenhill); the dangers of nuclear (counter)proliferation (Art and Greenhill, Castillo, Volpe, and Sechser); and the viability of deterring and/or quashing terrorist and insurgent activity (Fraiman, Krause, Walsh, and Long).

Third, a number of the chapters apply classic security studies and coercion-related concepts to new domains. These include but are not limited to Crawford's expansion and extension of George and Simons's "isolation of the adversary" in his exploration of diplomatic coercion; Krause's adaptation of balance-of-power theory to intragroup dynamics within insurgencies and national movements; Lindsay and Gartzke's application of traditional military force-on-force concepts to the realm of cyberspace; Sechser's expansion and relaxation of some long-accepted tenets about the nature of coercive bargaining and the significance of coercers' objectives, some of which are in turn profitably illustrated in Haun's case study; and Greenhill's explication of how and why cross-border population movements can be an effective coercion by punishment strategy. Markowitz draws upon traditional theories about institutions, interests, and state behavior to make predictions about future competition and conflicts, while Volpe integrates insights about the significance of credible assurances in facilitating successful coercion to the realm of proliferation.

Fourth, the grouping of the chapters by theme permits instructors to teach theoretical concepts in a fairly broad-based way. In addition to the current groupings of chapters by section, a number of other disparate chapters can be effectively coupled. These include but are not limited to the study of cross-domain coercion (Lindsay and Gartzke, Greenhill, Markowitz, and Haun); the critical role of information in coercion (Fraiman, Lindsay and Gartzke, Long, and Sechser); the role of regime type in influencing coercion processes and/or outcomes (Downes, Drezner, Markowitz, and Greenhill); and the particular dynamics of multilateral *and* multilevel coercion (Crawford, Drezner, Fraiman, Greenhill, and Krause). Finally, in addition to being an effective stand-alone overview of coercion, Art and Greenhill's introductory essay can be usefully assigned with any and all of the aforementioned units as a bridge from Cold War precepts to twenty-first-century applications.

In sum, *Coercion* combines classic tenets with contemporary innovations and applications. It is intended to connect and synergize scholarship on a broad array of exciting and timely topics and, in the process, help reinvigorate a crucial subfield of security studies and foreign policy. The volume has been designed to appeal to scholars, practitioners, and instructors who engage with coercion and foreign policy generally and with diplomacy, terrorism, sanctions, protest, refugees, nongovernmental organizations, and proliferation more specifically.

PART I | Coercion

A Primer

CHAPTER 1

Coercion

An Analytical Overview

ROBERT J. ART AND KELLY M. GREENHILL

JUST AS THE COLD WAR spawned a great deal of scholarly study about deterrence, so too has the unipolar era spawned a great deal of study of compellence.[1] The Cold War featured a nuclear standoff between two superpowers, one in which the survival of both countries was thought to be at stake. It is not surprising that deterrence of war, the avoidance of escalatory crises, and the control of escalation were paramount in the minds of academic strategists and political-military practitioners during this period. The bulk of the innovative theoretical work on deterrence, especially nuclear deterrence, was produced from the late 1940s through the mid-1960s. Most of the creative works during the subsequent years were, and continue to be, refinements of and elaborations on those foundations.[2]

With the advent of the unipolar era, the United States found itself freed from the restraints on action imposed by another superpower and began more than two decades of issuing military threats against or launching conventional military interventions into smaller countries, or both: Iraq (1990–91), Somalia (1992–93), Haiti (1994), North Korea (1994), Bosnia (1995), Kosovo and Serbia (1998–99), Afghanistan (2001), Iraq again (2003–11), Libya (2011), Syria (2014–), and Iraq yet again (2015–). Unsurprisingly, strategists and practitioners during the unipolar era became focused on various forms of compellence—compellent threats, coercive diplomacy, and the limited and demonstrative uses of force—and especially on the reasons those forms of compellence, when employed by the United States, more often than not failed and subsequently

[1] We thank Victoria McGroary for invaluable research assistance.

[2] For an excellent overview of the state of knowledge about deterrence through the 1970s, see Robert Jervis, "Deterrence Theory Revisited," *World Politics* 31 (1979): 289–324. For a representative view of the nature of deterrence today, see Patrick M. Morgan, "The State of Deterrence in International Politics Today," *Contemporary Security Policy* 33 (2012): 85–107.

required more robust military action for the United States to prevail. As a consequence of the unipolar era's change of focus, the literature on compellence burgeoned.[3]

More recently, and particularly in the aftermath of the game-changing terrorist attacks on September 11, 2001, there has also been a heightened focus on nonstate actors (NSAs). Academic works have focused on how NSAs employ coercion against states and against other NSAs (see, for instance, chapter 7); how states can most effectively deter and compel NSAs (and how such strategies may differ from coercion wielded by states; see chapter 6); and how NSAs attempt to compensate for their relative weaknesses through the use of asymmetric means (see chapters 8–10). In this period, there has been a nearly simultaneous increase in the nuance and breadth of scholarship that examines how coercion works when using tools other than (or in addition to) traditional military force and by actors other than the unipole. Such tools include targeted sanctions (see chapter 12), cyber weapons (see chapter 9), migration or demographic bombing (see chapter 10), and drones (see chapter 8). There has also been a growth in research that examines how coercive tools in one domain (for instance, cyber) can be used to influence outcomes in another (for instance, military capabilities), which Erik Gartzke and Jon Lindsay refer to as cross-domain coercion.[4]

While not providing a comprehensive review of all the theoretical and empirical scholarship on deterrence and compellence to date, this chapter does highlight the big findings about coercion, and by extension the big gaps in our understanding of it, as well as summarizes the contributions that the essays in this volume make to our understanding of coercion. The chapter proceeds as follows: Part one briefly defines coercion to include both deterrence and compellence, and shows why it can be hard to distinguish between the two in practice. Part two highlights salient points about deterrence, distinguishes among four types of deterrence, and discusses why deterrence can fail. Part three outlines the key contributions to our understanding of compellence that the past three decades of scholarship have revealed. Finally, Part four concludes with two sets of propositions about coercion—one that summarizes the state of our current collective knowledge and one that highlights new contributions proffered in this volume.

Coercion

Coercion is the ability to get an actor—a state, the leader of a state, a terrorist group, a transnational or international organization, a private actor—to do something it does not want to do. Coercion between states, between states and nonstate actors, or between nonstate actors is exercised through threats or

[3] For a partial list of works on compellence, see note 18.
[4] Erik Gartzke and Jon Lindsay, eds., *Cross-Domain Deterrence*, unpublished manuscript.

through actions, or both, and usually, but not always, involves military threats or military actions. Threats can be implicit or explicit. Coercive action may also utilize positive inducements. Offering such inducements may increase chances of success, but coercion is not coercion if it consists solely of inducements. Coercion always involves some cost or pain to the target or explicit threats thereof, with the implied threat to increase the cost or pain if the target does not concede.

The Two Faces of Coercion

Coercion comes in two basic forms: deterrence and compellence. Often the terms *coercion* and *compellence* are used interchangeably, but that erroneously implies that deterrence is not a form of coercion. This chapter therefore reserves the term *coercion* for the broad category of behavior that can manifest as either deterrence or compellence.

Used this way, deterrence is a coercive strategy designed to prevent a target from changing its behavior. "Just keep doing what you are doing; otherwise I will hurt you" is the refrain of deterrence. It operates by threatening painful retaliation should the target change its behavior. A state issues a deterrent threat because it believes the target is about to, or will eventually, change its behavior in ways that will hurt the coercer's interests. Thus getting an actor not to change its behavior, when its preference is to change its behavior, is a form of coercion. Compellence, on the other hand, is a coercive strategy designed to get the target to change its behavior.[5] Its refrain is "I don't like what you are doing, and that is why I am going to start hurting you, and I will continue to hurt you until you change your behavior in ways that I specify." Compellence, either through threat or action, is a form of coercion because the target's preference is not to change its behavior, but it is being forced to do so. So deterrence is a coercive strategy, based on threat of retaliation, to keep a target from changing its behavior, whereas compellence is a coercive strategy, based on hurting the target (or threatening to do so), to force the target to change its behavior. In both cases, the target is being pressured to do something it does not want to do.

Is It Deterrence or Compellence?

Defining the analytical distinction between deterrence and compellence is easy; applying the distinction in practice can be more difficult, for two reasons. First, in confrontational situations, there is the eye-of-the-beholder problem; second, particularly during crises, the deterrer may resort to compellent actions to shore up its deterrent posture.

---

[5] Thomas Schelling coined the term *compellence*. See Thomas C. Schelling, *Arms and Influence* (New Haven, CT: Yale University Press, 1966), 71.

In the eye-of-the-beholder problem, two actors look at the same action and see two different things. Just as one person's terrorist can be another person's freedom fighter, so too can one actor's deterrent posture look to the deterrent target as a form of compellence. When this occurs, the target of deterrence reasons thus: "With your threat to retaliate against me if I attempt to alter the status quo, you are, in effect, forcing me to accept the status quo, which I find illegitimate, disadvantageous, and unfair. It benefits you, but it harms me." Too often deterrence carries the connotation that the deterrer is justified in its actions, whereas the actor trying to change the status quo is viewed as the aggressor. (This is akin to asserting that he who attacks first is the aggressor, which may or may not be true.) Determining which actor is the aggressor hinges not on which actor is trying to overturn the status quo but instead on making a judgment about the legitimacy of the status quo. If the status quo is viewed by an uninvolved observer as just, then the actor trying to alter it will be viewed as the aggressor; if the status quo is viewed by the observer as unjust, then the actor trying to preserve it will be viewed as the aggressor. Assessing who is the aggressor is a different exercise than determining which state is the coercer and which the target. To be analytically useful, therefore, the concepts of deterrence and compellence must be separated from the exercise of assessing the legitimacy of the status quo.

The second reason distinguishing between deterrence and compellence can be difficult is that compellent actions are often undertaken in a crisis by a coercer in order to shore up its deterrent posture. Thomas C. Schelling put it well: "Once an engagement starts . . . the difference between deterrence and compellence, like the difference between defense and offense, may disappear."[6] For example, during the 1962 Cuban Missile Crisis, President Kennedy instituted a blockade around Cuba to prevent the Soviet Union from putting more missiles on the island. This was meant to demonstrate that Kennedy was serious about getting the missiles out by showing he was prepared to escalate the use of force. Blocking more missiles from coming in was a form of compellence.

Although the distinction between deterrence and compellence can sometimes blur in specific situations, and although compellence can be resorted to in order to shore up deterrence, the two concepts nevertheless retain their analytical distinctiveness and validity. After all, there remains a fundamental difference between trying to prevent changes to the status quo and trying to stop or reverse changes to the status quo. Preventing a target from changing its behavior is different from forcing a target to change its behavior. From these differences flow many important consequences for the use of military force and for its role in statecraft.

---

[6] Ibid., 80.

Deterrence

Deterrence can manifest in four distinct ways across space and time: homeland and extended, general and immediate. The first pairing refers to the territory being protected, the second to the temporal dimension in its use. Homeland deterrence, which is sometimes referred to as "direct deterrence," uses threats to dissuade an adversary from attacking a state's home territory and populace or any territories that it may have abroad. What is being protected is the territory over which the state exercises its sovereignty. Extended deterrence uses threats to prevent an adversary from attacking an ally or another state over which the defender is extending its security blanket. What is being protected is the territory of a third party or parties, often called the client state. General deterrence is about the long-term state of the military balance between two adversaries; immediate deterrence is about a specific crisis between them at a specific time.

Homeland and Extended Deterrence

One of the foundational propositions of deterrence theory is that homeland deterrence is easier to achieve than extended deterrence. The reason is that extended deterrence has less inherent credibility than homeland deterrence to a potential challenger. A potential challenger is more likely to believe that a deterrer will retaliate with force against the challenger if the challenger attacks the deterrer's homeland than if it attacks the client state's homeland. This is because, in either case, should the deterrer retaliate against the challenger's attack, the challenger is likely to counterretaliate against the deterrer. If this is the case, then which piece of territory is a deterrer likely to value more and, consequently, risk more: its own or that of its client state? Put simply: dissuading an attack on one's homeland is more credible than dissuading an attack on a client's homeland. Thus states that make extended deterrent pledges struggle to make them credible to both the client state and its potential attacker. Protectors have resorted to all sorts of mechanisms to make their pledges credible, including stationing the protector's troops (and in the case of nuclear-armed protectors, also tactical nuclear weapons) on the client's territory, providing reassurances through frequent policy pronouncements about the importance of the client to the protector, bending military strategy to satisfy political imperatives, and making shows of military force when necessary.

If homeland deterrence is inherently more credible than extended deterrence, then we should find fewer challenges to the former than to the latter. Although there is a scarcity of empirical work on this foundational proposition, a notable exception by Paul Huth, Christopher Gelpi, and D. Scott Bennett found that, for all the deterrence encounters among Great Powers between 1816 and 1984, 69 percent were cases of extended deterrence and 31 percent of homeland deterrence.[7] This result comports with the logic of the foundational

[7] See Paul Huth, Christopher Gelpi, and D. Scott Bennett, "The Escalation of Great Power Militarized Disputes: Testing Rational Deterrence Theory," *American Political Science Review* 87 (1993): Table

proposition. Ideally we would also like to know how many would-be challengers to homeland and extended deterrence decided, after assessing relative costs and benefits, not to challenge the status quo. However, this is somewhere between difficult to impossible to determine because the incentives for a would-be challenger are to keep such calculations from public view.

There are two other interesting insights to be gleaned from Huth et al. First, when the 1816–1984 period is taken as a whole, there seems to be no essential difference between success rates in forcing a challenger to back down in homeland deterrence cases and in extended deterrence cases. Of the 30 identified cases of homeland deterrence encounters, 17 were successful and 13 were failures (a 56 percent success rate). For the 67 extended deterrence encounters, 36 were successful and 29 were failures (a success rate of 55.4 percent). This success rate accords well with the pioneering work on extended deterrence undertaken by Bruce Russett and Paul Huth, who, after examining the universe of 54 cases of extended deterrence between 1900 and 1980, found that extended deterrence was successful 31 out of 54 times (a success rate of 57 percent).[8] Therefore the case for the inherently greater credibility of homeland deterrence compared to extended deterrence rests on the greater frequency of extended deterrence encounters, not on a difference in success rates once a deterrence encounter or crisis is entered into, assuming Huth et al.'s data set is valid.

The second insight is that extended deterrence was more successful from 1945 to 1984 than between 1816 and 1945. The data reveal not a trend over a long period of time toward greater success but rather a distinct break after World War II; extended deterrence was markedly more successful after 1945. The difference in success rates is most likely due to the impact of nuclear weapons on Great Power politics: those weapons made the superpowers, which were involved in the lion's share of the extended deterrent encounters from 1945 to 1984, more cautious in challenging one another. Fearon confirmed the heightened success rate of extended nuclear deterrence after reanalyzing the Huth and Russett data set. Fearon found that in the encounters where the deterrer

---

A-1, 620–21. The percentages are our calculations based upon the data in Table A-1. There were 30 cases of homeland deterrence crises and 67 cases of extended deterrence crises, for a total of 97 of what Huth et al. refer to as "deterrence encounters among the great powers." Danilovic found even more striking results: in her data set of deterrence crises from 1895 to 1985, there were 44 cases of extended deterrence crises but only four cases of direct or homeland deterrence failures. See Vesna Danilovic, *When the Stakes Are High: Deterrence and Conflict among Major Powers* (Ann Arbor: University of Michigan Press, 2002), 60 and Tables 3.2 and 3.3.

[8] See Paul Huth and Bruce Russett, "What Makes Deterrence Work? Cases from 1900–1980," *World Politics* 36 (1984): 505, Table 1. Also see Paul Huth and Bruce Russett, "Testing Deterrence Theory: Rigor Makes a Difference," *World Politics* 42 (1990): 466–501, in which they updated their data but with no substantial change in their conclusions. In their 1990 article, Huth and Russett were responding to a critique of their 1984 article by Richard Ned Lebow and Janice Gross Stein, "Deterrence: The Elusive Dependent Variable," *World Politics* 42 (1990): 336–69.

possessed nuclear weapons, extended deterrence worked 80 percent of the time, significantly more often than the 55–57 percent success rates identified above.[9]

What is the logic behind the increased caution of a challenger once nuclear weapons are introduced, and how are matters resolved if it comes to a deterrence encounter?[10] As argued earlier, protector states that issue deterrent pledges have to take steps beyond simply stating to any and all would-be challengers, "I will defend my client state with all means necessary, so don't mess with me—or else." Talk is cheap, so actions of some sort have to accompany such talk to establish credibility. This is true whether the protector and would-be challenger are just conventionally armed or one or both possess nuclear weapons.

When both protector and challenger have nuclear weapons, matters become even more complicated because nuclear weapons have a double effect—one on the protector, the other on the would-be challenger. On the one hand, nuclear weapons make it harder for the protector to convince a would-be challenger that it will retaliate, when to do so potentially subjects the protector to the challenger's (nuclear) retaliation. On the other hand, the second effect works on the would-be challenger's propensity for risk taking. The fear of loss of control—that things could escalate during a crisis to nuclear use—makes the challenger cautious about pushing too hard, even against a suspicious extended deterrence pledge. But if the challenger proceeds to launch a challenge, then the protector has to consider whether to respond, and it must then worry about the loss of control that *its* response could bring about. How matters are ultimately resolved, given these cross pressures, depends on the value the protector and would-be challenger put on their own respective interests, as well as on their estimates of how much the other values its interests.

During the Cold War, inherent doubts about extended deterrence were often phrased thus: "Would the United States risk Washington to defend Bonn against the Soviet Union?" Today we would phrase it "Will the United States risk Washington to defend Tokyo against Beijing?" There is always a level of doubt in the client leader's mind about how far its protector will go to defend it if the protector, by doing so, risks severe damage to its own populace and territory in the process. Nuclear weapons make this conundrum quite severe for the protector, but it exists with conventionally armed states as well because within the anarchic structure of international politics, no state can fully trust another to protect its interests.

---

[9] See James Fearon, "Signaling versus the Balance of Power and Interests: An Empirical Test of a Crisis Bargaining Model," *Journal of Conflict Resolution* 38 (1994): 253–55.

[10] What we are here calling a deterrence encounter is generally termed a "general deterrence failure" or an "immediate deterrence crisis," as will be explained shortly.

General and Immediate Deterrence

Immediate deterrence refers to a crisis, when a challenger is threatening to upset the status quo. General deterrence is about maintaining the status quo over the long term and keeping the deterrer so strong and capable that a potential challenger will never consider any alteration of the status quo.[11] Patrick Morgan puts it well: "General deterrence is to ensure that thinking about an attack never goes very far, so crises don't erupt and militarized disputes don't appear and grow."[12] Immediate deterrence deals with a situation wherein a challenger's thinking about an attack has advanced rather far, the parties are in a crisis, and they are clearly engaged in a militarized dispute (a situation where military threats are being used or when smaller scale military actions are taking place). General deterrence is closely related to the balance of power between two adversarial states. If the balance is stable, then general deterrence should remain strong. If general deterrence is unstable, then either an asymmetry in overall capabilities between the two adversarial states has emerged and it favors the challenger, or an advantage for the challenger in a specific locale has materialized—each of which will make the likelihood of a challenge more likely. In short, immediate deterrent crises can break out when general deterrence has failed.[13]

Deterrence Success and Failure

Finally, we must consider the circumstances that enable deterrence to succeed or fail. The elements of successful deterrence, about which vast amounts have been written, are actually simple in substance and few in number, although not always easy to obtain. Deterrence is most likely to succeed when the following conditions are satisfied. First, the deterrer has the capability to execute its deterrent threat, and the would-be challenger believes the deterrer has the capability to execute its deterrent threat, or the deterrer does not have the capability but the challenger thinks it does because the deterrer is a good bluffer. Second, the deterrer possesses the resolve (defined as the willingness of an actor to bear costs) to execute its deterrent threat should that be necessary, and the would-be challenger believes the deterrer has the resolve to do so and that the deterrer's resolve is stronger than its own. Third, the would-be challenger is a rational actor, which means that its behavior is purposive and that it

---

[11] It was Morgan who first made the distinction between general and immediate deterrence. See Patrick Morgan, *Deterrence: A Conceptual Analysis*, 2nd ed. (Beverly Hills, CA: Sage, 1983). Also see Patrick Morgan, *Deterrence Now* (Cambridge: Cambridge University Press, 2003), 80–86.

[12] Morgan, *Deterrence Now*, 80.

[13] The emphasis here is on the word *can*, not *will*. Danilovic found that out of 153 instances of general deterrence failure among major powers between 1895 and 1985, 105 cases (68.6 percent) never escalated into crises of immediate deterrence (*When the Stakes Are High*, 61 and Tables 3.1 and 3.2). For additional analyses of general deterrence, see Morgan, *Deterrence Now*, chapter 3, especially 159; Paul Huth and Bruce Russett, "General Deterrence between Enduring Rivals: Testing Three Competing Models," *American Political Science Review* 87 (1993): 61–73.

makes means-ends calculations based on cost-benefit considerations. Fourth, the would-be challenger believes that the deterrer's threat, if executed, would make the costs it incurs by challenging the status quo so much greater than the benefits it can possibly glean that it demurs from challenging the status quo. Ultimately, therefore, the credibility of a deterrent threat lies in the eyes of a would-be challenger.

How, then, can deterrence fail? In any number of ways, but essentially deterrence failure occurs if one or more of the above elements are absent. For purposes of simplifying the analysis of deterrence failure, Alexander George and Richard Smoke created a useful typology that describes the three circumstances in which an adversary might challenge the status quo and bring on an immediate deterrence crisis: the fait accompli, the limited probe, and the controlled pressure tactic.[14] All three challenger strategies have one element in common: the challenger believes that the potential dangers its actions create are both calculable (the risks are known) and controllable (the risks can be limited). The latter is key: the challenger must believe that it can control escalation so as to contain the costs that it might have to bear.

Where the three strategies differ is in the challenger's beliefs about the nature of the defender's commitment. In a fait accompli strategy, the challenger believes there is no commitment by the defender to protect the territory or people in question, and so it launches a swift blow, or swiftly takes some other type of action, in order to create a done deed, which gives the putative defender little or no time to change course, make a commitment, and block the challenger. If the fait accompli works, it forces the putative defender to accept the new status quo because the defender calculates that the costs to return to the previous status quo are too high.

A limited probe strategy is an immediate deterrence failure in which the challenger provokes a crisis to reveal the nature and extent of the defender's commitment. The challenger believes that the defender's commitment is uncertain, and the limited probe—a circumscribed challenge—is designed to make the defender take actions (or not) in order to reveal how strongly, if at all, it cares about this commitment. The limited probe is meant to be provocative, but not so provocative as to trigger a full-blown response. In this case, the situation remains controllable because the challenger's actions, by definition, are limited, and the challenger can quickly retreat if it finds that the defender not only cares but cares greatly.

In a controlled pressure strategy, the challenger believes the defender's commitment is unequivocal but soft, and so the challenger applies pressure, in increasing amounts if necessary, to convince the defender that the costs of fulfilling its commitment are more than it is willing to bear, or to chip away at the defender's commitment and in the process convince the defender's ally that it cannot defend the ally. In this case the challenger believes that it can

[14] Alexander L. George and Richard Smoke, *Deterrence in American Foreign Policy: Theory and Practice* (New York: Columbia University Press, 1974), 536–48.

control the costs of escalation because the defender will not pay much to meet its commitments.

These three types of deterrence failure make clear that in order to avoid an immediate deterrence crisis, a defender must make crystal clear to any potential attacker what the defender's red lines are by clearly stating its commitment, by clearly communicating them to the potential challenger, by pointing out the costs the challenger will bear should it cross the red lines, and by making unequivocally clear that it will respond robustly should the challenger cross the red lines. In addition, the defender must demonstrate to the putative challenger that it possesses the capabilities to fulfill its commitments, either by retaliating against the challenger or by defeating its attempts to alter the status quo. To demonstrate resolve, the defender must make clear that it is willing to bear high costs (or as high as is necessary) to prevent the challenger from crossing the red lines, or to push it back across them should they be crossed. If the defender can convince the challenger that its own resolve is high, it then becomes difficult for the challenger to conclude that it can control escalation, thereby undercutting its belief that it can control the costs it would have to bear. Will ("I intend to have my way on this issue"), capability ("I have the means to get my way"), and resolve ("I care so much that I am willing to pay high costs")—these are essential ingredients to prevent immediate deterrence failures.

However, although these three ingredients may be essential, they are not sufficient to prevent every immediate deterrence failure. There is a fourth type of failure about which George and Smoke do not say much: situations in which a highly committed challenger faces off against a highly committed defender.[15] The defender has made clear its strong will, sufficient capability, and high resolve to the challenger, all of which the challenger has understood. Still, an immediate deterrence failure occurs because the challenger is so highly motivated to overturn the status quo that it does not care about controlling the costs it has to bear and is willing to see the crisis escalate. If we assume actors are rational, the challenger's motivation therefore appears to be the most important of all the ingredients in assessing whether and why an immediate deterrence failure occurs. After reviewing a large number of empirical studies, Morgan aptly concludes, "Challenger motivation is the most important factor in deterrence success or failure, especially if 'motivation' covers both the desire to challenge and a willingness to take risks. The deterrer doesn't control the situation unless that motivation is low enough to permit it."[16]

It is difficult to determine whether and why deterrence succeeded in any given situation or, to be more precise, why a deterrence encounter never took

---

[15] George and Smoke, *Deterrence in American Foreign Policy*, 547–48. For more on the issue of highly motivated challengers, see James D. Fearon, "Selection Effects and Deterrence," *International Interactions* 28 (2002): 5–29.

[16] Morgan, *Deterrence Now*, 164. In this volume, Sechser concludes the same thing regarding compellence.

place. For example, did the Soviet Union not attack Western Europe during the Cold War because of the U.S. deterrent pledge to retaliate against the Soviet Union? Was it because the Soviet Union was a status quo power in Europe, not a revisionist one, and throughout the course of the Cold War never ever had the intention of trying to seize Western Europe militarily? Was it because the Soviets were consumed first with reconstruction after World War II and then later with the Chinese threat, and hence did not have the resources to take Western Europe even if they had the desire? In short, were U.S. actions central to or largely irrelevant to the fact that the Soviets did not attack? Henry Kissinger put the matter thus: "Since deterrence can only be tested negatively, by events that do *not* take place, and since it is never possible to demonstrate why something has not occurred, it became especially difficult to assess whether the existing policy was the best possible policy or a just barely effective one. Perhaps deterrence was even unnecessary because it was impossible to prove whether the adversary ever intended to attack in the first place."[17]

Kissinger exaggerates when he says that we can never explain why something has not happened. After all, we can explore possible reasons why a dog did not bark: perhaps its owner had its vocal cords cut; perhaps the dog was trained never to bark; perhaps the dog was asleep. The point is not that it is impossible to explain why something did not happen; the point is that it is generally easier and more plausible to show why something did happen. Similar quandaries arise when trying to account for why we do not see more mass-casualty terrorist attacks than we do. Is it because of restraints imposed by violent nonstate actors (VNSAs), or because of the efficacy of deterrence, or because of VNSAs' lack of capacity? Or is it due to a lack of intent? Thus the insights and shortcomings that pertain to state-to-state deterrence can be equally valid when applied to the nonstate actor context. Such is also the case for compellence.

Compellence

Compellence can be employed not just in wartime but also in situations short of war, and it can be used strategically for purposes of denial, punishment, or risk. When used in war, we term compellence *wartime compellence*; when used in situations short of war, we term it *coercive diplomacy*.[18]

---

[17] Henry Kissinger, *Diplomacy* (New York: Simon and Schuster, 1994), 608, quoted in Danilovic, *When the Stakes Are High*, 50–51.

[18] Although strictly speaking we should call coercive diplomacy *compellence diplomacy*, because the term *coercive diplomacy* has become the convention we too employ it. Alexander L. George first coined the term. See Alexander L. George, David K. Hall, and William E. Simons, *The Limits of Coercive Diplomacy: Laos, Cuba, Vietnam* (Boston: Little, Brown, 1971). Other important earlier books on coercion and coercive diplomacy include Alexander L. George, *Forceful Persuasion: Coercive Diplomacy as an Alternative to War* (Washington, DC: U.S. Institute of Peace Press, 1991); Alexander L. George and William E. Simons, *The Limits of Coercive Diplomacy*, 2nd ed. (Boulder, CO: Westview Press, 1994); Robert A. Pape, *Bombing to Win: Airpower and Coercion in War* (Ithaca, NY: Cornell University Press, 1996); Robert J. Art and Patrick M. Cronin, eds., *The United States*

Wartime Compellence and Coercive Diplomacy

Wartime compellence means that two parties are at war with one another.[19] War involves large numbers of military forces clashing with one another and (often significant) loss of life; coercive diplomacy, by contrast, entails limited or no contact between rival military forces and little or no loss of life. Wartime compellence usually includes economic measures—sanctions and embargoes—along with the use of force. Coercive diplomacy can involve only the use of force (threats or actual use), only economic means, or a combination of force and economic measures.[20]

Coercive diplomacy can utilize force at three distinct levels. First, coercive diplomacy can consist of just threats: "This is what I will do to you if you do not do as I say." Threats are mostly talk; no military action is taken by the coercer, other than moving military forces around and positioning them to strike with lethal force, should that decision be made. The purpose of such movement is to signal intention and resolve. Signaling involves actions that are akin to flexing one's muscles but not actually punching the other fellow. Second, coercive diplomacy can employ demonstrative military action: "Okay, you did not take my threat seriously; here, let me show you what I can do to you if you do not do what I want." Force is used physically but in a limited way in order to increase the strength of the threat made by demonstrating what one's use of force can do. This is equivalent to punching the adversary once, for example, but not with a knockout blow. Militarily, it could involve destroying one of the adversary's bridges so as to demonstrate that you have the capability to destroy all its bridges if it does not give way. Third, coercive diplomacy can employ limited force: "Since my demonstration did not impress you, let me do more than simply demonstrate what I can do to you; let me hurt you a little more. I will take out four of your bridges surrounding your capital city." If the limited use of force fails to sway the target, the coercer can then move to war: "You did not listen to me; now I am going to hurt you really, really badly." Once that line is crossed, we have moved from the realm of coercive diplomacy into the realms of wartime compellence and victory.

Unfortunately the line between limited force and actual war is not always clear-cut. Take the 1999 Kosovo War, for example. NATO conducted an

---

and Coercive Diplomacy (Washington, DC: U.S. Institute of Peace Press, 2003); Daniel Byman and Matthew Waxman, *The Dynamics of Coercion: American Foreign Policy and the Limits of Military Might* (Cambridge: Cambridge University Press, 2002); Peter Viggo Jakobsen, *Western Use of Coercive Diplomacy after the Cold War* (New York: St. Martin's Press, 1998); James W. Davis Jr., *Threats and Promises: The Pursuit of International Influence* (Baltimore: Johns Hopkins University Press, 2000).

[19] By convention, a war is defined as a military conflict between two or more states in which there are at least 1,000 battle deaths.

[20] If only economic measures are used, and no use of force is involved, we refer to that as *economic compellence*, an eventuality that has grown increasingly common in recent years, albeit to mixed reviews. See, for instance, Richard N. Haass, "Economic Sanctions: Too Much of a Bad Thing," *Brookings Policy Brief Series* 34 (June 1998); Ella Shagabutdinova and Jeffrey Berejikian, "Deploying Sanctions While Protecting Human Rights: Are Humanitarian 'Smart' Sanctions Effective?," *Journal of Human Rights* 6 (2007): 59–74.

eleven-week bombing campaign against Serb targets within the province of Kosovo and in Serbia proper to compel Serb forces to withdraw from the beleaguered province. Was this campaign a case of coercive diplomacy because it resulted in relatively little loss of life for both noncombatants and military forces and because there were no NATO boots on the ground? Or was it war, given the length and extent of bombing that took place, even if loss of life was small? The answer has implications for assessing success and failure as well as the general coding of cases as coercive diplomacy (a failure) or wartime compellence (arguably a draw).

There are three additional important points worth noting about wartime compellence and coercive diplomacy. First, coercive diplomacy is closely related to militarized interstate disputes. Such disputes are defined as situations in which parties are in conflict; military force is threatened, deployed, or physically used, but total battle deaths are fewer than 1,000. Anything over 1,000 battle deaths is, by convention, no longer a militarized dispute, but war. The larger the number of lives lost, the greater are the chances that the conflict will intensify and expand. Coercive diplomacy is intended to be "compellence on the cheap"; killing large numbers of the adversary is generally the worst way to get something on the cheap.

Second, successful coercion in war is not the same thing as victory in war. Achieving victory means that one of the adversaries has defeated the military forces of the other adversary (or adversaries), to the degree that the latter is (are) no longer capable of putting up effective organized military resistance. Victory by one entails defeat of the other. Successful wartime coercion, by contrast, means that the coercer has bent the target to its will without having to completely defeat the target's military forces. Successful coercion occurs short of military victory because, as Robert Pape points out, "If a coercive attempt is made [that leads to war] but the war ends only when one side is decisively defeated, then coercion has failed, even if the coercer wins the war."[21] So actors have three different paths to get what they want when employing military force: coercive diplomacy, wartime compellence, and victory.

While it is relatively easy to state the difference between what constitutes successful wartime compellence and what constitutes victory in war, in practice it can sometimes be devilishly difficult to distinguish between them. Germany's seeking an armistice in early October 1918 illustrates the point. After the failure of the de facto commander of Germany's military forces, Erich Ludendorff, to break Allied resistance with a series of spring and summer offensives on the western front, the Allies struck back and launched a series of withering counteroffensives, made more effective with the addition of U.S. troops. Sustaining heavy losses, in September Ludendorff ordered the German armies to fall back to the Hindenburg Line, Germany's last line of defense beyond the homeland.

[21] Pape, *Bombing to Win*, 15.

On September 29 Ludendorff advised the kaiser and chancellor that Germany seek an armistice to keep the Allies from entering the homeland.[22]

Was Germany's suing for an armistice a case of successful compellence in war or of victory in war? The case for the former rests on two assertions: first, the Allies had demonstrated that they would be able to defeat German forces if the war dragged on; second, Allied victory had not yet been achieved because German forces could still put up effective resistance, even if not indefinitely. The case for victory, in contrast, is that Ludendorff saw the handwriting on the wall: it was only a matter of time, and short time at that, before the homeland was invaded; organized resistance would therefore be futile and would not prevent the inevitable. It is not necessary to decide which is the case here. The point of the example is to show that distinguishing between victory (destruction of the adversary's military forces) and wartime compellence (showing the adversary that its military forces will be destroyed unless it ceases to fight) can be tricky.[23] Destruction of the adversary's forces is easy to see once it has taken place; demonstrating that the adversary's forces can continue to put up organized resistance and are not yet defeated requires an estimate of how much "residual capacity to resist" the losing armed forces retain. That is not easy to assess.

Third, the few studies that exist indicate there is little difference between the success rates of *interstate* coercive diplomacy and *interstate* wartime compellence.[24] More research needs to be done, especially on wartime interstate compellence, to determine whether this conclusion holds. This is important because if a state knows that the odds of success for coercive diplomacy are low, but also knows that success rates of wartime compellence are high, then a coercer might be tempted to skip coercive diplomacy and proceed to wartime compellence. Alternatively, the challenger might engage in more coercive diplomatic gambits than it might otherwise, believing that it might get lucky but also knowing if it did not, it could always proceed to wartime compellence and still get its way. Hence the higher the perceived rate of wartime compellence success, the more likely is war, all other things being equal. On the other hand, if a potential coercer knew that the success rates for both types of compellence were low and roughly the same, it might be less tempted to go down either route, and hence the less likely war would be.

Two studies of coercive diplomacy suggest that failure is more frequent than success. Robert Art and Patrick Cronin found a success rate of 33.3 percent, based on 15 cases of the U.S. exercise of coercive diplomacy against small

---

[22] See John Keegan, *The First World War* (New York: Knopf, 1999), 392–414.

[23] Ibid., 412–13.

[24] The most extensive scholarship on wartime compellence consists of studies of air power (see note 27). Little has been done on assessing the efficacy of sea power blockades during war. One notable exception is John Mearsheimer's *The Tragedy of Great Power Politics* (New York: Norton, 2000), chapter 4. Mearsheimer found one successful case out of nine instances when one Great Power successfully blockaded another since 1789, for a success rate of 11 percent.

to medium-size states between 1992 and 2001.[25] In a more comprehensive study, Todd Sechser found a success rate of 41.4 percent for interstate coercive diplomacy, based on his Militarized Compellent Threat data set (MCT) of 210 distinct interstate compellent threat episodes between 1918 and 2001, which involve mainly, although not exclusively, Great Powers trying to compel smaller states.[26]

The extant data sets on the success rate of interstate wartime compellence deal only with the effects of air power: one was compiled by Pape and the other by Michael Horowitz and Dan Reiter.[27] Pape's analysis demonstrates that the compellence success rate through air power is 40 percent (16 successes out the universe of 40 cases between 1917 and 1991). Horowitz and Reiter expanded Pape's data set to 53 cases through 1999 and found 19 successes out of 53 cases (36 percent). Both data sets, however, contain cases of coercive diplomacy as well as states attacking and trying to coerce rebel forces, neither of which is an example of interstate wartime compellence. When we remove those cases from Pape's data set, we are left with 29 cases of wartime compellence, of which 13 succeeded (44.8 percent). Doing the same thing with the Horowitz-Reiter data set removes 12 cases from their 53, yielding 15 successes out of 41 cases (36.6 percent). If we compare these two modified data sets to the MCT data set, the difference between a success rate of 36.6 or 44.8 percent for wartime compellence through air power, on the one hand, and 41.4 percent via coercive diplomacy through a variety of military means, on the other, is insufficiently large to favor one or the other. If these findings are correct, what would likely persuade a state to rely more heavily on coercive diplomacy than wartime compellence are cost considerations: coercive diplomacy is cheaper than wartime compellence to execute. At the same time, any decision to attempt either wartime compellence or coercive diplomacy depends on a whole host of factors, only one of which is cost. Another is capabilities: relative success rates mean nothing to a state that does not have the means to compel a given target by any method.

Why Is Coercive Diplomacy Hard?

What accounts for the relatively low success rate of coercive diplomacy? Why does it fail more often than it succeeds, especially for the United States, which is so much more powerful than the target states it has tried to coerce? Six distinct explanations have been offered.

---

[25] We removed one of the terrorism cases from the data set because it was not an interstate example so as to make it comparable with the Sechser data set. See Art and Cronin, *The United States and Coercive Diplomacy*, 385–87.

[26] Todd S. Sechser, "Militarized Compellent Threats, 1918–2001," *Conflict Management and Peace Science* 28 (2011): 389.

[27] See Pape, *Bombing to Win*, Tables 1 and 2. See Michael Horowitz and Dan Reiter, "When Does Aerial Bombing Work?," *Journal of Conflict Resolution* 45 (2001): 147–73, especially appendix A, 166–67.

First, coercive diplomacy is hard because compellence is hard. Successful compellence requires that the target publicly give way to a coercer's demands, whereas in a successful general deterrent situation, the target can claim that it never intended to do what the deterrer was trying to prevent.[28] Giving way to a compeller involves public humiliation and damage to the target's reputation, which do not happen in a general deterrent situation when a target merely continues doing what it has been doing.[29] In a general deterrent situation, the target has "plausible deniability" ("I never intended to do that"); in a compellent situation, it does not ("I had to change my behavior because you forced me to do so").[30]

Second, for a variety of psychological and material reasons, defenders of the status quo tend to be more highly motivated—that is, their resolve is greater—than challengers of the status quo. One psychological theory, known as "prospect theory," that purports to explain this tendency posits that actors are risk-acceptant to prevent losses but risk-averse to achieve gains.[31] Compellers are asking targets to give up something by changing their behavior. The targets are therefore the defenders of the status quo, while compellers are the would-be challengers of the status quo. If defenders of the status quo are willing to take greater risks to keep what they have, and if challengers to the status quo are less willing to take risks to overturn it and gain more, then defenders should generally prevail over compellers.

Third, when the target gives way to the compeller, that act has not only reputational costs but also power costs. Giving way once can weaken the target enough militarily that it is harder to stand up to the compeller if it comes back for more concessions. As a consequence, the target is more likely to dig in at the outset, resist giving way to the compeller's demands, and hope the compeller does not care as much as it does about the issues in contestation.[32]

Fourth, and relatedly, when the compeller is considerably more powerful than the target, the compeller cannot credibly commit that it will not come back in the future and demand further concessions. The inability of a powerful compeller to make believable commitments about its future behavior derives from the capability-intention dilemma: state intentions can change swiftly; capabilities, however, change much more slowly. The compeller's vast superiority makes its commitment not to come back and ask for more seem hollow

[28] We have appended the qualifier *general* to deterrence because this assertion is valid for general deterrent situations but not for immediate deterrent crises.

[29] Robert J. Art, "To What Ends Military Power?," *International Security* 4 (1980): 9.

[30] Schelling was the first to argue that compellence is harder than deterrence. His reasoning was that compellent threats tend to be vaguer in what they ask of a target: " 'Do nothing' is simple. 'Do something' is ambiguous." If the target is unclear about what it is supposed to do, then compliance will become a hit-or-miss affair. See Schelling, *Arms and Influence*, 72–73. We do not agree with this reasoning. There is nothing inherent in a compellent threat that makes it vaguer than a deterrent threat. "Stop attacking my friend" is just as clear as "Don't attack me."

[31] Robert Jervis, "The Political Implications of Loss Aversion," *Political Psychology* 13 (1992): 187–204.

[32] See Art and Cronin, *The United States and Coercive Diplomacy*, 366–67.

because it has the power to come back and take more if it so decides. Moreover this problem becomes greater as the asymmetry in power between compeller and target increases.[33] Absent a world government, there is no built-in safeguard in international politics to ensure that powerful states do not change their minds.

Fifth, in those cases where the United States is the compeller, the credibility of its threats is weakened by the way it executes them. The "American way of war," argues Dianne Chamberlain, relies on technology, especially air power and intelligence collection, to keep U.S. casualties to a minimum. This may save lives, but the focus on force protection sends a clear signal that the United States does not care enough about the issue under contestation to expend its blood as well as its treasure to get its way. Chamberlain calls this American way of war a "cheap threat" and hence a weak signal of U.S. resolve, so it generally fails.[34]

Sixth, compellent threats more often than not fail because the United States has too great an appetite; it asks more of states than they are willing to give.[35] As Phil Haun argues in chapter 4, the United States often makes insatiable demands. It wants everything, including literally the head of the head of the current regime. As Alexander Downes discusses in chapter 5, U.S. demands threaten the very sovereignty and survival of the regime, leaving incumbents little choice but to resist. For example, when Saddam Hussein agreed in February 1991 to vacate Kuwait, but only under the condition that he could remove all the military equipment in Kuwait along with his Iraqi troops, the United States said no because its goal had moved beyond merely liberating Kuwait from Iraqi occupation to cutting down Iraq's military power so that it would be less of a menace to the region. The Iraqi leader surrendered only after his forces and their equipment were subsequently smashed in Kuwait and the remnants of both were heading back to Iraq.

In sum, whichever and how many of these six mechanisms are at work in any given case, they help explain why the more powerful do not invariably prevail against the weaker. A great preponderance of power does not guarantee coercive diplomacy success, although it may well guarantee successful compellence during war, and even victory in war. These are key lessons to keep in mind in an era when exercises and coercive uses of force are very common—the United States, for instance, has been involved in a military operation on average every 17 months since the end of the Cold War—while full-blown high-intensity Great Power wars are nonexistent.

---

[33] See Todd S. Sechser, "Goliath's Curse: Coercive Threats and Asymmetric Power," *International Organization* 64 (2010): 627–60.

[34] Dianne Pfundstein Chamberlain, *Cheap Threats: Why the United States Struggles to Coerce Weak States* (Washington, DC: Georgetown University Press, 2015), introduction and chapter 1.

[35] See also Phil Haun, *Coercion, Survival and War: Why Weak States Resist the United States* (Stanford: Stanford University Press, 2015), chapter 2.

Denial and Punishment Strategies

Whether used during war or in coercive diplomatic gambits, a compeller can employ its military forces against the target for three different strategic purposes: military denial, civilian punishment, and risk.[36] Denial is thwarting the target's military operations, punishment is targeting and killing its population, and risk is promising punishment or more punishment.

Compellence by denial means that the compeller has sought out the target's military forces and attacked them, with the purpose of degrading, crippling, or destroying them.[37] For a denial strategy to be successful, the coercer must demonstrate to the target that its military strategy can be or is being undermined by the compeller's military countermeasures. The coercer may be able to do this with only threats or limited uses of force, but wartime denial is easier to achieve when significantly larger amounts of force are used. If a strategy of denial is to succeed when the compeller only threatens or uses limited amounts of force, the target must imagine what the compeller can do to it. During war, however, imagination is not required because the compeller can produce demonstrable adverse effects on its military forces. However employed, denial strategies work by convincing the target that it will be unable to attain its political goals through force. Remember, however, that thwarting the target's military operations does not imply its complete military defeat. Successful military denial compels the target to give way short of militarily defeating it.

Compellence via punishment is achieved by attacking a target's population and cities and inflicting unacceptable pain, although killing large numbers of military forces is sometimes also done for punishment purposes. The goal is to convince the target that the costs and risks it has to bear by persevering with its chosen course of action far outweigh the achievable potential gains. The purpose of the pain, in short, is not to undermine the target's military strategy but to weaken its resolve to carry on.

Compellence via risk is achieved by threatening to inflict punishment on the target. Risk is essentially the promise to inflict pain if no pain has yet been inflicted, or to inflict more (and more) pain if some has already been administered, in order to convince the target to concede. If the latter, more punishment can be delivered all at once with maximum force or at a gradually increasing rate. Whether a target is threatened once or serially, risk is a cheap form of punishment. As Keren Fraiman argues in chapter 6 of this volume, this kind of compellence, even if administered indirectly, can be quite effective at changing the decision-making calculations of nonstate targets and their state sponsors, often at relatively low cost. Greenhill finds the same thing with regard to the deployment of displaced populations as instruments of state-level

[36] See Pape, *Bombing to Win*, 18–20.

[37] "Denial by defense" means the target has successfully warded off a challenger's attack. "Dissuasion by defense" means the target has convinced the challenger through its defensive preparations that the attack is infeasible or not worth the costs that the attacker would bear.

coercion, through a kind of "demographic bombing"–driven mechanism that she details in chapter 10.

Because risk is a form of punishment, there are really only two basic compellent strategies: military denial and civilian punishment. Does one work better than the other? It depends on the circumstances. When the compeller threatens or actually uses its military forces directly against the target's military forces or its civilian population, military denial works better than punishment. However, when the compeller's military forces are used not to kill the target's civilians but to produce (or threaten to produce) large population movements across state borders, then punishment, as Greenhill shows, can be stunningly effective.

Pape has demonstrated that when the compeller's air power is applied directly against the target, it is more effective when used for military denial than for civilian punishment. Pape located 40 cases of coercive air power campaigns from 1917 through 1991 that involved military denial, civilian punishment, or both. The denial theory predicts accurately 37 out of 40 cases, or 92.5 percent.[38] That is, when denial was high or very high, compellent success mostly occurred, and when denial was medium or low, failure mostly occurred, irrespective of the value civilian vulnerability took. In the 14 cases when punishment was high or very high, success occurred eight times, or 57 percent.[39] In other words, when employing air power as the coercive instrument, denial was a far better predictor of the compellent outcome—success or failure—than was civilian punishment.[40]

In contrast, Greenhill has found that when displaced people are used as coercive weapons against well-chosen target states, coercion by punishment can be quite effective.[41] Of the 75 to 85 cases of demographic-bombing-driven deterrence and compellence between 1951 and 2015 that she has thus far identified, the success rate for partial compliance with the coercer's demands is about 73 percent; for full compliance, 57 percent. If one disaggregates the data, the success rate for deterrence only is 20 percent for full compliance, and the success rate for compellence only is 66 percent for full

[38] See Pape, *Bombing to Win*, 51–53. Pape coded 13 cases out of 40 where the threat of military denial or actual military denial through conventional bombing was high or very high. In those 13 cases, conventional military denial was successful 10 times, for a success rate of 77 percent. This rate is probably too high since in 4 of these denial successes, punishment was also high or very high. If we take out the 4 cases where both punishment and denial were high or very high, conventional military denial has a success rate of 45 percent (6 military denial-only successes out of 13 where denial was high or very high).

[39] Four of these cases were ones of nuclear coercion and all were successful. If we wish to keep the comparison between denial and punishment at the conventional level, punishment predicted only 4 successes out of 10.

[40] Muddying the comparison somewhat is the fact that there were eight cases where both punishment and denial were high or very high. Of these, two were failures and six were successes. Of those six, four were cases where nuclear punishment or nuclear risk was involved. Even if we throw out those cases, however, the more accurate predictive power of denial compared to punishment still stands, although the percentages change.

[41] Kelly M. Greenhill, *Weapons of Mass Migration: Forced Displacement, Coercion and Foreign Policy* (Ithaca, NY: Cornell University Press, 2010).

compliance.[42] It is worth noting that the 57 percent success rate for compellence by punishment is equivalent to the 55 to 57 percent overall success rate for extended deterrence discussed earlier, although not as high as the 80 percent success rate of extended deterrence when the deterrer possesses nuclear weapons.

These findings suggest the need for two significant amendments to our understanding of the relative efficacy of denial versus punishment strategies. First, what works best—in Pape's view, military denial—may not be universally applicable but rather contingent on the context (e.g., war vs. peacetime); the natures (e.g., state vs. nonstate actors), capabilities, and levels of resolve of the challenger and target; and, quite critically, the choice of coercive instrument(s) used.[43] Second, compellence may be not more difficult but in fact easier than deterrence when comparing a strategy of demographic bombing (punishment) to extended deterrence. Blanket statements about the relative ease of deterrence compared to compellence are not justified by the available evidence.

Demands, Assurances, and Inducements

Also important to assess are the effects on the target's resolve of the type of demands the coercer issues and the assurances and inducements it offers to the target. If much is demanded of the target, is compliance less likely? And is the reverse true: if less is demanded, is compliance more likely? In addition, what are the effects of offering assurances and inducements to the target on the latter's decision to resist or give way? Do assurances and inducements increase the chances of compellent success, and, if so, when should they be offered: before or along with the coercive threat, or only after it is made? These are important questions to resolve, but unfortunately we do not have a large number of studies to help us answer them. Therefore our conclusions must be viewed as tentative, pending further study.

The evidence that we have on demand type and coercive success is mixed. Alexander L. George and William E. Simons found that, indeed, there was an inverse relation between demand type and compellent outcome: the greater the compeller's demands, the lower the success rate. This conclusion, however, is based on a very small number of cases and cannot be considered definitive.[44] Chungshik Moon and Mark Souva found that democracies were good at making threats over some issues, such as policy, leadership, and reparations, but not over issues of territory. This would seem to suggest that regime change

[42] See also Kelly M. Greenhill, "Asymmetric Advantage: The Weaponization of Migration as an Instrument of Cross-Domain Coercion," in Gartzke and Lindsay, *Cross-Domain Deterrence*; Kelly M. Greenhill, "Demographic Bombing: People as Weapons in Syria and Beyond," *Foreign Affairs*, December 17, 2015.

[43] For further discussion and evidence that our understanding of what works, and doesn't, is conditioned by context and choice of coercive instrument, see the Gartzke and Lindsay, Crawford, and Drezner chapters in Part four of this volume. For further discussion of the significance of the nature of actors involved, see the chapters by Fraiman, Walsh, and Krause in Part three.

[44] George and Simons, *The Limits of Coercive Diplomacy*, 15.

(leadership) is less important than state territory, a questionable result.[45] With a data set about twice as large as that of George and Simons, Art and Cronin found no correlation between demand type and compellent success. Success and failure seemed randomly distributed and unrelated to what was being demanded of the target.[46] In chapter 5 of this volume, Downes finds, surprisingly, that regime change, surely a "demanding" demand because of its equivalence to regime suicide, had a success rate of 80 percent. However, Downes does not believe that the past is prologue because the special conditions that gave rise to such a high success rate are not likely to be duplicated in the future.[47] In chapter 3 of this book, Sechser argues that the more the compeller asks of the target, the less likely is the target to comply, and the less it asks of the target, the more likely is the target to comply. However, Sechser's conclusion is based on deductive logic rather than empirical demonstration. In sum, the weight of the available evidence favors the counterintuitive conclusion that there is no firm relationship between how much is demanded of the target and the likelihood of compellent success, but until additional studies are done, this conclusion must be treated with caution.

Evidence about the role that both assurances and inducements play in compellence outcomes is also limited, but that which exists suggests that assurances and inducements can be helpful in producing target compliance. Assurance, or what some call "reassurance," is not to be confused with inducements.[48] Assurance, as Schelling instructs, refers to the coercer's promise not to change the terms of the implicit contract between coercer and target once the target complies with the coercer's demand: "Any coercive threat requires corresponding *assurances*; the object of a threat is to give somebody a choice. To say, 'One more step and I shoot,' can be a deterrence threat only if accompanied by the implicit assurance, 'And if you stop I won't . . . . The assurances that accompany a compellent action—move back a mile and I won't shoot (otherwise I shall) and I won't then try again for a second mile—are harder to demonstrate in advance, unless it be through a long past record of abiding by one's own verbal assurances."[49] If assurances are akin to contracts, inducements are akin to side payments. When a compeller offers an inducement, it is saying "I am hurting you now (or threatening to) because you refuse to comply with my wishes, but if you do comply, not only will I stop hurting you, but I will also offer you some sort of reward." Assurance signifies that the compeller will stick by its agreement once the target complies; inducement is a reward,

---

[45] Chungshik Moon and Mark Souva, "Audience Costs, Information, and Credibility Commitment Problems," *Journal of Conflict Resolution* 60 (2016): 434-58.

[46] Art and Cronin, *The United States and Coercive Diplomacy*, 391–97. When the difficulty of the demand in their dataset is categorized, no firm conclusions can be drawn about demand type and coercive success.

[47] Downes qualifies his conclusion by attributing the high rate to selection effects: compellers demanded regime change only when they thought the target was unable to resist.

[48] For a useful discussion of strategies of assurance, see Jeffrey W. Knopf, "Varieties of Assurance," *Journal of Strategic Studies* 35 (2012): 375–99.

[49] Schelling, *Arms and Influence*, 74–75.

something other than the promise not to continue hurting the target once it complies. Assurance is a promise not to hurt the target more; inducement, the promise of some "goodies" for compliance.

Schelling's assertion that assurances must accompany coercive threats has generally been taken as axiomatically true, but not much systematic empirical work has been done to support it. Two exceptions stand out: Sechser's argument about power asymmetries and Haun's argument about U.S. demands for regime change both represent confirmation, albeit indirect, about the importance of assurances for target compliance. If a powerful actor is either unable (Sechser) or unwilling (Haun) to commit not to come back at the target once it gives way, then Sechser and Haun found that the target is unlikely to comply with the compeller's initial demand. By extension, we can draw the inference that offers of assurances will help produce target compliance. In their detailed study of why the Libyan dictator Muammar Qaddafi decided to give up his nuclear weapons program, Bruce Jentleson and Christopher Whytock found just that: U.S. assurances not to seek regime change were an important factor in securing Qaddafi's compliance.[50] Tristan Volpe, in an innovative adaptation of the role that reassurance can play in coercive diplomacy, demonstrates in chapter 15 how a state that is threatening to acquire nuclear weapons can use reassurances that it will not do so in order to wrest (compel) concessions from those states trying to halt its nuclear weapons program.[51]

With respect to inducements, we can make two opposing arguments.[52] The first is that inducements should make the target more willing to give way because it is receiving compensation for its compliance.[53] The second is the reverse argument: inducements should make the target less willing to give way because they signal that the compeller wants the target's compliance badly and therefore that resisting longer will produce additional gains for the target. The little evidence we have favors the first argument. Art and Cronin found that in 4 of their 16 coercive diplomacy cases, positive inducements were offered and 3 achieved success (75 percent), in comparison to the success rate of 33 percent for the 16 cases taken as a whole. In addition, George and Simons found that both cases in which positive inducements were offered were successes, whereas all five cases in which no inducements were offered were failures or were ambiguous in outcome.[54]

Similarly it should be the case that the timing of inducements matters. Logic dictates that inducements should be offered only after the compellence gambit

---

[50] Bruce W. Jentleson and Christopher A. Whytock, "Who 'Won' Libya? The Force-Diplomacy Debate and Its Implications for Theory and Policy," *International Security* 30 (2005–6): 47–86.

[51] Also see Tristan Volpe, "Proliferation Persuasion: Coercive Bargaining with Nuclear Technology" (Ph.D. dissertation, George Washington University, 2015).

[52] There is more evidence regarding the role of inducements in economic coercion than for compellence that involves threats or use of force. For example, see David A. Baldwin, "The Power of Positive Sanctions," *World Politics* 24 (1971): 19–38.

[53] See also Haun, in this volume.

[54] Art and Cronin, *The United States and Coercive Diplomacy*, 393–97; George and Simons, *The Limits of Coercive Diplomacy*.

has begun. To lead with inducements is likely to signal that the compeller is weak or lacks resolve and is likely to give way if pressed. Compellence situations are crises akin to the game of chicken, and such situations demand firm resolve at the outset, in both the conventional and the nuclear realm. Of the four cases in which Art and Cronin found positive inducements were offered, three were offered after threats were made or force used, and two of those three were successes.[55] Thus while the logic of offering inducements after threats are issued or force is used is powerful, the evidence to support it is thin.

Unconventional Weapons and Actors: Nuclear and Nonstate Compellence

The Challenges of Nuclear Compellence

Writing on nuclear compellence has come in two waves. The first flowering of studies began in the early 1980s and lasted about a decade.[56] A second wave began in the early twenty-first century and is ongoing.[57] As with studies on the relation between demand type and compellent success, the efficacy of nuclear compellence is hotly contested, but the weight of the available evidence suggests that nuclear compellence can, but often does not, work.

In their book on nuclear threats, Sechser and Fuhrmann identified 19 cases of nuclear coercive diplomacy, none of which in their view was a success. If coercive success was achieved, it was due to nonnuclear threats and actions that the compeller issued. Nuclear compellent threats in these cases failed for two key reasons: signaling problems and low threat credibility. In terms of signaling, too often the threats were vague, so targets were uncertain about the seriousness of the threat, or even whether a threat was being made. With

---

55 Art and Cronin, *The United States and Coercive Diplomacy*, 394–95.

56 Among the more important of the first wave of works on nuclear compellence are Barry M. Blechman and Douglas M. Hart, "The Political Utility of Nuclear Weapons: The 1973 Middle East Crisis," *International Security* 7 (1982): 132–57; Richard K. Betts, *Nuclear Blackmail and Nuclear Balance* (Washington, DC: Brookings, 1987); Richard K. Betts, "A Nuclear Golden Age? The Balance before Parity," *International* Security 11 (1986–87): 3–33; Morton H. Halperin, *Nuclear Fallacy: Dispelling the Myth of Nuclear Strategy* (Cambridge, MA: Ballinger, 1987); Scott D. Sagan, "Nuclear Alerts and Crisis Management," *International Security* 9 (1985): 99–140; Marc Trachtenberg, "The Influence of Nuclear Weapons in the Cuban Missile Crisis," *International Security* 10 (1985): 137–64; Gordon H. Chang, "To the Nuclear Brink: Eisenhower, Dulles, and the Quemoy-Matsu Crisis," *International Security* 12 (1988): 96–123; H. W. Brands Jr., "Testing Massive Retaliation: Credibility and Crisis Management in the Taiwan Strait," *International Security* 12 (1988): 124–52; Roger Dingman, "Atomic Diplomacy During the Korean War," *International Security* 13 (1988–89): 50–92; Rosemary J. Foot, "Nuclear Coercion and the Ending of the Korean Conflict," *International Security* 13 (1988–89): 92–113; Pape, *Bombing to Win*, chapter 4.

57 Representative works of the second wave are Todd S. Sechser and Matthew Fuhrmann, *Nuclear Weapons and Coercive Diplomacy* (Oxford: Oxford University Press, 2016); Matthew Kroenig, "Nuclear Superiority and the Balance of Resolve: Explaining Nuclear Outcomes," *International Organization* 67 (2013): 141–73; Kyle Beardsley and Victor Asal, "Winning with the Bomb," *Journal of Conflict Resolution* 53 (2009): 278–301; Bradley A. Thayer and Thomas M. Skypeck, "Reaffirming the Utility of Nuclear Weapons," *Parameters* 43 (2013): 41–45.

regard to credibility, a nuclear compellent threat simply is not as credible to a would-be target as a threat of nuclear retaliation is to a would-be attacker. The stakes in nuclear compellence situations are rarely as high for a compeller as the stakes are to a deterrer involved in either homeland or extended deterrence gambits. Nuclear deterrence works well when existential threats are in play, as they are for homeland deterrence and often in extended deterrence situations. Existential stakes are usually not in play for a compeller. Nothing possesses as much credibility as a nuclear threat to retaliate against an attacker if the attacker struck the target's homeland, as argued earlier. Extended deterrence commitments are also highly credible if they involve protection of objects highly valued by the deterrer. Therefore the stakes for a compeller in nuclear coercive diplomatic situations rank a distant third, behind the stakes for a deterrer in homeland and extended deterrent situations. In turn, the lower the stakes for the compeller, all other things being equal, the less credible is its threat. Consequently, as a general rule, nuclear compellent threats are less credible than nuclear deterrent threats.

There is one clear exception to this rule: the situation wherein a deterrer has to issue a compellent threat or take a compellent action in order to shore up deterrence in an immediate deterrence failure situation, as was discussed at the outset of this chapter. In this type of situation, compellence is employed to protect something of very high value to a state that is simultaneously engaging in compellence and deterrence.

Sechser and Fuhrmann's skepticism about the efficacy of nuclear compellence is justified, but there are three cases for which it can be credibly argued that nuclear compellence played some role in producing a successful outcome. The first involves wartime compellence: the U.S. use of two atomic bombs against Japan in early August 1945. In a comprehensive analysis of the Japanese government's deliberations after the atomic bombs were dropped, Pape concludes that nuclear compellence played some role in Japan's decision to surrender.[58] While the Japanese Army was largely unmoved by their use, nuclear weapons reportedly had an effect on Emperor Hirohito. When told of the first reports of the bomb's effect on Hiroshima, the emperor was reported to have said, "Under these circumstances, we must bow to the inevitable. No matter what happens to my safety, we must put an end to this as speedily as possible so that this tragedy will not be repeated."[59] The emperor switched positions, and that helped tip the internal debate within the Japanese government to sue for peace earlier than would have been the case.

Two additional cases of nuclear compellent success—comprising nuclear threats issued by the United States against China during the Taiwan Strait crises of 1954–55 and 1958—are instances of coercive nuclear

---

[58] See Pape, *Bombing to Win*, chapter 4, especially 109–33. See also Leon Sigal, *Fighting to a Finish: The Politics of War Termination in the United States and Japan, 1945* (Ithaca, NY: Cornell University Press, 1988).

[59] Pape, *Bombing to Win*, 122.

diplomacy.[60] In both cases, compellent threats were issued by a deterrer (the United States) to shore up deterrence against a challenger (the People's Republic of China) in the midst of an immediate deterrence crisis. Strong circumstantial evidence suggests the explicit threats made by the United States were effective. They were both received and understood by Mao's regime, and, in both cases, after the threats were issued, China called for negotiations. This is compellence pure and simple: the United States issued threats to persuade China to change its behavior, and, in response, China's behavior did change, although precisely how much of a role the compellent threats played is unclear.[61]

In sum, successful nuclear compellence is not impossible, but it is exceedingly difficult and dangerous to execute. If such gambits occur in the future, we should expect successful outcomes to be exceedingly rare; such scenarios are discussed in some detail by Jasen Castillo in chapter 14 of this volume.

Nonstate Compellence: Terrorism, Insurgency, and Social Movements

While scholars such as Martha Crenshaw and Thomas Schelling laid the foundations of our understanding of nonstate coercion decades ago, scholarship in this arena exploded after 9/11.[62] Shared conclusions have thus far been elusive, however. There is, for instance, widespread disagreement with regard to assessing the success rate of nonstate coercion. Robert Pape, David Lake, Andrew Kydd and Barbara Walter, and Jakana Thomas, among others, have argued that coercion by VNSAs in the form of terrorism frequently works; they point to governmental overreaction and terrorists' imposition of unacceptable costs as reasons for its effectiveness.[63] However, Stathis Kalyvas, Max Abrahms, Audrey Kurth Cronin, Seth Jones and Martin Libicki, and Page Fortna argue that, consistent with Crenshaw and Schelling's earlier claims, coercive terrorism tends to be ineffective due to its indiscriminate nature and the ability of states to eliminate or ignore nonstate coercers without conceding.[64]

The fundamental disagreement between the two camps appears to be largely an artifact of two sets of divergent methodological choices: case selection

---

[60] See Peter J. Roman, *Eisenhower and the Missile Gap* (Ithaca, NY: Cornell University Press, 1995); Marc Trachtenberg, *A Constructed Peace: The Making of the European Settlement, 1945–1963* (Princeton, NJ: Princeton University Press, 1999).

[61] See, for instance, Sechser and Fuhrmann, *Nuclear Weapons*, chapter 6.

[62] Martha Crenshaw, "Theories of Terrorism: Instrumental and Organizational Approaches," *Journal of Strategic Studies* 10 (1987): 13–31; Thomas Schelling, "What Purposes Can 'International Terrorism' Serve?," in *Violence, Terrorism, and Justice*, ed. R. G. Frey and Christopher Morris (Cambridge: Cambridge University Press, 1991).

[63] Robert Pape, *Dying to Win: The Strategic Logic of Suicide Terrorism* (New York: Random House, 2005); David Lake, "Rational Extremism: Understanding Terrorism in the Twenty-First Century," *Dialog-IO* 1 (2002): 15–29; Andrew Kydd and Barbara Walter, "The Strategies of Terrorism," *International Security* 31 (2006): 49–80; Jakana Thomas, "Rewarding Bad Behavior: How Governments Respond to Terrorism in Civil War," *American Journal of Political Science* 58 (2014): 804–18.

[64] Stathis Kalyvas, "The Paradox of Terrorism in Civil War," *Journal of Ethics* 8 (2004): 97–138; Max Abrahms, "Why Terrorism Does Not Work," *International Security* 31 (2006): 42–78; Audrey Kurth Cronin, *How Terrorism Ends: Understanding the Decline and Demise of Terrorist Campaigns* (Princeton, NJ: Princeton University Press, 2009); Seth G. Jones and Martin C. Libicki, *How Terrorist Groups*

criteria and metrics of coercive success and failure. With regard to differences in case selection criteria, for instance, Pape asserts that his study includes the universe of cases of suicide terrorism, while Abrahms principally draws his cases from the set of campaigns by actors on the U.S. State Department's Foreign Terrorist Organization list. The inclusion of some additional cases in Abrahms's data set that are absent from Pape's—such as the campaign by the Real Irish Republican Army—drives down Abrahms's aggregate success rate relative to Pape's, even though both scholars concur on what transpired in all of the cases that appear in both of their data sets. Thus which cases are included and excluded from study materially affects assessments of success and failure of coercive terrorism.

Scholars have also employed different coding criteria in assessing success and failure within the same cases. So while Pape and Abrahms, for example, agree on the facts of what terrorism did and did not accomplish in specific cases, they disagree as to whether these achievements should be coded as successes or failures, with Pape generally setting the bar for what constitutes a success significantly lower than Abrahms does. For instance, in the case of Hamas's terrorist campaign, the release of a prisoner would be coded as a success by Pape because it represented a new concession by the Israeli government, but it would not be coded as a success by Abrahms because the campaign did not yield a new Palestinian state, a stated objective of the movement. Such disagreements reveal that the magnitude of a coercer's demand may be a factor in determining whether or not coercion succeeds or fails. This provisional finding reveals the need for further research and should cause us to revisit again the role that magnitude of demands may play in state-to-state coercion.

As Krause has observed, the finding that coding differences have generated divergent assessments of terrorism's utility as a coercive instrument also informs our understanding of disagreements over the efficacy of insurgency.[65] Timothy Wickham-Crowley, for instance found that only 8 percent of insurgencies succeed, whereas Jason Lyall and Isaiah Wilson reported a success rate of 57 percent. This apparently striking difference can be readily explained by the fact that radically different measures of success are employed in the two studies: nothing short of the achievement of social revolution is coded as a success by Wickham-Crowley, whereas Lyall and Wilson deem an insurgency a success if it results in either a military withdrawal or a stalemate.[66] These examples suggest many apparently significant scholarly disagreements may be more illusory than real, since seemingly contradictory findings yield

End (Santa Monica, CA: RAND, 2008); Virginia Page Fortna, "Do Terrorists Win? Rebels' Use of Terrorism and Civil War Outcomes," *International Organization* 69 (2015): 1–38.

[65] Peter Krause, "The Political Effectiveness of Non-State Violence: A Two-Level Framework to Transform a Deceptive Debate," *Security Studies* 22 (2013): 259–94.

[66] Timothy Wickham-Crowley, *Guerrillas and Revolution in Latin America: A Comparative Study of Insurgents and Regimes since 1956* (Princeton, NJ: Princeton University Press, 1992); Jason Lyall and Isaiah Wilson, "Rage against the Machines: Explaining Outcomes in Counterinsurgency Wars," *International Organization* 63 (2009): 67–106.

comparable success rates when similar case selection criteria are applied and success and failure criteria are standardized.

Other strands of new research on VNSAs reinforce our assessment that received wisdom about success and failure of coercion involving nonstate actors may require reevaluation. In chapter 6 of this volume, for instance, Fraiman argues that "transitive compellence"—whereby states that seek to affect the behavior of VNSAs do so by targeting the states that host them—is both more common and far more effective than is generally understood. This misapprehension exists, Fraiman argues, because the conventional wisdom regarding host capabilities and motivations—that is, they are as a rule both too weak and too reluctant to take effective action against VNSAs—is itself misguided. In chapter 8, on the use of drones, James Igoe Walsh finds that while drones offer noteworthy operational and technological advantages, they also frequently instigate retaliatory and signaling counterattacks by insurgents and other VNSAs, which can in turn exercise deleterious effects on counterintelligence campaigns and undermine efforts at coercion.[67]

In addition to highlighting the importance of the magnitude of the coercer's demands, recent studies have advanced our understanding of the dynamics and outcomes of nonstate coercion by discarding the unitary actor assumption that lies at the foundation of most studies of conventional coercion. Scholars have analyzed the unity, fragmentation, and balance of power among different nonstate actors within the same movement—such as armed groups in an insurgency or political parties and nongovernmental organizations in a social movement—to assess how the dynamics *within* a group affect the use and effectiveness of coercion *without*.[68] For instance, Wendy Pearlman has persuasively shown that the process of "spoiling" can serve as an effective means of coercion against external opponents, as well as an effective method of within-group political contestation.[69] Likewise, in chapter 7 of this volume, Krause demonstrates that the distribution of power within social movements affects the capacity of individual groups within the movement to coerce state and other nonstate actors.

Works such as these represent a research program with significant potential not only to advance our understanding of nonstate coercion but also to shed

---

67 For a divergent perspective on the efficacy of drones, see Anoop Sarbahi and Patrick Johnston, "The Impact of U.S. Drone Strikes on Terrorism in Pakistan and Afghanistan," *International Studies Quarterly* 60 (2016): 203–19.

68 Wendy Pearlman, "Spoiling Inside and Out: Internal Political Contestation and the Middle East Peace Process," *International Security* 33 (2008): 79–109; Kathleen Cunningham, "Divide and Conquer or Divide and Concede: How Do States Respond to Internally Divided Separatists?," *American Political Science Review* 105 (2011): 275–97; Peter Krause, "The Structure of Success: How the Internal Distribution of Power Drives Armed Group Behavior and National Movement Effectiveness," *International Security* 38 (2013–14): 72–117.

69 Pearlman, "Spoiling Inside and Out." *Spoiling* refers to the process of using violence to oppose or resist the conclusion or implementation of peace processes. On the coercive possibilities of spoiling, see Stephen John Stedman, "Spoiler Problems in Peace Processes," *International Security* 22 (1997): 5–53; Kelly M. Greenhill and Solomon Major, "The Perils of Profiling: Civil War Spoiling and the Collapse of Intrastate Peace Accords," *International Security* 31 (2006–7): 7–40.

light on the many issues previously highlighted concerning state coercers who have generally, if perhaps too simplistically, been assumed to be unitary actors. While some of the parameters have shifted and the aperture has broadened, the power to hurt remains a key feature of international politics in the twenty-first century and a critical area of study in international relations and security studies.

Summary

Based on the preceding analysis, we offer a brief summary of what we think we know about coercion and what we still need to know:

1. Homeland deterrence is easier to achieve than extended deterrence, although we have only indirect evidence to that effect. We need direct evidence that this is the case.
2. The challenger's strength of motivation (its resolve) is probably the most important factor in determining whether there will be an immediate deterrence failure. This proposition needs to be tested.
3. Deterrence and compellence often come in pairs during an immediate deterrence failure because the deterrer tries to shore up deterrence through compellent threats and actions against the challenger. This proposition needs to be tested.
4. Extended deterrence is easier than compellence when we are speaking of compellence by denial, but the situation appears to be the reverse when we are speaking of compellence by punishment.
5. Coercive diplomacy is difficult because threats to use force, as well as demonstrative and limited uses of force, are less effective than actions that employ force or employ it in significant amounts.
6. There appears to be no significant difference between the success rates of wartime compellence and coercive diplomacy, but more study of this proposition is necessary to confirm it.
7. Whether denial works better than punishment (or vice versa) depends on the context of its use, the nature of the coercer and target, and the type of coercive instrument(s) used.
8. Compellence appears to work better when combined with both reassurances and inducements, but the evidence we have is suggestive only, and more research is necessary to verify what seems deductively sound.
9. There appears to be no strong correlation between what a compeller asks of a target (its demand) and whether the target complies, at least among states. More research on this is necessary.

10. A coercer's superiority in capabilities over a target does not necessarily translate into success, but in fact may hinder the successful exercise of coercive diplomacy.
11. The greater the disparity in power between the compeller and the target, the less likely the former is to get its way vis-à-vis the latter.
12. Nuclear extended deterrence has a high success rate, whereas successful nuclear compellence appears to be a rare event.
13. Nonstate coercion in the form of terrorism and insurgency has a mixed record. Initial studies indicate that the magnitude of the demand, the discriminate nature of the violence, and the unitary nature of the coercer are the key factors in explaining variation in outcome, although further study is necessary.

The essays in this volume build upon these insights. In the main they make three different types of contribution. Some apply traditional coercive concepts to new subject areas. Some refine further our long-held understandings of coercion-related concepts. Others add new insights to what we thought we knew. Here are some of the insights of the subsequent chapters:

1. Compellence is a bargaining process in which the shadow of the future matters a great deal.
2. Relative capabilities of coercers and targets are poor overall predictors of success. This is the case because weak actors may select into crises only where their resolve is great and because strong actors tend to make large demands and offer few incentives, leading to higher rates of coercive failure; that is, weak actors can successfully compel strong actors and successfully resist compellence by them.
3. Many classic coercion concepts can be both profitably and easily mapped onto new domains and applied to new issue areas. Such concepts include the stability-instability paradox, force majeure, escalation dominance, balance of power, and isolation of the adversary.
4. Accurate intelligence is a key variable in coercive diplomatic gambits.
5. Foreign imposed regime change in the past has been highly effective, but only against highly vulnerable targets: those that are relatively weak and geographically close to the compeller and in which the regime leaders possess exit options—three conditions that are unlikely to be duplicated in the future for any given regime.
6. Nonmilitary and cross-domain forms of coercion are common and often effective; nevertheless their significance is generally still underappreciated. Such tools include diplomatic isolation, economic sanctions, resource-related blackmail, using people as weapons, and cyber attacks.
7. Relaxation of the unitary actor assumption is necessary to fully understand intragroup coercion dynamics, such as within insurgencies and national movements.

8. Coercion, even when successful in the short run, can generate blowback and lead to longer-term failures.

Coercion, especially when it involves the threat or actual use of force, is a nasty business. This is important to keep in mind when deciding when and how to employ forceful coercion of either the deterrent or compellent variety. Adding to our knowledge about the power to hurt is essential whether we aim to assess, deploy, respond to, or stop coercion in the most effective and humane manner possible.

CHAPTER 2 | Intelligence and Coercion

A Neglected Connection

AUSTIN LONG

INTELLIGENCE AND COERCION HAVE long been recognized as important elements of international security. From the intelligence gaps that allowed the Allies to be blindsided by Japanese and German attacks in World War II to similar gaps before the 1973 Yom Kippur War and the attacks of September 11, 2001, the importance of intelligence to security is widely appreciated.[1] Similarly, coercion (compellence and its cousin, deterrence) has been a major subject of scholarly effort. As Robert J. Art and Kelly M. Greenhill note in their chapter in this volume, there have been several waves of study of the phenomenon since 1945.[2]

However, there has been much less effort to systematically examine the connections between intelligence and coercion. This chapter explores three central ways the two are linked. First, by providing a coercer with an understanding of a target's values, resolve, and capabilities, intelligence collection and analysis are crucial to evaluating how and to what extent coercion is possible. Indeed, in some cases intelligence is critical to even determining if coercion has succeeded. Second, intelligence collection and analysis is also essential to directing the tools of coercion—whether military force or economic sanctions—at specific elements of a target's political, economic, or military assets. Third, covert action, often though not always conducted by intelligence organizations, provides a discrete mechanism for coercion that lies between the overt use of military force

[1] See, inter alia, Roberta Wohlstetter, *Pearl Harbor: Warning and Decision* (Stanford: Stanford University Press, 1962); Ernest May, *Strange Victory: Hitler's Conquest of France* (New York: Hill and Wang, 2001); David E. Murphy. *What Stalin Knew: The Enigma of Barbarossa* (New Haven, CT: Yale University Press, 2005); Uri Bar-Joseph, *The Watchman Fell Asleep: The Surprise of Yom Kippur and Its Sources* (Albany, NY: SUNY Press, 2005); *The Report of National Commission on Terrorist Attacks upon the United States* (New York: W.W. Norton, 2004).

[2] See also Thomas Schelling, *Arms and Influence* (New Haven, CT: Yale University Press, 1966); Robert Pape, *Bombing to Win: Air Power and Coercion in War* (Ithaca, NY: Cornell University Press, 1996); Daniel Byman and Matthew Waxman, *The Dynamics of Coercion: American Foreign Policy and the Limits of Military Might* (New York: Cambridge University Press, 2002).

TABLE 2.1 The Functions of Intelligence for Coercion

FUNCTION	DESCRIPTION	ROLE IN COERCION CAMPAIGN
Analysis of target (precoercion)	Understanding adversary values, capabilities, and objectives	Helps coercer identify which threats are likely to be effective
Analysis of target (postcoercion)	Understanding adversary response to coercion	Necessary to know when coercion has succeeded or failed
Analysis of coercer	Gauging the intentions and capabilities of the coercer	Helps target assess the credibility of the threat
Targeting	Finding and holding military and nonmilitary targets at risk	Required to threaten assets, especially mobile ones, with military force or nonmilitary means (e.g., asset forfeiture)
Campaign analysis	Evaluating effects of coercive tools and integrating tools in an overall campaign	Required to maximize coercion effectiveness
Covert action	Use of coercion via intelligence organizations in a clandestine and/or deniable fashion	Adds a coercive tool that may be less costly and more effective

and other nonviolent mechanisms of coercion. After analyzing these functions of intelligence for coercion (summarized in Table 2.1), the chapter concludes by examining the challenges of using intelligence capabilities in coercion and the need for a more sustained research agenda focused on intelligence.

Knowing the Enemy: How Intelligence Drives the Perception and Success of Coercion

The link between intelligence and coercion effectiveness is perhaps the most studied of the connections between the two. As Daniel Byman, Matthew Waxman, and Eric Larson have noted, "successful coercion requires not only the collection of accurate data but a sophisticated integration of those data to generate the total profile of the adversary necessary to design appropriate coercive threats."[3] Art and Greenhill echo this conclusion, underscoring the need in deterrence interactions to know "the value the protector and would-be challenger put on their own respective interests, as well as on their estimates of how much the *other* values its interests." Without this understanding a coercer does not even know what or how much to threaten.

[3] Daniel Byman, Matthew Waxman, and Eric Larson, *Air Power as a Coercive Instrument* (Santa Monica, CA: RAND, 1999), 44.

For example, during the Cold War there were serious questions about how much nuclear targeting of Soviet cities would enable the United States to deter the Soviet Union in a crisis. In the 1970s this led to several studies on what the Soviets really cared about, which concluded that leadership and regime survival were more important to threaten than cities or even military forces.[4] The United States adjusted its nuclear coercion strategy accordingly.

A similar evolution in understanding adversary values took place during the Kosovo air war. NATO targeting of Serbian military assets did not have the desired coercive effect in part due to weaknesses in targeting intelligence (discussed in the next section of this chapter) and in part due to not threatening the appropriate targets. Once the campaign shifted to holding the assets of Serbian elites at risk, those elites began to pressure the Serbian government to accede to NATO demands.

Even when a coercer threatens something the target values, intelligence is required to understand how that threat interacts with other threats. Furthermore the target needs intelligence to understand how seriously to take the threat. A lack of quality intelligence on the side of the coercer or the target can thus lead to coercion failure.

The confrontation between Iraq and the United States over Iraq's alleged weapons of mass destruction (WMD) program in 2002–3 represents one of the most striking examples of coercion failure due to inadequate intelligence. Iraq failed to appreciate the seriousness of the U.S. threat to invade until very late, and the United States failed to appreciate how its threat interacted with other threats to Iraq, most notably those concerning the regime stability of Iraqi dictator Saddam Hussein. The United States also failed to detect that its coercive effort to compel Iraq to abandon its WMD program had already succeeded.[5]

As is now apparent, in 2002 Iraq had no WMD. U.S. coercion had therefore already succeeded, even before the crisis. However, Saddam still sought to use the threat of WMD for deterrence, relying on a formula that one Iraqi general termed "deterrence by doubt."[6] This required maintaining high levels of ambiguity in complying with UN inspectors from 1991 until 2003. As stated in the "Comprehensive Report of the Special Advisor to the Director of Central Intelligence on Iraq's Weapons of Mass Destruction" (a.k.a. the Duelfer Report), "The Iran-Iraq war and the ongoing suppression of internal unrest taught Saddam the importance of WMD to the dominance and survival of the

---

[4] William Odom, "The Origins and Design of Presidential Decision-59: A Memoir," in *Getting MAD: Nuclear Mutual Assured Destruction, Its Origins and Practice*, ed. Henry D. Sokolski (Carlisle Barracks, PA: Strategic Studies Institute, 2004).

[5] For an alternative interpretation see Phil Haun, *Coercion, Survival, and War: Why Weak States Resist the United States* (Stanford: Stanford University Press, 2015).

[6] "Interview: Lt. Gen. Raad al-Hamdani," *Frontline*, PBS, n.d., http://www.pbs.org/wgbh//pages/frontline/shows/invasion/interviews/raad.html. Hamdani is widely regarded as one of the most non-political, competent Iraqi generals; he commanded the II Republican Guard Corps during Operation Iraqi Freedom.

Regime. Following the destruction of much of the Iraqi WMD infrastructure during Desert Storm, however, the threats to the Regime remained; especially his perception of the overarching danger from Iran. In order to counter these threats, Saddam continued with his public posture of retaining the WMD capability. This led to a difficult balancing act between the need to disarm to achieve sanctions relief while at the same time retaining a strategic deterrent."[7] The need to maintain secrecy regarding the actual extent of the WMD program was so high that many senior Iraqi military and political figures were unaware of the extent of disarmament.[8]

The U.S. intelligence community not only failed to detect Iraq's deception; it also did not appreciate Iraq's threat calculus, which ranked internal threats as most dangerous, followed closely by threats from neighboring Iran. These two threats were highly interrelated, as the Shia government of Iran might lend support to Iraqi Shia. From Saddam's perspective, the United States was a distant third to these two threats. Both internal enemies and the Iranian regime were believed to have much higher credibility in terms of willingness to carry out threats than the United States.

Despite its overwhelming power, Iraqi leadership did not believe that the United States would do much to punish the regime for noncompliance. At most, the Iraqi leadership believed the United States might use its massive air power to support a Shia revolt.[9] This failure meant Iraq, the target of compellence, did not believe the United States would execute its threat.

The influence of Saddam's personal biases on this threat calculus was considerable. He simply could not imagine that the United States would have the stomach to commit ground troops, particularly if the United Nations did not support the invasion. The United States had left Vietnam, he said, after losing 58,000 troops. During the Iran-Iraq War, Iraq had lost that many in the battle for the al Faw peninsula alone. He made specific references to Somalia (allegedly even giving out copies of *Black Hawk Down* to military officers) and even Operation Enduring Freedom as indicative of Americans' fear of casualties. In addition, he had faith that France and Russia would prevent a UN resolution. So as long as he could ride out the bombardment and uprisings, he would survive. Worst case, he would lose the far south of Iraq (around Basra) as he had lost the far north to the Kurds after the 1991 Gulf War.[10] Better Iraqi intelligence might have helped disabuse him of these notions of U.S. timidity, and better U.S. intelligence might have helped policymakers understand Saddam's skewed threat assessment.[11] Either would have made coercion failure less likely.

---

[7] "Comprehensive Report of the Special Advisor to the Director of Central Intelligence on Iraq's Weapons of Mass Destruction" (hereafter Duelfer Report), vol. 1, section 1, p. 34.

[8] Duelfer Report, vol. 1, section 1, pp. 64–65; Kevin Woods, et al., The *Iraqi Perspectives Project: A View of Operation Iraqi Freedom from Saddam's Senior Leaderhip* (Norfolk, VA: U.S. Joint Forces Command, 2006) (hereafter Iraqi Perspectives), 91–92.

[9] *Iraqi Perspectives*, 25–28.

[10] Ibid., 29–31.

[11] While Iraqi intelligence was extremely limited, it was much more focused on—and to some extent more effective in—evaluating the Iranian threat. For evidence of this, based on captured Iraqi

In contrast to the perceived weakness of U.S. resolve, Iran had fought an incredibly bloody eight-year war with Iraq. The credibility of the Iranians was never in doubt among the Iraqi leadership, who had experienced the effects of Iranian "human wave" attacks and had seen Iranian troops occupy Iraqi soil. Given the atrophy in the conventional Iraqi military after the Gulf War, Saddam felt that his ambiguous WMD threat was his only card for deterring Iran. Thus an intelligence failure led Saddam to maintain an illusion of WMD to deter Iran and internal enemies, even though that illusion invited U.S. attack. U.S. intelligence failed to understand the broader threats to Iraq and also could not determine that Iraq had no WMD and little chance of restarting its program.

Deterrence by doubt began to crumble as the United States and its allies moved to prepare for war in late 2002. Saddam finally began to believe that the U.S. coercive threat might be credible. He was forced to reveal to his senior leadership that in fact no WMD would be available in a conflict with the United States. According to former deputy prime minister Tariq Aziz, morale plummeted after this revelation.[12] The regime then moved to cooperate with inspectors and rushed to clean up any remaining hints or fragments of WMD programs.[13]

However, this rush was too little, too late to prevent a U.S. invasion. These problems were amplified by the unwillingness of Iraqi intelligence to accurately assess both Iraqi and U.S. capabilities. Information passed up the chain of command was tailored to please Saddam and was filled with distortions, half-truths, wishful thinking, and outright lying.[14] After interviewing the notorious "Chemical Ali," the authors of the Duelfer Report dryly noted, "Asked how Saddam treated people who brought him bad news, 'Ali Hasan Al Majid replied, 'I don't know.' ISG assesses that 'Ali Hasan Al Majid has never known any instance of anybody bringing bad news to Saddam."[15] Clearly Saddam had poor intelligence not only on the U.S. threat but also on the actual readiness of the Iraqi state and military for war.

In the other direction, distortions flowing down the chain of command had deleterious effects on the execution of Saddam's orders. For example, his decision to fully comply with inspectors in late 2002 was met with disbelief by members of Iraq's Military Industrialization Commission (MIC) that oversaw work on military technology. They feared that this order, so at odds with Saddam's long-standing policy, was some sort of ruse or loyalty test. Knowing that disloyalty was readily punished by summary execution and/or torture, members of the MIC were hesitant to comply. Not until the Iraqi vice president came and spoke to them for several hours in early 2003 about the legitimacy

---

records, see "Iraqi Human Intelligence Collection on Iran's Nuclear Weapons Program, 1980–2003," *Studies in Intelligence* 57, no. 4 (December 2013): 23–30

[12] Duelfer Report, vol. 1, section 1, p. 65.

[13] Duelfer Report, vol. 1, section 1, pp. 63–64; *Iraqi Perspectives*, 91–95.

[14] See Duelfer Report, vol. 1, section 1, pp. 11–12; *Iraqi Perspectives*, 6–10.

[15] Duelfer Report, vol. 1, section 1, p. 11. ISG is the Iraq Survey Group, the organization tasked to review Iraq's WMD program.

of the order did they accept it as genuine.[16] Even prior to this, elements of the MIC had been deceiving the regime's own National Monitoring Directorate, charged with ensuring compliance with UN resolutions.[17]

The resultant confusion among Iraqis about whether they were to comply with or continue to deceive inspectors may have contributed to the U.S. and UN interpretation of the events of late 2002 and early 2003. Conditioned by years of deception, the international community saw the confused and haphazard Iraqi attempts at full compliance as evidence of continuing deception. In fact this fragmented response to directives was simply symptomatic of the nature of the regime.[18] Thus both U.S. and Iraqi intelligence failures interacted to produce a "failure" of coercion, followed by brute force war, when in fact coercion had already succeeded.

The converse of this bizarre situation of coercion failure is also possible, as without good intelligence a coercer could believe that coercion has succeeded when it has in fact failed. This is one of the principal concerns about a potential agreement over Iran's nuclear program. Without highly effective monitoring, any agreement that Iran makes (short of fully abandoning its nuclear ambitions) could be subject to cheating through the use of clandestine facilities. The Joint Comprehensive Plan of Action that Iran and the international community agreed to thus has substantial monitoring provisions that create intelligence collection opportunities.[19]

One could imagine a similar problem in the Cuban Missile Crisis. Without U.S. overhead imagery and photographic interpretation, the U.S. government would have had neither the ability to detect Soviet missiles before they were fully deployed nor the ability to verify that the Soviets had withdrawn the missiles.[20] Similar logic applies to verification of arms control agreements, though they are often not a result of coercion per se (although the Intermediate-Range Nuclear Forces (INF) Treaty was a result of U.S. nuclear deployment decisions that had a coercive element).[21] Without intelligence, it is difficult, if not impossible, to determine compliance or noncompliance.

---

[16] Duelfer Report, vol. 1, section 1, p. 9.

[17] Duelfer Report, vol. 1, section 1, pp. 53–55.

[18] See Duelfer Report, vol. 1, section 1, pp. 10, 63–64; *Iraqi Perspectives*, 92–94. In addition to the official report, see Charles Duelfer, *Hide and Seek: The Search for Truth in Iraq* (New York: Public Affairs, 2009) and Charles Duelfer and Stephen Dyson, "Chronic Misperception and International Conflict: The U.S.-Iraq Experience," *International Security* 36, no. 1 (Summer 2011): 73-96

[19] See Austin Long, "If You Really Want to Bomb Iran, Take the Deal," in *Iran and the Nuclear Deal* (Washington, DC: Project on Middle East Political Science, 2015).

[20] On the importance of imagery in the Cuban Missile Crisis, see Dino Brugioni, *Eyeball to Eyeball: The Inside Story of the Cuban Missile Crisis* (New York: Random House, 1992).

[21] For a recent assessment of intelligence and verification in the nuclear realm, see Defense Science Board, *Assessment of Nuclear Monitoring and Verification Technologies* (January 2014), http://www.acq.osd.mil/dsb/reports/2010s/NuclearMonitoringAndVerificationTechnologies.pdf. On the coercive elements of Intermediate-Range Nuclear Forces Treaty negotiations, see Russell Sherrett, "Dual Track Decision and the Intermediate-Range Nuclear Force Treaty: The Role of the Cruise and Pershing II Missiles" (Master's thesis, U.S. Army Command and General Staff College, 1992).

The INF Treaty highlights the complication this imposes on coding success of coercion, which, as Art and Greenhill point out, is often difficult to begin with. Beginning in 2014 the United States accused the Russian Federation of violating the treaty (presumably based on intelligence sources). It then began "to review a broad range of military response options and to consider the effect each option could have on convincing Russian leadership to return to compliance with the INF Treaty and on countering the capability of a Russian INF Treaty prohibited system."[22] "Convincing" Russian leadership with military options sounds like tacit acknowledgment of coercion, but how will the United States know it has succeeded, given that Russia still maintains it is not in violation? The intelligence requirement to confirm the Russians are no longer in violation, as opposed to merely better at hiding the violation, will be even higher than finding the violation initially.

In some cases, simply demonstrating that the coercer has quality intelligence is enough to amplify the effect of coercive threats by making them more credible. Bruce Jentleson and Christopher Whytock describe the power of intelligence that the United States and United Kingdom demonstrated by intercepting both Libyan communications and a ship carrying WMD components. These intelligence triumphs had a psychological effect on the Libyans, as they came to understand how much was known about their WMD and terrorist activity, and it contributed to the successful campaign to coerce Libya to relinquish its WMD program.[23]

A similar phenomenon can be observed with the Soviet Union in the 1970s and 1980s. Human intelligence successes enabled the Soviets to understand significant aspects of U.S. technical intelligence collection. The Soviets began to take certain U.S. threats much more seriously and indeed to overestimate U.S. credibility in some cases.[24]

Intelligence is thus an underappreciated linchpin of coercion effectiveness; it merits its own place on the list of mechanisms for coercion success or failure. Without intelligence, coercers cannot know what target assets to threaten, and it is difficult if not impossible for them to know whether their coercive threats have actually succeeded. It is likewise difficult for the targets of coercion to assess the nature and credibility of coercive threats without adequate intelligence.

---

[22] Statement of Brian McKeon, Principal Deputy Undersecretary of Defense for Policy, before the House Armed Services Committee Subcommittee on Strategic Forces, December 1, 2015, p. 4.

[23] Bruce Jentleson and Christopher Whytock, "Who 'Won' Libya? The Force-Diplomacy Debate and Its Implications for Theory and Policy," *International Security* 30, no. 3 (Winter 2005): 75–76. See also Michael Crawford, "Exploring the Maze: Counter-proliferation Intelligence," *Survival* 53, no. 2 (April–May 2011): 131–58.

[24] See discussion in Austin Long and Brendan Rittenhouse Green, "Stalking the Secure Second Strike: Intelligence, Counterforce, and Nuclear Strategy," *Journal of Strategic Studies* 38, nos. 1–2 (2015): 38–73; also see Brendan Rittenhouse Green and Austin Long, "The MAD Who Wasn't There: Soviet Reactions to the Late Cold War Strategic Balance," *Security Studies* (forthcoming).

Deploying Coercive Tools: Intelligence to Find and Fix Targets

In addition to helping coercers understand what to threaten, intelligence provides a crucial mechanism for deploying the tools by which threats are carried out. This is true not only of straightforward military force, such as bombing, but also more subtle tools such as sanctions. All require intelligence in order to be effective. Conversely, intelligence can also allow the target of coercion to take certain actions to preempt or mitigate a coercer's threat.

For example, during the Cuban Missile Crisis, once U.S. intelligence had determined that holding Soviet leadership at risk was important for coercion in a general sense, improved intelligence was required to be able to target the leadership with nuclear forces. While this would initially seem to be an easy task—simply bomb Moscow—in fact the Soviet leadership had invested heavily in mobile and underground facilities to ensure they survived. The United States needed to develop the ability to locate these facilities and destroy them in order to threaten Soviet leadership.[25]

Another effort to potentially coerce the Soviet Union during a conventional war centered on intelligence for antisubmarine warfare. The U.S. Navy planned to target Soviet ballistic missile submarines during the opening conventional phases of any war with the Soviet Union. Destroying these valuable components of the Soviet Union's nuclear force structure would, it was believed, have a strong coercive effect and help bring the Soviets to the peace table.[26]

While some analysts believed this strategy would provoke the Soviets rather than coerce them, the ability to even make the threat hinged on intelligence. The United States therefore invested heavily in acoustic and signals intelligence in order to track elusive Soviet submarines. During the Cold War these programs were highly classified, but based on subsequent revelations it seems clear that the United States had significant success in collecting actionable intelligence and therefore could potentially have carried out this threat.[27]

Intelligence can also play a critical role in countering coercive threats. Some threats rely on surprise to be effective and credible, so intelligence that provides a warning can allow targets of coercion to mitigate the impact. In other cases, targeting intelligence can allow for preemptive or reactive attacks to neutralize the threat.

For example, one of the most feared threats that Iran could use for counter-coercion is to close the Strait of Hormuz with military forces. A major portion

[25] See Odom, "The Origins and Design of Presidential Decision-59."
[26] Barry R. Posen, *Inadvertent Escalation: Conventional War and Nuclear Risks* (Ithaca, NY: Cornell University Press, 1991); Long and Green, "Stalking the Secure Second Strike."
[27] See Christopher Ford and David Rosenberg, *The Admiral's Advantage: U.S. Navy Operational Intelligence in World War II and the Cold War* (Annapolis, MD: Naval Institute Press, 2005); Sherry Sontag and Christopher Drew, *Blind Man's Bluff: The Untold Story of American Submarine Espionage* (New York: Public Affairs, 1998); and especially Owen Cote, *The Third Battle: Innovation in the U.S. Navy's Silent Cold War Struggle with Soviet Submarines* (Newport, RI: Naval War College, 2003).

of the world's oil and gas flows out of the Persian Gulf through the Strait, so closing it would have a major disruptive effect on world energy prices. Iran has developed a significant capability for mine warfare and antiship attacks that could make it extraordinarily hazardous to attempt to transit the Strait, so the threat would have some credibility.

However, one of the best unclassified analyses of the Iranian threat to the Strait argues that Iranian success is highly dependent on surprise. According to Caitlin Talmadge, if Iran were able to plant a large number of mines in the Strait without detection, then even the U.S. Navy and its allies would have a hard time clearing the Strait and restoring the free flow of commerce. Yet if Iran's mine-laying effort was detected early, the United States could immediately take preventive action that would greatly limit the threat.[28] Intelligence is thus the linchpin to countering this potential Iranian coercive threat.

Another potential Iranian coercive threat is the use of medium-range ballistic missiles and intermediate-range ballistic missiles to target oil facilities in the Gulf state allies of the United States, especially Saudi Arabia. While a comprehensive assessment of Iranian abilities suggests that this threat is currently overstated, if Iranian missile accuracy improves, it could become significant.[29] Antiballistic missile systems might mitigate this threat to some degree, but a large enough volume of missiles could saturate defenses and allow missiles to get through.

One countercoercion option would be to attack Iranian missiles before launch. Yet many of Iran's missiles are mobile, so targeting them would require detailed real-time intelligence. The United States and its allies were not particularly successful in targeting similar Iraqi missiles in the 1991 Gulf War. However, improvements in intelligence in the past two decades combined with a dedicated effort to track Iranian missiles before a crisis (which was totally absent with Iraq before 1991) could make such an endeavor much more effective and therefore an effective countercoercion capability.[30]

Similarly, one of North Korea's major coercive threats is to target the South Korean capital of Seoul and other locations with conventional artillery based along the Demilitarized Zone. Much of this artillery is not only mobile but operates from hardened artillery shelters, making it an extremely difficult target. Yet modern precision-guided munitions, combined with excellent real-time intelligence, could potentially ameliorate this threat by degrading the artillery, either preemptively or even reactively after a North Korean attack began.[31]

There are limits, at least at present, to the potential effectiveness of such intelligence-based countercoercion capabilities. The Israeli Air Force

---

[28] Caitlin Talmadge, "Closing Time: Assessing the Iranian Threat to the Strait of Hormuz," *International Security* 33, no. 1 (Summer 2008): 82–117.

[29] Joshua Shifrinson and Miranda Priebe, "A Crude Threat: The Limits of an Iranian Missile Campaign against Saudi Arabian Oil," *International Security* 36, no. 1 (Summer 2011): 167–201.

[30] See discussion in Long and Green, "Stalking the Secure Second Strike."

[31] See Joseph Bermudez, "North Korea's Long Reach in Profile," *Jane's International Defence Review*, November 1, 2003; Austin Long, *From Cold War to Long War* (Santa Monica, CA: RAND, 2008).

attempted to limit the coercive threat of Hezbollah rockets and missiles using real-time intelligence and precision-guided weapons during the 2006 war in Lebanon. While it appears to have had extraordinarily good success in eliminating the threat of long-range Hezbollah systems, it had much less success against shorter range (and therefore smaller, more numerous, and less detectable) weapons.[32]

Beyond direct use of force for both coercion and countercoercion, intelligence is also critical to deploying other coercive instruments. Whether sanctions or no-fly zones, almost every form of coercion depends on some degree of intelligence in order to be effective.

For example, one of the most potent coercive tools developed in the past decade is the use of financial sanctions based on access to the global banking system. While financial sanctions are not new, the newer versions, introduced after the attacks of September 11, 2001, rely on access to U.S. banking to incentivize private banks and other institutions to dissociate from sanctioned entities. The penalty for failing to do so is severe fines, as demonstrated by the unprecedented $10 billion fine levied on BNP Paribas for allegedly violating sanctions on Iranian financial entities.[33]

These new financial sanctions require extensive development and use of intelligence in order to be effective. First, intelligence is critical to identifying the crucial financial actors that need to be sanctioned. States (and nonstate actors) often go to extraordinary lengths to conceal their connections to financial entities when under sanctions, so this is a nontrivial problem.

For example, in 2013 the United States seized the skyscraper located at 650 Fifth Avenue in New York from the nonprofit Alavi Foundation and two other companies.[34] The owners were determined to be fronts for the Iranian government, a determination made jointly between U.S. law enforcement and intelligence organizations.[35] Without extensive financial intelligence, it is unlikely that this seizure would have been possible.

Second, even when targets of financial sanctions have been identified, intelligence is crucial to convince banks, both inside and outside of the United States, that a target is actually in violation of sanctions. Peter Feaver and Eric Lorber highlight the importance of intelligence in this context: "Banks and governments compliant with U.N. and U.S. sanction

[32] David Makovsky and Jeffrey White, *Lessons and Implications of the Israel-Hizballah War: A Preliminary Assessment* (Washington, DC: Washington Institute for Near East Policy, 2006), 51; Benjamin S. Lambeth, *Air Operations in Israel's War against Hezbollah: Learning from Lebanon and Getting It Right in Gaza*, (Santa Monica, CA: RAND, 2011), 92–110. Lambeth notes that the longest range rockets, the Zelzals, were never fired during the war despite Hezbollah rhetoric about using them to target Tel Aviv, suggesting either complete Israeli success in preemptively destroying them or extreme pressure from Iran on Hezbollah not to use them.

[33] Sean Farrell, "BNP Paribas Faces Fine of More than $10bn in US Sanctions Investigation," *Guardian*, May 30, 2014.

[34] Julie Satow, "Seizing Iran's Slice of Fifth Avenue," *New York Times*, September 24, 2013.

[35] Michael Farrell, "What's Known about Iran-Linked Alavi Foundation?," *Christian Science Monitor*, November 14, 2009.

policies have also been collaborating in this effort, and states regularly feed intelligence about the nature of Iran's illicit activities to banks that conduct business with them, or related enterprises."[36] This intelligence is crucial to convincing banks that the risk to their reputation and bottom line is not worth the returns from conducting transactions with the sanctioned entities.

This need to share intelligence highlights one crucial difference between financial intelligence for deploying sanctions and intelligence for deploying traditional military forces. While the latter targeting can be done unilaterally, the interconnected nature of global finance requires intelligence cooperation from a variety of allied countries and private sector financial institutions. Feaver and Lorber underscore the complications associated with using intelligence for financial sanctions:

> Interestingly, the presentation of sensitive information linking Iran's Revolutionary Guards to different Iranian banks to non-U.S. companies presented a tricky task for senior government officials and required significant coordination both between the United States and its allies and partner countries, as well as between U.S. government bureaucracies. U.S. officials could not present extremely detailed information to these banks because of classification issues, and therefore these banks sometimes doubted the credibility of the information being shown . . . . By approaching host governments and showing them sensitive information regarding the illicit firms, U.S. government officials were able to prevent recalcitrant banks from using their host governments' position as an argument for not reducing their transactions with the illicit firms.[37]

These financial sanctions, backed by robust intelligence and intelligence sharing, have seemingly been substantially more effective than previous generations of sanctions. Assessments in late 2013 indicated that Iran's currency was collapsing, its ability to sell oil was greatly curtailed, and its economy was generally under intense pressure. While perhaps not the only factor in bringing Iran to the table to negotiate on its nuclear program, many analysts highlight the role financial sanctions played in coercion (although Iran, not surprisingly, denies this).[38]

While Iran has been perhaps the most high-profile target of these new financial sanctions, it is not the only target. North Korea and now Russia have also been targeted, along with specific individuals and nonstate actors.

---

[36] Peter Feaver and Eric Lorber, "Coercive Diplomacy: Evaluating the Consequences of Financial Sanctions," Legatum Institute (November 2010), 30.

[37] Feaver and Lorber, "Coercive Diplomacy," 36.

[38] Thomas Erdbrink, "Iran Staggers as Sanctions Hit Economy," *New York Times*, September 30, 2013; "Iran Dismisses Barack Obama's Claim That Sanctions Prompted Nuclear Talks," *Guardian* (citing Agence France-Presse), January 30, 2014.

Lebanese Canadian Bank, for example, was targeted as the center of a major money-laundering scheme tied to Lebanese Hezbollah. The bank was essentially destroyed by this designation, as it was fined and then liquidated and its assets were bought by another bank. Intelligence was again critical to the success of sanctions, though so far coercion of Hezbollah appears to be less successful than that of Iran.[39]

Note that while financial sanctions require intelligence sharing in order to be effective, in contrast to military force that can be applied unilaterally, intelligence collection on a global scale almost always requires alliance and liaison with other intelligence services. Even the United States, which has the largest (by budget) intelligence community in the world, needs allied support. It relies heavily on its alliance with the United Kingdom, Australia, Canada, and New Zealand (the "Five Eyes") to support its global collection of signals intelligence.[40] Similarly the United States derives a significant amount of its intelligence from liaison relationships with a variety of foreign intelligence services around the world.[41]

This reliance on intelligence from allies and partners is important, as it means that while the coercive tool (military force) can be used unilaterally, it often requires intelligence that cannot be collected unilaterally to be effective. Coercion often thus has a multilateral nature even when it appears to be unilateral. This then requires agreement (even if only tacit and nonpublic) from alliance partners that the coercive act is appropriate, which in turn requires alliance management and quiet diplomacy for even the most unilateral-seeming efforts.

Few uses of military power, whether for coercion or simply brute force, are perceived to be more unilateral than U.S. drone strikes. Yet drone strikes are simply not possible without intelligence support that inevitably requires allies.[42] An example of this is the drone strikes allegedly conducted by the United States from Camp Lemonnier in Djibouti. According to open-source reports, these operations in Somalia, Yemen, and elsewhere are enabled not only by the cooperation of the government of Djibouti but also by the cooperation of

---

39 Jo Becker, "Beirut Bank Seen as a Hub of Hezbollah's Financing," *New York Times*, December 13, 2011; Nate Raymond, "Lebanese Bank to Pay U.S. $102 Million in Money-Laundering Case," Reuters, June 25, 2013.

40 The original "British-U.S. Communications Intelligence Agreement," March 5, 1946, was declassified in 2010 and is available online at NSA/ CSS, https://www.nsa.gov/news-features/declassified-documents/ukusa/assets/files/agreement_outline_5mar46.pdf. See also Jeffrey T. Richelson and Desmond Ball, *The Ties That Bind: Intelligence Cooperation between the United Kingdom/United States of America Countries—United Kingdom, United States of America, Canada, Australia and New Zealand Countries* (Boston: Allen & Unwin, 1985).

41 Daniel Byman, "The Intelligence War on Terrorism," *Intelligence and National Security* (December 2013): 837–63.

42 This point is discussed in more detail in Austin Long, "Dueling Asymmetries: International Terrorism, Insurgency, and Drone Warfare in the 21st Century," in *The Future of Warfare in the 21st Century* (Abu Dhabi: Emirates Center for Strategic Studies and Research, 2014).

the United Kingdom, which provides a communication relay and likely other intelligence support to the camp.[43]

Coercive Covert Action and the Necessity of Intelligence

In addition to enabling coercion via other tools, such as military strikes or sanctions, intelligence can provide a mechanism to directly coerce: covert action. Covert action in this case means an action whose effects (political or military) may be observable but whose origin cannot be determined or can be plausibly denied. Covert action thus provides an intermediate step between the overt use of military force and powerful but indirect levers like financial sanctions.[44] While covert action is not exclusively the province of intelligence organizations, it is typically conducted by such organizations if for no other reason than they are typically the best placed to do so. In addition, covert action requires the same sort of intelligence for targeting noted above for overt action or sanctions.

One major type of covert action that has been widely noted as a coercive tool is proxy warfare.[45] In proxy warfare, a state sponsors a third-party proxy to attack a desired target while the sponsor remains unknown (or at least can plausibly deny charges of support). While proxies seldom directly threaten the survival of a regime in the way that overt military action does, they can nonetheless impose significant costs.

Intelligence organizations, whether civilian or military, are almost always the part of a state's security apparatus that is responsible for proxy warfare. These organizations are by design opaque, allowing states to maintain plausible deniability for their support to proxies. Understanding proxy warfare thus requires understanding intelligence and intelligence organizations.[46]

An example of proxy warfare for coercion is the case of Iran and Iraq in the 1970s. The two states had a variety of territorial disputes, particularly regarding the Shatt al-Arab waterway along the Iran-Iraq border. Iran, through intelligence organizations, supported the Iraqi Kurds as a proxy force to coerce the Iraqi government into recognizing Iranian claims. While not the only source of pressure on Iraq, the result of Iranian support was the eventual recognition of Iran's claims in the 1975 Algiers Accord. In exchange, Iran ended support for the Iraqi Kurds.[47] Although the Algiers Accord proved transient after the fall of the shah of Iran, it highlights the potential effectiveness of proxy warfare.

---

[43] Mark Ballard, "UK Helping US Military Build Intelligence Software for Drone Targeting," *Computer Weekly*, May 7, 2014; Craig Whitlock, "Remote U.S. Base at Core of Secret Operations," *Washington Post*, October 25, 2012.

[44] See also Austin Carson, "Secrecy, Acknowledgement, and War Escalation: A Study in Covert Competition" (Ph.D. dissertation, Ohio State University, 2013).

[45] See Byman et al., *Air Power as a Coercive Instrument.*

[46] See Erica Borghard, "Friends with Benefits? Power and Influence in Proxy Warfare" (Ph.D. dissertation, Columbia University, 2014).

[47] F. Gregory Gause, *The International Relations of the Persian Gulf* (New York: Cambridge University Press, 2009).

However, proxy warfare also has a number of shortcomings. First, the interests of the coercer and the proxy are seldom more than partially aligned. This can weaken the effectiveness of coercion if, for example, the proxy's actions in pursuit of its interests do not impose significant costs on the target of coercion Alternatively the target of coercion may be willing to make concessions to the interests of the proxy, but not the coercer.

Intelligence is thus vital to determining how to coerce the target and in selecting and managing an effective proxy. Failure to understand the proxy can result in much less effective coercion due to divergence of interest. At worst it can lead to blowback, where the proxy's actions directly or indirectly strengthen the intended target of coercion.

In addition, proxy warfare for coercion becomes more complicated if the coercer is not geographically close to the proxy. While Iran had an easy time supporting Iraqi Kurds in territory adjacent to Iran, many would-be proxies are not so conveniently located. This, then, often requires a coercer to ally with another, adjacent state (or states). This further complicates coercion, as the interests of the adjacent state, the coercer, and the proxy may all be quite distinct. Typically both the coercer and the adjacent state will use their intelligence organizations as agents and interlocutors. The result can be a tangle of competing agendas that, even when successful in coercion, can produce a variety of unintended consequences.

The U.S. support to the Afghan mujahedin in order to impose costs and ultimately coerce the Soviets into withdrawing from Afghanistan is perhaps the most notable example of this phenomenon. Lacking proximity, the United States, via the Central Intelligence Agency, had to turn to Pakistan to provide the conduit and staging area for proxy support. Pakistan, represented by its Inter-Services Intelligence, wanted a strong say in which mujahedin were supported. The divergence between Pakistan, the United States, other supporters of the mujahedin (such as Saudi Arabia's General Intelligence Directorate and the United Kingdom's Secret Intelligence Service), and the mujahedin factions led to a disjointed effort against the Soviets and frequent in-fighting among the mujahedin. This greatly weakened the effectiveness of the mujahedin, and when the Soviets withdrew and the communist regime in Afghanistan fell, civil war emerged that created opportunities for both the Afghan Taliban and Al Qaeda.[48]

Moreover some of the proxies that the United States supported in the 1980s would subsequently become its most dangerous enemies as their interests diverged. The Haqqani network is the paramount example of this. In the 1980s, Jaluddin Haqqani, a Pashtun mujahedin commander from eastern Afghanistan, was one of the most effective leaders in the fight against

[48] Milt Bearden and James Risen, *The Main Enemy: The Inside Story of the CIA's Final Showdown with the KGB* (New York: Random House, 2003); Steve Coll, *Ghost Wars: The Secret History of the CIA, Afghanistan and Bin Laden: From the Soviet Invasion to September 10, 2001* (New York: Penguin Books, 2004).

the Soviets. U.S. Congressman Charlie Wilson, the most vocal supporter of the mujahedin, allegedly called Haqqani "goodness personified." Yet decades later Haqqani and his sons led one of the most lethal components of the anti-U.S. insurgency in Afghanistan, with continued support allegedly coming from Pakistan.[49]

In addition to proxy warfare, states have other covert action options for coercion. One is the direct use of covert forces against the target of coercion. While this is similar in some ways to overt use of force, the scale is frequently much smaller and it faces unique challenges, not least of which is maintaining plausible deniability for the coercer. Nevertheless such use of force is not infrequently part of a coercive campaign. Intelligence organizations are typically at the forefront of such activities.

An example of direct covert action for coercion from the early Cold War is the British campaign to impose costs on Indonesia during the period of Indo-Malaysian confrontation (also known as Konfrontasi). The British military sought to coerce Indonesia into accepting the formation of the Malaysian Federation, which Indonesia opposed, instead supporting an insurgency on the island of Borneo against the new Malaysian government and its British allies.

The British did not want to escalate the conflict significantly, so its coercion options were limited.[50] Direct covert action by British forces against Indonesian targets just over the border on Borneo allowed the British to impose costs while minimizing the risk of escalation for at least two years. These punitive raids were small and kept highly classified, but they ultimately played a significant part in coercing Indonesia into ending Konfrontasi.[51]

Direct covert action was also part of an alleged Israeli campaign to coerce Iraq and France to abandon nuclear cooperation in the 1970s, which Israel feared would ultimately lead to Iraq's acquiring nuclear weapons. This covert action campaign, allegedly conducted by Israel's foreign intelligence service, Mossad, included assassination of Iraqi nuclear scientists, sabotage of a reactor core being assembled in France for shipment to Iraq, and attacks on French companies.[52] While this campaign had some coercive success, allegedly causing the French to stipulate that they would provide oversight of the Iraqi reactor for a decade, it ultimately did not succeed in ending Franco-Iraqi cooperation. As a result, Israel escalated to overt brute force military action against the reactor, destroying it in June 1981.

---

[49] See Coll, *Ghost Wars*; Emma Graham-Harrison, "Haqqani Network Is Considered Most Ruthless Branch of Afghan Insurgency," *Guardian*, September 7, 2012.

[50] For other examples, see Carson, "Secrecy, Acknowledgement, and War Escalation."

[51] Thomas Mockaitis, *British Counterinsurgency in the Post-Imperial Era* (Manchester: Manchester University Press, 1995), 32–39.

[52] Bennett Ramberg, "Osirak and Its Lessons for Iran Policy," *Arms Control Today*, May 2012; Rodger W. Claire, *Raid on the Sun: Inside Israel's Secret Campaign That Denied Saddam the Bomb* (New York: Broadway Books, 2004).

A similar campaign, also orchestrated by Israeli intelligence, is alleged to be currently under way against Iran, with the goal of coercing Iran to abandon its nuclear program. This campaign has included assassination of Iranian nuclear scientists and sabotage of facilities. As with the campaign against Iraq, it has not (yet) succeeded.[53]

However, one significant difference between the campaign against Iraq's nuclear program and the similar one against Iran's program is the introduction of sabotage through cyber rather than physical means. This was most clearly demonstrated by the so-called Stuxnet computer virus, which was introduced into the control systems for critical components of Iran's nuclear program through clandestine means. This opens up new potential mechanisms for coercion but also demonstrates the need for extensive intelligence collection and preparation in order to utilize such tools. Stuxnet required extensive technical understanding and human penetration (either witting or unwitting) of the Iranian nuclear program to be even modestly effective.[54]

Cyber therefore represents an evolution in covert action, but not a total revolution. Other cyber attempts at sabotage after Stuxnet have been less effective in part because of the requirement for some level of physical penetration to cross the so-called air gap into critical systems. Air gaps are physical disconnects between networks and the Internet, which limits the ability of typical cyber approaches to penetrate the network. As an example, the so-called Shamoon virus, launched via email against Saudi ARAMCO allegedly in retaliation for Stuxnet, corrupted business data but did not affect oil production, as those critical systems were air-gapped.[55] Thus even fairly sophisticated cyber covert action requires intelligence for targeting and some level of physical intervention to target air-gapped systems, presumably from recruited human agents. This underscores the criticality of overall intelligence capabilities for any sort of coercion.

Cyber efforts can also add to more traditional mechanisms of coercion. The United States is alleged to have used cyber attacks on Serbian air defense in conjunction with more traditional electronic warfare to enable the air campaign against Serbia during the 1999 Kosovo war. As with the other cyber actions noted above, this likely relied on extensive intelligence preparation. This is underscored by the fact that the United States debated using but did not use similar techniques against Libya in 2011 as they would take too long

---

[53] Yaakov Katz and Yoaz Hendel, *Israel vs. Iran: The Shadow War* (Washington, DC: Potomac Books, 2012).

[54] Jon Lindsay, "Stuxnet and the Limits of Cyber Warfare," *Security Studies* 22, no. 3 (2013) 365-404; Ralph Langner, "To Kill a Centrifuge: A Technical Analysis of What Stuxnet's Creators Tried to Achieve," The Langner Group (November 2013), https://www.langner.com/wp-content/uploads/2017/03/to-kill-a-centrifuge.pdf; Jon Lindsay and Eric Gartzke, "Weaving Tangled Webs: Offense, Defense, and Deception in Cyberspace," *Security Studies*, forthcoming; Lindsay and Gartzke, this volume.

[55] Christopher Bronk and Eneken Tikk-Ringas, "The Cyber Attack on Saudi Aramco," *Survival* (April–May 2013).

to implement, implying that the intelligence preparation against Libyan air defense was lacking at the time.[56]

In addition to covert action that causes direct damage, whether via armed proxies or cybernetic sabotage, there are more subtle methods of intelligence-based coercion. One example is the counterfeiting of currency in order to impose economic costs. Allegedly this was done by both sides during the wars in Indochina and Vietnam during the 1950s and 1960s.[57]

Similarly so-called black propaganda can indirectly impose costs for coercion. Black propaganda differs from ordinary propaganda in that its origin cannot be attributed to the source because it is propagated through clandestine means. This almost inevitably means such operations are conducted by intelligence organizations. Such operations are often intended to sow internal dissent by, for example, presenting an alleged alternative to a regime. In Vietnam, the United States created a fictitious underground organization that was allegedly opposing the North Vietnamese government. This nonexistent organization was intended to inflame discontent in the North over issues such as land reform in order to coerce the North Vietnamese to accept the status quo division of Vietnam.[58]

Intelligence and Multifaceted Coercive Campaigns

Intelligence underpins not only individual coercive tools but also overall coercive campaigns. Coercive campaigns integrate a variety of tools with a variety of effects, making assessment of the campaign's progress complex. Intelligence provides feedback to the coercer on the progress of the campaign and also how well the tools are (or are not) mutually supporting. This adjustment and orchestration is often overlooked by scholars but not by policymakers. Intelligence is thus critical to strategies of coercion.

The current alleged Russian campaign to coerce Ukraine into accepting a place in Russia's sphere of influence is an example of such a campaign. The Russian campaign has integrated a variety of tools, ranging from economic (manipulating gas prices and supply to Ukraine) to proxy warfare in eastern Ukraine. Russia's extensive intelligence apparatus has been a major component of many of these tools, but it has also provided an overall mechanism for orchestrating these tools and gauging their effect. While unclassified reporting is thin at present, at least one account based on NATO and former U.K. intelligence officials argues that Russian success is due to "a

---

[56] William Arkin, "The Cyber Bomb in Yugoslavia," *Washington Post*, October 25, 1999; Ellen Nakashima, "U.S. Cyberweapons Had Been Considered to Disrupt Gaddafi's Air Defenses," *Washington Post*, October 17, 2011.

[57] Douglas Porch, *The French Secret Services: A History of French Intelligence from the Dreyfus Affair to the Gulf War* (New York: Farrar, Straus and Giroux, 2003); John Plaster, *SOG: The Secret Wars of America's Commandos in Vietnam* (New York: Onyx, 1998).

[58] Plaster, *SOG*.

well-resourced intelligence machine" that "has very effectively employed all of the tools of power: information, diplomacy, politics, military might—both overt and unconventional—and economic."[59]

The U.S. campaign to coerce Iran into accepting significant limits on its nuclear ambitions is another example of such an integrated campaign. As noted earlier, intelligence underpins tools as diverse as financial sanctions and cyber covert action. The Obama administration, including the president, allegedly took a deep interest in monitoring the intelligence analysis of how well the coercion campaign was working.[60]

Complications of Intelligence and Coercion

While intelligence is a critical building block of both coercive tactics and coercion strategy, it can be complicated to utilize. A principal difficulty is in using clandestine intelligence assets for coercion without fatally compromising their effectiveness. For example, if a coercer utilizes communications intercepts from a target as part of a coercive campaign (e.g., to target coercive tools, whether financial or explosive) there is a serious risk that the target will realize its communications are being intercepted. This realization could then lead the target to adopt more secure communications, depriving the coercer of that asset. This deprives the coercer of a particular coercive tool in the present and also access to the target's communications in the future.

A probable concrete example of this phenomenon was the U.S. effort to compel India to cease preparations for a nuclear test in 1996. As part of this effort, the U.S. ambassador to India revealed U.S. satellite imagery that demonstrated that the United States was well aware of India's preparations. While this coercive effort succeeded in 1996, it is likely that the Indians learned enough about U.S. monitoring that they were able to defeat it through denial and deception operations. In 1998, India tested a nuclear weapon without the United States detecting the preparations in time to marshal a coercion effort against it.[61]

This problem of using clandestine assets is particularly acute for cyber tools and covert action, which rely on very specific vulnerabilities in computer code and frequently in physical security as well. Any use of the tools that produces a detectable effect (and sometimes even without effect) can reveal those vulnerabilities and allow the target to take steps to repair them. For example, both Siemens and Microsoft released patches to their respective operating systems

---

59 Sam Jones, "'Masterly' Russian Operations in Ukraine Leave NATO One Step Behind," *Financial Times*, June 8, 2014.

60 David Sanger, *Confront and Conceal: Obama's Secret Wars and Surprising Use of American Power* (New York: Broadway Books, 2012).

61 Jeffrey Richelson, *Spying on the Bomb: American Nuclear Intelligence from Nazi Germany to Iran and North Korea* (New York: Norton, 2006).

to fix vulnerabilities revealed in the Stuxnet attack on Iran.[62] While there may always be other vulnerabilities in those systems, those particular exploitable flaws are no longer usable for other cyber covert actions.

Yet some revelation of clandestine capabilities is often required for coercive success. In his seminal article, "Rationalist Explanations for War," Fearon describes how private information (such as information about war plans or intelligence capabilities) can lead to war because it limits the ability of potential combatants to rationally evaluate their respective strengths. If they were able to do so, they could strike a bargain that would achieve the same results without war—in other words, successful coercion by the stronger party.[63]

In addition to needing to reveal coercive capabilities in some instances, forgoing the use of certain clandestine capabilities may also undermine coercion. For example, the United States needs to maintain surveillance of Iran's nuclear program even if coercion succeeds. Failure to successfully detect cheating by Iran could allow it to covertly produce fissile material for a nuclear weapon, which would be tantamount to a coercion failure. The United States thus has strong incentives to use all available intelligence means to ensure compliance—even if using certain assets (whether specific communications intercept capabilities or human sources) places those assets at risk.

Failure to deploy intelligence assets is often difficult to discern particularly in cases of coercion, where there are seldom detailed postmortems on intelligence. In contrast, some high-profile deterrence failures, where postmortems are frequent, illustrate the dangers of failing to deploy sensitive intelligence assets for fear of compromising them. Notably Uri Bar-Joseph claims that in 1973 Israeli Military Intelligence refused to activate a sensitive collection asset that was intended to provide insight into the highest levels of Egyptian military decision-making. This asset could likely have provided warning of the impending Egyptian offensive, which in turn could have allowed a timely and effective Israeli mobilization that might have deterred the Egyptians.[64] A similar pattern may be true of intelligence and coercion.

Decisions about employing intelligence assets for coercion are therefore likely to be fraught with peril. Using some assets may risk (or even guarantee) losing them, yet failing to use them may likewise cause coercion to fail. Policymakers and intelligence professionals thus need to engage in a serious dialogue about the use of these assets. Yet there is little evidence such dialogue exists in anything but a rudimentary fashion.[65]

---

[62] David Kushner, "The Real Story of Stuxnet," *IEEE Spectrum*, February 26, 2013.
[63] James D. Fearon, "Rationalist Explanations for War," *International Organization* 49, no. 3 (1995): 379-414.
[64] Bar-Joseph, *The Watchman Fell Asleep*; Uri Bar-Joseph, 'The 'Special Means of Collection': The Missing Link in the Surprise of the Yom Kippur War," *Middle East Journal* 67, no. 4 (Autumn 2013): 531–46.
[65] Though there was some thought given to this late in the Cold War. See Kevin Lewis, *Getting More Deterrence out of Deliberate Capability Revelation* (Santa Monica, CA: RAND, 1989).

Summary

Successful coercion requires knowledge of the capabilities, will, and credibility of the coercer and target; identification of the best assets to target and discovery of their locations; understanding of the past, present, and future behavior of the target to adjust strategy and assess effectiveness; and, sometimes, the ability of the coercer to issue and carry out threats covertly. Each of these factors requires quality intelligence and the organizations that generate it. Perfect knowledge in all of these areas is improbable, but success without intelligence in any of them is impossible.

Intelligence issues remain one of the critical underexplored topics in modern social science as applied to issues of international security. While there are exceptions, intelligence scholars have not generated a sustained research program relative to those devoted to more conventional topics, such as nuclear weapons or civil wars. This chapter has underscored the need for such an agenda for both political scientists and policymakers.

For political scientists, explicit recognition of the role of intelligence in coercion could breathe new life into older research agendas, such as the study of sanctions effectiveness. By including intelligence capabilities as a variable, researchers can generate more accurate assessments of the overall capability of states to coerce through sanctions. Scholars could analyze coercion strategy in light of the intelligence picture available to each party at the time, as opposed to the 20/20 hindsight that is often utilized to explain actions and outcomes. It could also allow political scientists to develop more holistic theories of coercion that account for the fact that states seldom apply only a single coercive tool but rather orchestrate campaigns that are always built on the foundation of intelligence.

For policymakers, an appreciation of the intelligence foundations of coercion could lead to more systematic evaluation of the need for certain kinds of intelligence (such as financial intelligence) that might otherwise be neglected. It could also help generate a more informed dialogue with intelligence professionals about the trade-offs in using and/or revealing certain intelligence capabilities for coercion.

PART II | Coercion in an Asymmetric World

CHAPTER 3 | A Bargaining Theory of Coercion

TODD S. SECHSER

Subjugating the enemy's army without fighting is the true pinnacle of excellence.

—SUN TZU, *The Art of War (c. 500 B.C.E.)*

IN THE AUTUMN OF 1939, the Soviet Union engaged in an ambitious coercive campaign against Finland. For over a year, Josef Stalin had watched Adolf Hitler apply his expansionist agenda in central Europe, and now he began preparing for the day the German army turned against the Soviet Union. High on Stalin's agenda was the security of Leningrad, which would be vulnerable to German attack in the event that Finland was unable—or unwilling—to stop a Nazi invasion. Stalin's solution was to obtain a series of territorial concessions from Finland, which would allow the Soviets to expand the defense perimeter around Leningrad and install island fortifications in the Gulf of Finland to prevent a naval assault. The Soviets initially attempted to achieve this objective with a strategy of "friendly persuasion," but soon escalated to threats of war.[1]

After months of unsuccessful negotiations, however, the Soviets concluded that coercive diplomacy had failed. The Finnish government refused to yield to Stalin's demands, and on November 30, 1939, the Soviet Union launched a multipronged military assault against Finland. After more than three months of winter combat, Finland sued for peace, ultimately ceding even more territory than the Soviets had originally demanded. The Soviets paid a heavy price for these gains: the war cost the lives of perhaps 127,000 Soviet soldiers;[2] the Finnish army destroyed thousands of Soviet aircraft and tanks; and the

[1] The most complete account is Max Jakobson, *The Diplomacy of the Winter War: An Account of the Russo-Finnish Conflict, 1939–1940* (Cambridge, MA: Harvard University Press, 1961). See also Anthony F. Upton, *Finland, 1939–1940* (London: Davis-Poynter, 1974); Väinö Tanner, *The Winter War: Finland against Russia, 1939–1940* (Stanford: Stanford University Press, 1957).

[2] Grigori F. Krivosheev, ed., *Soviet Casualties and Combat Losses in the Twentieth Century* (London: Greenhill, 1997).

surprising ferocity of Finland's resistance dealt a severe blow to the prestige and morale of the Red Army.

The Soviet Union's strategy during the 1939 crisis offers a useful glimpse into the challenges inherent in coercive diplomacy. Stalin found himself with two competing objectives during the negotiations. On one hand, he sought to wring as many concessions as possible from Finnish negotiators. At various points during the crisis, he demanded the establishment of a Soviet naval base on the strategic peninsula of Hankö; a revision of the Soviet-Finnish border in the Karelian Isthmus; anchorage rights in critical Finnish ports; and ownership of a variety of islands in the Gulf of Finland, among other territories.[3] The more territory and bases he could secure, Stalin reasoned, the better he could protect Leningrad against a Nazi assault.

On the other hand, however, Stalin also sought to avoid war with Finland. While he believed the Soviets could easily defeat the Finnish army (an assessment that later proved far too optimistic), he also sought to avoid distractions as the Soviets prepared for a war in Europe. Fighting the Finns also risked provoking intervention by the United States, Britain, or France—a potentially disastrous outcome. Yet the more Stalin demanded, the more motivated Finland would be to stand firm. Throughout the negotiations Stalin had several opportunities to accept Finnish counteroffers, and at several points even moderated his demands.[4] Ultimately, however, he decided to escalate the crisis rather than accept a suboptimal deal.

The Russo-Finnish crisis of 1939 therefore highlights three important realities about coercion in international relations.[5] First, coercion is fundamentally about *bargaining*. Achieving one's coercive objectives entails a process of demands, offers, counteroffers, concessions, and trades. In this respect, coercive diplomacy is no different from the sort of negotiations one might observe in a used-car lot: bargaining takes place along a continuum, with each side trying to obtain the best possible deal. The negotiations between Finland and the Soviet Union in 1939 spanned several months, each side staking out positions

---

[3] Jakobson, *The Diplomacy of the Winter War*, 115–16.

[4] Upton, *Finland*, 40. See also Albin T. Anderson, "Origins of the Winter War: A Study of Russo-Finnish Diplomacy," *World Politics* 6, no. 2 (1954): 169–89.

[5] The literature about coercive diplomacy is extensive. Among the many studies of the topic, see Barry M. Blechman and Stephen S. Kaplan, *Force without War: U.S. Armed Forces as a Political Instrument* (Washington, DC: Brookings Institution, 1978); Alexander L. George and William E. Simons, *The Limits of Coercive Diplomacy*, 2d ed. (Boulder, CO: Westview, 1994); Lawrence Freedman, *Strategic Coercion: Concepts and Cases* (New York: Oxford University Press, 1998); Daniel Byman and Matthew C. Waxman, *The Dynamics of Coercion: American Foreign Policy and the Limits of Military Might* (New York: Cambridge University Press, 2001); Robert J. Art and Patrick M. Cronin, eds., *The United States and Coercive Diplomacy* (Washington, DC: U.S. Institute of Peace, 2003); Peter Viggo Jakobsen, *Western Use of Coercive Diplomacy after the Cold War: A Challenge for Theory and Practice* (New York: St. Martin's Press, 1998); Kenneth A. Schultz, *Democracy and Coercive Diplomacy* (New York: Cambridge University Press, 2001); Kelly M. Greenhill, *Weapons of Mass Migration: Forced Displacement, Coercion, and Foreign Policy* (Ithaca, NY: Cornell University Press, 2010); Todd S. Sechser, "Militarized Compellent Threats, 1918–2001," *Conflict Management and Peace Science* 28, no. 4 (2011): 377–401; Todd S. Sechser and Matthew Fuhrmann, *Nuclear Weapons and Coercive Diplomacy* (New York: Cambridge University Press, 2017).

it hoped would maximize its own gains while not pushing the adversary past its breaking point. What makes coercive diplomacy unique is not the subject matter of the bargaining but rather the fact that it takes place against the background of the threat of military force.

Second, coercers operate in an environment of imperfect information. Like poker players in a high-stakes game, coercers can see the hand they have been dealt, but others' hands are hidden to them. Choosing a coercive demand would be straightforward if coercers knew their adversary's level of resolve: the coercer could then demand precisely enough to maximize its gains while still avoiding war. Leaders, however, cannot read minds. Worse, leaders have reasons to exaggerate their resolve in order to encourage their opponents to make more favorable offers. Stalin's negotiators in 1939 spent several months trying to establish Finland's precise level of resolve, at one point pointing to a map and repeatedly asking, "Would you perhaps give up *this* island?"[6] Ascertaining the opponent's level of resolve is a basic feature of coercive diplomacy.

Third, coercers must choose their demands wisely.[7] In coercive diplomacy, coercers have two basic objectives: they want to wrest the largest possible concessions from the target, and they prefer to win those concessions without having to pay the costs of war, if possible. Yet these two objectives are often in tension: demanding larger concessions carries a greater risk of war. Large demands increase the potential rewards for success but decrease the likelihood that success will be achieved without war. Coercers therefore must strike a careful balance between maximizing gains and minimizing risk. The Soviet position in 1939 nicely illustrates this fundamental tension. Emboldened by his belief that the Finns would not dare stand up to Soviet power, Stalin budged little from his original demands. Yet had Stalin foreseen the costly war that would follow the 1939 crisis, he might have revised his position. Likewise, the Finnish leadership engaged in extensive debate about just how much risk they could bear—and how much territory would be worth giving up to mitigate that risk. In the end, each side overplayed its hand.

This chapter considers the implications of the bargaining perspective for coercive diplomacy. In particular, it applies the logic of bargaining to better understand the choices faced by coercers. How do coercers weigh their desire for gains against the risk of war? How do power and information play into these calculations? And most important, how does this perspective reshape our understanding of the dynamics of coercive diplomacy?

To explore the choices and dilemmas faced by coercers, this chapter presents a simple bargaining model of international conflict. One important advantage of utilizing a formal model is that it requires considering the perspective of all

[6] Yohanan Cohen, *Small Nations in Times of Crisis and Confrontation* (Albany, NY: State University of New York Press, 1989), 255. Finnish negotiators, realizing immediately what the Soviets were up to, refused to play along.

[7] Todd S. Sechser, "Goliath's Curse: Coercive Threats and Asymmetric Power," *International Organization* 64, no. 4 (2010): 627–60.

sides in a coercive bargaining encounter. To completely specify a mathematical model, every player's strategies, outcomes, and preferences must be stated. This requires imagining a crisis from each player's viewpoint, envisioning not only choices made but also options that are discarded. The analysis yields several surprising implications. First, the model tells us something about the conditions under which scholars are likely to observe successful coercive diplomacy in international relations. Most theories of coercive diplomacy tell us that coercive threats are most likely to fail when targets are highly resolved. But the model turns the conventional wisdom on its head: by accounting for coercers' incentives to adjust their demands to avoid war, the model shows that successful coercive diplomacy is, counterintuitively, more likely when the targets of coercive threats are resolved. Second, the model underscores the double-edged nature of military power in coercive diplomacy. While military power is useful for intimidating adversaries into backing down without a fight, it also motivates coercers to make larger and riskier demands. Powerful coercers therefore may not be more likely to win without a fight; indeed, they may even be less likely to do so.

Coercion as a Bargaining Process

In a civil lawsuit, there is typically a period of negotiation in which the parties attempt to settle the lawsuit before it ever reaches a courtroom. The reason is that going to trial is costly: even if one is fortunate enough to win, litigation costs time and money, mitigating the gains from victory at trial. Furthermore, the outcome of a trial is uncertain beforehand. The parties therefore have significant incentives to settle the dispute before expensive attorneys' fees begin to accumulate.[8] Behind these negotiations, however, is an implicit threat from the plaintiff. If the settlement offered by the defendant is not attractive enough, the plaintiff might decide to take the case to court, an outcome that could be costly for everyone. The plaintiff, in effect, hopes to use the threat of a courtroom trial to coerce the defendant into offering a lucrative deal.

This picture of pretrial negotiations bears an important resemblance to international conflicts: both typically center around allocation of a scarce resource. In a civil context, that resource generally takes the form of monetary damages. The plaintiff hopes to receive as much money as possible, whereas the defendant prefers to pay nothing at all. In an international setting, disputed issues can include territory, trade policies, treatment of an ethnic group, a country's leadership, or a variety of other issues. In each case, however, the disputing parties have opposing preferences: each wants to "win" as much

[8] The puzzle of why civil legal disputes ever end in trial rather than settlement has been a persistent question in the legal studies field for decades. See, for instance, Robert H. Mnookin and Lewis Kornhauser, "Bargaining in the Shadow of the Law: The Case of Divorce," *Yale Law Journal* 88, no. 5 (1979): 950–97; George L. Priest and Benjamin Klein, "The Selection of Disputes for Litigation," *Journal of Legal Studies* 13, no. 1 (1984): 1–55.

of the issue as possible. The central problem therefore is how to allocate that resource.

Characterizing these settings as problems of resource allocation highlights a second important similarity between pretrial negotiations and international disputes: coercion plays a key role in both. In both settings, the disputants hope to use the threat of a costly "outside option" for resolving the dispute—a courtroom trial or a war—to compel the adversary to agree to a deal beforehand. The ability to successfully compel a settlement stems from one's ability to shape that costly outcome. For instance, a litigant that appears very likely to prevail in a jury trial, or whose legal costs are being covered by a wealthy third party, stands to negotiate a more favorable settlement because the litigant does not fear the costs of a trial. Likewise, a state that is sure to prevail in war, or whose population does not particularly fear the costs of fighting, should also be able to drive a better bargain.

In short, a bargaining perspective sees both coercive *threats* and military *force* as central elements of coercive diplomacy. Violence and negotiation are not distinct entities; they are both part of the same bargaining process. As Thomas Schelling wrote nearly 50 years ago, "Coercion requires finding a bargain, arranging for [the adversary] to be better off doing what we want—worse off not doing what we want—when he takes the threatened penalty into account."[9]

A Basic Model of Coercion

This section elaborates the assumptions of the bargaining perspective and explores the dynamics of coercion using a simple model of bargaining. The model draws its inspiration from the famous "ultimatum game," a bargaining model often used by economists to represent situations in which one actor attempts to impose its will on another.[10] The format of the basic ultimatum game is elegantly simple: one actor proposes a division of a valuable item (usually a pot of money), and the second actor may accept or reject the proposal. If the second actor rejects the offer, however, both parties get nothing.

The ultimatum game is useful for thinking about coercive diplomacy for several reasons. First, it describes a situation in which one actor makes a clear demand and the other must respond. Coercive encounters in international relations often fit this mold, with one side making a demand and the other deciding between accepting or rejecting it.[11] President John F. Kennedy's demand that the Soviet Union remove its missiles from Cuba in 1962, for example, left little room for a counteroffer and carried an assurance that the only two

---

[9] Thomas C. Schelling, *Arms and Influence* (New Haven, CT: Yale University Press, 1966), 4.
[10] Werner Güth, Rolf Schmittberger, and Bernd Schwarze, "An Experimental Analysis of Ultimatum Bargaining," *Journal of Economic Behavior and Organization* 3, no. 4 (1982): 367–88.
[11] For examples of ultimatums in international crises, see Paul Gordon Lauren, "Ultimata and Coercive Diplomacy," *International Studies Quarterly* 16, no. 2 (1972): 131–65.

options available to the Soviets were total compliance or war. Similarly, George W. Bush's message to Saddam Hussein prior to the 2003 invasion of Iraq was a clear ultimatum: "Saddam Hussein and his sons must leave Iraq within 48 hours. Their refusal to do so will result in military conflict, commenced at a time of our choosing."[12] The ultimatum game allows us to analyze the bargaining dynamics of these encounters.[13]

Second, the proposer in the ultimatum game must think strategically about its demand. If it demands too much, it risks the possibility that the recipient will reject the demand and leave it with nothing. Indeed, behavioral economists have found that individuals are quite willing to reject ultimatum offers they believe to be unfairly low, even though this means a lower payoff for themselves.[14] The proposer therefore must weigh the temptation of larger gains against the risk that if it overshoots, it may get nothing at all. At the same time, however, it could be costly to be too cautious. If the proposer asks for too little, its demand will surely be accepted, but the gains from the deal will be small.

A third useful aspect of the ultimatum game is that there is a price to be paid for failing to reach a bargain. In coercive diplomacy, failing to reach a settlement might lead to a costly military conflict. Both sides therefore have an incentive to strike a deal. Similarly, in the ultimatum game, if the recipient rejects the proposer's offer, the two sides receive nothing, leaving the pot of money on the table.

While the ultimatum format is a useful representation of coercive encounters, it is important to be clear about its limitations. Perhaps the most important one is that it does not allow the recipient to make a counteroffer: it can only accept or reject the original proposal without modifying it. In reality, of course, international negotiations are much more freewheeling. Leaders in international disputes are not bound by strict rules that stipulate who makes offers, what those offers may look like, and how many rounds of negotiation may take place before the game ends. Further, these rules are not a trivial matter: bargaining models are notoriously sensitive to minor changes to the rules.[15] The advantage of the ultimatum model lies in its simplicity and ease of analysis, but it is important to acknowledge that it offers a first glimpse at the problem of coercion, not the final one.[16]

---

[12] George W. Bush, "Bush's Speech on Iraq: 'Saddam Hussein and His Sons Must Leave,'" *New York Times*, March 18, 2003.

[13] It may seem odd to classify the ultimatum game as a bargaining model since it does not actually contain any back-and-forth haggling. The term is used here in its broadest sense, referring to the fact that the model requires the players to decide how to divide a valuable, scarce resource, even though the rules of negotiation are quite restrictive.

[14] For examples, see Colin F. Camerer, *Behavioral Game Theory: Experiments in Strategic Interaction* (Princeton, NJ: Princeton University Press, 2003), chapter 2.

[15] See, for example, Drew Fudenberg and Jean Tirole, *Game Theory* (Cambridge, MA: MIT Press, 1991), 398–99; Jeffrey S. Banks, "Equilibrium Behavior in Crisis Bargaining Games," *American Journal of Political Science* 34, no. 3 (1990): 599–614.

[16] It is important not to exaggerate this point, however. Even though the ultimatum game employs restrictive rules, changing them would not necessarily alter the findings of the model. Rubinstein, for example, analyzed a model with a more fluid back-and-forth bargaining protocol, but the first-round equilibrium offer turns out to be exactly the same as the equilibrium offer in an ultimatum

Before applying the ultimatum model to coercive international bargaining, a few modifications are required. First, the model will retain the two-player format of the original ultimatum game, but henceforth the players will be labeled the "coercer" and the "target." Next, it is stipulated that the item in dispute is already owned by the second actor. In international relations, there are few equivalents to an unclaimed $100 bill in the middle of the street; most objects of value already have an owner. In this respect, then, the game resembles Schelling's characterization of a "compellent" threat: one actor demands something from an adversary and threatens some kind of punishment if the adversary does not act.[17] Finally, the outcome of the game must be adjusted. In the standard version of the ultimatum game, the parties receive nothing if they fail to reach an agreement. However, this outcome is modified such that the parties fight a winner-take-all war over the disputed item if the proposer's offer is rejected. In this war, each side enjoys some probability of winning the entire item but also pays a fixed cost for fighting whether it wins or loses—though not necessarily the same cost as its opponent.[18] In other words, a rejection of the coercer's threat triggers a "costly lottery" in which both sides pay a price for a chance at winning the entire item. This sequence of events is illustrated graphically in Figure 3.1.[19]

In this interpretation of the ultimatum game, "success" occurs when the target accepts the coercer's demand, and "failure" occurs when the target rejects it. To be clear, however, these terms refer to the narrow outcome of the threat itself, not whether the overall encounter is a foreign policy success or failure for the coercer. The reason is that failed threats sometimes precede successful military operations in which coercers achieve their broader objectives by force. In 1990 and 1991, for example, the United States issued a coercive threat against Iraq, with President George H. W. Bush demanding that Iraqi forces evacuate Kuwait. The threat was unsuccessful, but the ultimate outcome of the crisis was a U.S. victory: U.S. forces expelled Iraqi troops from Kuwait after just six weeks of combat. At the same time, the United States surely would have preferred to

---

game. Further, in equilibrium Rubinstein's model lasts only one round, just as in the ultimatum model. See Ariel Rubinstein, "Perfect Equilibrium in a Bargaining Model," *Econometrica* 50, no. 1 (1982): 97–109; Robert Powell, "Stability and the Distribution of Power," *World Politics* 48, no. 2 (1996): 239–67, especially 252–55.

[17] Thomas C. Schelling, *The Strategy of Conflict* (Cambridge, MA: Harvard University Press, 1960), 195–99.

[18] The basic model described here was first used in an international relations context by Fearon. See James D. Fearon, "Threats to Use Force: Costly Signals and Bargaining in International Crises" (Ph.D. dissertation, University of California, Berkeley, 1992); James D. Fearon, "Rationalist Explanations for War," *International Organization* 49, no. 3 (1995): 379–414. A number of scholars following in this research program have adopted some form of this model, although others have abandoned it in an effort to gain leverage on problems of wartime and postwar bargaining.

[19] Reducing war to a single-shot lottery seems unnatural, particularly in light of Clausewitz's admonition that "war does not consist of a single short blow." See Carl von Clausewitz, *On War*, ed. and trans. Michael Howard and Peter Paret (1832; Princeton, NJ: Princeton University Press, 1976), 79. Yet while the model neglects to delve into wartime negotiations, the lottery represents each side's expectations about the likely payoffs from fighting. Since the focus here is on the prewar process of coercive bargaining, this simplification is a worthwhile trade-off.

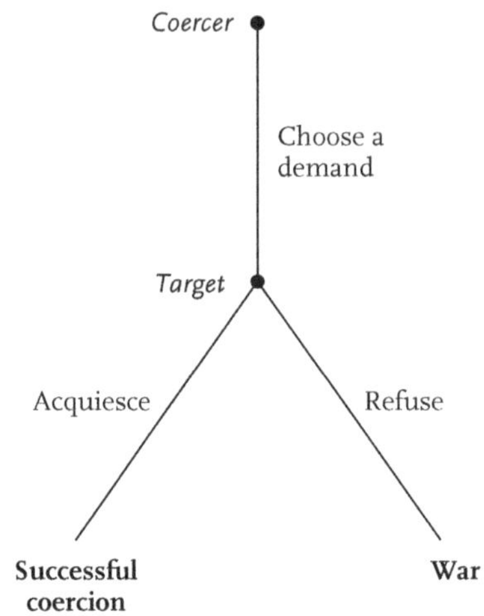

FIGURE 3.1 A Basic Model of Coercion

achieve this outcome without any fighting at all. This is precisely the aim of a coercive threat. The outcome of interest in this discussion therefore is the success or failure of coercive threats rather than broader crisis outcomes.[20]

Some additional assumptions are in order. The first and most basic of these is an assumption about the actors in a coercive encounter: the model assumes that the players are rational and that they seek to maximize their gains (or minimize their losses) from the encounter. Stipulating that the actors are rational does not imply that they are all-knowing, but it does mean that they are able to make optimal decisions given the information available to them. Second, the model assumes that military conflict takes only one form. In other words, the coercer does not choose how much military force to employ. Third, the analysis stipulates that the players have full and accurate information about one another's payoffs. While this assumption will be relaxed shortly, it is useful to begin with this assumption to establish a baseline for analysis. Finally, assume that the players in the model are very slightly risk-averse, such that when peace and war offer identical expected payoffs, they prefer peace.

The model immediately reveals a central feature of coercive diplomacy: the objective of a coercive demand is not to provoke war but rather to prevent it. Coercion relies on the threat of military punishment to achieve political objectives, but enacting that punishment is costly even if it achieves its ultimate coercive objective. Wars entail substantial human, material, and psychological costs that leaders would prefer to avoid if possible. As Schelling wrote in his seminal book on coercion, *Arms and Influence*, "successful threats are those

[20] For further discussion of this point, see Alexander B. Downes and Todd S. Sechser, "The Illusion of Democratic Credibility," *International Organization* 66, no. 3 (2012): 457–89.

that do not have to be carried out."[21] For a coercer, then, the basic challenge is to devise a threat that attains the greatest gain at the least possible cost.[22]

Analysis of the Basic Model

With these assumptions, the model can be analyzed in order to illuminate its implications for coercive diplomacy. The first step is to assign mathematical terms to represent the model's various components. The game begins with the coercer's decision about how much to demand. For simplicity, stipulate that the coercer and target are negotiating over an item with a value of 1. The coercer must choose how much, if any, of that item to demand. The term x will serve as a placeholder for the coercer's demand, noting that x can range anywhere from 0 to 1. Using this terminology, the outcome of a successful coercive threat can now be defined: if the target accepts the coercer's demand, the coercer receives x and the target keeps $1-x$.

The other possible outcome of the game is a military conflict. If the parties fight a war over the disputed item, each stands a chance of winning the entire item. Stipulate that the coercer's probability of winning is represented by p. The target's probability of winning is therefore $1-p$. Since the balance of power plays a central role in determining each side's odds of prevailing in a military contest, it is plausible to say that p represents the coercer's relative share of military capabilities: the more military power it possesses, the higher p will be.[23] Further, each player pays a cost for participating in this military "lottery." The notation c_C will represent the coercer's cost, and c_T represents the target's cost. Further stipulate that the costs of war are also loosely related to the balance of power, with more powerful actors able to inflict greater costs on their opponent.[24] Recall that the players must pay these costs whether they win or lose.[25] Each player's "expected" payoff from fighting a war can now be described: for the coercer, that payoff is $1(p-c_C)+0(1-p-c_C)$, which simplifies to $p-c_C$. For the target, the expected payoff of war is $1(1-p-c_T)+0(p-c_T)$, which simplifies to $1-p-c_T$.

What is the result of this coercive bargaining encounter? This question can be answered by solving for the Nash equilibrium of the game, which is described in the online appendix for this chapter. The coercer makes the largest demand that it knows will be accepted, which turns out to be $x=p+c_T$. The target in turn accepts this demand, and war is avoided.

---

[21] Schelling, *Arms and Influence*, 10.

[22] Clausewitz recognized this as well when he wrote, "The aggressor is always peace-loving . . . . He would prefer to take over our country unopposed" (*On War*, 370).

[23] More formally, stipulate that p is defined as the coercer's share of military capabilities (m_i) in the dyad. Therefore: $p = \frac{m_C}{m_C+m_T}$.

[24] To be precise about it, let c_C and c_T be determined by some monotonic function $f_i(p, m_i)$ such that p and c_T are positively related, p and c_C are negatively related, and m_i and c_i are negatively related.

[25] Although this is a standard assumption in bargaining models of war, one might argue that the costs for fighting depend in part on the outcome: victorious wars might cost less to fight than unsuccessful wars. While incorporating this assumption into the model would complicate the equilibrium solution somewhat, it would not change the thrust of the conclusions below.

The first thing to note is that, in equilibrium, this encounter always ends in successful coercion. In other words, war is never an equilibrium outcome. The reason is that the coercer has the luxury of complete information: it knows exactly what its opponent's payoffs are, so it chooses its demand strategically to maximize the coercer's gains without provoking a costly war. Because the target expects to receive $1-p-c_T$ from fighting, and the coercer knows this, the coercer can adjust its demand so that the target is left with exactly this amount (or very slightly more) by acquiescing to the demand. Since the coercer will receive $p+c_T$ from this demand, but only $p-c_C$ from a war, it has no incentive to provoke a conflict by demanding more. The coercer knows how far it can push, and pushes no further. This model therefore underscores the importance of accounting for strategic behavior on the part of the coercer. To understand coercive outcomes, one must understand not only the target's incentives, but also the coercer's strategy.

A second observation relates to the role of military power in this coercive encounter. The balance of power shapes the outcome of the crisis, but not in the way that is often assumed in coercive diplomacy scholarship. The standard view is that the balance of power influences the likelihood of coercive success: coercers that can threaten greater punishment are more likely to have their demands accepted.[26] In this view, power enters the scene in the final stage of a crisis, when the target chooses between capitulation and war. But this is not how power works in the ultimatum model. Instead, the primary role of power is to shape the coercer's demand: coercers with a military advantage (that is, a higher p) make larger demands, whereas weaker coercers settle for small demands. In other words, the coercer incorporates the balance of power into its initial demand, taking into account how its demand will be received by the target. Ultimately, all equilibrium demands have the same likelihood of success, irrespective of the balance of power.[27]

Yet this model is unsatisfying. It is implausible to assume that the coercer knows the target's level of resolve with such precision. Indeed, this assumption begs the question, since a central question in coercive diplomacy is how coercers and targets can communicate their resolve through signals and other diplomatic measures.[28] The following section relaxes this assumption.

The Role of Information in Coercive Diplomacy

One of the most important insights to emerge from international relations scholarship about war is that wars are often a consequence of incomplete

[26] George and Simons, *The Limits of Coercive Diplomacy*; Byman and Waxman, *The Dynamics of Coercion*; Art and Cronin, *The United States and Coercive Diplomacy*.
[27] See also Fearon, "Threats to Use Force," 24.
[28] James D. Fearon, "Signaling Foreign Policy Interests: Tying Hands versus Sinking Costs," *Journal of Conflict Resolution* 41, no. 1 (1997): 68–90; James D. Fearon, "Signaling versus the Balance of Power and Interests: An Empirical Test of a Crisis Bargaining Model," *Journal of Conflict Resolution* 38, no. 2 (1994): 236–69; James D. Morrow, "The Strategic Setting of Choices: Signaling, Commitment, and

information. Adversaries in a dispute, in other words, must make educated guesses about the other side's resolve, military capabilities, and other factors. When leaders miscalculate about these factors, war can be the result.[29] Understanding the outcomes of coercive encounters therefore requires first understanding the information environment in which the actors are operating. In short, one must answer this question: How much does each side know about its opponent?

In the original ultimatum model of coercive bargaining, each player knew all the relevant facts about its opponent: its military capabilities, its costs for fighting, and its value for the issue at hand. But what happens when this assumption is relaxed to allow for the possibility of error? This can be investigated by introducing a small amount of uncertainty into the game. Stipulate that the coercer is facing a target whose resolve it does not know. The target can be one of two types: a "tough" type and a "weak" type. A "tough" target is distinguished by having lower costs for fighting wars, so it is generally more willing to risk war by resisting a coercive threat. But, crucially, the coercer does not know whether it is facing a tough or a weak target.[30] The coercer is not completely in the dark, however: there is some probability that it is facing each type of target, and it is aware of this probability. But it must devise its strategy without being certain about the other side's resolve.

The two types of targets are defined as follows. A tough target is one whose cost for war is $\underline{c}_T$. A weak target's costs for war are $\overline{c}_T$, where $\overline{c}_T < \underline{c}_T$. Further, both cost terms are tethered to the balance of power, p, such that the ratio of the two cost terms, $\frac{\overline{c}_T}{\underline{c}_T}$, remains constant across all values of p. Last, the probability that the target is tough must be defined. Call that probability τ, which implies that $1-\tau$ is the probability that the target is weak. At the outset of the game, the target's type is determined with these probabilities, but the outcome is not revealed to the coercer.

How does the outcome change when uncertainty is introduced into this model of coercive diplomacy? Working backward provides the answer. As before, the coercer seeks to demand as much as possible without pushing the target to resist. Yet while the coercer can in principle demand anything between 0 and 1, in equilibrium there are actually only two demands that a coercer might want to make: $\underline{x} = p + \underline{c}_T$ and $\overline{x} = p + \overline{c}_T$.[31] The logic here is straightforward. From the coercer's point of view, its demand can have one of just three discrete probabilities of succeeding. First, its demand will never

Negotiation in International Politics," in *Strategic Choice and International Relations*, ed. David A. Lake and Robert Powell (Princeton, NJ: Princeton University Press, 1999), 77–114.

[29] For example, see Geoffrey Blainey, *The Causes of War* (London: Macmillan, 1973); James D. Morrow, "Capabilities, Uncertainty, and Resolve: A Limited Information Model of Crisis Bargaining," *American Journal of Political Science* 33, no. 4 (1989): 941–72; Fearon, "Rationalist Explanations for War."

[30] On the notion of using "types" with different utility functions to represent uncertainty, see John C. Harsanyi, "Games with Incomplete Information Played by 'Bayesian' Players, I: The Basic Model," *Management Science* 14, no. 3 (1967): 159–82.

[31] Note the new notation: $\overline{x}$ to refer to the higher demand and $\underline{x}$ to refer to the lower one.

succeed if it demands so much that both tough and weak targets would rather fight than capitulate (i.e., $x > p + \overline{c}_T$). This is never optimal since the coercer would prefer to have at least a chance of avoiding the costs of fighting. At the other end of the spectrum, the coercer can be assured of a successful demand if it demands so little that both tough and weak targets will acquiesce ($x \leq p + \underline{c}_T$). The coercer's third option is to demand somewhere in between, where the probability of success is equal to the probability that the target is weak ($1 - \tau$). For a demand in this range ($p + \underline{c}_T < x \leq p + \overline{c}_T$), a tough target will refuse, while a weak target will accept. The coercer therefore must first decide which risk level it prefers—low, medium, or high—and then select the maximum demand within that range.

How much will the coercer demand? The answer to this question depends on the likelihood that the target is tough. If that likelihood is sufficiently high, then the coercer will make the maximum possible demand within the "low" range, which turns out to be $x = p + \underline{c}_T$. But if the coercer is confident enough that the target is weak—in other words, if τ is sufficiently low—then it will be emboldened to make a demand in the "middle" range: specifically, $x = p + \overline{c}_T$. However, it is never optimal for the coercer to make a demand beyond this level, since it will assuredly trigger a war. Thus, for practical purposes the coercer is left with only two possible demands: "high" ($\overline{x}$) and "low" ($\underline{x}$). This is illustrated in Figure 3.2, which tracks the likelihood of successful coercion as the coercer's demand increases.

Now that the coercer's choices have been narrowed down to just two possible demands, the coercer's strategy can be identified. In equilibrium the coercer will issue the high demand (i.e., $\overline{x} = p + \overline{c}_T$) if the probability of facing a tough target falls below a critical value τ^*.[32] Otherwise, it will make the low demand, $\underline{x} = p + \underline{c}_T$. In other words, under conditions of uncertainty, the coercer makes a high demand only if it is sufficiently confident—although not necessarily certain—that the target is a weak type and will accept the demand.

The Effects of Uncertainty on Coercive Outcomes

The introduction of uncertainty into the model has an immediate and important effect: coercive failures now become possible. The coercer no longer has the luxury of peering into the adversary's mind to determine exactly how much to demand, so there is a real possibility that it will guess incorrectly and issue a demand that is rejected. To be precise, the likelihood of coercive failure is τ so long as the coercer is motivated to issue the higher of its two possible equilibrium demands. Under conditions of incomplete information, then, there will always be a chance that coercion will fail. This is not, however, the result of a strategic error on the part of the coercer: indeed, the coercer is playing its optimal strategy, given the information it has. But since its information

[32] Specifically, this critical value is $\tau^* = \frac{\overline{c}_T - \underline{c}_T}{c_C + \overline{c}_T}$.

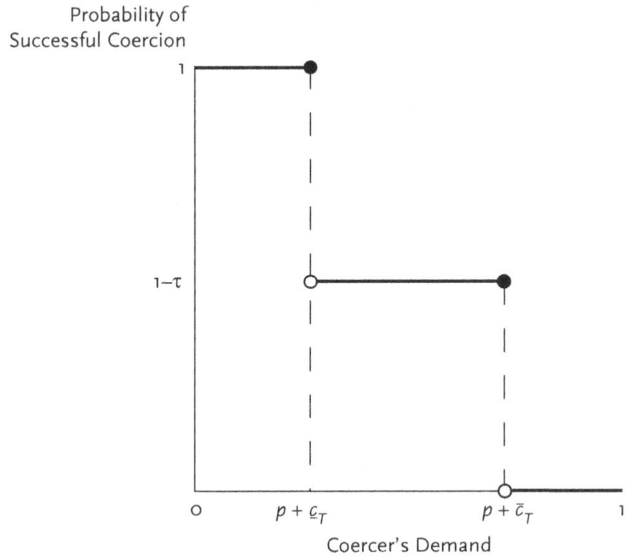

FIGURE 3.2 The Probability of Successful Coercion as the Coercer's Demand Varies

is necessarily incomplete, it may issue a demand that turns out to exceed the target's threshold of tolerance.

Coercion and the Shadow of the Future

We now add one final wrinkle into this model of coercive diplomacy. In the models described so far, there is only one coercive episode. In reality, however, there is no artificial limit on the number of coercive encounters two opponents might experience. The United States, for example, issued coercive demands on multiple occasions against Iraq between 1990 and 2003. Japan engaged in a long string of coercive attempts against China during the 1930s; Germany likewise made multiple coercive demands against Czechoslovakia, Austria, and Poland prior to World War II. In short, coercion is not necessarily a one-time affair. This section therefore builds on the previous model by incorporating a second coercive episode: once the outcome of the initial confrontation has been decided, the coercer may have the opportunity to make a new demand on another issue. Since the future cannot be known with certainty, however, it is useful to stipulate that this second opportunity arises with some known probability. The players do not know beforehand whether a second crisis will occur, but they do know how likely this event is. The incomplete-information component of the previous game remains: the coercer does not know whether it is facing a tough or a weak target.

To account for the shadow of this potential future crisis, a "discount factor" is introduced into the model. Let δ represent the value of the item in the

TABLE 3.1 Summary of Formal Notation

	TERM	INTERPRETATION	RESTRICTIONS
Players	C	Coercer	
	T	Target	
Payoffs	x_n	C's demand in round n	$0 \leq x_n \leq 1$
	c_C	Expected cost of war for coercer	$c_C \geq 0$
	$\underline{c}_T$	Expected cost of war for "tough" target	$\underline{c}_T \geq 0$
	$\overline{c}_T$	Expected cost of war for "weak" target	$0 \leq c_T < \overline{c}_T$
Beliefs	p	Probability that C will win a war against T	$0 \leq p \leq 1$
	m_i	Military power of player i	
	τ	Ex ante probability that T is "tough"	$0 \leq \tau \leq 1$
	δ	Net present value of second-round item	$\delta \geq 0$

second dispute, adjusted to account for the uncertainty that a second crisis will even take place. This modification allows each player to calculate its strategy in light of its expectations about the second round.[33] Table 3.1 reviews the notation utilized in the models thus far.

The discount factor, represented by δ, deserves a brief discussion here. Because δ represents the net present value of the second-round pie (i.e., its value to the players at the outset of the game), it is best conceived as the product of three factors. The first factor is the value of the object, which is assumed to be equal to 1, just as in the first round.[34] The second factor is a discount placed on future gains, reflecting each player's preference for obtaining gains sooner rather than later. The third factor is the probability that a second opportunity for a dispute will even arise. This uncertainty exerts a discounting influence on the present value of the second-round item because if the likelihood of a second round is very small, then the expected gains from that round must also be proportionately small.[35]

Coercive Outcomes in the Multiround Model

The introduction of a possible second coercive encounter changes the equilibrium of the game in a number of respects. These changes can be seen

[33] To accommodate this additional round, let x_n represent the coercer's demand in round n.

[34] This assumption does not undermine the generality of the analysis, but does simplify the equilibrium calculations.

[35] Note that if δ is equal to zero—that is, the players are certain that no second round will take place—the game becomes identical to the one-round, incomplete-information model evaluated above.

by first analyzing the coercer's strategy. As in the one-round version of the game, if the probability of encountering a tough target is sufficiently low, the coercer will be willing to make a "high" demand. That demand turns out to be $p+\bar{c}_T-\delta(\bar{c}_T-\underline{c}_T)$. If the likelihood of facing a tough target is too high, however, the coercer will make a smaller first-round demand $(p+\underline{c}_T)$. This demand is calibrated to persuade all weak targets to capitulate and all tough targets to resist in the first round. The outcome of the first round therefore helps the coercer identify tough opponents so that it can accurately calibrate its demand in the second round. In game-theoretic terms, this is called a separating equilibrium: the coercer issues a demand that "separates" the two types of targets. In other words, the types identify themselves by their response to the coercer's first-round demand. This is optimal for the coercer because it can then exploit its newfound knowledge to maximize its gains in the second round. In short, the risk of coercive failure in the first round is a necessary price it must pay in order to obtain information that could be useful in the second encounter.

How do weak targets respond to the coercer's strategy? Compared to the one-round version of this model, a weak target must adopt a different approach when there is the possibility that a second coercive encounter may occur. Previously, a weak target would have been willing to acquiesce to any demand less than $p+\bar{c}_T$, but now it will reject a larger set of demands; specifically, it will reject any demand greater than $p+\bar{c}_T-\delta(\bar{c}_T-\underline{c}_T)$. In other words, there is a range of demands that was once agreeable to the weak target but becomes unacceptable when the weak target develops an expectation that the game might be repeated. This is illustrated in Figure 3.3, which compares the first-round equilibrium strategies of both types of targets in the one- and two-round games. As the figure demonstrates, weak targets become more difficult to coerce in the two-round game, whereas tough targets maintain the same

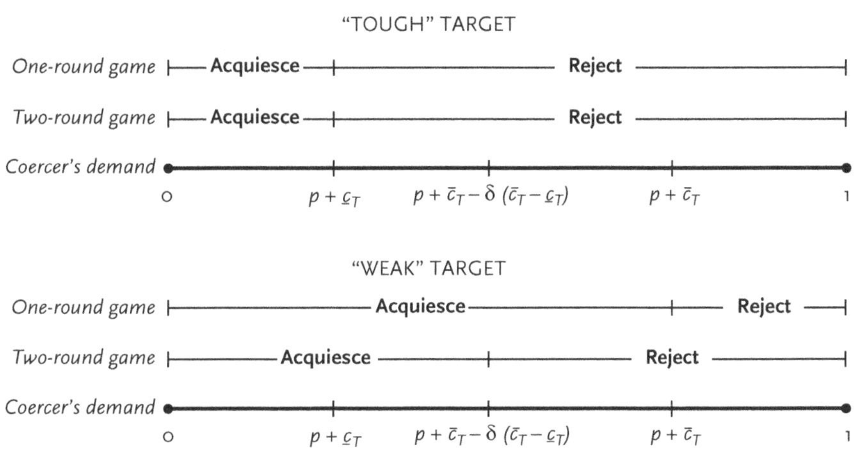

FIGURE 3.3 Comparison of Targets' Equilibrium Responses to First-Round Demands in the Coercion Game

strategy in both games. To persuade a weak target to acquiesce in the two-round game, a coercer must reduce its demands.

What is going on here? To understand why the weak target has become less agreeable, consider a weak target's fortunes if it instead played the same strategy as it played in the one-round game. Given a sufficiently low τ, the coercer would begin by demanding $x_1 \leq p + \overline{c}_T$, to which the weak target would agree. The coercer, realizing its target was a weak type, would then make the same demand again in the second round, giving the target an overall payoff of $(1 - p - \overline{c}_T) + \delta(1 - p - \overline{c}_T)$. In contrast, resisting this demand in the first round and paying the costs of fighting causes the coercer to make a lower second-round demand ($x_2 = p + \underline{c}_T$), which the weak target will accept, for a total payoff of $(1 - p - \overline{c}_T) + \delta(1 - p - \underline{c}_T)$. This outcome is strictly better than the alternative of capitulating in the first round.[36]

To put it differently, weak targets are motivated to resist otherwise acceptable demands because doing so allows them to masquerade as tough targets. By resisting demands they would really prefer to accept, weak targets can secure lower demands in the second round. Fighting, in other words, is a signal of resolve: by paying the price of war today, targets can deter unfavorable offers in the future. The coercer, aware of this incentive, issues a demand in the first round that helps it obtain information about the target's true resolve. It calibrates its first threat so that tough targets resist while weak targets capitulate. The coercer then uses this new knowledge to make a second-round demand that ensures maximal gains without provoking war. These dynamics play out, however, only when the coercer is bold enough to play a risky first-round strategy. If there is a sufficiently high likelihood that the target is tough to begin with, the coercer will play a conservative strategy in both rounds, gleaning no information whatsoever from the first-round result.

Therefore, despite the coercer's best efforts, there remains some probability that its threats will be rejected in the first round of the game.[37] The likelihood that this initial encounter will end in coercive failure can now be calculated. That likelihood turns out to be $\frac{(\tau^*)^2}{2}$, which represents the probability of two events occurring in succession: (1) the coercer is sufficiently confident that the target is weak that it issues a "high" demand in the first round, and (2) the target is actually tough, and therefore rejects the demand. In its expanded form, the probability that a coercer's first-round threat will fail therefore is $\frac{(\overline{c}_T - \underline{c}_T)^2}{2(\overline{c}_T + c_C)}$.

Implications: Power and Coercion

This analysis yields some interesting conjectures about the role of military power in coercive diplomacy. Recall that military power appears in the model

---

[36] Tough targets, by contrast, do not change their equilibrium strategy in this game, and reject all demands greater than $p + \underline{c}_T$ in both rounds.

[37] Because of the information it learns in the first round, however, the coercer is always able to make a successful second-round demand.

indirectly via four terms: p, which represents the balance of military capabilities, $\frac{m_C}{m_C+m_T}$; $\underline{c}_T$, a tough target's value for the costs likely to be inflicted on it in wartime; $\overline{c}_T$, a weak target's value for an identical amount of military punishment; and c_C, the coercer's expected costs for fighting. These relationships reflect the fact that greater military power conveys an enhanced ability to inflict costs on one's opponent as well as an ability to limit damage to oneself.[38] Recall also that the model assumed the ratio of the targets' cost functions—that is, $\frac{\overline{c}_T}{\underline{c}_T}$—to be constant. This assumption is not particularly stringent, tantamount to assuming that a state that values 1,000 battlefield casualties twice as much as another state would also value 10,000 casualties twice as much as the other state.[39]

In light of these relationships, how does military power influence the likelihood of successful coercion? At first glance, the balance of power appears to have no effect here, since p does not appear in the equation for the likelihood of coercive failure.[40] Yet, while the balance of power does not appear independently as a parameter in the probability of war, it nonetheless plays a role by influencing the coercer's costs of fighting—and therefore the demands it is willing to make. More powerful coercers can inflict greater costs on their opponents—and limit damage to themselves. As a result, as a coercer's military advantage grows, its costs decline while the target's costs increase.

When these effects of military power are incorporated into the calculations, they yield a surprising conclusion: *as a coercer's military power increases, its coercive threats become more likely to fail.* How can this be? The reason is that as the coercer's power increases, it becomes more profitable for the coercer to assume the risk of a failed threat by playing a "separating" strategy—in other words, a high demand in the first round, instead of a safe demand. War is now less costly for the coercer, so the coercer is more willing to risk it. Further, since the weak and tough target's costs increase proportionately, the gap between them—that is, the difference between $\overline{c}_T$ and $\underline{c}_T$—widens. When there is a large difference in resolve between weak and tough targets, determining "who's who" becomes even more valuable for the coercer. Weak targets can be exploited more in the second round, while tough targets are to be avoided even more diligently. In short, militarily powerful coercers have more to gain and less to lose by making risky, high-stakes threats in coercive diplomacy. As a coercer's power increases, it is willing to endure a higher probability of failure because the rewards from success are higher as well. Coercers are willing to launch riskier probes as they grow more powerful.

---

38 Branislav L. Slantchev, "The Power to Hurt: Costly Conflict with Completely Informed States," *American Political Science Review* 97, no. 1 (2003): 123–33 provides a nice discussion of these two effects of military power.

39 The conclusions below also hold under some conditions if the assumption of a fixed ratio is relaxed. The mathematical appendix for this chapter, available at faculty.virginia.edu/tsechser, contains a proof that derives these conditions.

40 This is consistent with some previous work on costly lottery bargaining models in international politics. See, for instance, Fearon, "Threats to Use Force"; Robert Powell, *In the Shadow of Power: States and Strategies in International Politics* (Princeton, NJ: Princeton University Press, 1999).

The idea that military power might be associated with lower rates of coercive success is quite counterintuitive, contradicting traditional scholarship on coercive diplomacy as well as common sense. But it is important to understand the nuance of the argument. Although the balance of power plays a key role in the target's decision-making process, that is not where the action is. Rather, the effects of military power manifest earlier in the crisis, when the coercer must decide how much to ask for. The coercer has two choices at this stage: issue a high demand that has a large payoff but is also more likely to be rejected, or issue a safe demand that is certain to be accepted but is less lucrative. How does the coercer balance these competing pressures? This is where military power comes into play. When the coercer is weak, it has a low tolerance for risk and will issue the "high" demand only when it is relatively sure that the target will accept it. This is because the costs of being wrong are high. But as the coercer grows more powerful, those costs dwindle. As a result, its appetite for risk increases, and it becomes willing to issue a "high" demand in situations where it once would have shied away.

Empirical evidence seems consistent with the notion that coercive challenges from powerful states may be more likely to fail. The Militarized Compellent Threats database, a collection of 210 coercive episodes between 1918 and 2001, indicates that coercers are actually less likely to make successful threats when the target enjoys a military advantage.[41] Likewise, coercers with an advantage in nuclear weapons capabilities tend to experience higher failure rates.[42] However, this is not because military power is a disadvantage in coercive diplomacy—quite the contrary. Coercers with a military advantage enjoy higher expected payoffs in the crisis bargaining model analyzed above, but they achieve those payoffs in part by taking greater risks.

Implications: Reputations and Coercive Diplomacy

A second result relates to the role of reputations in international relations. Reputation plays a central role in the model analyzed here: the way a target state behaves in the first round shapes the coercer's beliefs about its resolve. However, reputation does not always play a role: indeed, the coercer revises its beliefs about the target only when it devises a first-round demand that is specifically designed to generate new information. If it selects the "low" demand, however, the target's response carries no information about whether it is tough or weak. In other words, under some conditions, targets may capitulate to coercive threats without suffering any damage to their reputation. This carries an important implication for empirical research about reputations: in

[41] Sechser, "Militarized Compellent Threats"; Todd S. Sechser, "Reputations and Signaling in Coercive Bargaining," *Journal of Conflict Resolution*, forthcoming.
[42] Todd S. Sechser and Matthew Fuhrmann, "Crisis Bargaining and Nuclear Blackmail," *International Organization* 67, no. 1 (2013): 173–95. On the role of nuclear weapons in coercive diplomacy, see the chapters by Jasen J. Castillo and Tristan Volpe in this volume.

coercive diplomacy, *acquiescence does not necessarily damage a target's reputation.* However, this is not because reputations do not matter in the model; they matter a great deal. But their primary effect may be to push coercers into courses of action that yield no reputational inferences.

A related observation is even more counterintuitive: *coercive success is more likely against targets that have reputations for resolve.*[43] The reason is that a coercer will issue a risky "high" demand only if it is sufficiently confident that the target is weakly resolved. If the coercer already believes the target to be strong—in other words, if the target's reputation is good—then it will issue a low demand that is more likely to be accepted. This result obtains because war is an inefficient means of getting what one wants, so the coercer seeks to issue the highest possible demand without prompting a fight. Since coercers have some information about a target's resolve before formulating a coercive threat, they utilize that information to locate this optimal demand. A successful threat only means that the coercer has done this successfully. In short, successful coercive threats tell us more about the coercer than about the target. Capitulating to a coercive threat does not necessarily reveal low resolve.[44]

The implications of this logic for empirical research are significant. Several scholars have observed that states often do not develop reputations for being irresolute when they capitulate to coercive threats.[45] When scholars observe a successful coercive demand—in other words, acquiescence—it may only mean that the coercer was intimidated enough to moderate its demands ahead of time. In this scenario, coercers may draw no inferences at all from the conciliatory behavior of their opponents. But again, this does not mean that reputation plays no role. The lesson here is that reputations may indeed matter, but they may operate primarily prior to crises rather than during them.[46]

Implications: Threats and Reassurances

Schelling observed in *Arms and Influence* that reassurance is critical to success in coercive diplomacy: "any coercive threat requires corresponding assurances" that acquiescence will not invite future depredations.[47] The analysis here is consistent with this view. The two-round game revealed

[43] Specifically, as τ increases, it becomes increasingly likely that the coercer will select a pooling strategy, which in equilibrium results in capitulation by both weak and tough targets.

[44] Empirical studies, however, often make precisely this leap, assuming that capitulation implies weak resolve. See, for example, Joe Clare and Vesna Danilovic, "Multiple Audiences and Reputation Building in International Conflicts," *Journal of Conflict Resolution* 54, no. 6 (2010): 860–82.

[45] For example, Glenn H. Snyder and Paul Diesing, *Conflict among Nations: Bargaining, Decision Making, and System Structure in International Crises* (Princeton, NJ: Princeton University Press, 1977); Ted Hopf, *Peripheral Visions: Deterrence Theory and American Foreign Policy in the Third World, 1965–1990* (Ann Arbor: University of Michigan Press, 1995); Jonathan Mercer, *Reputation and International Politics* (Ithaca, NY: Cornell University Press, 1996); Daryl G. Press, *Calculating Credibility: How Leaders Assess Military Threats* (Ithaca, NY: Cornell University Press, 2005).

[46] See also Sechser, "Goliath's Curse," which explores the dynamics of reputations and asymmetric power in coercive diplomacy in greater detail.

[47] Schelling, *Arms and Influence*, 74.

an often-overlooked dynamic about coercive diplomacy: targets must consider not only the issues at stake in today's crisis but also how their actions might influence the outcomes of future crises. In the model, targets that believed future crises to be likely were more difficult to coerce than targets that believed today's crisis to be the last. It would be a mistake, then, for coercers to think solely about how to make their threats more potent. While threats are undoubtedly a central aspect of coercion, reassurances can also play a critical role. Coercers that can credibly promise not to make further demands are likely to be more successful in coercing their adversaries. The challenge for coercers, then, is to find ways to credibly tie their own hands and make promises of restraint believable.[48]

Limitations and Conclusions

Explaining coercive outcomes requires understanding the decisions made by both coercers and coercive targets. In other words, coercion is a process of strategic bargaining. In the competitive setting of coercive diplomacy, actors must consider not only their own objectives but also the anticipated reactions of their adversaries. This chapter has explored a series of models of coercive diplomacy, in which two actors bargain in the shadow of military conflict. The discussion paid special attention to the strategic calculations of coercers in an attempt to understand the conditions under which coercion succeeds and fails. The results of this analysis have several implications for understanding the outcomes of coercive episodes.

First, coercive outcomes depend critically on choices made in the early stages of a crisis. The first of these choices is the coercer's decision to initiate the crisis and, secondarily, what (or how much) to demand. While a coercer would like to win the largest possible concession from the target, demanding too much could result in a costly conflict. The possibility of war disciplines the coercer's calculations, compelling it to consider the target's likely reactions when formulating a threat. Coercive diplomacy is fundamentally about balancing risk and reward.

Second, information plays a starring role in coercive bargaining. Coercers and targets base their decisions around assumptions about the adversary's capabilities and resolve, but uncertainty can complicate these calculations. In reality, it can be difficult to know the other side's military strength, willingness to fight, and values. Coercive outcomes therefore depend not simply on the actors' military capabilities and resolve, but also on their ability to learn (or communicate) this information. This insight points scholars of coercive diplomacy in two related directions. First, the study of coercion would benefit greatly from the insights of scholarship on intelligence. A coercer's ability to obtain information about its opponent can mark the difference between success and failure, so understanding intelligence capabilities is central to

---

[48] Sechser, "Reputations and Signaling in Coercive Bargaining."

explaining coercive outcomes.[49] Second, a better understanding of signaling would improve scholarly theories of coercion. While there is an extensive literature on signaling in international relations, the insights of this literature have not yet been fully integrated into the study of coercive diplomacy.[50] Scholars and practitioners alike would benefit from a sharper understanding of what signals are available to leaders, and how effective they are.

Third, the role of military power in coercive diplomacy is more complex than scholars have acknowledged. In the traditional story about coercion, power plays a role primarily in intimidating the adversary. Actors that possess greater military capabilities can threaten more punishment, in this view, and therefore can more easily compel their adversaries to make concessions. This story, however, is incomplete. It overlooks an important fact: power influences not only the adversary's calculations but also one's own calculations. Military power simultaneously intimidates and emboldens. Actors with more power can make bigger demands and take greater risks.[51] The implications for the study of coercion are profound: instead of being associated with success, military power may be associated with coercive failure. Stronger actors can afford to take greater risks, leading to higher rates of failure.

Where Do We Go from Here?

The analysis also highlights several areas for further exploration in the study of coercive diplomacy. The first area involves coercion involving nonstate actors. The modeling exercise in this chapter generally treated the primary actors as states, but this need not be the case. In principle, the model ought to apply equally well to coercive encounters involving insurgent groups, actors in civil wars, terrorist organizations, and other nonstate entities.[52] At the same time, it is possible that these types of entities are a poor fit for the assumptions used to derive the conclusions in this chapter. For example, the concept of a winner-take-all conflict to resolve a dispute that escalates to war makes little sense when the target is a terrorist organization, since groups such as Al Qaeda likely resort to terrorism precisely because they stand no chance of defeating conventional armies in open battle. Other assumptions of the model may prove ill-fitting as well. Nevertheless the model offers a useful starting

[49] See, for example, Austin Long's chapter in this volume.

[50] For examples of empirical work on signaling, see Schultz, *Democracy and Coercive Diplomacy*; Brian Lai, "The Effects of Different Types of Military Mobilization on the Outcome of International Crises," *Journal of Conflict Resolution* 48, no. 2 (2004): 211–29; Matthew Fuhrmann and Todd S. Sechser, "Signaling Alliance Commitments: Hand-Tying and Sunk Costs in Extended Nuclear Deterrence," *American Journal of Political Science* 58, no. 4 (2014): 919–35; Todd S. Sechser and Abigail S. Post, "Hand-Tying versus Muscle-Flexing in Crisis Bargaining," paper presented at the annual conference of the American Political Science Association, San Francisco, September 5, 2015; Sechser, "Reputations and Signaling in Coercive Bargaining."

[51] For example, the chapter by Alexander B. Downes in this volume finds that more powerful states are more likely to demand what is arguably the greatest concession a leader can make: complete abdication.

[52] Several of the chapters in this volume, including contributions by Keren Fraiman, Peter Krause, and James Igoe Walsh, evaluate the logic of coercion in the context of insurgencies.

point for thinking about how coercion involving nonstate organizations may resemble—or deviate from—models of interstate coercive diplomacy.

On a similar note, more research is needed in the area of nonmilitary coercion. Whereas the analysis in this chapter emphasized coercive bargaining in the shadow of military force, states in fact have many coercive tools at their disposal, including economic sanctions, cyber warfare, and other forms of economic and political punishment.[53] Do standard models of military coercion apply to these scenarios? If not, how do these models need to be revised in order to account for nonmilitary coercive tools?

Finally, one limitation of the foregoing analysis is the absence of third-party actors. Third parties—including allies, other adversaries, neutral observers, and domestic political actors—often play a central role in coercive encounters.[54] The two-actor engagements analyzed in this chapter surely are too simple, overlooking a rich set of dynamics involving outside actors. A fruitful avenue for coercive diplomacy research would be to begin incorporating these actors into models of coercion.

[53] For sophisticated discussions of coercion using nonmilitary means, see the chapters in this volume by Daniel Drezner, Jon Lindsay and Erik Gartzke, Kelly M. Greenhill, and Jonathan Markowitz.

[54] See, for instance, Timothy W. Crawford's chapter in this volume.

CHAPTER 4

Air Power, Sanctions, Coercion, and Containment

When Foreign Policy Objectives Collide

PHIL M. HAUN

ON OCTOBER 6, 1994, as Deputy Prime Minister Tariq Aziz of Iraq denounced United Nations sanctions before the General Assembly, elements of two Iraqi Republican Guard armored divisions rumbled toward the border of Kuwait, as they had done before the August 1990 invasion.[1] Intelligence sources observed the troop movement, which, unlike in 1990, prompted a quick and forceful U.S. response. The United States demanded that Iraq not invade Kuwait and return its forces above the southern no-fly zone. The Pentagon repositioned naval assets and announced the deployment of hundreds of warplanes to back these demands with the threat of cruise missiles and airstrikes on Baghdad. On October 10, Iraq announced the removal of its forces from the border with the claim that it had only been conducting exercises. By the 17th, the troops were once again in garrison, where they would remain until 2003.

The onset of this crisis was brought about by Iraq's response to a U.S. policy of containment. After the Gulf War, the White House had kept in place the UN sanctions originally intended to compel the Iraqi Army to withdraw from Kuwait. The trade and arms embargo prevented Iraq from rebuilding its military and undermined President Saddam Hussein's regime. By 1994 four years of blockade had devastated Iraq's economy. The U.S. containment strategy also included air power, which encroached on Iraqi sovereignty by enforcing the safe haven for the Kurds in the north and the no-fly zone in the south.

Following the redeployment of the Republican Guard, Saddam made an additional concession by recognizing the Kuwaiti border in order to obtain

The views of the author do not represent those of the Department of Defense or the U.S. Navy.

[1] "Tariq Aziz Addresses U.N. General Assembly," Baghdad Republic of Iraq Radio Network, October 7, 1994, Foreign Broadcast Information Service (FBIS)-Near East and South Asia (NES)-94-196 on October 11, 1994.

Russian support in the UN Security Council to have the sanctions lifted. Instead of relaxing sanctions, however, the United States worked to maintain them, even as international criticism and evidence mounted that sanctions would never drive Saddam from power and only caused suffering for the most vulnerable segments of the Iraqi population. After this crisis, economic sanctions were no longer effective in coercing Iraq, leaving the United States reliant on the threat of airstrikes.

The 1994 Kuwaiti border crisis is a case where the United States used economic sanctions and air power to coerce a weaker state. In such asymmetric interstate conflicts, the inherent disparity in military capability allows the United States to choose whether to accommodate a weak state or to escalate the conflict into crisis. Should it escalate, the United States can either adopt a brute force strategy to seize its objectives or choose a coercive strategy, threatening or employing economic sanctions and/or limited force to convince the target to change its behavior. In theory, coercion should succeed, as a rational challenger will not incur the costs of a coercive strategy if the weak state is expected to resist.[2] In practice, however, asymmetric coercion often fails because the United States continues to impose sanctions or conduct military operations even after a target makes concessions, thus providing the target no incentive to modify its behavior amid an invariable U.S. strategy of containment.

This chapter proceeds as follows. First, a model of asymmetric interstate coercion is developed and equilibrium conditions identified to show that such coercion should succeed, in theory. The second section introduces an explanation for coercion failure based on a competing strategy of containment. Third, U.S. foreign policy with Iraq in the 1990s is analyzed with particular attention given to the 1994 Kuwaiti border crisis.

Asymmetric Interstate Coercion

A crisis arises when a conflict between states has an associated time constraint and there is an increased likelihood of violence.[3] In an asymmetric interstate crisis, the distribution of power is so askew that a powerful challenger, such as the United States, has the military capacity to threaten the existence of a much weaker target state, but not vice versa.[4] The disproportionate power of the United States gives it the luxury to escalate a conflict into a crisis or to accommodate (appease) a weak state to end the conflict.[5] Accommodation is

---

[2] This chapter refers to the more powerful state as the "challenger" in each scenario. If the challenger opts to coerce a weaker state, it could rightly be labeled a "coercer" as well.

[3] Charles Hermann, *Crises in Foreign Policy: A Simulation Analysis* (Indianapolis: Bobbs-Merrill, 1969), 414.

[4] Andrew Mack, "Why Big Nations Lose Small Wars," *World Politics* 27 (1975): 181.

[5] Alexander George and William Simons, *The Limits of Coercive Diplomacy* (Boulder, CO: Westview Press, 1994), 7. Daniel Treisman, "Rational Appeasement," *International Organization* 58 (2004): 345; D. C. Watt, "Appeasement: The Rise of a Revisionist School?," *Political Quarterly* 36 (1965): 191–213; Robert Beck, "Munich's Lessons Reconsidered," *International Security* 14 (1989): 161–91.

the preferred option for most conflicts in which nonvital interests are at stake or for which the expected costs of employing economic sanctions or military force outweigh the benefits. At times, however, issues are so vital that the United States employs its economic and military options in coercive or brute force strategies.

Military coercion threatens or employs limited violence to convince a target to comply with demands, while economic coercion employs sanctions to do the same.[6] The United States often threatens airstrikes as part of a military coercive strategy, while its economic sanctions include trade and arms embargos, the freezing of financial assets, the restriction of access to financial services, and the targeting of sanctions to specific individuals or firms. On occasion, the United States will begin a crisis by adopting economic sanctions and later augment them with the threat of military force. At other times, the issue may be so pressing that it turns directly to threatening airstrikes. Coercion requires that the United States issue demands and threats, the credibility of which are communicated by costly signals. Demands are either deterrent (i.e., for the target not to change what it is doing) or compellent (i.e., for the target to stop what it is doing). Threats are either punishment or denial. (See Art and Greenhill's chapter in this volume for a discussion of demands and threats.)

The United States uses coercion to realize its foreign policy goals. Coercion succeeds when the target complies with U.S. ex ante demands *and* the United States accepts the target's concessions. Coercion fails when the target continues to resist, when the United States rejects a target's concessions, or when the United States abandons coercion for a brute force strategy.

While successful coercion requires both the challenger and the target to accept the outcome, with a brute force strategy the United States attempts to simply seize its objectives. Brute force thus has the advantage of not needing to convince the target to comply with demands. Brute force war can achieve high-level objectives by seizing territory or imposing regime change through a campaign of invasion and occupation.[7] While the benefits gained by brute force are usually greater than those of coercion, so too are its costs. Although the United States chooses coercion more often than brute force, it has, on occasion, resorted to brute force war such as in Afghanistan in 2001 and Iraq in 2003.[8] In both cases, the benefits of regime change were accompanied by the high costs of war in terms of blood and treasure, most of which were expended not in the initial invasion but in the subsequent occupation.

---

[6] Thomas Schelling, *Arms and Influence* (New Haven, CT: Yale University Press, 1966), 3; Lawrence Freedman, *Deterrence* (Malden, MA: Polity Press, 2004), 27; Robert Pape, *Bombing to Win* (Ithaca, NY: Cornell University Press, 1996), 4; Daniel Byman and Matthew Waxman, *The Dynamics of Coercion: American Foreign Policy and the Limits of Military Might* (Cambridge: Cambridge University Press, 2002), 30; Carl von Clausewitz, *On War*, ed. Michael Howard and Peter Paret (Princeton, NJ: Princeton University Press, 1976), 75.

[7] Pape, *Bombing to Win*.

[8] Phil Haun, *Coercion, Survival and War: Why Weak States Resist the United States* (Palo Alto, CA: Stanford University Press, 2015).

A rational model of asymmetric coercion incorporates a powerful challenger's choice between a coercive or brute force strategy and, when coercion is chosen, the target's decision to concede or resist.[9] This does not suggest that states, their ruling regimes, or leaders always behave rationally. Rather, a rational choice model provides a framework from which to begin analyzing real-world cases. Central to this model is the assumption that decision-making is sequential in asymmetric interstate crises. The powerful coercer, without its survival at risk, has the latitude to choose whether to escalate a conflict to a crisis and, if it chooses coercion, to optimize the demands and threats made. Only once the coercer chooses coercion does the target get a vote, and its decision is whether to resist or concede.

Interstate conflicts arise over a variety of issues, from relatively minor matters such as a state's domestic policy toward an ethnic group, to higher order issues over territory or regime change. A rational challenger chooses the strategy with the best expected outcome from among the foreign policy options available to it: accommodation, coercion, or brute force. It can opt to accommodate, and the conflict concludes without crisis, in which case the challenger forfeits its interest in the issue in dispute and incurs the reputational costs as an appeaser. If instead a coercive or brute force strategy offers a better expected outcome, the challenger can escalate the conflict into crisis (see Figure 4.1).

With brute force war, the expected outcome for the powerful challenger depends on the value it places on the issue in question, discounted by the probability of victory. Although the challenger has an overwhelming advantage in power, the probability of victory need not equal the ratio of military forces between the two states. Military power can be diffused by distance and affected by both terrain and climatology. In addition, with its survival at risk, the target state may demonstrate higher resolve, which may partially or fully overcome the challenger's military advantage. Along with the anticipated benefits of war, the challenger must factor in the expected costs of fighting. While a brute force strategy can achieve high-level objectives such as the seizure of territory or the imposition of regime change, the high price associated with invasion and occupation may make the expected outcome of a brute force war less attractive than that of accommodation or coercion.[10]

Instead of accommodation or brute force, the powerful challenger may choose coercion. When implementing a coercive strategy, the coercer makes a demand that the target concede a portion of the issue in conflict. The challenger backs the demand with a threat, the credibility of which is communicated by a costly signal. In response, the weak state concedes or resists.[11] If it concedes, the expected outcome for the target is the amount it retains of the

[9] For the formal model see Haun, *Coercion, Survival and War*, appendix B.
[10] Patricia L. Sullivan, "War Aims and War Outcomes: Why Powerful States Lose Limited Wars," *Journal of Conflict Resolution* 51 (2007): 496–524.
[11] The model does not allow for partial concession by the target, though in the real world this clearly happens.

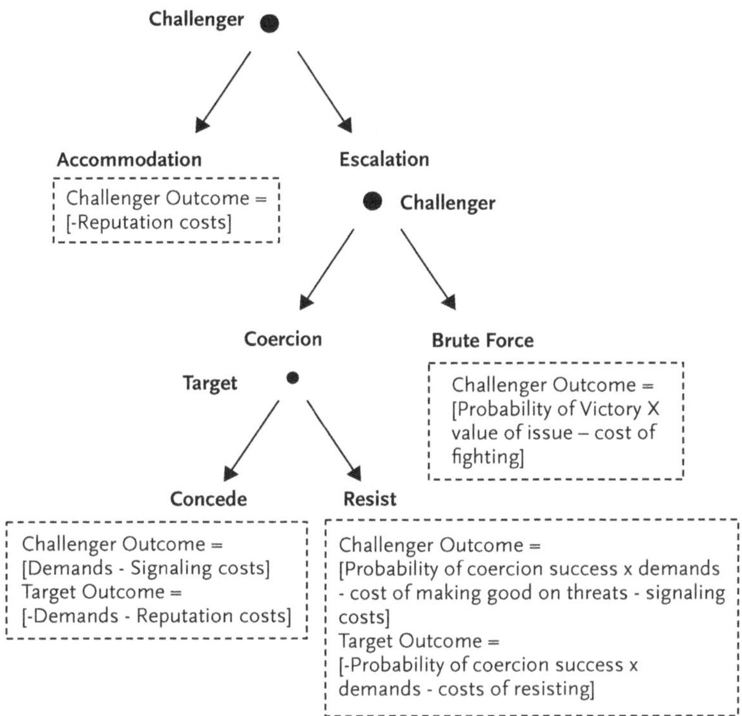

FIGURE 4.1 Asymmetric Coercion Model

issue at stake less the reputation costs for acquiescing. Should the weak state initially resist, then the crisis outcome depends on the likelihood the challenger will carry through on its threats and that this, in turn, will convince the target to change its mind. Under these conditions, the chance that coercion succeeds can be thought of as a lottery, with the odds being the probability that the target concedes once the coercer makes good on its threats.

Along with the benefits gained by resisting, the target state's expected outcome must also include the costs of resisting. This is the suffering the target endures when the challenger carries out its threats. For punishment strategies, these are the economic costs and civilian casualties suffered from sanctions or airstrikes. For denial strategies, these costs are measured by the degradation of a target's defenses. These imposed costs provide an explanation for coercion failure, whereby the target's losses are part of a coercer's containment strategy.

Turning to the powerful challenger's calculations, its expected outcome for coercion success depends on the value it places on its objective. Should the target initially resist, the challenger's expected benefit is discounted by the probability coercion will later succeed once it makes good on its threats. For example, when NATO commenced its threatened air strikes in the Balkans in 1999, Serbia, though initially resolute, eventually conceded control of Kosovo. NATO's expected benefit before the air strikes was discounted by the noncertain probability that Serbia would ultimately give in. Also included are the challenger's signaling costs along with the expected costs of making good on its threat. If the weak state continues to resist, the coercer can then either accept failure or abandon coercion and resort to brute force war.

Having just examined the expected outcomes for target concession or resistance, now consider how a rational challenger chooses its mix of demands and threats. The equilibrium condition for the model is the highest demand for which the target is indifferent to conceding or resisting.[12] Calculating this demand, however, is only half of the challenger's maximization problem. The demand must also be backed by a threat, and signaling the credibility of that threat is costly. Assuming decreasing marginal benefits for the conflict issue and increasing marginal costs for signaling, an interior solution exists whereby the challenger's optimal coercive offer limits both the demands and the threats made. The intuition is that a powerful challenger gains by increasing its demands, but the marginal benefits from additional demands accrue at a diminishing rate. The threats to back these larger demands must likewise be raised, which, to be seen as credible, requires additional signaling costs. Unlike benefits, the marginal cost of signaling accrues at an increasing rate, particularly when military action crosses the threshold of violence. Exemplary uses of force, such as military exercises, deployments, and mobilizations, are costly, but not nearly as costly as combat operations, with the risks of battlefield casualties and conflict escalation. As a result, the coercer optimizes by increasing its demands until the marginal benefits are offset by the increase in the marginal costs of signaling. If no interior solution exists, the challenger should not coerce but instead should select the upper bounded solution of brute force war.[13]

Containment as an Explanation for Coercion Failure

As the model suggests by its equilibrium conditions, coercion should succeed because a rational coercer would not choose coercion unless it had a better expected outcome than brute force war or accommodation. This is the case only if the coercer concludes the weak state is willing to concede to demands. While it should succeed in theory, coercion often fails in practice. International relations scholars have viewed coercion failure as the result of mistakes made by states, regimes, and leaders not acting rationally. In addition to nonrational explanations, other scholars have pointed to uncertainty, private information, and commitment problems as being responsible for coercion failure. Since all crises contain some elements of nonrational behavior, uncertainty, and

[12] A common modeling assumption is made in that if the target is indifferent between concession or resistance, it will concede.
[13] The lower bounded solution represents accommodation.

commitment concerns, these explanations are less useful in predicting coercion success or failure and better suited for understanding crisis onset.[14]

This chapter considers an explanation for coercion failure resulting from the simultaneous imposition of a containment strategy while the challenger attempts to coerce the target state via punishment. The economic and military costs imposed upon the target by the challenger carrying out its coercive threats serve to keep the target weak and unable to undertake significant military action. In such a case, the United States accepts coercion failure as the price paid for successful containment.

The Conflict between the United States and Iraq

Other than having developed an exceptionally large military, by 1988 Iraq had little to show for eight years of fighting Iran. Iraq's economy had shrunk to half its prewar size, and interest payments on its $50 billion in war debt—half of which was owed to Saudi Arabia and Kuwait—consumed a quarter of the Iraqi budget.[15] To remedy his economic problems, Saddam ordered the Republican Guard to invade Kuwait on August 2, 1990 (see Figure 4.2).[16] This aggression threatened the stability of President George H. W. Bush's "new world order," as well as U.S. economic interests due to the resultant spike in global oil prices.[17] Through the UN Security Council, the United States adopted a coercive strategy by demanding Iraq unconditionally withdraw from Kuwait and imposing economic sanctions that cut Iraqi imports by 90 percent and oil exports by 97 percent.[18] Saddam responded by annexing Kuwait.[19] Unconvinced sanctions alone would compel Iraq, Bush announced in November a buildup of a half million U.S. troops in the Middle East, which were intended to lead an international coalition authorized by the Security Council to liberate Kuwait.[20]

In the early hours of January 17, 1991, the coalition commenced Operation Desert Storm with airstrikes against strategic targets in and around Baghdad. Within days, however, the majority of strikes shifted to attriting the 336,000

---

[14] Haun, *Coercion, Survival and War*, 26–31.

[15] Efraim Karsh and Inari Rautsi, *Saddam Hussein: A Political Biography* (New York: Free Press, 1991), 161.

[16] "Confrontation in the Gulf; Excerpts from Iraqi Document on Meeting with U.S. Envoy" *New York Times*, September 23, 1990; James Baker, *The Politics of Diplomacy* (New York: G. P. Putnam's Sons, 1995), 272.

[17] George Bush, "Remarks at the Aspen Institute Symposium in Aspen Colorado, 2 August 1990," http://www.presidency.ucsb.edu/ws/?pid=18731; George Bush, "Address before a Joint Session of the Congress on the Persian Gulf Crisis and Budget Deficit," September 11, 1990, http://www.presidency.ucsb.edu/ws/?pid=18820.

[18] Clyde Farnsworth, "The Iraqi Invasion; Bush, in Freezing Assets, Bars $30 Billion to Hussein" *New York Times*, August 3, 1990; United Nations Security Council, "Resolution 661 (1990), 6 August 1990," https://www.treasury.gov/resource-center/sanctions/Documents/661.pdf.

[19] "Text of Saddam Husayn Initiative on Situation," Baghdad Domestic Service, 1990, FBIS-NES-90-156, August 13, 1990.

[20] George Bush, "President's News Conference on the Persian Gulf Crisis," November 8, 1990, http://www.presidency.ucsb.edu/ws/?pid=18792.

FIGURE 4.2 Iraq and Its Neighbors (1993)
SOURCE: University of Texas Libraries, http://www.lib.utexas.edu/maps/atlas_middle_east/iraq.jpg.

Iraqi troops in Kuwait and southern Iraq.[21] On February 24, the coalition executed its brute force strategy by invading Kuwait, and one hundred hours later, the White House unilaterally declared a ceasefire.

The initiation of the Gulf War confirmed that economic sanctions and coercive air power had failed to coerce Iraq's withdrawal from Kuwait. The brute force invasion of Kuwait subsequently severely attrited Iraq's overall military power and degraded its ability to project power across its borders.[22] Though the coalition never did completely annihilate the Iraqi Army, it did capture or destroy 75 percent of its tanks, 54 percent of its armored personnel carriers,

[21] Thomas A. Keaney, *Gulf War Airpower Survey* (Washington, D.C.: U.S. Government Printing Office, 1993) 2:254; Thomas A. Keaney, *Gulf War Airpower Survey Summary* (Washington, D.C.: U.S. Government Printing Office, 1993), 106.
[22] U.S. Congress, Senate Committee on Intelligence, *US Intelligence Community's Pre-War Intelligence Assessments on Iraq* (Washington, DC: GPO, 2004), 378; http://nsarchive.gwu.edu/NSAEBB/NSAEBB254/doc12.pdf,

and 89 percent of its artillery pieces in Kuwait.[23] By war's end the million-man Iraqi Army had been reduced by 66 percent and Saddam's elite Republican Guard had been reduced by nearly 50 percent, from 12 to 7 divisions.[24] In addition to the problem of reorganizing what was left of Iraq's military, Saddam now faced domestic unrest sparked by his defeat, prompting him to send the surviving units of the Republican Guard to suppress Shiite and Kurdish uprisings. To constrain his regime's ability to use force against these groups, the United States established a northern safe area and a southern no-fly zone. While prohibiting Iraqi troops to enter the north, no such restrictions were placed on troop deployments in the south.[25]

Through another Security Council Resolution, passed in April 1991, the United States ordered sanctions to be kept in place until Iraq agreed to acknowledge the Kuwaiti border, abandon its weapons of mass destruction (WMD) program, and cooperate with UN Special Commission (UNSCOM) and International Atomic Energy Agency monitors.[26] In January 1993, Iraq began to test the determination of the United States in enforcing the no-fly zone and weapons inspections. Iraqi aircraft repeatedly violated the southern no-fly zone, and Iraqi officials impeded the work of UN inspectors. To induce cooperation in his final days in office, President Bush ordered airstrikes on Iraqi air defenses and a nuclear facility.[27] This did not, however, compel Iraq to cease its efforts to undermine the United States. In April, Iraqi intelligence attempted to assassinate the former president during his visit to Kuwait. This prompted a June 1993 retaliatory cruise missile strike by the Clinton administration on Iraq's intelligence headquarters.

Even though Saddam chafed against the Security Council's resolutions, continued economic sanctions and air power had the potential to coerce him into making policy changes. What they could not do, however, was compel Iraq to remove Saddam from power. Although the CIA attempted to encourage domestic groups to overthrow him, the United States was unwilling at this point to incur the high costs of a brute force war to impose regime change.[28] The White House settled instead on a dual policy of employing sanctions to coerce Iraq into abandoning its WMD program and sanctions and air power to contain Iraqi military power. It was the resulting conflict between these competing strategies that led to another coercion failure.

---

[23] Keaney, *Gulf War Airpower Survey*, 2:261.

[24] Michael R. Gordon and Bernard E. Trainor, *The Generals' War* (Boston. MA: Little, Brown, 1995), 459; International Institute for Strategic Studies *The Military Balance* (London: Brassey's, 1990–92).

[25] R. W. Apple, "After the War: The Overview; U.S. Says Iraqi Generals Agree to Demands 'On All Matters'; Early P.O.W. Release Expected," *New York Times*, March 4, 1991; Gordon and Trainor, *The Generals' War*, 444–47.

[26] UN Security Council, Resolution 687, April 3, 1991,https://documents-dds-ny.un.org/doc/RESOLUTION/GEN/NR0/596/23/IMG/NR059623.pdf?OpenElement.

[27] Michael R. Gordon, "Raid on Iraq; U.S. Leads Further Attacks on Iraqi Antiaircraft Sites; Admits Its Missile Hit Hotel; Raids in 2 Regions," *New York Times*, January 19, 1993.

[28] Michael Knights, *Cradle of Conflict* (Annapolis, MD: Naval Institute Press, 2005), 151.

Three years of continual sanctions eventually placed such a burden on the Iraqi people that even a tyrant like Saddam could no longer ignore their plight. Inflation spiraled out of control, leaving most Iraqis unable to afford food and dependent on meager government rations.[29] As a result, in November 1993 Saddam was compelled to change his policies and began to cooperate with UNSCOM inspectors in the hope that this would convince the Security Council to lift sanctions. By the summer of 1994, UNSCOM had made significant progress, destroying all known chemical and nuclear weapons and production equipment, while also installing video surveillance equipment at key production facilities.[30] Economic sanctions had succeeded in convincing Iraq to concede to demands regarding WMD, but the United States was not willing to remove the sanctions out of concern that Saddam might rebuild Iraq's WMD.

In terms of the asymmetric coercion model, the United States, as the powerful coercer, chose not to accommodate Iraq with regard to its WMD program after the Gulf War. The United States also chose not to employ a brute force strategy of invasion, but instead adopted a coercive strategy by issuing demands that Iraq allow inspections and the monitoring of potential WMD facilities. The United States backed its demands with the threat of Iraqi economic collapse signaled by the continuation of the economic blockade. After two years of sanctions, Iraq agreed to the inspections and monitoring. This concession to U.S. core demands was not sufficient, however, for the United States to relax the sanctions. The United States was also pursuing a policy of containment, which was designed to prevent Saddam's regime from projecting its military power to the north and south within its borders or threaten its foreign neighbors. Containment required keeping Iraq economically weak through the sanctions and using air power to enforce the northern safe area and southern no-fly zone.

The Security Council reviewed the sanctions bimonthly, and in September 1994 Saddam was counting on a positive recommendation from UNSCOM. By now, Iraq had exhausted its foreign currency reserves for purchasing foodstuffs and begun to halve rations to well below subsistence levels.[31] UNSCOM's chief instead recommended additional time to ensure Iraqi compliance.[32] Incensed, Saddam reversed course, threatening to deny inspectors further access unless sanctions were immediately lifted.

---

[29] Youssef Ibrahim, "Baghdad's Burden—A Special Report; Iraq Is Near Economic Ruin but Hussein Appears Secure," *New York Times*, October 25, 1994.

[30] Paul Lewis, "U.N.'s Team in Iraq Sees Arms Gains," *New York Times*, July 26, 1994.

[31] Baghdad Iraqi News Agency, "'Temporary' Changes Made to Ration Card Quotas," September 25, 1994, FBIS-NES-94-187, September 27, 1994; Ibrahim, "Baghdad's Burden."

[32] UNSCOM, "Report of the Secretary-General on the Status of the Implementation of the Special Commission's Plan for the Ongoing Monitoring and Verification of Iraq's Compliance with Relevant Parts of Section C of Security Council Resolution 687 (1991)," S/1994/1138 Security Council Distribution General: United Nations, October 7, 1994; Barbara Crossette, "Threats in the Gulf: The U.N.; Iraq's Attempt to Have Sanctions Lifted Quickly May Have Backfired," *New York Times*, October 11, 2009.

He further ordered to the Kuwaiti border a deployment of armored elements of two Republican Guard divisions consisting of 14,000 troops. [33] These events coincided with the October 6, 1994, address by Deputy Prime Minister Aziz, demanding that the UN General Assembly take action to remove the sanctions.[34]

The Iraqi backlash against the continuation of sanctions brought about a new conflict between the United States and Iraq over the deployment of troops along the Iraqi-Kuwaiti border. The United States escalated the conflict into a crisis by choosing a coercive strategy, demanding the troops not invade Kuwait and instead return to their barracks north of the southern no-fly zone. The United States backed its demands with threats of cruise missiles and air strikes, the credibility of these threats being signaled by the deployment of ships and aircraft to the region capable of targeting Baghdad.

The 1994 Kuwaiti Border Crisis

As Aziz spoke before the General Assembly, U.S. intelligence sources had already identified the movement of the Republican Guard units, prompting an immediate military response. On October 7, the Pentagon dispatched a navy carrier group from the Adriatic to the Red Sea, which included destroyers armed with conventional cruise missiles. (See Table 4.1 for chronology.)[35]

On October 8, the Pentagon signaled the credibility of the threat of force by taking the unusual step of announcing deployment orders by disclosing the repositioning of its forces, the airlift of 4,000 soldiers to join prepositioned equipment in Kuwait, and the deployment of ships from Diego Garcia bearing equipment for another 15,000 troops.[36] The United States placed on alert U.S. Air Force combat wings in the United States and Europe, along with a stateside U.S. Army mechanized division.

Concurrent with its deployment announcement, the Pentagon issued the deterrent demand that "Iraq respect the territorial integrity of Kuwait." Military spokesmen reinforced the threat of U.S. airstrikes by highlighting the U.S. capability to strike Baghdad with air and cruise missile attacks.[37] President Clinton further signaled U.S. willingness to use force by warning Saddam that

---

[33] "West Urged to Maintain Sanctions against Iraq," *Times* (London), October 4, 1994, FBIS-NES-94-192.

[34] "Tariq Aziz Addresses U.N. General Assembly."

[35] Kenneth Bacon, "DoD News Briefing: Mr. Kenneth H. Bacon, ATSD PA," October 28, 1994, http://archive.defense.gov/Transcripts/Transcript.aspx?TranscriptID=65,.

[36] Such deployment orders are typically kept secret. John Sheehan and Pat Hughes, "DoD News Briefing: Lieutenant General John Sheehan," October 8, 1994, http://archive.defense.gov/Transcripts/Transcript.aspx?TranscriptID=60; Eric W. Herr, "Operation Vigilant Warrior: Conventional Deterrence Theory, Doctrine, and Practice" (Master's thesis, School of Advanced Airpower Studies, Montgomery, AL, 1996), chapter 3.

[37] Sheehan and Hughes, "DoD News Briefing: Lieutenant General John Sheehan."

TABLE 4.1 Chronology of Kuwaiti Border Crisis

DATE	KEY EVENTS
October 6, 1994	– Deputy Prime Minister Tariq Aziz of Iraq addresses the UN General Assembly and demands lifting of sanctions. – U.S. intelligence observes two Republican Guard armor divisions begin to deploy toward Kuwait border.
October 7	– U.S. deploys USS *George Washington* Carrier Group from Adriatic to Red Sea.
October 8	– Pentagon announces deployment of Carrier Group, 2,000 marines, 4,000 soldiers, and prepositioned equipment ships from Diego Garcia. – Pentagon warns of capability of forces to conduct punishment strikes on downtown Baghdad.
October 10	– Iraq announces troop withdrawal. – President Clinton announces deployment of 36,000 troops and 350 combat aircraft.
October 11	– U.S. intelligence observes commencement of Iraqi troop withdrawal.
October 12	– U.S. acknowledges Iraqi troop movement but continues deployment.
October 13	– Several Republican Guard units delay south of 32nd parallel. – Russia announces commencement of negotiations with Iraq to recognize Kuwaiti border.
October 14	– U.S. submits Resolution 949 to Security Council demanding Iraq continue pulling back its forces to home bases.
October 15	– UN Security Council adopts Resolution 949.
October 16	– Iraq accepts Resolution 949.
October 17	– U.S. intelligence determines remaining Republican Guard units are moving north.

"it would be a grave error for Iraq to repeat the mistakes of the past or to misjudge either American will or American power."[38]

It did not take long for Iraq to respond. After consultation and urging by Russia, Iraq announced on October 10 that it would remove the forward-deployed Republican Guard units near the border. In an effort to reduce reputation costs for backing down, Iraq claimed their deployment had merely been part of scheduled military exercises, though there was some evidence the Iraqis had also been establishing logistics sites, just as they had in late July 1990.[39] That evening, Clinton stated that there was not yet evidence of a

[38] William J. Clinton, "Remarks on Iraq," October 8, 1994, *American Presidency Project*, http://www.presidency.ucsb.edu/ws/index.php?pid=49261&st=Iraq&st1.

[39] Baghdad INA, "Al-Sahhaf Announces Troop Withdrawal," October 10, 1994, FBIS-NES-94-196, October 11, 1994; Elaine Sciolino, "Threats in the Gulf: The Overview; U.S. Offers Plan to Avoid Threat from Iraq Again," *New York Times*, October 13, 1994; William Clinton, "Letter to Congressional

withdrawal and that the U.S. policy of containment would "not allow Iraq to threaten its neighbors or intimidate the United Nations as it ensure[d] that Iraq [would] never again possess . . . weapons of mass destruction." With that, he announced the additional deployment of 350 aircraft and 36,000 troops.[40]

On October 11, forward Iraqi units began pulling back from the border, and on the following day, Iraq announced that most of its troops had been withdrawn.[41] Uncertain as to whether the Iraqi troops were indeed returning to their garrisons, the United States indicated that it would continue with troop deployments and keep 155,000 on alert.[42]

On October 13, U.S. intelligence noted two brigades from one Republican Guard division stopping near the town of Nasiriya, south of the no-fly line at the 32nd parallel. It also observed Iraqi forces just north of Basra at Qalat Salih, delaying their retreat. [43] On the 14th, the United States submitted Resolution 949 to the Security Council, which was then adopted on the following day. It demanded "that Iraq immediately complete the withdrawal of all military units recently deployed to southern Iraq to their original positions." It further demanded that Iraq not threaten its neighbors or UN operations in Iraq, that it not redeploy units to the south, and that it cooperate fully with UNSCOM.[44] On October 16, Iraq accepted the Security Council resolution, and by the 17th the crisis had come to an end for the United States with intelligence reports of Iraqi troops again on the move toward their garrison.[45]

When the troop withdrawal was announced on the October 10, Iraq had confirmed that the decision had been made in consultation with Russia.[46] Three days later, the Russian foreign minister, Andrey Kozyrev, met with Saddam and issued a joint statement: "Russia has called for adopting decisive steps to prevent the escalation of the situation and to return the situation to the course of political and diplomatic efforts. These efforts will eventually lead to achieving solid security and stability in the region, to the cancellation of the sanctions imposed on Iraq, and to setting up good neighborly relations between

---

Leaders Reporting on Iraq's Compliance with United Nations Security Council Resolutions," October 27, 1994, *American Presidency Project*, http://www.presidency.ucsb.edu/ws/index.php?pid=49379&st=&st1=,

[40] William Clinton, *My Life* (New York: Knopf, 2004), 624; Michael Gordon, "Threats in the Gulf: The Military Buildup; At Least 36,000 U.S. Troops Going to Gulf in Response to Continued Iraqi Buildup," *New York Times*, October 10, 1994; William Clinton, "Address to the Nation on Iraq," October 10, 1994, *American Presidency Project*, http://www.presidency.ucsb.edu/ws/index.php?pid=49264&st=Iraq&st1=.

[41] Robert S. Greenberger, "U.S. Plan to Block Future Iraqi Moves on Kuwait amid Signs of Withdrawal," *Wall Street Journal*, October 12, 1994.

[42] Michael R. Gordon, "Threats in the Gulf: The Tactics; U.S. Sees Signs of Iraqi Retreat but Continues Buildup," *New York Times*, October 12, 1994.

[43] Michael R. Gordon, "Threats in the Gulf: The Strategy; U.S. Plans to Keep Planes and Tanks in the Gulf Area," *New York Times*, October 14, 1994.

[44] UN Security Council Resolution 949, October 15, 1994, https://documents-dds-ny.un.org/doc/UNDOC/GEN/N94/401/71/PDF/N9440171.pdf?OpenElement.

[45] Steven Greenhouse, "U.S. Says Iraq Appears to Resume Pullback from Kuwait Border," *New York Times*, October 17, 1994.

[46] Baghdad INA, "Al-Sahhaf Announces Troop Withdrawal"; "Al-Sahhaf Defends Position, Criticizes U.S.," Paris Radio Monte Carlo, October 11, 1994, FBIS-NES-94-197, October 12, 1994.

Iraq and Kuwait."[47] The meeting also produced a proposal that Iraq formally acknowledge the Kuwaiti border, in response to which the UN would lift sanctions. Kozyrev conveyed this proposal to the Kuwaiti government and then traveled to New York to present it to the Security Council.[48] The Russians' diplomacy proved only partially successful. On November 10, Iraq did formally recognize "the sovereignty of the State of Kuwait, its territorial integrity and political independence."[49] Subsequent Russian efforts to have the Security Council lift sanctions, however, proved fruitless.

Prompt U.S. military actions had signaled a credible threat that compelled Iraq to withdraw its forces from the Kuwaiti border and brought this crisis to a close. This crisis was not settled solely by the threat of military action, however. The Russian promise of support in the Security Council to have the economic sanctions lifted helped prompt Iraq to withdraw its troops and to acknowledge the Kuwaiti border in November 1994.

Though the Kuwaiti border crisis had been resolved, Iraqi WMD remained a U.S. concern, which led to a continuation of its containment strategy and sanctions. The August 1995 defection of Saddam's son-in-law Hussein Kamel, responsible for Iraqi WMD, resulted in UNSCOM obtaining a wealth of additional documentation on Iraq's biological and nuclear weapons program.[50] Yet this discovery only increased U.S. uncertainty over the amount of WMD that remained.

The 2003 invasion would later reveal how weak Iraq's conventional military forces had become and that Iraq had previously eliminated its WMD programs. Yet this information was unknown to the United States at the time, and a series of events led it to question the long-term viability of its containment strategy. First, in December 1995 the UN Food and Agriculture Organization reported a fivefold increase in Iraqi childhood mortality rates.[51] This in turn placed international pressure for the Security Council to reoffer the Oil-for-Food program, which Saddam had rejected in 1991 but agreed to in May 1996.[52] Iraq began pumping oil again in December, and though the Iraqi government did not directly receive the revenue from oil sales, Saddam now had some control over which countries received contracts and who in Iraq received food. In addition, the UN restructured its sanctions regime. Instead of banning all

---

[47] Baghdad Republic of Iraq Network, "Joint Statement Issued," October 13, 1994, FBIS-NES-94-199, October 14, 1994.

[48] Barbara Crossette, "Threats in the Gulf: The Diplomacy; Russia and Iraq Work Out Plan to Ease Gulf Tension," *New York Times*, October 14, 1994; Barbara Crossette, "U.S. Is Demanding a Quick U.N. Vote on Iraqi Pullback," *New York Times*, October 15, 1994.

[49] Barbara Crossette, "Iraqis to Accept Kuwait's Borders," *New York Times*, November 11, 1994.

[50] United Nations Special Commission, "Chronology of Main Events," http://www.un.org/Depts/unscom/Chronology/chronologyframe.htm,.

[51] Barbara Crossette, "Iraq Sanctions Kill Children, U.N. Reports," *New York Times*, December 1, 1995.

[52] UN Security Council Resolution 706, August 15, 1991, https://documents-dds-ny.un.org/doc/RESOLUTION/GEN/NR0/596/42/IMG/NR059642.pdf?OpenElemen, Citing issues of sovereignty and restrictions on the use of revenues, Saddam refused for nearly five years to cooperate with the UN. David Malone *The International Struggle over Iraq: Politics in the U.N. Security Council 1980–2005* (Oxford: Oxford University Press, 2006), 117.

goods unless specifically allowed, the onus on inspections was reversed, with all goods now allowed unless specifically prohibited.[53]

Second, Saddam began pushing back on the U.S. enforcement of the northern safe area and southern no-fly zone. In September 1996, Iraq tested the United States by deploying troops to Irbil to intervene in a Kurdish dispute. U.S. air power patrolling the northern safe area was incapable of responding directly to the Republican Guard's actions; instead the United States retaliated weakly, with limited air strikes against Iraq's air defense systems in the southern no-fly zone.

Third, Iraq began to resist WMD inspections by limiting access to facilities and harassing UN inspectors. For the next two years, Iraq adopted "cheat and retreat" tactics concerning both the southern no-fly zone and UN inspections, whereby it repeatedly entered the no-fly zone and hindered inspectors, only to relent when faced with a new Security Council resolution threatening airstrikes.[54]

The United States eventually abandoned coercion and the hope that sanctions and/or air strikes would convince Iraq to comply with its demands. This shift in policy was made explicit when Congress passed the Iraq Liberation Act in 1998, making Iraqi regime change a U.S. mandate.[55] In December 1998, UN inspectors departed Iraq in anticipation of the Desert Fox air raids and would not return until 2002.[56] These airstrikes were no longer meant to coerce Iraq but to degrade and destroy Iraqi conventional and unconventional military power. Though regime change was now its official policy, the United States did not abandon containment for a brute force strategy until after the events of September 11, 2001. After toppling the Taliban in Afghanistan, President George W. Bush then removed Saddam from power in 2003.

Over the course of the 1990s, the United States had employed both economic sanctions and air power to both coerce and contain Iraq's WMD and conventional military capabilities. Over time, however, the unwillingness of the United States to relax sanctions when Iraq chose to cooperate with UN inspections eventually undermined their coercive impact, particularly once Saddam accepted the Oil-for-Food program. Finally, the United States gave up its pretext of coercion as it began to question economic sanctions and air power's ability to contain Saddam's ambitions in the long run.

---

[53] UN Security Council Resolution 986, April 14, 1995, http://www.uncc.ch/sites/default/files/attachments/documents/res0986.pdf, ; U.N. Security Council, "Letter Dated 20 May 1996 from the Secretary-General Addressed to the President of the Security Council," May 26, 1996, http://www.un.org/ga/search/view_doc.asp?symbol=S/1996/356, For a chronology of the Oil-for-Food program see "Office of the Iraq Programme Oil-for Food," http://www.un.org/Depts/oip/background/chron.html.

[54] The Security Council adopted seven such resolutions during this period: June 1996 (UNSCR1060), June 1997 (1115), October 1997 (1134), November 1997 (1137), March 1998 (1154), September 1998 (1194), and November 1998 (1205). It finally withdrew inspectors from Iraq on December 16, 1998, in anticipation of the Desert Fox airstrikes.

[55] H.R. 4655 (1998), Iraq Liberation Act of 1998, https://www.congress.gov/105/plaws/publ338/PLAW-105publ338.pdf,

[56] For specifics on Operation Desert Fox see Knights, *Cradle of Conflict*, 200–10.

Containment and Coercion at Cross Purposes

As this case of U.S. foreign policy with Iraq during the 1990s demonstrates, simultaneously employing strategies of coercion and containment can work at cross purposes. Economic sanctions and air power can be used to punish a target state's economy and attrit its military forces, but in order for coercion to succeed the threat of force must be accompanied by the credible promise to remove the threat once the target complies with demands. By contrast, a containment strategy may require that sanctions and air power be kept in place in order to keep a target weak and unable to project its power.

The asymmetric coercion model predicts coercion should succeed, but in practice it often fails. This chapter examined one reason for coercion failure: the simultaneous employment of coercive and containment strategies. In this case, the means of containment, that of keeping sanctions and air power in place regardless of policy concessions, work at cross purposes with that of coercion, resulting in coercion failure.

Two policy implications stand out based on these findings. First, for sanctions and air power to be effective tools of coercion, the United States must be willing to reduce or remove these threats once the target state complies with demands. Coercion is a type of bargaining, which requires compromise to reach a settlement. In order to achieve coercion success, the United States must also be willing to relinquish some of its objectives and still be willing to suspend sanctions and air strikes in order to end a crisis. Second, this case demonstrates that at times the United States has multiple strategies employed against a target that can work at cross purposes. Coercing Iraq to cooperate with WMD inspections assisted the U.S. containment strategy, but not vice versa, as the continuation of sanctions eliminated the incentive for Iraq to continue to cooperate with inspections if it had no hope of having any relief from sanctions. Policymakers should understand that under such conditions, coercion failure may be the price of containment success. Such an outcome should not necessarily be considered a strategic mistake or foreign policy failure.

Finally, these insights are useful for dealing with current conflicts, such as Iran and its nuclear program. The utility of economic sanctions in coercing Iran on WMD will be undermined if the Iranians come to believe that the United States is not likely to lift sanctions regardless of their actions. Given that many U.S. policymakers seek regime change in Iran, they must come to terms with the fact that keeping all options on the table actually takes some potential successes off it.

CHAPTER 5 Step Aside or Face the Consequences

Explaining the Success and Failure of Compellent Threats to Remove Foreign Leaders

ALEXANDER B. DOWNES

WHY DO COMPELLENT THREATS demanding that foreign leaders give up power succeed in some instances but not others?[1] The deck would appear to be stacked against the success of such "regime change" threats.[2] It is well known, for example, that compellence is difficult in international relations.[3] Complying with a compellent threat requires that a target take a visible action in response to an observable demand, which involves greater loss of face than complying with a deterrent threat, where the target can claim that it had no intention of taking any action in the first place. As Robert Art has put it, "The target has no . . . plausible deniability in the case of compellence because its overt submission is required."[4]

In addition to the difficulty of compellence in general, a demand for regime change is one of the most ambitious concessions one state can request from another. Since all leaders, whether dictators or democrats, prefer to remain in office, they are naturally inclined to resist demands that they abdicate. Foreign demands for regime change may also require that leaders flee into exile or face prosecution, potential imprisonment, or even execution at the hands of

---

[1] A previous version of this chapter was presented at the 2015 annual meeting of the American Political Science Association in San Francisco. The author thanks Bob Art, Allan Dafoe, Todd Sechser, and the editors of this volume for helpful comments.
[2] Technically, *regime change* is broader than *leadership change*. Regime change always includes a change in the effective leader of the target state, but may also entail transforming the target's political institutions, such as from autocratic to democratic. Unless otherwise noted, however, this chapter uses the terms synonymously to refer only to a change in the target state's political leadership.
[3] Thomas C. Schelling, *Arms and Influence* (New Haven, CT: Yale University Press, 1966).
[4] Robert J. Art, "Coercive Diplomacy: What Do We Know?," in *The United States and Coercive Diplomacy*, ed. Robert J. Art and Patrick M. Cronin (Washington, DC: U.S. Institute of Peace Press, 2003), 362.

the coercer, none of which is likely to appeal to threatened leaders. In short, foreign threats to compel regime change seem to be exactly the kind of threat that targets are most likely to resist. As Art puts it, a demand for regime change "should be the most difficult because it requires a regime in power to commit suicide, and regimes do not willingly do that."[5]

Indeed, the recent history of threats for regime change appears to bear out the contention that such demands rarely succeed. In the post-Cold War era, the United States has issued such threats against Manuel Noriega of Panama (1989), Raoul Cédras of Haiti (1994), Saddam Hussein of Iraq (2003), and Muammar Gaddafi of Libya (2011). In three of these four cases, the threat failed: with the lone exception of Haiti, the United States had to use decisive military force to unseat the targeted leader, including launching major invasions with ground forces in two instances.[6] Even in the successful case of Haiti, Cédras did not agree to leave power until the 82nd Airborne Division was en route to remove him by force. Such cases support the argument that leaders are unlikely to give up power without a fight, and thus that compellent threats demanding regime change are likely to fail.[7]

But this is not the whole story. In the past, threats of regime change—by the United States and other powers—have succeeded at a much higher rate than more recent threats. The United States successfully used militarized threats to evict leaders in Nicaragua, the Dominican Republic, and Costa Rica between 1909 and 1919.[8] Germany compelled Chancellor Kurt Schuschnigg of Austria to step down in favor of Nazi interior minister Arthur Seyss-Inquart in March 1938, and the Soviet Union similarly coerced the leaders of the Baltic republics of Latvia, Lithuania, and Estonia to hand over power in June 1940.[9] These successes are not uncommon. In the Militarized Compellent Threat (MCT) data set, a compilation of all compellent threats from 1918 to 2001, demands for leadership change succeeded in a shocking 82 percent of cases, compared to only 40 percent of demands involving other issues.[10]

---

[5] Art, "Coercive Diplomacy," 389–90.

[6] In the third case, Libya, the United States and its NATO partners limited their participation to airpower.

[7] Studies supporting this conclusion include Alexander L. George and William E. Simons, *The Limits of Coercive Diplomacy*, 2nd ed. (Boulder, CO: Westview Press, 1994), 269, 270, Table 2; Art, "Coercive Diplomacy," 401.

[8] On Nicaragua (1909 and 1910), see Michel Gobat, *Confronting the American Dream: Nicaragua under U.S. Imperial Rule* (Durham, NC: Duke University Press, 2005), 70; Yann Kerevel, *Re-examining the Politics of U.S. Intervention in Early 20th Century Nicaragua: José Madriz and the Conservative Restoration*, Research Paper Series, No. 43 (Albuquerque: University of New Mexico Latin American Institute, November 2006), 23. On the Dominican Republic (1912, 1914, and 1916), see Bruce J. Calder, *The Impact of Intervention: The Dominican Republic during the U.S. Occupation of 1914–1924* (Austin: University of Texas Press, 1984), 5–19. On Costa Rica (1919), see Marc Edelman and Joanne Kenen, eds., *The Costa Rica Reader* (New York: Grove Weidenfeld, 1989), 69.

[9] On Austria, see A. J. P. Taylor, *The Origins of the Second World War* (New York: Simon and Schuster, 1961), 147–49. On the Baltics, see Alexander Shtromas, *The Soviet Method of Conquest of the Baltic States: Lessons for the West* (Washington, DC: Washington Institute for Values in Public Policy, 1986), 15–24.

[10] On the MCT data set, see Todd S. Sechser, "Militarized Compellent Threats, 1918–2001," *Conflict Management and Peace Science* 28, no. 4 (2011): 377–401. The dataset is available online at Harvard

Understanding why compellent threats for regime change succeed and fail is important for at least three reasons. First, analysts of compellence tend to treat compellent episodes over different issues as instances of the same phenomenon. But there may be important differences in the dynamics of compellent threats over different issues. In particular, whereas territory in principle is divisible, demands that a country change its political leader are not: only one person can rule at a time. This inherent indivisibility may make demands for leader change more likely to fail. Second, demands for regime change are not uncommon in international politics, and thus it is important to understand when such demands will succeed. The MCT data set, for example, contains 28 leadership threats spread over 85 years, or roughly one every three years. As noted earlier, the United States has issued four such demands since 1989, an average of one every seven years. For the foreseeable future, the United States will possess the military wherewithal to intervene in all corners of the globe. Washington may choose to issue threats backed by force to try to remove regimes it finds objectionable or threatening, as it has in the past.[11] Third, the analysis in this chapter helps adjudicate the debate on the role of power in explaining compellent threat success. Traditionally, scholarship on the credibility of threats and promises in international relations has argued that commitments are likely to be viewed as credible when the state has the capability to carry them out.[12] Recent studies, by contrast, contend that power can be a liability in compellence: powerful states are more likely to have their threats rejected than accepted.[13]

This chapter explores the determinants of success and failure of compellent threats that demand regime change by examining cases contained in the MCT data set. The chapter argues that the unexpectedly high success rate for leadership threats is explained by the fact that challengers possess crushing material superiority over their targets, which also tend to be located in close geographic proximity to challengers and have few if any allies to protect them. It also argues that this is no accident: challengers issue leadership demands only against weak and isolated targets. We simply do not observe challengers issuing regime change threats in peacetime against equally powerful targets,

---

Dataverse, https://dataverse.harvard.edu/dataset.xhtml?persistentId=hdl:1902.1/17315. On the success of leadership demands relative to other types of demands, see Todd S. Sechser, "Reputations and Signaling in Coercive Bargaining," *Journal of Conflict Resolution*, forthcoming.

[11] The Obama administration, for example, publicly called for the ouster of Syrian president Bashar al-Assad in August 2011 but did not threaten to remove him by force. See Scott Wilson and Joby Warrick, "Syria's Assad Must Go, Obama Says," *Washington Post*, August 18, 2011.

[12] Daryl G. Press, *Calculating Credibility: How Leaders Assess Military Threats* (Ithaca, NY: Cornell University Press, 2005).

[13] Todd S. Sechser, "Goliath's Curse: Coercive Threats and Asymmetric Power," *International Organization* 64, no. 4 (Fall 2010): 627–60; Sechser, "Reputations and Signaling in Coercive Bargaining"; Phil Haun, *Coercion, Survival, and War: Why Weak States Resist the United States* (Stanford: Stanford University Press, 2015); Dianne Pfundstein Chamberlain, *Cheap Threats: Why the United States Struggles to Coerce Weak States* (Washington, DC: Georgetown University Press, 2016).

presumably because such extreme demands would likely be rejected and the challenger would then face an unpalatable choice between a costly, uncertain war and an embarrassing diplomatic reversal.[14] The surprising success of regime change threats is thus due in large part to a selection effect: such threats succeed where previous literature suggests they should fail because challengers issue them only when the target is virtually defenseless. This finding is in line with Todd Sechser's bargaining theory of coercion (in this volume): a preponderance of power leads challengers to issue ambitious demands. In the case of leadership demands, however, the power disparity between challenger and target is so great that challengers are highly confident that targets have little option but to comply.

Three other factors contribute to the success of regime change demands. First, leadership threats are more likely to obtain compliance when challengers signal that they intend to deploy their crushing superiority against targets, such as by mobilizing or deploying their military forces. Second, challengers that allow targeted leaders safe egress from power are somewhat more likely to succeed. However, the increasingly hostile international environment facing former dictators in recent times—where they can hardly escape prosecution—may help explain the failure of regime change threats since the end of the Cold War. Third, threats against personalist dictators may be particularly likely to fail because these regimes prioritize internal threats and tend to discount the seriousness of external threats.

Compellence: Definition and Literature

Coercion is the art of manipulating costs and benefits to affect the behavior of an actor. Coercion takes two particular forms. Deterrence consists of threats of force designed to persuade a target to refrain from taking a particular action. Compellence, by contrast, utilizes force—or threats of force—to propel a target to take an action, or to stop taking an action it has already started. Both deterrence and compellence can take place in peace or war. This chapter focuses on compellence during peacetime. Specifically, it focuses on *compellent threats*, which are composed of two parts: (1) a verbal or written demand that a target undertake a material change in the status quo, coupled with (2) a threat to use military force if the target fails to comply. Although the demand must be explicit, the militarized threat may be explicit or implicit; for example, it can be articulated in speech or written form by the challenger or consist of a tacit signal of preparation or intent to use force, such as the mobilization, movement, or deployment of military

[14] This is distinct from wartime demands for regime change, which are sometimes issued in dyads of roughly equal power, such as between belligerents in the two world wars. Wartime compellence is excluded from this analysis, which focuses on the efficacy of threats for achieving leadership change.

assets. Both of these two aspects—a demand for a change in the status quo and a threat (verbal or tacit) to use force—must be present for a compellent threat to exist.[15]

Compellent threats are similar to what others have called "coercive diplomacy," defined by Robert Art as "the attempt to get a target—a state, a group (or groups) within a state, or a nonstate actor—to change its objectionable behavior through either the threat to use force or the actual use of limited force."[16] Both concepts, for example, allow the coercer to use low-level violence. As Art writes, "If we conceive of coercion to have three phases—threats to use force, demonstrative use of force, and full-scale use of force (or war)—coercive diplomacy encompasses only the first two phases."[17] Similarly, compellent threats allow for states to signal their resolve by mobilizing or maneuvering forces—or using limited amounts of force—in support of a threat.[18] Coercive diplomacy and compellent threats each fail if the challenger seizes the disputed item (or otherwise resolves the dispute) by force, or if the target's compliance is clearly unrelated to the challenger's threat. The key difference between the two concepts is that compellent threats require the issuance of an explicit demand accompanied by a militarized threat, whereas demands and threats may remain implicit in episodes of coercive diplomacy.

Previous Literature on Compellence Outcomes

Studies of compellence in international relations confirm Thomas Schelling's argument that success is elusive. Table 5.1 compares the success rates for compellence, coercive diplomacy, and compellent threats from five empirical studies. The clear message is that forceful attempts short of war to compel adversaries to change their behavior are unlikely to work. Success rates range from a low of 18 percent to a high of 41 percent; averaged across all 336 cases in the five studies, compellence succeeds in 35 percent of them.[19] Studies of deterrence, by contrast, find a significantly higher rate of success of between 50 and 57 percent.[20]

---

[15] Sechser, "Militarized Compellent Threats," 380. See also Alexander B. Downes and Todd S. Sechser, "The Illusion of Democratic Credibility," *International Organization* 66, no. 3 (Summer 2012): 475.

[16] Robert J. Art, introduction to *United States and Coercive Diplomacy*, 6. On the definition of coercive diplomacy, see also George and Simons, *Limits of Coercive Diplomacy*, 7–11; Alexander L. George, *Forceful Persuasion: Coercive Diplomacy as an Alternative to War* (Washington, DC: U.S. Institute of Peace Press, 1991), 5–6. See also the Art and Greenhill chapter in this volume.

[17] Art, "Coercive Diplomacy," 360.

[18] Sechser, "Militarized Compellent Threats," 384–85.

[19] These success rates are similar to those for compellence with air power during war (40 percent) and economic sanctions (34 percent). Robert A. Pape, *Bombing to Win: Air Power and Coercion in War* (Ithaca, NY: Cornell University Press, 1996), 52; Gary Clyde Hufbauer, Jeffrey J. Schott, and Kimberly Ann Elliott, *Economic Sanctions Reconsidered*, 3rd ed. (Washington, DC: Peterson Institute for International Economics, 2007), 159.

[20] See, respectively, Vesna Danilovic, *When the Stakes Are High: Deterrence and Conflict among Major Powers* (Ann Arbor: University of Michigan Press, 2002); Paul K. Huth and Bruce Russett, "What Makes Deterrence Work? Cases from 1900–1980," *World Politics* 36, no. 4 (July 1984): 505.

TABLE 5.1 Success Rates for Compellence, Coercive Diplomacy, and Compellent Threats

TYPE	SOURCE	SUCCESSES/TOTAL	SUCCESS RATE (%)
Compellence	Blechman and Kaplan	5/28	18
Compellence	Petersen	16/67	24
Coercive Diplomacy	George and Simons	2/7	29
Coercive Diplomacy	Art (summary judgments)	2/8	25
Coercive Diplomacy	Art (expanded data set)	5/16	31
Compellent Threats	Sechser	87/210	41
Total		117/336	35

SOURCES: Barry M. Blechman and Stephen S. Kaplan, *Force without War: U.S. Armed Forces as a Political Instrument* (Washington, DC: Brookings Institution, 1978), 92; Walter S. Petersen, "Deterrence and Compellence: A Critical Assessment of the Conventional Wisdom," *International Studies Quarterly* 30, no. 3 (September 1986): 283; Alexander L. George and William E. Simons, *The Limits of Coercive Diplomacy*, 2nd ed. (Boulder, CO: Westview Press, 1994), 270; Robert J. Art, "Coercive Diplomacy: What Do We Know?," in *The United States and Coercive Diplomacy*, ed. Robert J. Art and Patrick M. Cronin (Washington, DC: U.S. Institute of Peace Press, 2003), 376–78, 385–87; Todd S. Sechser, "Militarized Compellent Threats, 1918–2001," *Conflict Management and Peace Science* 28, no. 4 (2011): 377–401.

It is thus well established that compellence is hard. But what explains variation in the success and failure of coercive diplomacy and compellent threats? Previous scholarship has focused on four factors.[21]

Power. It has long been thought in international relations that powerful states get their way; as Thucydides put it, "The strong do what they can and the weak suffer what they must."[22] Yet empirical work on coercive diplomacy and compellent threats has never supported this axiom. Studies of the U.S. experience with coercive diplomacy, as is evident from Table 5.1, consistently find that U.S. threats fail more often than they succeed. Recent work on compellent threats explains why power may in fact be a significant impediment to threat success.[23] Sechser argues that targets facing compellent threats must consider the effect that their behavior in response to the current threat will have on the likelihood they will be challenged again. Coercers, in turn, must consider the cost to the target's reputation it suffers from backing down. Anything that makes a repeated challenge more likely—such as a powerful

[21] For a discussion of other factors that might matter in compellence, see George and Simons, *Limits of Coercive Diplomacy*, 279–87; Art, "Coercive Diplomacy," 393–401.

[22] Robert Strassler, ed., *The Landmark Thucydides: A Comprehensive Guide to the Peloponnesian War* (New York: Free Press, 1996), 352. Other studies that argue that material power enhances the credibility of threats include Press, *Calculating Credibility*; George and Simons, *Limits of Coercive Diplomacy*, 285–86; Art, "Coercive Diplomacy," 399.

[23] Sechser, "Goliath's Curse."

or proximate coercer—causes the target to increase its assessment that it will be challenged again, and thus to place a higher value on its reputation. This gives targets incentives to resist the initial threat to convince the coercer that it is a "tough" type.[24] Coercers, however, tend to underestimate the target's concern for its reputation and thus offer too little compensation to obtain the target's acquiescence. The target's fear for its reputation and the challenger's unwillingness to lower its demands or offer side payments to compensate the target for the damage to its reputation cause the target to resist threats from powerful states. Sechser demonstrates the logic of this argument in a case study of the failed Soviet compellent threat against Finland in 1939 and shows quantitatively that threats from powerful and proximate coercers are less likely to succeed.[25]

Interests. It is widely argued that the side with the greater interests at stake will prevail in compellence.[26] This is another way of saying that the side that cares more about the issue in dispute will win. How much an actor cares about prevailing dictates its resolve: the costs it is willing to pay and the risks it is willing to run to achieve its objective. Actors with high levels of resolve have an advantage in compellence scenarios because they are willing to suffer more pain to achieve their objectives.

Relying on concepts like interests and resolve to explain compellence outcomes is problematic because, as Art points out, they are inherently difficult to measure. "Before the fact," writes Art, "the coercer can never know for certain whose resolve is stronger—its own or the target's."[27] Even if one could determine an adversary's level of resolve before a crisis, it can change as the crisis unfolds (as can the state's own level of resolve). According to another widely believed axiom in international relations, a different difficulty with interest-based arguments is that defenders of the status quo are always more strongly motivated than challengers. This is especially true in compellence episodes because targets cannot conceal giving in to a compellent threat, and thus cannot avoid the costs to reputation or political survival entailed by capitulating. And it is unclear why challengers cannot simply adjust their demands downward to account for the target's stronger interests in the dispute.[28]

Regime type. A third factor commonly believed to influence compellent threat success is challenger regime type. In particular, threats issued by democracies are thought to be more likely to elicit compliance than threats

---

[24] Moreover, Sechser's model in this volume shows that challengers increase their demands as they grow more powerful, thereby generating a higher chance of war should the target turn out to be highly resolved.

[25] Sechser, "Goliath's Curse"; Sechser, "Reputations and Signaling in Coercive Bargaining." For similar arguments applied specifically to the United States, see Haun, *Coercion, Survival, and War*; Pfundstein Chamberlain, *Cheap Threats*.

[26] George and Simons, *Limits of Coercive Diplomacy*, 281.

[27] Art, "Coercive Diplomacy," 365.

[28] Sechser, "Goliath's Curse," 630.

from nondemocracies because of the audience costs that would be suffered by a democratic leader who issues a threat but subsequently backs down.[29] Studies have found that democracies are less likely to have militarized interstate disputes reciprocated and are more likely to prevail in international crises, and that publics disapprove of leaders who make threats and then back down.[30] Recent scholarship has questioned these findings, however, showing that some types of autocracies are also capable of generating audience costs; that compellent threats from democracies are no more likely to elicit compliance than are threats from nondemocracies; and that democratic leaders can avoid audience costs by providing justifications for refraining from carrying out threats.[31]

Demand type. The success and failure of compellence could vary with the nature of the challenger's demand. Intuitively, demands issued over minor issues, such as a change in policy, should be more likely to succeed than threats over regime change or sovereignty.[32] The evidence on this point, however, is mixed. Art, for example, finds no support for the idea that more extreme demands, such as regime change, are less likely to elicit compliance than demands over issues of lesser salience.[33] His sample contains only two demands for leadership change, however, one of which (Haiti, 1994) succeeded, whereas the other (Somalia, 1992–93) failed. Similarly, economic sanctions fared only slightly worse than average (31 vs. 34 percent) when the goal sought by the coercer was regime change.[34] In the MCT data set, by contrast, leadership demands succeed twice as often as demands over territory, policy, reparations, or other issues.[35]

Most of these studies, of course, examine compellence in general rather than threats directed solely at leaders. We now turn to the MCT data set to compile and analyze a list of threats demanding regime change.

---

[29] James D. Fearon, "Domestic Audience Costs and the Escalation of International Disputes," *American Political Science Review* 88, no. 3 (September 1994): 577–92.

[30] Kenneth A. Schultz, *Democracy and Coercive Diplomacy* (Cambridge: Cambridge University Press, 2001); Christopher F. Gelpi and Michael Griesdorf, "Winners or Losers? Democracies in International Crises, 1918–1994," *American Political Science Review* 95, no. 3 (September 2001): 633–47; Michael Tomz, "Domestic Audience Costs in International Relations: An Experimental Approach," *International Organization* 61, no. 4 (Fall 2007): 821–40.

[31] Jessica L. Weeks, "Autocratic Audience Costs: Regime Type and Signaling Resolve," *International Organization* 62, no. 1 (Winter 2008): 35–64; Downes and Sechser, "Illusion of Democratic Credibility"; Jack Snyder and Erica Borghard, "The Cost of Empty Threats: A Penny, Not a Pound," *American Political Science Review* 105, no. 3 (August 2011): 437–56; Matthew S. Levendusky and Michael C. Horowitz, "When Backing Down Is the Right Decision: Partisanship, New Information, and Audience Costs," *Journal of Politics* 74, no. 2 (April 2012): 323–38.

[32] Sechser's model in this volume implies that coercers facing resolved targets will make smaller demands and that these demands are more likely to be accepted.

[33] Art, "Coercive Diplomacy," 401.

[34] Hufbauer et al., *Economic Sanctions Reconsidered*, 159.

[35] Sechser, "Militarized Compellent Threats."

Compellent Threats for Regime Change in the Militarized Compellent Threats Data Set

Logic and recent evidence indicate that trying to intimidate foreign leaders into leaving office is hard. All political leaders seek to remain in power and generally resist stepping aside unless they lose an election (in a democracy) or are forced out at the point of a gun (in a nondemocracy). Agreeing to forfeit leadership at the behest of a foreign power is risky, especially when removal is likely to be accompanied by exile, prosecution, or worse. Indeed, the Archigos data set on leaders, which compiles information on the manner in which leaders leave office and their fate after removal (no punishment, exile, imprisonment, or death), shows that only 21 percent of leaders avoid some type of additional punishment after being ousted by foreign powers. Fifty-five percent of leaders removed in this way are forced to leave the country, while 22 percent are sent to jail.[36] Faced with fates like these, leaders should surely resist demands by foreign powers that they leave office. Compellent threats for regime change therefore should be likely to fail.

This section examines the empirical record of compellent threats demanding regime change. To do so, it uses the most comprehensive data set of compellent threats compiled to date: Sechser's Militarized Compellent Threat data set, which covers the period from the end of World War I through 2001.

The MCT Data Set

A militarized compellent threat is defined as "an explicit demand by one state (the challenger) that another state (the target) alter the status quo in some material way, backed by a threat of military force if the target does not comply."[37] Several points about this definition deserve elaboration. First, the data set adopts the current material status quo as a reference point in order to distinguish compellence from deterrence. As Sechser points out, whether a threat is deterrent or compellent is often "in the eye of the beholder" because the two states disagree about what constitutes the legitimate status quo. The data set's rules thus maintain that "compellent threats aim to alter the material status quo, whereas deterrent threats aim to preserve it."[38] For this reason, the data set excludes faits accomplis, whereby a state seizes a disputed item and then demands that another state renounce its claim. In such cases the material status quo has already been altered, and the threat simply demands that the target recognize the new status quo.

---

36 H. E. Goemans, Kristian Skrede Gleditsch, and Giacomo Chiozza, "Introducing *Archigos*: A Data Set of Political Leaders, 1875–2003," *Journal of Peace Research* 46, no. 2 (March 2009): 276. These proportions are broadly similar to those of leaders removed in domestic coups or revolutions, except that 20 percent of these leaders are killed, as opposed to only 1 percent killed after removal by foreign forces.

37 Sechser, "Militarized Compellent Threats," 380.

38 Ibid., 382.

Second, the MCT data set includes only demands backed by threats and limited demonstrations or uses of force; instances where challengers seize an item without making a demand are excluded, as are intrawar instances of compellence. The data set thus focuses clearly on the efficacy of threats for obtaining target compliance rather than the efficacy of force for achieving objectives. Third, demands in compellent threat episodes must be made explicit in order to "ensure that the dataset contains only cases in which both sides agreed about the nature and extent of the challenger's threat."[39] Explicit demands also establish a clear reference point by which to code whether or not the target complied with the challenger's demand. Finally, although demands must be made explicit, the accompanying threat of military force can be explicit or implicit, "transmitted through explicit verbal communication or through public military maneuvers or demonstrations that coincide with the demand."[40]

The data set contains 210 compellent threat episodes; because some cases include multiple challengers, there are a total of 242 challenger-target dyads.

Leadership Threats in the MCT Data Set

The MCT data set codes compellent threats as falling into five nonexclusive issue areas: territory, leadership, policy, reparations, and other. Sechser defines leadership demands as including "all demands to remove or replace particular individuals within the target's government."[41] Leadership demands as defined by MCT, however, are not always synonymous with demands for regime change. Importantly, leadership demands need not be directed at heads of state but may seek the ouster of lower level officials as well.[42] For example, in February and March 1938, Hitler issued two compellent threats for leadership change against Austria. The second of these was a classic regime change threat, as Hitler demanded that Chancellor Schuschnigg give way to Austrian Nazi Party leader Seyss-Inquart or face invasion. Schuschnigg quickly acquiesced, Seyss-Inquart was appointed chancellor and promptly invited the Germans to occupy and annex Austria. The prior threat, however, demanded only that Schuschnigg appoint Seyss-Inquart as minister of the interior and other Nazis to various cabinet posts or face immediate invasion.[43] This threat also succeeded.

Table 5.2 lists all 28 challenger-target dyads—representing 23 separate episodes—in which a compellent threat over leadership was issued in the MCT data set. Strikingly, as shown in Figure 5.1, compellence succeeded in over

39 Ibid., 382.
40 Ibid., 380.
41 Ibid., 384.
42 Ibid., n14. Below, these threats are removed to see if they inflate the success rate of leadership threats. For the moment, however, they are included in the analysis.
43 Alfred D. Low, *The Anschluss Movement, 1918–1931, and the Great Powers*, vol. 185 (Boulder, CO: East European Monographs, 1985), 365.

TABLE 5.2 Compellent Threats over Leadership in the MCT Data Set

MCT CODE	CHALLENGER	TARGET	YEAR	TARGETED LEADER	OUTCOME	LEADER FATE
1919-7	United States	Costa Rica	1919	Federico Tinoco	Success	Exile
1920-4	Russia	Azerbaijan	1920	Nasib bey Yusifbeyli	Success	Killed
1920-6	Russia	Armenia	1920	Simon Vratsyan	Success	Exile
1921-2	*Yugoslavia*	*Hungary*	*1921*	*King Karl I*	*Success*	*NA*
1921-2	*Czechoslovakia*	*Hungary*	*1921*	*King Karl I*	*Success*	*NA*
1921-2	*Romania*	*Hungary*	*1921*	*King Karl I*	*Success*	*NA*
1921-5	*Romania*	*Hungary*	*1921*	*King Karl I*	*Success*	*NA*
1921-5	*Czechoslovakia*	*Hungary*	*1921*	*King Karl I*	*Success*	*NA*
1921-5	*Yugoslavia*	*Hungary*	*1921*	*King Karl I*	*Success*	*NA*
1935-2	*Japan*	*China*	*1935*	*Mayor of Tientsin, Governor of Hebei*	*Success*	*NA*
1936-1	*Japan*	*China*	*1936*	*Mayor of Tientsin*	*Failure*	*NA*
1938-1	*Germany*	*Austria*	*1938*	*Interior Minister*	*Success*	*NA*
1938-2	Germany	Austria	1938	Kurt Schuschnigg	Success	Prison
1939-1	Germany	Czechoslovakia	1939	Emil Hacha	Success	OK*
1939-3	Hungary	Carpatho-Ukraine	1939	Augustyn Voloshyn	Success	Exile
1940-3	Russia	Lithuania	1940	Antanas Smetona	Success	Exile
1940-4	Russia	Estonia	1940	Konstantin Pats	Success	Prison
1940-5	Russia	Latvia	1940	Karlis Ulmanis	Success	Prison
1940-11	Germany	Greece	1940	Ioannis Metaxas	Failure	Natural Death

(continued)

TABLE 5.2 Continued

MCT CODE	CHALLENGER	TARGET	YEAR	TARGETED LEADER	OUTCOME	LEADER FATE
1940-11	Italy	Greece	1940	Ioannis Metaxas	Failure	Natural Death
1945-1	Russia	Romania	1945	King Michael I	Success	Exile
1961-3	United States	Dominican Republic	1961	Ramfis Trujillo	Success	Exile
1967-3	*Turkey*	*Greece*	*1967*	*Gen. Georgios Grivas*	*Success*	*NA*
1968-2	Russia	Czechoslovakia	1968	Alexander Dubcek	Success	Prison
1979-4	*Libya*	*Chad*	*1979*	*Defense Minister*	*Failure*	*NA*
1989-1	United States	Panama	1989	Manuel Noriega	Failure	Prison
1994-4	South Africa	Lesotho	1994	King Letsie III	Success	OK
1994-5	United States	Haiti	1994	Raoul Cédras	Success	Exile

NOTE: The numbering system for the MCT cases reflects the year-incident system used in version 1.0 of the data set (not yet released) rather than the old system in version 0.9. Italics indicate threats directed against individuals who were not heads of state.

* Hacha remained in office as a figurehead president after Germany annexed the remainder of Czechoslovakia in March 1939, so his fate is coded as OK. At the end of World War II he was arrested and imprisoned by the Soviets.

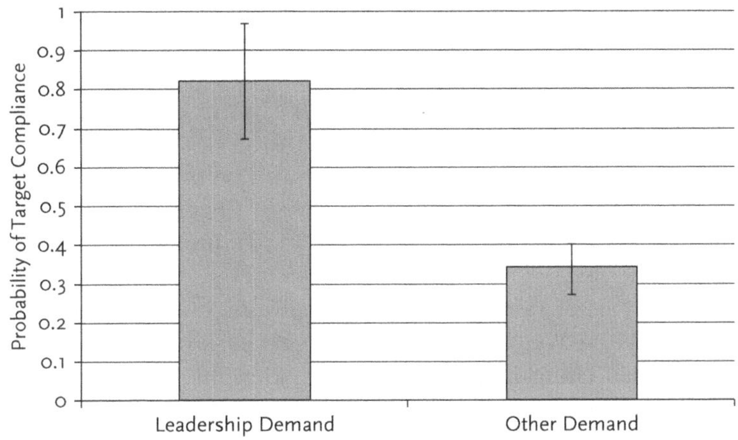

Note: Solid bars indicate probability of target compliance; capped lines inside each bar indicate 95 percent confidence intervals. The probability that compliance rates with leadership demands and other types of demands are the same is vanishingly small ($p < 0.0001$).

FIGURE 5.1 Compliance with Compellent Threats Demanding Leadership Change in the MCT Data Set

82 percent of these dyads. This figure remains almost identical when threat episodes are the unit of analysis rather than challenger-target dyads: challengers obtained target compliance in 19 of the 23 episodes (83 percent). This is more than double the rate at which compellent threats succeed over other issues, a difference that is highly statistically significant.[44] What explains this unexpectedly high rate of success?

A glance at Table 5.2 suggests that the success rate of leadership threats may be inflated by the inclusion of two types of cases that do not constitute regime change. The first type of case, as already discussed briefly, involves demands for the resignation of government officials below the level of head of state. This type of case occurs several times in the MCT data set. Japan, for example, issued two threats against China in the 1930s, demanding that the Chinese government remove local officials. In May 1935, Japanese authorities in the city of Tientsin sent an ultimatum to the commander of Chinese forces in North China demanding (among other things) that the mayor of Tientsin and the governor of Hebei province be removed following the assassination of two pro-Japanese newspaper editors (MCT-1935-2). At the direction of Chiang Kai-shek, the commander, He Yingqin, acquiesced and removed the two officials. Similarly, in MCT-1936-1 in January 1936, Japanese officials again demanded the removal of the mayor of Tientsin, but this time the demand was refused.[45]

[44] This significance persists in multivariate analyses. Sechser, "Reputations and Signaling in Coercive Bargaining."

[45] Two other Japanese threats (MCT-1935-6, Wuhan, in September 1935, and MCT-1937-2, Marco Polo Bridge, in July 1937) appear to involve demands for the removal of leaders, but the officials in

There are two other cases of this type that appear in the MCT data set. In response to an attack in which Greek Cypriot forces overran two Turkish Cypriot villages on November 15, 1967, the Turkish government demanded that Greece dismiss the commander of Greek Cypriot forces, Gen. Georgios Grivas, and send him home to Greece (MCT-1967-3). On November 19, the Greek government agreed to Grivas's removal. The other case occurred in Chad in June 1979, when Libya tried to coerce Chadian leader Goukouni Oueddei to dismiss Defense Minister Hissène Habré, a demand that was rejected (MCT-1979-4).

The second type of case that does not involve regime change occurred in the two post–World War I crises in which Czechoslovakia, Yugoslavia, and Romania targeted Hungary. In both of these cases, the three allies sought to prevent Karl I, the former Habsburg ruler of Austria-Hungary, from taking power in Hungary. Karl had gone into exile in Switzerland shortly after the war ended but had not actually abdicated his throne. On March 27, 1921, he returned to Hungary and stated his claim as the rightful ruler of the country. In response, Czechoslovakia, Yugoslavia, and Romania (known as the Little Entente) announced that they would declare war if Karl were allowed to take power. Hungarian regent Miklos Horthy refused to step down, and a majority of the Hungarian Diet also opposed Karl's ascension to office. Karl relented and returned to Switzerland on April 5. The crisis recurred in October, however, when Karl reentered Hungary and rallied some of his supporters to march on Budapest. The Little Entente reiterated its ultimatum that Karl be prevented from taking power and threatened to invade. Hungarian authorities immediately arrested Karl and handed him over to the Entente. These two cases, although they were clearly disputes over who would lead Hungary, involved threats aimed not at changing the Hungarian regime but rather at preventing Karl—who was not at the time the Hungarian head of state—from attaining power.

For the purposes of studying the efficacy of compellent threats for achieving regime change, these two sets of cases are not relevant since they demand that targets remove officials who are not heads of state. States may also be less resistant to removing lower-level officials than top leaders, which could bias the success rate of leadership threats upward. Deleting these 11 challenger-target dyads (seven separate episodes) leaves 17 dyads and 16 compellent threats that actually demanded regime change. Dropping these cases, however, barely affects the success rate for such threats, which succeeded in 82 percent of dyads and 81 percent of threat episodes. The way the MCT data set codes leadership demands does not falsely inflate the success rate of demands for regime change, which remains virtually unchanged when demands against lower level officials (or nongovernment officials, like Karl I) are excluded.

---

question were military officers. Sechser excludes demands for the dismissal of officers from his coding of leadership threats.

Explaining the Success and Failure of Leadership Demands in the MCT Data Set

Even after excluding leadership demands that are not aimed at regime change, compellent threats against foreign leaders still succeed at a much higher rate than compellent threats in other types of issues. What explains the difference? Regime change threats succeed so often because of a selection effect: such threats are issued only when the challenger possesses such an overwhelming advantage in material power that the target has almost no chance of resisting an invasion. Therefore target leaders are better off capitulating to the threat than resisting, since besides losing office they would also suffer the additional costs of fighting. Moreover, leaders who acquiesce to regime change threats might be able to obtain a better personal outcome, such as the ability to flee into exile rather than facing imprisonment or execution at the hands of the challenger. Geographic proximity, diplomatic isolation, and demonstrations of force further enhance the credibility of leadership threats.

Power and Selection

One facet of the relationship between challengers and targets that becomes apparent on close inspection is the overwhelming advantage in material power possessed by challengers. Table 5.3 summarizes the percentage of total capabilities in the challenger-target dyad accounted for by the challenger in the year a threat of regime change was made on five common indicators of power in international relations: military expenditures, military personnel, iron and steel production, primary energy consumption, and the CINC score, which measures the percentage of total world capabilities held by each state in a given year. As is evident from the table, the results are extremely lopsided: the challenger in each dyad controls more than 97 percent of the capabilities in each category of power. Indeed, the lowest percentage held by any

TABLE 5.3 Challenger-Target Power Relations in Regime Change Threats

INDICATOR	CHALLENGER'S AVERAGE PERCENTAGE OF CAPABILITIES
Military Expenditures	0.988
Military Personnel	0.975
Iron and Steel Production	0.983
Primary Energy Consumption	0.978
CINC Score	0.977

NOTE: The table includes only regime change threats rather than all leadership threats.

SOURCE: Correlates of War National Material Capabilities data set, v4.0, available at Correlates of War Project, http://correlatesofwar.org/.

challenger in any category is 89, the proportion of primary energy consumption accounted for by Germany in the Germany-Czechoslovakia dyad in 1939. In the key categories of actual military power—military expenditures and military personnel—the lowest percentage controlled by a challenger is Italy in its dyad with Greece in 1939 (91 percent), yet Italy's threat in this case was issued jointly with Germany. Combined, the two Axis powers accounted for 99.7 percent of military expenditures in their confrontation with Greece, which is just shy of the median value (99.8 percent) for this variable, a figure that corresponds roughly to the advantage the Soviet Union held over Lithuania in 1940. The smallest advantage in military personnel is the 93 percent (782,000 vs. 58,000) German preponderance over Austria in 1938, but the median value of this variable (99.1 percent) is similar to the U.S. advantage over the Dominican Republic in 1961.

This extreme imbalance of power between challengers and targets appears to be uniquely the case for leadership threats. Threats over other issues in the MCT data set are not characterized by such a skewed balance of power. The highest percentage of capabilities controlled by the challenger in the two key categories of actual military power—military expenditure and military personnel—for threats over issues other than regime change is 73 percent (military expenditure in threats over policy and "other"). In fact, t-tests show that the challenger's mean proportion of capabilities for regime change threats is significantly greater than the challenger's share of capabilities for the four other issue areas at the 99 percent level of confidence in all five categories of power.[46]

Two conclusions can be drawn from these figures. The first is that a major reason compellent threats for regime change succeed is that the challengers in these cases possess crushing material superiority over their targets. The second is that challengers make regime change threats only when they possess crushing material superiority over targets, and targets understand that challengers could easily remove them by force if necessary. Precisely because demands for regime change are so extreme and thus so likely to be rejected by targets, challengers are likely to issue them only when targets have virtually no ability to defend themselves and thus little choice but to acquiesce.

It is striking, for example, that of the 17 compellent threats demanding regime change in the MCT data set, all but two—Hungary versus Carpatho-Ukraine in 1939 and South Africa versus Lesotho in 1994—were issued by a Great Power against a minor power.[47] Major powers simply do not demand regime change of each other, most likely because such threats lack credibility. The United States, for instance, enacted a policy to contain the expansion of Soviet power in the early years of the Cold War, but the long-term goal of containment was not defensive. Rather, as elaborated in NSC-68, it was "to foster

[46] This is also true (at the 95 percent level of confidence) for the broader category of leadership threats in every category of power except iron and steel production.

[47] Even in these two minor power dyads, the power disparity between challenger and target is vast.

a fundamental change in the nature of the Soviet system," that is, to promote regime change in the Soviet Union.[48] This policy, however, was expounded behind closed doors in Washington, not in public demands directed at Soviet leaders, who would rightly have wondered how the United States intended to enforce their demand if Moscow defied it.

The exception to this rule occurs only when Great Powers are already at war and the actions of the adversary convince its opponent that the war cannot be safely terminated without a change of leadership.[49] This is precisely what happened in both world wars. In World War I, Germany's attack convinced British leaders that a Prussian military clique controlled the German government and that any negotiated peace would not last without a change of regime.[50] In World War II, the nature of German and Japanese aggression similarly persuaded Britain and the United States that agreeing to peace terms with Berlin and Tokyo would be pointless since these regimes were inherently aggressive.[51] Decisions regarding which objectives to fight for once war has begun, however, are fundamentally different from decisions about which objectives can be attained by threats of force in peacetime. Demands like regime change—which any leader with a choice will surely reject—thus tend to be issued only when target leaders don't have a choice: when challengers can quickly and easily remove them by brute force.

Power Projection

A second factor that facilitates the success of regime change demands, as well as the selection of which states to make such demands of, is geographic proximity. In every episode in the MCT data set in which a leadership threat was issued, not only was the challenger much more powerful than the target, but it was able to bring its tremendous advantage in capabilities directly to bear because it was contiguous to the target on land or across a short stretch of water. The ability to project power against the target's homeland no doubt increased the credibility of the challenger's threat because it could immediately invade with ground forces. Even leaders beset by internal threats and rebellions cannot afford to ignore a militarized threat from a proximate Great Power. Soviet threats against small states in the Caucasus, Baltics, and Eastern Europe were no doubt highly credible because there was nothing to block the overpowering might of the Red Army from swiftly occupying these countries.[52] Similarly, the overwhelming power of the U.S. military combined with its ability to project

---

48 "A Report to the National Security Council—NSC 68," April 12, 1950, 9.

49 Alex Weisiger, *Logics of War: Explanations for Limited and Unlimited Conflicts* (Ithaca, NY: Cornell University Press, 2013).

50 Lorna S. Jaffe, *The Decision to Disarm Germany: British Policy towards Postwar German Disarmament, 1914–1919* (Boston: Allen and Unwin, 1985), 7–20.

51 Weisiger, *Logics of War*; Dan Reiter, *How Wars End* (Princeton, NJ: Princeton University Press, 2009).

52 Indeed, in some cases the Red Army was already present inside these states.

that power across the short distances of the Caribbean with its unmatched navy made U.S. threats more difficult to resist.

Diplomatic Isolation

Working in tandem with geographic proximity is a third factor, diplomatic isolation. Challengers typically choose targets for regime change threats that have little hope that a third party will intervene on their behalf to prevent regime change from occurring. On the one hand, this is because, as remarked earlier, challengers make leadership threats against countries in the immediate vicinity and within their sphere of influence. Targets of U.S. regime change threats in the Americas, for example, such as Costa Rica, Panama, Haiti, and the Dominican Republic, had no hope that they would be saved by an external power. In addition, many targets lack a long history of independence or were until recently part of the challenger state. This was the case for Armenia and Azerbaijan in 1920 and the Baltic states in 1940, all former territories of the Russian Empire. Similarly, there was little possibility of U.S. interference when the Soviets made regime change demands against Romania in 1945 and Czechoslovakia in 1968, given that the Soviets occupied both countries.

Movement of Forces

Given that challengers who make regime change demands generally do so only when they are likely to succeed, are there additional factors that increase the likelihood that threats of regime change will obtain compliance? Consistent with the emphasis on costly signals in the previous literature on interstate coercion, analyses of the MCT data set have found that threats accompanied by demonstrations of force—"whether the challenger mobilized troops or conducted conspicuous military maneuvers after issuing a compellent threat"—are significantly more likely to succeed than threats where such actions are absent.[53] Analysis of the subset of leadership threats that actually demanded regime change strongly supports this view. Ninety-three percent of regime change threats accompanied by a demonstration of force elicited full compliance from the target, as opposed to only 33 percent of those where the challenger did not undertake a movement of forces.[54] The evidence thus supports the supposition that compellent threats for regime change are more likely to obtain compliance when the challenger supports its threat with demonstrations of force.

---

[53] Sechser, "Militarized Compellent Threats," 391. Costly signals consist of statements or actions by a state that make it costly for that state to abandon a commitment. James D. Fearon, "Signaling Foreign Policy Interests: Tying Hands versus Sinking Costs," *Journal of Conflict Resolution* 41, no. 1 (February 1997): 68–90. On the importance of demonstrations of force in the MCT data set, see Sechser, "Militarized Compellent Threats," 391; Sechser, "Reputations and Signaling in Coercive Bargaining."

[54] Even with only 17 cases, this difference is statistically significant ($p < 0.05$).

Leader Fate

As documented, only one-fifth of all leaders who leave office in response to a compellent threat escape punishment of some kind, such as exile, imprisonment, or death. This is also true of leaders who are forced from office by external powers explicitly in threats that demand regime change, only 24 percent of whom avoided additional punishment. One might suspect, however, that regime change threats would be more likely to succeed if the challenger promised to refrain from punishing the targeted leader after he left office. Furthermore, fleeing into exile—although hardly an attractive prospect—is surely more palatable for deposed leaders than going to jail or facing execution. This logic implies that threats should be more successful if targeted leaders have the ability to escape to a neighboring country.

Examining the data on compliance with regime change threats and the fate of leaders reveals some limited support for the relationship between personal survival and threat success. Although only two leaders—Emil Hacha of Czechoslovakia and King Letsie III of Lesotho—avoided some form of postregime change punishment, in both cases the threat succeeded. Similarly, in all seven cases in which leaders fled into exile, compellent threats for regime change achieved compliance. Threats where former leaders wound up in jail, however, still succeeded in four out of five cases. Further research is needed to discover whether challengers promised these leaders they would be allowed to go into exile but later reneged, or whether these leaders thought they could evade capture but were unsuccessful. The one threat wherein a former leader was killed—the Soviet threat against Azerbaijan in 1920—succeeded, but the leader, Nasib bey Yusifbeyli, was killed not by the invading Red Army but by bandits a month after he had fled Baku. This case thus does not provide evidence against the view that personal survival for leaders facilitates the success of regime change threats.

Compellent Threats for Regime Change beyond the MCT Data Set

This exploration of compellent threats for regime change in the MCT data set has revealed that even after excluding leadership threats that do not demand the removal of the target's sitting head of state, these threats still succeeded about 80 percent of the time. This surprising result was largely a function of the crushing imbalance in material power between the challenger and the target, which itself is produced by the fact that challengers make regime change threats only when they are vastly more powerful than the target, the two are in close geographic proximity, and the target is diplomatically isolated. Challengers can further increase their prospects for success by showing that they mean business by deploying military assets or using limited amounts of force, and perhaps also by allowing the targeted leader to flee abroad rather than incarcerating or killing him. The argument that demonstrations of force enhance threat credibility is consistent with previous studies that have used the MCT data, but the others are seemingly in conflict with Sechser's argument that power and proximity hinder compellent threat success. The contradiction can be explained by arguing that the relationship between power and threat success—at least for leadership threats—is curvilinear: up to a point, increasing the challenger's power decreases the likelihood of target compliance because powerful challengers cannot commit not to issue another challenge in the future, giving targets incentives to stand firm today. Beyond a certain threshold, however, targets simply become unable to resist. Moreover, if the challenger seeks to replace the current leadership or annex the target, this erases the probability of a future challenge and thus the shadow of the future disappears, rendering resistance to the current threat less likely.

This argument fits well with the pattern of successes and failures of U.S. compellent threats historically. The United States is the most prolific practitioner of regime change in modern history, toppling a total of 31 individual leaders in 28 separate episodes.[55] It is also one of the most frequent issuers of compellent threats, its 21 demands trailing only Japan, Russia, and Great Britain.[56] Of the four U.S. regime change threats that appear in the MCT data, all four targets—Costa Rica (1919), Dominican Republic (1961), Panama (1989), and Haiti (1994)—were dwarfed by U.S. power and located in the country's backyard. Three of these four threats succeeded in dislodging the targeted leader, the only failure coming when U.S. forces had to invade Panama to capture and remove Noriega. Similarly, in the decade before the MCT data set begins, the United States issued seven regime change threats against leaders in Nicaragua, Honduras, the Dominican Republic, and Mexico, all of which were successful.[57] In each case, the target was literally defenseless in the face of threatened U.S. intervention: each country was dwarfed by U.S. capabilities, located close to the United States, and had no third party willing to help. Several were also further weakened by civil strife and U.S. control over their finances.

Since 2001, however, U.S. threats demanding regime change failed to persuade Saddam or Gaddafi to leave power. What explains these recent compellent failures? The argument made in this chapter implies that the reason is that the United States is no longer selecting the types of targets that are likely to be overawed by U.S. threats. For example, both Iraq and Libya were substantially less powerful than the United States, but not nearly to the same

[55] Alexander B. Downes and Jonathan Monten, "Forced to Be Free: Why Foreign-Imposed Regime Change Rarely Leads to Democratization," *International Security* 37, no. 4 (Spring 2013): 90–131.
[56] Sechser, "Militarized Compellent Threats," 387.
[57] In addition to the sources listed in note 8, see (on Honduras) Stephen Kinzer, *Overthrow: America's Century of Regime Change from Hawaii to Iraq* (New York: Times Books, 2006), 75–76; and (on Mexico) Lester D. Langley, *The Banana Wars: United States Intervention in the Caribbean, 1898–1934*, 2nd ed. (Lanham, MD: Rowman & Littlefield, 2002), 82–109.

degree as the earlier cases.[58] This provides some support for the idea that there is a curvilinear relationship between power and threat success. Perhaps more important, neither country is located close to the United States, where U.S. intervention would be unopposed. Although neither Iraq nor Libya had many allies, Saddam reportedly believed that other Great Powers would oppose any U.S. attack in the UN Security Council.[59] The United States did deploy military forces in support of both threats, however, which should have increased their credibility.

Two other factors may also help explain these recent leadership threat failures. First, the likelihood that Saddam or Gaddafi could have escaped eventual punishment by fleeing into exile was low. Although there were rumors of exile deals in the works for both dictators, nothing concrete materialized.[60] But even if one of them had managed to broker an escape to a country that was not at the time a signatory of the International Criminal Court (ICC), that would not have guaranteed safety from prosecution. Contemporary international criminal law rests on the twin pillars of individual responsibility and universal jurisdiction, meaning that mass killers are responsible for their actions as individuals and may be apprehended and prosecuted anywhere. Any state—not just the ICC—could have indicted Saddam or Gaddafi and attempted to persuade the country harboring them to give them up. Witness the fates of former Liberian and Chadian dictators Charles Taylor and Hissène Habré, each of whom—promised immunity from prosecution by Nigeria and Senegal, respectively—went into exile, only to go on trial years later after outside pressure convinced those countries to bring the former leaders to justice. Recent research has found that leaders who commit atrocities are less likely to choose exile since the apprehension of former Chilean strongman Augusto Pinochet in London in 1998 at the behest of a Spanish judge, and that as a result civil wars involving such leaders are longer and bloodier than other civil wars.[61]

A second factor that bears additional examination is target regime type. Little work has been devoted to this variable, but the threat failures against Panama, Iraq, and Libya suggest that threats against personalist dictatorships may be particularly likely to fail. The evidence is clearest for Iraq, where Saddam simply did not believe that the United States would seek regime change in 2003. He remained focused on the internal threats to his regime from domestic uprisings and coups. As one study puts it, "Even with U.S. tanks crossing the

---

[58] The U.S. military was slightly more than three times larger than the Iraqi military in 2001 and almost 20 times larger than Libya's in 2007. Both countries were dwarfed, however, in the category of military spending.

[59] Kevin M. Woods, *The Iraqi Perspectives Report: Saddam's Senior Leadership on Operation Iraqi Freedom from the Official U.S. Joint Forces Command Report* (Annapolis, MD: Naval Institute Press, 2006), 28.

[60] On Saddam, see Karen DeYoung and Michael Abramowitz, "Report Says Hussein Was Open to Exile before 2003 Invasion," *Washington Post*, September 27, 2007. On Gaddafi, see David Smith, "Where Could Colonel Muammar Gaddafi Go If He Were Exiled?," *Guardian*, February 21, 2011.

[61] Daniel Krcmaric, "The Justice Dilemma: International Law, Mass Atrocities, and the Dynamics of Civil War" (Ph.D. dissertation, Duke University, 2014).

Iraqi border, an internal revolt remained Saddam's biggest fear."[62] The reason is that in regimes like Saddam's, the greatest danger to the leader's survival typically comes from domestic sources, especially the military. Moreover, having populated the upper ranks with family and tribe members, political loyalists, and sycophants, and instituted draconian punishments for bearers of unwelcome information, there was nobody to correct Saddam's chronic misperception of U.S. objectives or Iraq's ability to resist a U.S. attack.[63] In cases like this, domestic threats may trump external threats and cause leaders to underestimate the seriousness of the external threat and overestimate their ability to resist militarily, both of which might cause compellence to fail.

All told, these factors do not bode well for the likelihood that the United States would be able to compel regime changes in countries like Syria, Iran, or North Korea in the future.

---

[62] Kevin Woods, James Lacey, and Williamson Murray, "Saddam's Delusions: The View from the Inside," *Foreign Affairs* 85, no. 3 (May–June 2006): 3–4.

[63] On Saddam's underestimation of the U.S. threat in 2003, see Julia M. Macdonald, "Credibility in Crises: The Role of Leadership Beliefs in State Threat Assessments," (Ph.D. dissertation, George Washington University, 2016).

PART III | Coercion and Nonstate Actors

CHAPTER 6

Underestimating Weak States and State Sponsors

The Case for Base State Coercion

KEREN E. FRAIMAN

VIOLENT NONSTATE ACTORS (VNSAS) pose significant security challenges within the international system by undermining the sovereignty and stability of their host states. Across the globe, these violent groups have sought out opportunities to establish bases of operation within host states' sovereign territory (i.e., the "base state") and then proceeded to launch conventional attacks, insurgencies, and terrorist campaigns against other states, with or without the support of the base states. Between 1948 and 2008, there were 152 documented incidents of violent groups utilizing base states to launch external attacks.[1] This dynamic can be observed with Hezbollah in Lebanon vis-à-vis Israel; Al Qaeda in Afghanistan, Sudan, and Yemen vis-à-vis the United States, Spain, and Great Britain; and Lashkar-e-Taiba in Pakistan vis-à-vis India, among others.

A state threatened by this class of VNSAs has a variety of strategic options. First, it can target the violent group directly. Second, it can ignore the issue or focus on defending itself against attack. Third, it can target the state hosting the group in order to coerce it into "cleaning up its own backyard." This third strategy—what I call "transitive compellence"—is a central tenet of U.S. foreign policy and, especially following 9/11, one that is shared by states threatened by VNSAs, including Israel, Turkey, and the European Union, among others. States that serve as bases for violent groups are increasingly viewed as responsible for or tacitly complicit in their actions and have increasingly become legitimate targets of coercion for containing the threats that emanate from within their borders.[2]

---

[1] Belgin San-Acka, *Dataset on Non-State Violence, Supporters and Targets: External Support for Internal Conflict*, 2011, http://home.ku.edu.tr/~bakca/nagdataset.html.

[2] Tal Becker, *Terrorism and the State: Rethinking the Rules of State Responsibility* (Oxford: Hart Publishing, 2006).

Coercing states into containing VNSAs is a common policymaking strategy. Yet transitive compellence has received scant attention in the scholarly literature. When the strategy has been examined, it is usually assumed to be especially difficult to pursue because of base state characteristics. They are typically portrayed as either too weak to confront a VNSA on base state territory or as active sponsors of the VNSAs themselves. For example, the 2010 U.S. *National Security Strategy* explained, "Failing states breed conflict and endanger regional and global security."[3] The predominant concern regarding these states is that when states become weak, nonstate actors "can take opportunistic advantage of a deteriorating internal security situation to mobilize adherents, train insurgents, gain control of resources, launder funds, purchase arms, and ready themselves for assault on world order."[4] At the same time, base state sponsorship of VNSAs is "exceptionally difficult to stop," particularly for the most committed sponsors.[5] The empirical record is more complex, however; far from suggesting the difficulty of transitive compellence, it indicates the strategy can be quite successful at containing threats posed by VNSAs.

This chapter seeks to audit the conventional wisdom on transitive compellence. The central arguments it explores are how and why transitive compellence works and how it can be used to contain the threat of a VNSA residing within a base state. Focusing in particular on Turkish efforts to get Syria and Iraq to crack down on the Kurdistan People's Party (Partiya Karkari Kurdistan, PKK), the chapter discusses the dynamics, costs, and benefits of transitive compellence and highlights the strategy's potential even in ostensibly difficult cases of state sponsors and weak states. This chapter builds upon the traditional coercion literature highlighted in Art and Greenhill's chapter in this volume, wherein the state remains the dominant coercer and target. However, as in other chapters in this volume, it seeks to move beyond some of our assumptions and imposed constraints about the agency (or lack thereof) of weak states and incorporate the realities of nonstate actors' influence in the international system, as both Krause and Walsh emphasize in their chapters. As many of the chapters in this volume demonstrate, broadening the lens through which coercion is understood can better explain its influence and utility in the international system.

Transitive Compellence

Transitive compellence is a strategy whereby one state coerces another into containing a threat posed by a third party, which in this context refers to a

---

[3] *The National Security Strategy of the United States of America*, 2010, 7, https://obamawhitehouse.archives.gov/sites/default/files/rss_viewer/national_security_strategy.pdf.
[4] Robert I. Rotberg, "Nation-State Failure: A Recurring Phenomenon?," in *National Intelligence Council 2020 Project* (2003), http://www.au.af.mil/au/awc/awcgate/cia/nic2020/panel2_nov6.pdf.
[5] Daniel Byman, *Deadly Connections: States That Sponsor Terrorism* (Cambridge: Cambridge University Press, 2005), 6.

VNSA residing within its borders. If the base state elects to comply with the coercing state's demands, it can employ a variety of strategies toward the VNSA; however, in all cases the ultimate target of coercion is the violent non-state group rather than its host.

In his famous speech before a joint session of Congress on September 20, 2001, President George W. Bush articulated just such a strategy: "[The United States] will pursue nations that provide aid or safe haven to terrorism. Every nation, in every region, now has a decision to make. Either you are with us, or you are with the terrorists. From this day forward, any nation that continues to harbor or support terrorism will be regarded by the United States as a hostile regime."[6] The National Strategy for Combating Terrorism later echoed this sentiment: "When states prove reluctant or unwilling to meet their international obligations [to combat terrorism] . . . the United States . . . will take appropriate steps to convince them to change their policies."[7] When an incident arose from Yemen in 2010, Secretary of State Hillary Clinton proclaimed, "Yemen must take ownership of the challenges it faces, and of its internal affairs," once again promoting the preferred U.S. policy of each state taking control of extremists based within their own borders.[8]

The basing phenomenon is hardly new, nor is the remedy of coercing base states. For example, Israel utilized a transitive compellence strategy against states that hosted fedayeen fighters, including Jordan, Egypt, Syria, and Lebanon. In 1968 Moshe Dayan, then minister of defense, explained Israel's coercive policy in a lecture to military officers:

> We cannot guard every water pipeline from explosion and every tree from uprooting. We cannot prevent every murder of a worker in an orchard or a family in their beds. But it is in our power to set a high price on our blood, a price too high for the Arab community, the Arab army, or the Arab government to think it worth paying. We can see to it that the Arab villages oppose the raiding bands that pass through them, rather than give them assistance. It is in our power to see that Arab military commanders prefer a strict performance of their obligation to police the frontiers rather than suffer defeat in clashes with our units. We can cause the Arab governments to renounce a "policy of strength" towards Israel by turning it into a demonstration of weakness. The decision not to get into quarrels with Israel will only come if the Arabs have reason to suppose that otherwise they will have to reckon with sharp reactions from our side and be dragged into a conflict in which they would be the losers.[9]

---

[6] George W. Bush, "An Address to a Joint Session of Congress and the American People," September 20, 2001. Transcript available at: https://www.hsdl.org/?abstract&did=474298.

[7] U.S. National Security Council, *National Strategy for Combating Terrorism*, September 2006, http://purl.access.gpo.gov/GPO/LPS74421, 17.

[8] Paul Richter, "Hillary Clinton Urges Yemen to 'Take Ownership' of Its Problems," *Los Angeles Times*, January 27, 2010.

[9] Moshe Dayan, "Why Israel Strikes Back," in *Under Fire; Israel's 20-Year Struggle for Survival*, ed. Donald B. Robinson (New York: Norton, 1968), 120–23.

Dayan and other policymakers repeatedly made clear that the Israeli government held the Arab states accountable for attacks that emanated from within their borders and that these states would suffer military retaliation if they did not prevent the attacks.[10]

In each of these cases, transitive compellence was aimed at coercing the base state and its citizens to actively prevent infiltrations conducted by the fedayeen. Israeli policymakers issued their threats and elucidated their demands toward these states through both public and private channels. In addition, the Israelis utilized a combination of small and large reprisal operations aimed at economic, military, and civilian assets in order to punish these regimes and impose significant costs for noncompliance with their demands.[11]

When a state engages in transitive compellence, it seeks to undermine the existing equilibrium between a host state and the VNSA within it. In some circumstances, allowing a VNSA to use its territory as a base may not have been particularly disruptive and may even have conferred certain benefits on the host state.[12] In others, the VNSA may have posed problems for its host, but compared to other priorities, confronting the issue ranked relatively low on the base state's agenda. Irrespective of how the base state related to the VNSA prior to coercion, after it commences, there is at minimum a need to reconsider the status quo. Transitive compellence makes maintaining the status quo more costly, and base states need to evaluate whether it is worth trying to preserve it. Thus, if a coercer can credibly threaten or use limited action to increase the pain for a base state, such actions should cause the base state to at least evaluate the costs of compliance before rejecting the demands of the coercer.

Measuring Success

In the broadest terms, the goal of this kind of coercion is to compel the base state to take a specific action or actions against the violent group that will limit its ability to act against the external coercer. Thus success is measured through observation and evaluation of a base state's actions against a VNSA and, in particular, the nature of these actions in relation to the coercer's demands. Base state actions can take a variety of forms, including but not limited to better patrolling of base state borders, extradition of the VNSA's leadership, disarmament of the violent group, and closing training bases. A complete success is one in which the base state changes its behavior with respect to the violent group in the specific manner demanded by the coercer. However, success is rarely as straightforward or as dichotomous. Thus coercive success can also be measured on a sliding scale,

---

[10] See also Barry Blechman, "The Consequences of the Israeli Reprisals: An Assessment" (Ph.D. dissertation, Georgetown University, 1971).

[11] Between 1951 and 1969 the Israelis conducted 76 reprisal actions, of which 17 were significant and resulted in more than 10 fatalities and casualties. Barry Blechman, "Middle East Military Event Data, 1949–1969," https://doi.org/10.3886/ICPSR05202.v1.

[12] Daniel L. Byman, "Confronting Passive Sponsors of Terrorism," *Center for Middle East Policy Analysis Papers* (Washington, D.C.: Brookings Institution, 2005).

of lesser and greater success, depending on the extent to which a host has made the environment less hospitable for a VNSA on its soil. For example, although an external coercer may demand complete disarmament, widespread arrests of members of a VNSA can be considered a partial coercive success.

When evaluating coercive success and failure, it is essential to focus on the behavior of the base state as well as that of the VNSA. Naturally, when assessing the success of coercion, it is logical to observe and measure whether levels of VNSA activity have significantly changed and been reduced following coercion. A measurable decline in violent group activity would suggest that the status quo has shifted and the violent group has been contained in some fashion; thus other measurable changes in VNSA activity following transitive compellence may be indications of the impact of the strategy.

However, although observing spikes and dips of violent group attacks can be instructive to policymakers and analysts of the success or failure of the coercion, these measures can be misleading. By their nature, the number of attacks and perpetrators is driven by the autonomous strategy, tactics, and capabilities of the VNSA. Only attacks that were successfully implemented can be counted. Thus limiting observations to VNSA attacks may misleadingly suggest maintenance of the status quo while obfuscating the efforts of the base state in preventing attacks. Similarly, one can imagine a VNSA making a strategic decision to halt attacks for a limited period, which would appear data-wise as though the base state was successful even though the behavioral shift was unrelated to base state actions. Such issues are endemic in trilateral coercion; thus solely measuring changes in the rate and number of attacks is insufficient and, in isolation, might lead to inaccurate conclusions regarding the efficacy of transitive compellence.[13]

The Advantages of Transitive Compellence

Ultimately, transitive compellence is a preferred policy among states threatened by VNSAs for several complementary reasons. First, it places the onus of responsibility on base states for preventing violence emanating from their borders, as demanded by their sovereign responsibilities within the international system.[14] Second, base states may be best positioned to combat VNSAs, both

[13] For example, if a base state is willing to take costly action to contain the group, the coercer or others in the international community may be able to provide aid or intelligence to better implement the new policy.

[14] General Assembly Resolution 2625, *Declaration on Principles of International Law concerning Friendly Relations and Co-operation among States in accordance with the Charter of the United Nations*, (October 24, 1970), https://unispal.un.org/DPA/DPR/unispal.nsf/0/25A1C8E35B23161C852570C4006E50AB, United Nations Security Council, *Resolution 1373* (September 28, 2001), available from: https://documents-dds-ny.un.org/doc/UNDOC/GEN/N01/557/43/PDF/N0155743.pdf?OpenElement. This responsibility was most clearly articulated in Resolution 2625: "Every state has the duty to refrain from organizing, instigating, assisting or participating in acts of civil strife or terrorist acts in another state or acquiescing in organized activities within its territory directed towards the commission of such acts, when the acts referred to in the present paragraph involve a threat or

in terms of their informational advantages and domestic freedom of action.[15] Third, coercion against a state is a familiar and generally economical strategy for a coercer when compared to the brute force alternative. Fourth, passing the buck to base states permits coercers to avoid many of the pitfalls associated with dealing directly with VNSAs. Such challenges include the difficulty of identifying targetable assets, inflicting significant collateral damage, and maintaining sufficient resolve to alter the cost-benefit calculus of VNSAs.[16] Though transitive compellence has associated risks and costs—such as potential blowback and retaliation—when successfully pursued, it can deflect the most trying elements of containing violent groups onto base states.

What We Think We Know: Weak States and State Sponsors

As noted at the outset, base state coercion has received little attention in the literature and has not been examined systematically across cases. When the matter is addressed, treatment usually falls into two broad categories: (1) weak and failed states and (2) passive and active sponsorship of terror. Underlying these explanations are assumptions about why base states allow VNSAs to organize, train, recruit, and/or act within their borders.

Some scholars acknowledge the importance of base states but assume that such states are either weak or failed and therefore lack the capacity to take action. This strand of the literature acknowledges the potential threats that weak and failed states present but dismisses their capacity to act against these groups.

A second, related set of arguments focuses on the ways in which states purposely aid terrorist groups, including with financial support, training, recruitment, and basing.[17] This line of reasoning explains that states opt to back VNSAs for a variety of strategic reasons, including influencing one's neighbors, toppling an adversary's regime, and countering U.S. power. This argument assumes that the base state has accounted for the potential punishment that may result from its relationship with a VNSA and factored it into its

---

use of force." These responsibilities were further elaborated following the 9/11 attacks in Security Council Resolution 1373. For the full text view: https://unispal.un.org/DPA/DPR/unispal.nsf/0/25A1C8E35B23161C852570C4006E50AB.

[15] For example, the Jordanians closely monitored the Fedayeen throughout 1950–70 and even during moments of relative weakness used the Jordanian Intelligence Services to infiltrate these groups and keep tabs on their activities. Kamal S. Salibi, *The Modern History of Jordan* (London: I. B. Tauris, St. Martin's Press, 1993), 228.

[16] These challenges may also be present for the base state in some cases; however, from the perspective of the coercer, if it is possible to buck-pass to the base state, this is to their advantage. Daniel L. Byman and Matthew C. Waxman, *The Dynamics of Coercion: American Foreign Policy and the Limits of Military Might* 21, pp. 190 (Cambridge,; Cambridge University Press, 2002); Paul K. Davis and Brian Michael Jenkins, *Deterrence and Influence in Counterterrorism: A Component in the War on Al Qaeda* (Santa Monica, CA: RAND, 2002).

[17] See, e.g., Byman, *Deadly Connections*; Zeev Maoz and Belgin San-Akca, "Rivalry and State Support of Non-State Armed Groups (NAGS), 1946–2001," *International Studies Quarterly* 56, no. 4 (2012): 720–34.

strategic calculation.[18] External actors consequently should have a hard time severing these relationships; that is, transitive compellence should be unlikely to succeed.

Both of these pieces of conventional wisdom underestimate coercers' abilities to reshape a base state's relationship with a violent group, but for different reasons. The weak state argument hinges on the assumption that, despite the imposition of coercive costs, base states lack the capability to alter the status quo, while the sponsorship argument assumes base states are too committed to relationships with VNSAs and thus lack the will to contain them. Ultimately both frameworks suggest we should be pessimistic about transitive compellence efforts.[19] However, a closer examination of cases indicates a far more nuanced reality, one that ultimately reveals opportunities for success.

Turkish Transitive Compellence and the PKK

In order to simultaneously test conventional wisdom and explore the potential efficacy of transitive compellence, it is helpful to examine cases wherein all of the key elements are present. A hard test of these premises should include cases of a weak state and a state sponsor who were each subject to a consistent transitive compellent strategy. As such, Turkey's use of transitive compellence directed at both the Kurdish Regional Government (KRG) and the Syrian regime in order to contain the PKK represents two cases that together formulate a hard test of the conventional wisdom.[20] Syria was a notorious state sponsor of the PKK, whereas the KRG was a weak quasi-state with significant limitations on its power. The conventional wisdom would predict that we should observe little to no transitive compellence success on account of the aforementioned characteristics of the base states. In the case of Syria, the 20-year-long sponsorship relationship with the PKK should be exceedingly difficult to sever. In contrast, the extremely limited capabilities of the KRG would lead us to expect that they would be incapable of taking effective action against the PKK.

---

[18] Byman, *Deadly Connections*, 4, 6.

[19] Juxtaposing will and capacity has been used to explain the likelihood of refugee cross-border violence. See Sarah Kenyon Lischer, *Dangerous Sanctuaries* (Ithaca, NY: Cornell University Press, 2006), 28–30.

[20] The case of Turkey's transitive compellence against both Syria and the KRG is consistent with other cases of transitive compellence, particularly for this region. To date, there is no complete data set that captures all instances of transitive compellence and their outcomes, although one is in progress. Furthermore, although not discussed in this chapter, many of these cases have addressed the issue of violent nonstate actor basing with coercive strategy over a prolonged period of time. This variation enables a close study of the relationship between the base state and the violent group, the coercive strategies employed, and, ultimately, the success of these tactics. The Turkish case presents particular benefits for study due to Turkey's steadfast usage of this strategy and the PKK's utilization of multiple base states. For more details see Keren E. Fraiman, "Not in Your Backyard: Transitive Compellence, Base States and Violent Non-State Groups" (Ph.D. dissertation, Massachusets Institute of Technology, 2014)

As discussed in some detail below, while neither state appeared to be a good candidate for transitive compellence, Turkey was ultimately successful in compelling both of them to take action against the PKK. In the case of Syria, Turkey attempted to compel the Syrians to act at separate junctures in 1992, 1996, 1997, and 1998. Of these, the first and the fourth attempts elicited a positive response from the Syrian government, representing one partial success and one complete success.[21] In the Iraqi case, Turkey utilized transitive compellence in 1991–92, 1995, and 1997. In the first and third cases, Turkey was able to successfully compel the KRG to take action against the PKK.[22] Although the Turks were not always successful in eliciting changes in behavior using coercion, they were certainly far more effective than the conventional wisdom would predict.

Two episodes of Turkish transitive compellence merit closer inspection: the 1998 Syrian crisis and the 1992 instance of the KRG in northern Iraq. Although the Turks utilized transitive compellence repeatedly, these two episodes unfolded at junctures when the two states most closely resembled their traditional classifications as state sponsors and weak states, respectively. These hard cases highlight the limitations of the prevailing wisdom and suggest that the study of base state coercion ought to move beyond these narrow approaches toward a more nuanced examination of the base state's relationship to the violent group.

The Challenge of the PKK for Turkey

In the summer of 1984, the PKK became embroiled in an increasingly violent campaign against Turkey.[23] The PKK presented a formidable challenge to Turkey's control of its Kurdish areas and served as a persistent terrorist threat throughout Turkey (see Figure 6.1). The PKK, headed by Abdullah Ocalan, aimed to incite a communist revolution and establish an independent Kurdish state that would include areas of Turkey, Syria, Iraq, and Iran.[24] The PKK's first target was the Turkish state and its government, as this was where the majority of Kurds, estimated at 13 million, resided within the four southeastern provinces of Turkey.[25] The PKK's violent campaign within Turkey ebbed and flowed between 1984 and 1998, but Turkish authorities estimate that the

---

[21] Ibid.

[22] Ibid.

[23] Prior to 1984, the PKK was a target of the Turkish state due to its political activity, but it had not yet initiated its violent campaign. In August 1984, the PKK's first attack targeted the military posts in Eruh and Semdilini. Aliza Marcus, *Blood and Belief: The PKK and the Kurdish Fight for Independence* (New York: New York University Press, 2007), 79; Gokhan Bacik and Bezen Balamir Coskun, "The PKK Problem: Explaining Turkey's Failure to Develop a Political Solution," *Studies in Conflict & Terrorism* 34, no. 3 (2011): 251.

[24] Elena Pokalova, "Framing Separatism as Terrorism: Lessons from Kosovo," *Studies in Conflict & Terrorism* 33, no. 5 (2010): 435; Nur Bilge Criss, "The Nature of PKK Terrorism in Turkey," *Studies in Conflict & Terrorism* 18, no. 1 (1995): 18.

[25] David McDowall, *A Modern History of the Kurds* (London: I.B. Tauris, 2004), 3.

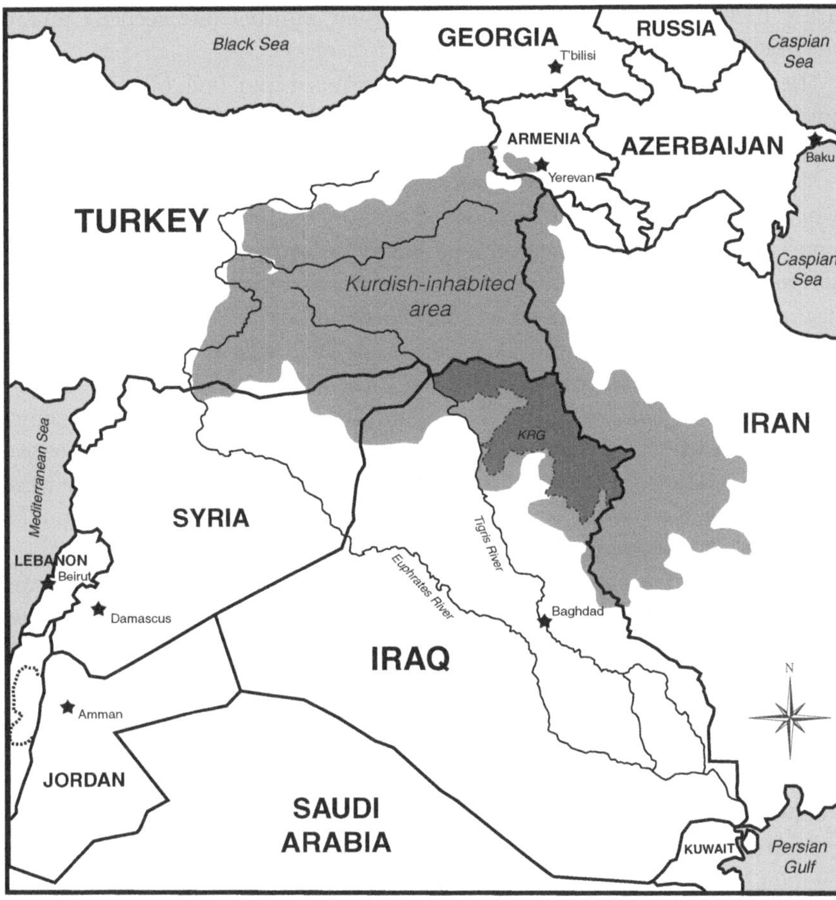

FIGURE 6.1 Kurdish Areas in Turkey and Neighboring States
SOURCE: University of Texas Libraries, http://www.lib.utexas.edu/maps/middle_east_and_asia/kurdish_lands_92.jpg

PKK claimed 30,000 to 35,000 lives within that period.[26] Between 1991 and 1997, it is estimated that Turkey spent $6 billion to $8 billion annually to quell PKK violence.[27] The increasing popularity of the PKK among Turkey's Kurdish population only further intensified their challenge to the state.[28] As of 1993,

[26] Alan Makovsky and Michael Eisenstadt, "Turkish-Syrian Relations: A Crisis Delayed?," *Washington Institute for Near East Policy*, October 17, 1998, http://www.washingtoninstitute.org/policy-analysis/view/turkish-syrian-relations-a-crisis-delayed; Svante E. Cornell, "The Kurdish Question in Turkish Politics," *Orbis* 45, no. 1 (2001): 123; Harmonie Toros, "Turkey Says It Is Prepared to Attack Kurdish Rebel Bases in Syria," *Washington Post*, October 5, 1998; Mahmut Bali Aykan, "The Turkish-Syrian Crisis of October 1998: A Turkish View," *Middle East Policy* 6, no. 4 (1999): 175.
[27] Robert Olson, "Turkey-Syria Relations since the Gulf War: Kurds and Water," *Middle East Policy* 5, no. 2 (1997): 168-93.
[28] Marcus, *Blood and Belief*, 176.

Turkey had officially designated the PKK their number one security threat, even ahead of Greece.[29]

The PKK threat extended into Syria and northern Iraq, both of which served as important operational bases. The Syrian base served three important functions. First, it became the PKK's organizational headquarters; Ocalan had resided within Syria since 1980 and successfully controlled the organization from there. Second, the PKK established training facilities within Syria proper, as well as within the Syrian-controlled Bekaa Valley in Lebanon. Third, in the mid- to late 1990s, the PKK began to use Syria as a launching pad for direct attacks into Turkey from the far western border of Syria. The PKK base within Syria was correctly perceived as a significant challenge in Turkey's broader counterinsurgency campaign against the PKK. Turkey viewed Syrian support for the PKK "as a *sine qua non* for that organization's ability to wage war against Turkey on all its Middle Eastern Borders."[30] In the midst of the 1998 coercive crisis, Prime Minister Mesut Yilmaz stated, "If Syria did not shelter the head of the bandits, if it did not set up camps and give money, then it would not be possible for this separatist bandit to continue his path."[31]

While the Syrian base was essential for PKK command and control, it was geographically ill suited for launching attacks into Turkey. The mountainous terrain of northern Iraq (Iraqi Kurdistan) was operationally more advantageous, which led Ocalan to establish a series of bases there to more easily launch attacks.[32] This staging area was crucial for the PKK, because without it PKK guerrilla attacks would have been launched almost entirely from within hostile Turkish territory. Furthermore, this region was exceedingly difficult to control. The steepness of the openings and the valleys made it difficult to penetrate. The rough, rolling terrain was difficult to navigate and favored the defender, because any invader can be seen from a great distance.[33] According to Turkish government sources, 3,533 PKK terrorist incidents occurred between 1984 and 1990, and those figures spiked to 15,146 events between 1991 and 1994.[34] The nearly 10-fold increase in attacks was attributed by many Turkish officials to be the direct result of the PKK's ability to operate more freely from the mountains of northern Iraq.[35] Removing the bases in northern Iraq and

---

[29] Umit Ozdag and Ersel Aydinli, "Winning a Low Intensity Conflict: Drawing Lessons from the Turkish Case," *Review of International Affairs*, 2, no. 3 (2003): 105, 114.

[30] Makovsky and Eisenstadt, "Turkish-Syrian Relations."

[31] "Turkey Warns Syria on Helping Kurd Rebels," *New York Times*, October 12, 1998. Interestingly, following the 1998 severance of the relationship, violence in Turkey was significantly reduced and the status of the PKK diminished, lending credence to Turkey's belief about the importance of Ocalan and the basing relationship in Syria.

[32] McDowall, *A Modern History of the Kurds*, 422; Michael M. Gunter, "Transnational Sources of Support for the Kurdish Insurgency in Turkey," *Conflict Quarterly* 11, no. 2 (1991): 260–62; Marcus, *Blood and Belief*, 59.

[33] Interview with a retired colonel, U.S. Army Special Forces, stationed at Zakho House in OPC and in northern Iraq in 2003, June 20, 2013.

[34] Kemal Kirisci and Gareth M. Winrow, *The Kurdish Question and Turkey: An Example of a Trans-State Ethnic Conflict* (London: Frank Cass, 1997), 27.

[35] Kirisci and Winrow, *The Kurdish Question and Turkey*, 27.

rolling up the PKK's Syria network ultimately became a focal point of Turkey's strategy for combating the PKK.

State Sponsorship in Syria and State Weakness in the KRG

In 1998 the Syrian state was considered notorious by Turkey and many Western states, including the United States. Sponsorship of VNSAs was not limited to the PKK. Rather, part of Syria's modus operandi for pursuing its grand strategic objectives included utilizing proxy groups that advanced its agenda or, at minimum, served as leverage against other states.[36] Since the Syrian-PKK partnership's nascent stages in 1980, the PKK had had a functional role in Syria's foreign policy. As they both viewed Turkey as a target, this overlap created an instrumental role for the PKK.[37] Generally Syria viewed Turkey as a regional rival, especially in light of its alignment with the West and subsequently with Israel, and thus sought to balance against it.[38] Following the end of the Cold War, Turkey's role as a regional player was growing, which invariably challenged the Syrian regime. Syrian leader Hafez al-Assad believed that the new world order that was emerging from the end of the Cold War was "profoundly biased against Arab and Syrian interests. The balance of power, he declared, had been upset [with the collapse of bipolarity] and the 'main winners have been the Arabs' enemies.'"[39] Ultimately Syria gained leverage against Turkey through its support of the PKK's violent campaign against Turkey.

In light of these known constraints, Assad sought to creatively balance against his foes while tempering his regional aspirations and taking pragmatic measures to avoid a direct military confrontation with any of his rivals.[40] In this respect, the PKK was instrumental, providing Assad with a violent group that was actively attacking Turkey, which could bleed the state and weaken its relative power. Thus, in Assad's broader balancing strategy, the PKK played a

---

[36] Syrian support for terrorist organizations included Palestinian al-Saiqa, Asbat al-Ansar, the Popular Front for the Liberation of Palestine–General Command (PFLP-GC); mercenary forces of Abu Nidal, Hizballah, Palestinian Islamic Jihad, and the Democratic Front for the Liberation of Palestine. Reuven Erlich, "Terrorism as a Preferred Instrument of Syrian Policy," *International Institute for Counter Terrorism*, October 12, 1998, https://www.ict.org.il/Article/754/Terrorism%20as%20a%20Preferred%20Instrument%20of%20Syrian%20Policy; Moshe Ma'oz, *Asad: The Sphinx of Damascus: A Political Biography* (New York: Weidenfeld & Nicholson, 1988), 171; Barry M. Rubin, *The Truth about Syria* (New York: Palgrave Macmillan, 2007), 77.

[37] Although the PKK and Syria both shared a common enemy in Turkey, their foreign policy goals were quite divergent. Despite its sponsorship and utilitarian use of the PKK, the Syrian state was never an advocate for the Kurdish cause and often took steps to work against the PKK's goal of establishing an independent Kurdistan. Robert Olson, "The Kurdish Question and Turkey's Foreign Policy towards Syria, Iran, Russia and Iraq since the Gulf War" in *The Kurdish Nationalist Movement in the 1990s: Its Impact on Turkey and the Middle East*, (Lexington, KY: University Press of Kentucky, 1996), 87; Ozdag and Aydinli, "Winning a Low Intensity Conflict," 105.

[38] Byman, *Deadly Connections*, 151.

[39] Assad quoted in Raymond A. Hinnebusch, *Syria: Revolution from Above: Contemporary Middle East* (London: Routledge, 2001), 160.

[40] For example, while Assad still sought to regain the Golan Heights from Israel and achieve Palestinian rights, he abandoned much of the Pan-Arab ideology and goals that had been dominant in the previous Ba'athist government. Hinnebusch, *Syria*, 151–60.

supporting role. To be clear, the exact objective behind supporting the PKK (and other armed groups) can only be inferred from the broader strategic context, as Assad continually denied his involvement with these groups. However, it appears that as a state sponsor of terrorism, Assad believed he could benefit by having an indirect and plausibly deniable hand in the affairs of his neighbors. This additional leverage could partially compensate for Syria's inferior conventional military forces.[41] Overall this type of sponsorship offered Syria an opportunity to engage in a relatively low-cost, low-risk conflict.[42]

It is precisely these types of calculations that suggest Assad would be reticent to succumb to Turkish coercion. By 1998, Syria had already been providing varying levels of support to the PKK for nearly 20 years, suggesting Assad had thoroughly calculated the costs and risks of maintaining the relationship. Thus adherents to the "strategic state sponsors" thesis would expect that the Turks in 1998 would meet major resistance when attempting to compel a change in Syrian behavior. This outlook is only reinforced when one considers Syria's notorious sponsorship of other VNSAs. Indeed, it is precisely for these reasons that observers at the time believed Syria would not bend.[43]

In contrast to the challenges of coercing a state sponsor, the KRG presented Turkey with the challenge of coercing a weak state. In the aftermath of the 1991 Gulf War, the KRG saw the two largest Iraqi Kurdish parties, the Kurdish Democratic Party (KDP) and the Patriotic Union of Kurdistan (PUK), take steps to consolidate Kurdish regional power. As a result of Operation Provide Comfort (OPC), in which the United States and its allies provided protection to Kurds fleeing the Iraqi government, the Kurds were able to establish "statehood by stealth."[44] By the end of 1992, the KRG held its first elections, created a state flag, and established a police force, a court system, security and intelligence forces, a bank, a postal service, and an agency for issuing passports.[45] In addition, the KRG relied on the peshmerga forces of the PUK and the KDP, estimated to be 20,000 regular fighters.[46] Importantly, Turkey also began to interact with the KRG and its associated political parties as a quasi-state. Consequently, Turkey expected that the KRG would patrol the border and contain PKK activity emanating from its territory. In essence, the Kurds had been granted, and subsequently established, a quasi-state.

---

[41] Byman, *Deadly Connections*, 118.

[42] Rubin, *The Truth about Syria*, 78. In many cases, even when Syria was clearly implicated, as in the murder of Jordan's prime minister in 1981, no direct action was taken against the Syrian regime.

[43] Makovsky and Eisenstadt, "Turkish-Syrian Relations."

[44] Kemal Kirisci and Gareth M. Winrow, *The Kurdish Question and Turkey*, (London; Portland, OR: Frank Cass, 1997) 161; Jonathan C. Randal, *After Such Knowledge, What Forgiveness? My Encounters with Kurdistan*, (New York: Farrar, Straus, and Giroux, 1997), 30.

[45] McDowall, *A Modern History of the Kurds*, 380–81; Michael M. Gunter, *The Kurds of Iraq: Tragedy and Hope*, (New York: St. Martin's Press, 1992), 87; Sheri Laizer, *Martyrs, Traitors, and Patriots: Kurdistan after the Gulf War*, (London: Zed Books, 1996): 110.

[46] Gunter, *Kurds of Iraq*, 40–41.

Despite the extensive efforts by the KRG to consolidate power and build state capacity, it remained an objectively weak state.[47] In 1991 the KDP and the PUK were reestablishing control over the region after enduring violent clashes with the Iraqi government, including the infamous chemical weapons attacks. During this period, the Kurds remained isolated and dependent on outside powers. The international community, through UN Security Council Resolutions 661 and 667, ultimately imposed significant financial and trade sanctions on Iraq.[48] These sanctions affected access to goods in northern Iraq as well. Furthermore, there was continued uncertainty about the Kurds' protection from Saddam Hussein's forces and whether their region would remain safe and secure.[49] Although both Jalal Talabani, the leader of the PUK, and Masoud Barzani, the leader of the KDP, strove to consolidate their collective power and establish a modicum of law and order in the region, the emerging quasi-state was still very weak. Thus, in this instance, the state capacity argument would predict that the KRG would be too weak to comply with the demands of the Turkish state and therefore would not act against the PKK.

The Outcomes of Turkey's Coercive Strategy

Turkey employed a transitive compellent strategy in order to quell the activity of the PKK within both Syria and northern Iraq. Despite differences in the PKK activity within the two states, Turkey had similar goals in both circumstances. In Syria the onus of the demands required Syria to expel the leadership of the PKK, in particular Abdullah Ocalan, the head of the PKK. In Iraq the primary demands required the prevention of cross-border attacks, which emanated from the mountain ranges bordering Turkey. Ultimately Turkey expected both states to take proactive measures to contain PKK activity and lessen the threat emanating from their respective borders.

1998 Syrian Crisis

In early 1998, after several failed attempts to resolve the issue through diplomacy, the Turkish National Security Council considered implementing a new round of coercive diplomacy and even contemplated using limited force to address Syrian basing of the PKK.[50] Turkey made a series of strong, public

[47] Unfortunately, there are no systematic data on the KRG's governance or economic or military spending in 1992, two traditional measures of state power. However, the nascent development of the region, coupled with the extensive sanctions and attacks from Saddam Hussein that immediately preceded the establishment of the KRG, allow one to characterize the KRG as extremely weak.
[48] Initially the sanctions were in response to Iraq's invasion of Kuwait, but after the war they were extended and linked to the removal of weapons of mass destruction.
[49] Charles Tripp, *A History of Iraq*, (Cambridge: Cambridge University Press, 2002), 272; "Worldwatch: Iraqi Troops Order Kurds to Leave," *Observer*, November 17, 1991; *CBS News Transcripts*, November 23, 1991.
[50] Aykan, "The Turkish-Syrian Crisis of October 1998," 176–77; Damla Aras, "The Role of Motivation in the Success of Coercive Diplomacy: The 1998 Turkish-Syrian Crisis as a Case Study," *Defence Studies* 9, no. 2 (2009): 216.

verbal threats toward Syria that clearly communicated Turkey's patience was quickly running out. These new threats were made publicly and included justifications for employing military force. In September, Gen. Atilla Ates, commander of the land forces, warned, "By supporting the bandit Apo [Ocalan], they [the Syrians] have confronted us with the plague of terrorism. Turkey has made necessary efforts for good relations. If Turkey does not receive any response to its efforts, it will have the right to take all appropriate measures. We have no more patience."[51] On October 1, President Suleyman Demirel declared "once more to the world that we have the right to retaliate against Syria."[52]

In addition to the public threats, for the first time Turkey set out to make its case in the international arena by utilizing the UN Security Council, the Conference on Security and Cooperation in Europe, and the Arab League.[53] Ankara formally identified Syria's offenses as (1) harboring Ocalan and top PKK leaders since 1979; (2) hosting multiple PKK congresses; (3) permitting military personnel to train PKK guerrillas, including Ocalan; (4) accommodating the growth of operations in the Hatay region since 1995; and (5) allowing the PKK to combine forces with Armenians and Greeks against Turkey.[54] In addition to the verbal assaults, Turkey created the impression that it was mobilizing large numbers of combat-ready troops on the 386-mile fortified border with Syria.[55] The serious nature of these threats was corroborated and conveyed by both American and Egyptian policymakers.[56] This military mobilization backed up the harsh rhetoric that was increasingly prevalent from Turkey's civilian and military leaders.

Syria's initial reaction to the Turkish coercive threats and mobilization in 1998 did not seem promising. In fact, statements from the Syrian embassy in Ankara blamed the crisis on an Israeli-Turkish military pact and held the Turkish government responsible for the lack of dialogue between the two states.[57] However, rifts in the Syrian camp soon became evident. Despite its outward resistance, Syria allowed Egyptian president Hosni Mubarak to mediate an agreement between itself and Turkey.[58] Additionally, divisions among Syria's civilian and military leaders began to become public, particularly because many Syrians were skeptical of a Syrian victory in the event that Turkey escalated to a full-scale war.[59]

Following these internal debates, Assad sent Turkey a verbal message through the Iranian foreign minister Kemal Kharrazi, stating that Syria had

---

[51] Quoted in Robert W. Olson, *Turkey's Relations with Iran, Syria, Israel, and Russia, 1991–2000: The Kurdish and Islamist Questions, Kurdish Studies Series* (Costa Mesa, CA: Mazda, 2001), 110.

[52] Quoted in Olson, *Turkey's Relations with Iran, Syria, Israel, and Russia*, 111.

[53] Aykan, "The Turkish-Syrian Crisis of October 1998," 176–77.

[54] Olson, *Turkey's Relations with Iran, Syria, Israel, and Russia*, 112.

[55] Olson, *Turkey's Relations with Iran, Syria, Israel, and Russia*, 111. Marcus, *Blood and Belief*, 270; Ozdag and Aydinli, "Winning a Low Intensity Conflict," 116.

[56] Interview with Henri Barkey, former U.S. State Department official, August 5, 2013.

[57] Aykan, "The Turkish-Syrian Crisis of October 1998," 176–77.

[58] Olson, *Turkey's Relations with Iran, Syria, Israel, and Russia*, 111.

[59] Aykan, "The Turkish-Syrian Crisis of October 1998," 178.

already begun to arrest PKK members and would expel Ocalan through private backchannels.[60] By October 9 Ocalan had left Syria for Moscow and began seeking asylum in Italy, Russia, the Netherlands, and Greece.[61] Ocalan explained that after Egypt confirmed that Turkey was serious about its military threats, Syrian officials communicated to him that they faced an unpleasant choice and requested that he leave the county—in other words, Assad agreed to expel Ocalan and not risk military confrontation with Turkey.[62] Though Syria did not fully comply with Turkey's demand to hand over Ocalan, his expulsion severely undermined the PKK command and control network in Syria and thus achieved the principal Turkish objective.[63]

By October 13, Syria had signaled through the Iranian and Egyptian foreign ministers that they were taking concrete actions against the PKK and were willing to begin unconditional talks with Turkey.[64] One week later, Turkey and Syria signed the Adana agreement. In response to the coercive demands laid out by Turkey, Damascus assured Ankara that Ocalan was not in Syria and would not be allowed to return and recognized the PKK as a terrorist organization.[65] The regime reaffirmed that the PKK camps were no longer operational and that the group would not be permitted to reestablish camps, other facilities or shelters, or conduct commercial activities within its borders. Likewise, Syria would no longer allow the transit of PKK members across the country. The state also confirmed that PKK members had already been arrested and the names of these individuals would be passed on to Turkish authorities.[66] Finally, in an effort to maintain quiet at the border, Syria agreed that it would not permit any activity from its territory that in any way jeopardized the security and stability of Turkey, including the flow of weapons, logistics, material or financial support, and propaganda.[67]

Ultimately, Turkey successfully coerced Syria into abdicating its relationship with the PKK and evicting its leader. This rapid reversal of policy occurred despite the fact that Syria had been a known state sponsor of the group for a prolonged period of time. Furthermore, although Syria had been quite intransigent in its previous dealings with Turkey, with the Adana agreement it met

---

60 Aykan, "The Turkish-Syrian Crisis of October 1998," 178.

61 McDowall, *A Modern History of the Kurds*, 443; see also Marcus, *Blood and Belief*, 279. On February 15, 1999, after several failed attempts by Turkey to extradite him, he was eventually apprehended in Nairobi as he attempted to fly to South Africa.

62 "Zebari: Turkey Was Behind Ocalan's 1998 Expulsion from Syria," *Rudaw*, November 11, 2013, http://rudaw.net/english/middleeast/iraq/17112013.

63 Marcus, *Blood and Belief*, 271; Alan Makovsky, "Defusing the Turkish-Syrian Crisis: Whose Triumph?," Washington Institute for Near East Policy, January–February 1999, http://www.washingtoninstitute.org/policy-analysis/view/defusing-the-turkish-syrian-crisis-whose-triumph.

64 Mahmut Bali Aykan, "The Turkish-Syrian Crisis of October 1998," 178; Aras, "Similar Strategies, Dissimilar Outcomes: An Appraisal of the Efficacy of Turkey's Coercive Diplomacy with Syria and in Northern Iraq," Journal of Strategic Studies 34, no. 4 (2011): 601.

65 "Minutes of the Agreement Signed by Turkey and Syria in Adana (Unofficial Translation)," (October 20, 1998). http://www.mafhoum.com/press/50P2.htm.

66 "Minutes of the Agreement Signed by Turkey and Syria in Adana."

67 Ibid.

Turkey's demands without preconditions. Before the ink had even dried on the agreement, Syria had proactively taken steps to evict the PKK from its territory, most importantly by expelling Ocalan. While the Turkish efforts were certainly intense, the crisis concluded rapidly without a single shot being fired.

Northern Iraq and the KRG

As in Syria, Turkey adopted a coercive strategy aimed at the Iraqi Kurdish political parties and the KRG. Using a variety of political, economic, and military levers, the Turkish government sought to coerce the Iraqi Kurdish parties to contain the PKK, which was based within their borders. Turkey's coercive leverage vis-à-vis the KRG was particularly strong in 1992. Turkey's pivotal role in OPC, coupled with its economic leverage and its willingness to use military force, provided the underpinnings for Turkey's coercive policy.

In the lead-up to the October 1992 raid, the Turkish government demanded the following three actions from the KRG: (1) dislodge the PKK from within the KRG's area of control, (2) monitor the border to prevent the use of bases to launch attacks, and (3) cooperate with the Turkish military in its raids. After the implementation of OPC and the subsequent meetings in Ankara, Turkey maintained that the Iraqi Kurdish parties were responsible for establishing a quiet border and preventing infiltrations by the PKK. This sentiment was reiterated clearly, both privately and publicly, throughout this period.[68]

Turkey possessed significant military leverage over the KRG.[69] Turkey had previously demonstrated its ability and willingness to invade Iraqi Kurdistan in pursuit of PKK militants, as well as to threaten Iraqi Kurds.[70] Well before the Kurdish parties had any level of autonomy in the region, they were the targets of Turkish military attacks. The military precedent set by Turkey led the Kurds to understand that the Turks were willing to use force and that, whether by accident or by design, their actions would likely lead to Iraqi Kurdish casualties.[71] "Iraqi Kurdish officials, struggling to build up their own administration . . . believed that the Turkish military wanted to send them a warning: either they help push the PKK out of the region, or they would be treated as part of the problem."[72] Lurking in the background behind the KRG's policy toward the PKK were military and economic sanctions that, if imposed,

---

[68] Interviews with a Kurdish policymaker, May 30, 2013; interview with Dr. Najmiddin Karim, governor of Kirkuk, June 12, 2013.

[69] The significant level of military leverage that the Turks possessed accords with many of the best practices delineated in the traditional coercion literature. However, its coercive attempts were not all successful. Thus, while employing coercive best practices is an essential component for yielding successful transitive compellence, it is often insufficient for predicting success. See Fraiman, "Not in Your Backyard."

[70] This period is outside the scope of my study because the KRG and the Kurdish parties were not autonomous at this time, and thus the coercion utilized was between a state and a nonstate group.

[71] Kemal Kirisci, "Turkey and the Kurdish Safe-Haven in Northern Iraq," *Journal of South Asian and Middle Eastern Studies* 19, no. 3 (1996): 30.

[72] Marcus, *Blood and Belief*, 200.

would significantly impact the viability of the Kurdish parties and the KRG more broadly.[73]

Importantly, as the Turks coerced the KRG, one of their primary demands was that they participate in the Turkish assaults against the PKK. The Turkish military was cognizant of its limitations in conducting combat operations in the mountains and understood the potential contribution of the Iraqi peshmerga fighters during the actual incursion.

In mid-October 1992 the Turkish military once again entered Iraq in order to attack PKK strongholds. This time the Turks successfully induced the Iraqi Kurds to participate in the operation. The KRG coordinated with the Turkish military in advance and played an important role in carrying out the assault. Leading up to the attack on the PKK, Turkish military officials and the Iraqi Kurdistan Front (IKF) met with greater regularity, which produced an agreement to curb PKK activities in the fall.[74] In the lead-up to the 1992 incursion, both Talabani and Barzani openly stated their shift in attitude toward the PKK; both appeared to have come to an agreement to support Turkey in their efforts against the PKK. Talabani declared that "both he and Barzani agreed that Turkey had every right to ensure its national security . . . . '[However,] we do not prefer that Turkey retaliates this way to maintain its security.' "[75] Additionally, both parties verbally declared their intention to combat and contain the PKK. The PUK Ankara spokesman, Sercil Kazzaz, described the PKK's actions as terrorism, while Siamed Bana of the KDP stated that the combined Kurdistan front created an initiative to combat threats to Turkey's security from Iraqi territory.[76] Similarly in February 1992, "IKF issued a warning to the PKK that if it failed to cease activities against Turkey, it would be purged from the region."[77]

Thousands of Turkish forces drove south, in the direction of Kurdish forces.[78] This particular attack was in response to a very costly PKK attack at the Turkish Derecik Jandarma border outpost, in which the PKK killed 23 soldiers and five Kurdish village guards.[79] Turkish soldiers pursued the militants

---

[73] In addition to the threat of military action, Turkey had significant political and economic coercive leverage over the KRG. Turkey's political leverage stemmed from its critical role in the implementation and maintenance of OPC, which secured the KRG's autonomy in northern Iraq. In particular, the continued use of the base at Incirlik was essential in maintaining the no-fly zone and dropping supplies. In addition, Turkey was the external economic lifeline for the Kurds, serving as the main outlet for trade and aid through the Khabur crossing. These coercive levers were utilized and understood by the KRG and enhanced the coercive threats of the Turks. Michael Gunter, "Kurdish Infighting: The PKK-KDP Conflict," in Olson, *The Kurdish Nationalist Movement in the 1990s*, 52; Philip Robins, *Suits and Uniforms: Turkish Foreign Policy since the Cold War*, (Seattle, WA: University of Washington Press, 2003), 333; Randal, *After Such Knowledge, What Forgiveness?*, 65.

[74] Robins, *Suits and Uniforms*, 325–26.

[75] Quoted in Gunter, *The Kurds of Iraq*, 74–75.

[76] Jonathan Rugman, "Turkey Launches Reprisal Raid on Kurdish Rebels," *Guardian*, October 26, 1991.

[77] Michael M. Gunter, "A De Facto Kurdish State in Northern Iraq," *Third World Quarterly* 14, no. 2 (1993): 306.

[78] McDowall, *A Modern History of the Kurds*, 436.

[79] The Turkish village guards were a Kurdish militia set up by the Turkish government to protect the Kurdish villages from the PKK. These village guards were often the target of PKK attacks because they collaborated with the government.

across the border, ultimately killing approximately 100 PKK fighters. Several days later, approximately 5,000 Iraqi Kurdish fighters attacked the PKK positions along the border with air support from Turkish bombing raids in the same area.[80] The IKF was essential to the success of the 1992 raid. During the fighting against the PKK, the IKF fielded between 5,000 and 6,000 KDP and PUK peshmerga that attacked the roughly 2,000 PKK militants who resided within Iraq.[81] In justifying their attacks on the PKK, the KRG expressed their desire for the PKK to shut down its base within Iraqi Kurdistan, while alluding to the role of international pressure. A couple of days after the clashes began, Nawshirwan Mustafa, Talabani's most senior representative, stated, "The Kurdish government is responsible for all the borders. The presence of PKK camps on our soil is provoking all the world against us. As far [as] the PKK's own tactics and strategies go, they are free to do as they choose in Turkish Kurdistan, but not here. We do not want the PKK to use Iraqi Kurdistan for its own objectives."[82]

The PKK commanders were not prepared for this onslaught. Many of the PKK militants quickly surrendered to the PUK peshmerga in order to avoid confrontation with the Turkish military or the KDP peshmerga.[83] In all, it was estimated that approximately 160 PKK fighters, 160 Iraqi Kurdish fighters, and a few Turkish soldiers were killed during this period.[84] At the conclusion of the confrontation, the Turkish government once again warned the Iraqi Kurds that it was their responsibility to keep the border quiet.[85]

The consequences of this clash were significant: the PKK had finally been flushed from their mountain stronghold and were moved en masse to Zeli camp, near the Iranian border, deep within the PUK-controlled areas.[86] The Turkish-KRG coalition was certainly not a perfect union, and the Turkish military publicly stated its frustration with what it perceived as a general unwillingness on the part of the Kurds to inflict sufficient casualties on the PKK.[87] Additionally, when the Turks asked their new Iraqi Kurdish allies to turn over the PKK militants who had been captured, Talabani responded that he had no intention of handing them over. Similarly, despite promises to the Turks to disarm the PKK upon their surrender, no such action materialized.[88] Despite these challenges, it is clear that the Iraqi Kurdish contribution to the incursion was essential, and, although incomplete, this episode can still be deemed a Turkish coercive success.

---

80 Marcus, *Blood and Belief*, 203.
81 Gunter, "A De Facto Kurdish State in Northern Iraq," 308; Marcus, *Blood and Belief*, 79, 203.
82 Quoted in Laizer, *Martyrs, Traitors, and Patriots*, 64.
83 Robins, *Suits and Uniforms*, 327.
84 Marcus, *Blood and Belief*, 205.
85 Ibid.
86 Ibid., 327.
87 Robins, *Suits and Uniforms*, 326.
88 Michael M. Gunter, *The Kurdish Predicament in Iraq: A Political Analysis*, (New York: St. Martin's Press, 1999), 118.

As in Syria, Turkish coercion was successful in inducing the nascent and weak KRG to utilize its limited resources to confront the PKK. Prior to the coercive episode, the KRG did not act to contain the PKK activity from within its borders, a policy that clearly shifted following Turkish threats. In this instance, the state capacity argument would have predicted that the KRG would be too weak to comply with the demands of the Turkish state and therefore would not act against the PKK. However, this period can instead be deemed a success and one wherein the PUK and the KDP acted against the PKK in cooperation with Turkish forces. The general weakness of the state did not preclude action against the 2,000 PKK fighters based in the region. This episode highlights that weak states and even quasi-states are capable of confronting VNSAs. We should be careful not to underestimate the capacity of any state that bases violent groups to contain and otherwise take effective action against them.

In the case of Syria and the KRG, the two approaches too broadly generalized the relationship between the base state and the violent group, thus overestimating the challenge of altering the status quo. While these static characterizations inform elements of this relationship, they fail to capture a wider variation present within these categories, which reveals the actual costs of compliance with greater precision. In particular, one must closely explore the foreign policy as well as the domestic political relationship between the violent group and the base state. As the underpinnings of the base state's cost-benefit calculation, they directly impact the state's willingness to comply with the coercer's demands.[89] An exploration of these ostensibly hard cases further highlights the need to systematically assess the specific cost calculations in each scenario. Ultimately an analysis of a group's state sponsor reveals that it does not inherently derive the same benefits from nor bear the same costs for containing a violent group within its borders. Similarly weak states can muster their capabilities to address these groups given the right set of incentives.

Summary

The basing of violent VNSAs continues to be a significant international security challenge. As these cases illustrate, one attractive and viable strategy is to compel hosts to contain or evict a group from its sovereign territory. Both Syria and the KRG responded to Turkish coercion, and the threat of force ultimately elicited the desired change in behavior and created a less hospitable environment for the PKK. These cases also demonstrated the relatively economical elements of the policy. In both cases, the actions of the Turkish government were relatively modest and certainly fell far short of addressing the PKK threat directly with brute force. Furthermore, both the Syrian regime and the KRG did appear to be best suited for confronting the PKK. Particularly in the case of the KRG, it was apparent that direct action by Turkey against the PKK failed

---

[89] Fraiman, "Not in Your Backyard."

in large part due to a lack of familiarity with the region as well as limited intelligence. Whatever the KRG lacked in manpower, it more than compensated for in its knowledge of the terrain. The KRG successfully drew upon that knowledge to eventually dislodge the PKK from its strategic mountain stronghold. Though not costless, these cases further illustrate the benefits of pursuing this strategic option.

In addition, both cases force us to rethink the categorization of states simply as state sponsors or weak states and the implications of these categories for classifying states in general and in relation to coercion. These two approaches have been increasingly prevalent in discussing the threats of terrorism and, importantly, in defining the types of policy options that are available. The case of the PKK underscores some of the shortcomings of relying on these frameworks and highlights the need to further explore the nuances of the relationship between VNSAs and base states. In particular, assessing the cost of compliance for these base states requires a move toward assessing both the foreign policy and the domestic relationship between the violent group and the state. Clearly, these are not always ironclad relationships, and thus it is essential to further explore how such ties can be loosened or severed. Even in cases where strategic support exists, such as in the case of Syria and the PKK, fissures in relationships can occur or be produced through coercion. Thus it is important to disaggregate differences within this category of states, as it is precisely these differences that may represent different opportunities for coercion success. Sponsorship of violent groups can vary dramatically over time, across different issues, and in regard to different strategies that a violent group employs. Some relationships may in fact possess these deeply ingrained ties, whereas other base states may have much more superficial relationships with these groups.

Similarly, observing the KRG's willingness and ability to act against the PKK highlights the potential for weak states to combat violent groups. This observation leads one to reevaluate what capacity, particularly what military capacity is actually necessary to contain VNSAs. Even absent coercion, one can observe ostensibly weak states acting with surprising force and competency against violent groups. For example, although Pakistan has hovered at the top of the Fragile State Index, an annual ranking that assesses political risk and early warning of conflict, its military offensive in the Swat Valley once again demonstrated that there existed latent capabilities that could be used effectively against the Taliban and Al Qaeda.[90] These examples of putatively weak states acting against VNSAs requires a deeper understanding of the actual limits of their power and whether their inaction is driven by a lack of will or interests on the part of the base state rather than the base state's weakness per se. Not all weak states are created equal, and it is necessary to examine why at

---

[90] "Special Report: 2010 Failed States Index. Interactive Map and Rankings," *Foreign Policy*, June 16, 2010, http://www.foreignpolicy.com/articles/2010/06/21/2010_failed_states_index_interactive_map_and_rankings.

times they mobilize their limited resources to confront these types of threats. From a policy perspective, it is clear that relying on aggregate measures of state capacity can mislead one to underestimate their actual capacity to act. As the United States and others select their strategies, targets, or partners in their fights against safe havens, it is crucial that they engage in these strategic choices with a firm understanding of the limits and possibilities of the states most confronted with these challenges.

Ultimately, placing the onus of containing violent groups back on the states that are hosting them is an attractive and a potentially efficacious strategy. While transitive compellence is not easy, the case of the PKK highlights that even surprising and ostensibly challenging bases can be coerced into taking meaningful action against the violent groups that reside within their borders. Even these states, in response to coercion, were able and willing to uphold their sovereign responsibilities as states within the international system.

CHAPTER 7

Coercion by Movement

How Power Drove the Success of the Eritrean Insurgency, 1960–1993

PETER KRAUSE

When there is no enemy within, the enemies outside cannot hurt you.

—AFRICAN PROVERB

WHEN AND WHY DO insurgencies and national movements succeed or fail?[1] Why, for instance, have the Algerians and Zionists achieved a state, but the Palestinians and Kurds have not? Why did the Eritrean insurgency fail for three decades, only to become Africa's first successful postcolonial national movement?

Each of these movements initiated numerous campaigns of coercion against its enemies, and yet we lack parsimonious and powerful theories to explain variation in their outcomes. As the other chapters in this volume demonstrate, studies of state coercion provide many of the building blocks—power, collective action, credibility, signaling. However, new theories of coercion are needed to explain the behavior and effectiveness of nonstate actors, whether as coercers or targets, as Fraiman's and Walsh's chapters in this volume analyze. Many studies treat insurgencies as unitary actors or narrowly focus on single groups, but the most powerful assessments of nonstate coercion are based on two-level models of groups that share a common strategic goal but are driven by their own selfish organizational interests.[2] Although these actors

---

[1] I would like to thank Eleanor Hildebrandt and the Project on National Movements and Political Violence for their research assistance, and Kelly M. Greenhill, Costantino Pischedda, and Michael Woldemariam for their excellent comments and suggestions.

[2] For studies that treat insurgencies as unitary actors, see Jason Lyall and Isaiah Wilson, "Rage against the Machines: Explaining Outcomes in Counterinsurgency Wars," *International Organization* 63, no. 1 (January 2009): 67–106; Erica Chenoweth and Maria Stephan, *Why Civil Resistance Works: The Strategic Logic of Nonviolent Conflict* (New York: Columbia University Press, 2011). For studies that focus on groups, see Max Abrahms, "Why Terrorism Does Not Work," *International Security* 31, no. 2 (Fall 2006): 42–78; Seth G. Jones and Martin Libicki, *How Terrorist Groups End*

and scenarios may be relatively new for coercion studies that have focused on strong, cohesive states coercing each other, they are some of the most ubiquitous historically. This chapter therefore provides fresh insight not only into the likely future dynamics of insurgencies in Syria, civil war in Ukraine, and clashing national movements in Israel and Palestine, but also into past political struggles across time and space.

In addition to scholars who point to external factors like regime type or the end of colonialism and the Cold War, some have begun to analyze the impact of movement structure on outcome.[3] These scholars analyze structure based on the number of groups in a movement or the existence of alliances among them, and then claim that either fragmented or united movements and insurgencies are most likely to succeed. The fundamental problem is that, despite elegant theories and impressive analyses of data sets and key historical cases, these studies largely overlook the key variable for understanding both the use and effectiveness of violence by national movements and insurgencies: power.[4]

The balance of power within a movement drives its outcome, and groups' positions within that balance of power drive their behavior. Although all groups prioritize their organizational strength and survival, hegemonic groups that dominate their movements are more likely to pursue the shared strategic objective of statehood because victory moves them from the head of a movement to the head of a new state. The hegemonic group's dominance also decreases the likelihood of counterproductive infighting, outbidding, chain-ganging, and spoiling among competing groups in the movement, while also allowing the movement to deliver a single clear, credible message about its objectives, threats, and guarantees. Movements with multiple significant groups (whether fragmented or united) are less likely to be effective because the leading and challenging groups will put less effort into the shared objective and will spend more time fighting one another, outbidding for support, spoiling each other's

---

(Santa Monica, CA: RAND, 2008); Audrey Kurth Cronin, *How Terrorism Ends: Understanding the Decline and Demise of Terrorist Campaigns* (Princeton, NJ: Princeton University Press, 2009). For two-level models, see Kristin Bakke, Kathleen Cunningham, and Lee Seymour, "A Plague of Initials: Fragmentation, Cohesion, and Infighting in Civil Wars," *Perspectives on Politics* 10, no. 2 (June 2012): 265–83; Paul Staniland, "Organizing Insurgency: Networks, Resources, and Rebellion in South Asia," *International Security* 37, no. 1 (Summer 2012): 142–77; Peter Krause, "The Political Effectiveness of Non-State Violence: A Two-Level Framework to Transform a Deceptive Debate," *Security Studies* 22, no. 2 (June 2013): 259–94.

[3] David Cunningham, "Veto Players and Civil War Duration," *American Journal of Political Science* 50, no. 4 (October 2006): 875–92; Kathleen Cunningham, "Divide and Conquer or Divide and Concede: How Do States Respond to Internally Divided Separatists?," *American Political Science Review* 105, no. 2 (May 2011): 275–97; Wendy Pearlman, *Violence, Nonviolence, and the Palestinian National Movement* (New York: Cambridge University Press, 2011); Jesse Driscoll, "Commitment Problems or Bidding Wars? Rebel Fragmentation as Peace Building," *Journal of Conflict Resolution* 56, no. 1 (February 2012): 118–49.

[4] One excellent exception is Fotini Christia, *Alliance Formation in Civil Wars* (Cambridge: Cambridge University Press, 2012), although her dependent variable is alliances among groups, not movement success.

negotiations, and sending mixed messages to the enemy they want to coerce. These are the key claims of what I call *Movement Structure Theory*.

This chapter will test Movement Structure Theory (MST) and its competitors using a longitudinal analysis of the Eritrean national movement from 1960 to 1993. The Eritrean movement had no impact on the creation and initial analysis of MST, which focused on the Middle East.[5] As Africa's first successful postcolonial national movement is becoming increasingly prominent within the literature on civil wars, insurgencies, and national movements, the Eritrean movement offers potential external validity for the theory as a crucial out-of-sample case.[6] It offers extensive variation on both the independent and dependent variables: the movement experienced periods of fragmented, united, and hegemonic structures as well as total failure and total success. This within-case variation allows for clear tests of competing arguments due to tight comparisons across coercive campaigns, as the movement structure changes but the actors and other key variables remain largely the same. As the analysis will show, a movement with the same actors, same foreign supporters, same demands, and same strategies failed in the 1960s and 1970s, yet succeeded in the 1980s and 1990s because the movement's balance of power shifted from fragmented and united to hegemonic.

These conclusions help explain when and why insurgencies are more likely to successfully coerce more capable state enemies. More specifically, they explain when and why insurgent groups will focus their efforts on coercing such external foes in the first place, instead of expending their energy on brute force struggles with internal rivals.

Movement Structure Theory: How Structure Drives Outcome

Groups in a national movement share the common strategic objective of independence, but that does not mean that independence is the top priority for each group.[7] On the contrary, groups care first and foremost about their survival and influence, which is secured through one essential factor: power. By securing

---

[5] Peter Krause, *Rebel Power: Why National Movements Compete, Fight, and Win* (Ithaca: Cornell University Press, 2017).

[6] Four of the best studies are Michael Woldemariam, "Why Rebels Collide: Factionalism and Fragmentation in African Insurgencies" (Ph.D. dissertation, Princeton University, 2011); Michael Woldemariam, "Battlefield Outcomes and Rebel Cohesion: Lessons from the Eritrean Independence War," *Terrorism and Political Violence*, (July 2014): 1–22; Nikolaos Biziouras, "The Genesis of the Modern Eritrean Struggle (1942–1961)," *Journal of the Middle East and Africa* 4, no. 1 (January 2013): 21–46; Costantino Pischedda, "Wars within Wars: Making Sense of Inter-Rebel Fighting" (Ph.D. dissertation, Columbia University, 2014). I thank Costantino Pischedda for suggesting the relevance of this case.

[7] Parts of this section are drawn from Peter Krause, "The Structure of Success: How the Internal Distribution of Power Drives Armed Group Behavior and National Movement Effectiveness," *International Security* 38, no. 3 (Winter 2013–2014): 72–116. © 2013 by the President and Fellows of Harvard College and the Massachusetts Institute of Technology, published by the MIT Press.

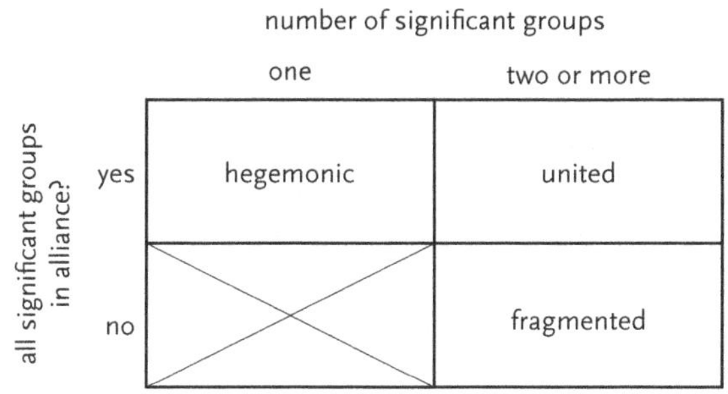

FIGURE 7.1 A Typology of Movement Structure

more members, guns, and money, nonstate groups increase their organizational strength, which is essential in an anarchical environment where the ruling regime, foreign states, and other groups in the same movement all seek their destruction. Although individuals in a movement may act selflessly at times, groups almost always prioritize their selfish organizational goals over the strategic goals they share with the movement.[8] Given group preferences and the fact that creating a new state is a costly endeavor, when and why would national movements ever succeed?

Groups are selfish, but the structure of their movement drives how they can best pursue that self-interest. The structure of a movement is defined by its internal balance of power, which is based on the number of significant groups it contains.[9] A *significant group* is either the strongest group in the movement or one with the strength to challenge for movement leadership.[10] The key distinction in structure is between those movements with one significant group and those with two or more—in other words, between movements with a competitive or a noncompetitive internal environment (see Figure 7.1).

Movements with one significant group are labeled hegemonic because they contain a single dominant group. The movement may contain any number of *subordinate* groups that pose no real threat to the *hegemon*, but a hegemonic movement contains no *challengers*. On the other hand, fragmented and united groups have a *leader* but no *hegemon*, because they contain one or more *challengers* that could overtake the movement *leader*. A united movement has all significant groups in an alliance, while a fragmented group does not. United movements are often not much different in actions or outcomes from fragmented movements, however, because alliances between nonstate actors are

[8] Krause, "The Political Effectiveness of Non-State Violence."

[9] As with great powers of the international system or effective parties of party systems, significant groups are the actors that drive campaign dynamics and whose number defines the structure of a movement.

[10] "Because the strength of armed groups is far more volatile than that of states, this study considers a group significant if its membership size, economic wealth, or seat distribution in common political institutions is one-third as large as that of the strongest group" (Krause, "The Structure of Success," 76).

so weak and wracked by commitment problems and struggles over relative power.[11] A group's position as a *hegemon, leader, challenger*, or *subordinate* drives its actions; a movement's position as hegemonic, united, or fragmented drives its outcome (see Table 7.1).

Hegemonic movements are far more likely to achieve success in the form of recognition by the United Nations, sovereign control of territory, and the creation of a new state than fragmented or united movements because of their complementary group incentives, lack of counterproductive mechanisms, and increased coherence and credibility.[12]

First, hegemonic movements are most effective because they align organizational and strategic goals. In other words, the thing that can best improve the hegemon's strength and security is movement victory, which means that the hegemon is far more likely to pursue it. In national movements, the achievement of statehood carries with it a collection of public, private, and club goods that largely accrue after victory. The balance of power inside the movement at the time of victory is likely to replicate itself inside the new state because stronger organizations are more likely to win any subsequent competitions against their weaker peers in armed conflicts or electoral campaigns. This means that although all individuals and groups in a particular movement enjoy the public good of removing a hated regime or military occupation, the strongest group is likely to capture most of the club and private goods of citizenship, political office, wealth, and status after independence is achieved.

Therefore the strongest group—whether the hegemon or the leader—is more likely to pursue the strategic objective than challengers or subordinate groups, which are less likely to capture any club or private goods. Hegemons are even more likely to pursue the strategic goal than are leaders, because—should the movement succeed—they are virtually assured of inheriting the leadership of the new state and its selective benefits. A leader, on the other hand, must be concerned that one or more of its challengers could capture some or all of these benefits given its relative strength. Furthermore, the only significant threat to the hegemon is the regime, whereas leaders must be concerned with both internal and external threats, making it less likely that they will put as many of their resources into pursuing the strategic objective. In sum, a group's pursuit of strategic objectives is driven by its position of power inside its movement. For a national movement in particular, it is best to be on top when the music stops, which means that hegemons will push hardest to win in short order, whereas weaker challengers will try to keep the party going until they assume the top spot.

Second, hegemonic movements are less likely to suffer the negative effects of infighting, outbidding, chain-ganging, spoiling, and foreign influence that

---

[11] When meaningful "unity" happens in the form of a formal merger, it is usually a significant actor swallowing a subordinate group, demonstrating again that relative power is the most important element of movement structure.

[12] Failure to achieve recognition from the UN, sovereign control of territory, or the creation of a new state is coded as "failure." Achievement of each objective is coded as "limited success," "moderate success," and "total success," respectively.

TABLE 7.1 Predictions of Movement Structure Theory

CAMPAIGN	MOVEMENT SYSTEM	MOVEMENT HIERARCHY	PREDICTED GROUP ACTIONS	PREDICTED MOVEMENT OUTCOME
Campaign 1	fragmented	1. group A 2. group B 3. group C	Groups C and B use violence to pursue pure organizational goals. Group A partially pursues strategic goals. Infighting and mixed messaging are likely.	failure
Campaign 2	fragmented	1. group C 2. group A 3. group B	Groups B and A use violence to pursue pure organizational goals. Group C partially pursues strategic goals. Infighting and mixed messaging are likely.	failure
Campaign 3	united	1. group C 2. group A 3. group B	Groups B and A use violence to pursue pure organizational goals. Group A partially pursues strategic goals. Infighting and mixed messaging are likely.	failure or limited success
Campaign 4	fragmented	1. group C 2. group A	Group A uses violence to pursue pure organizational goals. Group C partially pursues strategic goals. Infighting and mixed messaging are likely.	failure
Campaign 5	hegemonic	1. group C	Group C pursues strategic goals. Infighting and mixed messaging are unlikely.	moderate or total success

The predicted movement outcomes should be understood as probabilistic predictions of relative success between movement system types. Note that this table and Table 7.2 present the hierarchy among significant groups—hegemons, leaders, and challengers—for the purposes of simplicity, but each movement is likely to have many less powerful subordinates ranked below these groups as well.

SOURCE: Peter Krause, "The Structure of Success: How the Internal Distribution of Power Drives Armed Group Behavior and National Movement Effectiveness," *International Security* 38, no. 3 (Winter 2013–14): 79.

increase when groups compete for resources amid fragmentation. A fight between a hegemon and a subordinate has both a certain outcome and a brief time span, making it less likely to occur and less costly if it does. On the other hand, groups are far more likely to attack each other directly in a fragmented or united movement, as challengers can realistically employ violence in attempts to climb the movement ladder, and leaders can do the same in attempts to shove them down it. These internal fights between near equals are often costly in scarce human and monetary resources, and they divert movement effort away from the shared strategic objective.

Similarly, the increased probability of organizational success means that challengers are more likely than subordinates to attempt to violently outbid a leader, chain-gang the leader into an unwanted conflict, or spoil the leader's negotiations with the regime. Challengers have the unique combination of being more risk-acceptant than leaders or hegemons but also having enough capability that other groups find it difficult to restrain or simply ignore their attempts at outbidding, chain-ganging, or spoiling.[13] Although leaders and hegemons are both risk-averse given their pole position, hegemons find it far easier to ignore strategically counterproductive attempts at outbidding, chain-ganging, or spoiling due to their relative dominance. This makes the emergence of such counterproductive mechanisms less likely in hegemonic movements, which translates to more resources expended on external fights than internal ones, and subsequently greater strategic success.

In addition to these mechanisms, movements with multiple significant groups represent buyers' markets for foreign influence, allowing multiple rival states to control groups for their own ends. Hegemonic movements create the opposite situation, whereby a sellers' market for influence means that the hegemon is the only significant actor to support, giving it control over foreign donations and movement priorities. Given the hegemon's relative focus on strategic goals as compared to the leaders and challengers in fragmented and united movements, this makes strategic success more likely.

Third, a hegemonic movement has greater coherence in strategy, clarity in signaling, and credibility in threats and assurances. Because national movements rarely exterminate their foes, they generally must coerce the regime and international actors to change their policies, remove their troops, and recognize the new state. Fragmented and united movements have a difficult time doing so because their multiple significant groups send mixed messages about demands and threats. Furthermore, the lack of movement cohesion cripples the credibility of claims that movement actors will end the fighting or accept any concessions as final. By contrast, hegemonic movements are able to send clearer threats and guarantees, and their credibility is much higher due to the fact that a single powerful organization with a single leadership can more easily deliver any concessions and restrain any backlash.

[13] On the role of group strength and spoiling, see Kelly M. Greenhill and Solomon Major, "The Perils of Profiling Civil War Spoilers and the Collapse of Intrastate Peace Accords," *International Security* 31, no. 3 (Winter 2006–2007): 7–40.

The Eritrean National Movement: The Long Struggle for Hegemony and Independence

The campaigns of the Eritrean national movement summarized in Table 7.2 match up quite well with the predictions of Movement Structure Theory in Table 7.1. The Eritrean national movement was more successful when hegemonic than when united or fragmented due to a greater focus on strategic goals, less internal competition and infighting, and more clear and credible signaling. After analyzing the influence of the movement balance of power on group action and movement outcome, this section will engage with key competing arguments for the theory and the Eritrean case.

Eritrea 1891–1952: Fragmented Beginnings

According to many scholars, Eritrea is a prime case for the emergence of a fragmented national movement due to its extensive ethnolinguistic and topographical diversity.[14] Eritreans claim nine ethnolinguistic groups within their borders, a population nearly evenly divided between Christians and Muslims, and a mix of coastal lowlands, extensive highlands, and desert landscapes (see Figure 7.2). Many of these ethnic differences were reinforced under the Italians, who colonized Eritrea from 1891 to 1941 before being forced out of the strategic Red Sea territory by the Allies during World War II.[15] The British placed Eritrea under military administration while its future was debated in local, regional, and international circles.

Ruth Iyob writes, "Suddenly freed from colonial direction, [Eritrean actors] moved about the stage in confusion, animated by largely inchoate, contradictory, and competing nationalist agendas."[16] After the British lifted the ban on political parties in 1946, the nascent national movement experienced extensive fragmentation among groups like the Muslim League, the Liberal Progressive Party, and the Unionist Party, who variously sought immediate independence for Eritrea, a 10-year international trusteeship, and some form of union with neighboring Muslim Sudan and Christian Ethiopia. Despite proclamations of the need to work together and the fact that each party perceived itself as pursuing Eritrean nationalism, competition over political power and groups' associated prioritization of pan-African, Muslim, Christian, or secular national identity helped drive mistrust and infighting.[17]

---

[14] For discussions of relevant literature, see Donald Horowitz, *Ethnic Groups in Conflict* (Berkeley: University of California Press, 1985); James Fearon and David Laitin, "Ethnicity, Insurgency, and Civil War," *American Political Science Review* 97, no. 1 (2003): 75–90.

[15] Okbazghi Yohannes, *Eritrea: A Pawn in World Politics* (Gainesville: University Press of Florida, 1991), 8–16.

[16] Ruth Iyob, *The Eritrean Struggle for Independence: Domination, Resistance, Nationalism, 1941–1993* (Cambridge: Cambridge University Press, 1995), 4.

[17] Iyob, *The Eritrean Struggle for Independence*, 56–57, 72.

TABLE 7.2 Summary of Campaigns in the Eritrean National Movement, 1960–1993

TIME PERIOD	MOVEMENT SYSTEM STRUCTURE	HIERARCHY OF GROUPS AT START OF CAMPAIGN	SUMMARY OF GROUP ACTIONS	STRATEGIC OUTCOME OF CAMPAIGN
1960–62	fragmented	1. ELM 2. ELF	The newer, weaker ELF challenger strikes first and criticizes the ELM for being pacifist. Ethiopia abrogates the federation with Eritrea and makes it an Ethiopian province.	failure
1962–65	fragmented	1. ELF 2. ELM	After the ELM weakens and fighters flock to the ELF, the ELM launches its own operations in 1965, but its fighters are eliminated by the ELF.	failure
1965–70	united	1. ELF Zone 1 2. ELF Zone 2 3. ELF Zone 4 4. ELF Zone 3 5. ELF Zone 5	After the ELM fades away, the autonomous ELF zone commanders compete with one another for power before splitting starts in 1967. The ELF gains before an Ethiopian offensive nearly crushes it.	failure
1970–73	fragmented	1. ELF[1] 2. Ala group 3. PLF 4. Obel group	The ELF splinters; infighting and full-on civil war emerge in 1972 to the detriment of the movement.	failure
1973–75	fragmented	1. ELF 2. EPLF	The EPLF is created by the merger of Ala group, PLF, and members of the Obel group. Civil war continues as ELF fails to eliminate its growing rival while Ethiopians look on.	failure
1975–77	fragmented	1. EPLF 2. ELF	Harsh Ethiopian tactics and the downfall of the Selassie regime help the EPLF and ELF each gain new recruits and control of ~40% of Eritrea. The EPLF and ELF agree to focus on the Ethiopians, but infighting and splitting continue.	limited success
1977–83	fragmented	1. EPLF 2. ELF	The Ethiopian army pushes back against the EPLF and ELF, who accuse one another of treasonous retreats. The EPLF attacks the ELF, which weakens, splinters, and is no longer a challenger to the EPLF.	failure
1983–93	hegemonic	1. EPLF	The EPLF absorbs ELF splinters, makes diplomatic gains, defeats the Ethiopian forces on the battlefield, helps overthrow the Ethiopian regime, and wins independence.	total success

[1]The ELF label here refers to the core ELF group: the ELF General Command from 1969 to 1971 and the ELF Revolutionary Council from 1971 onward.

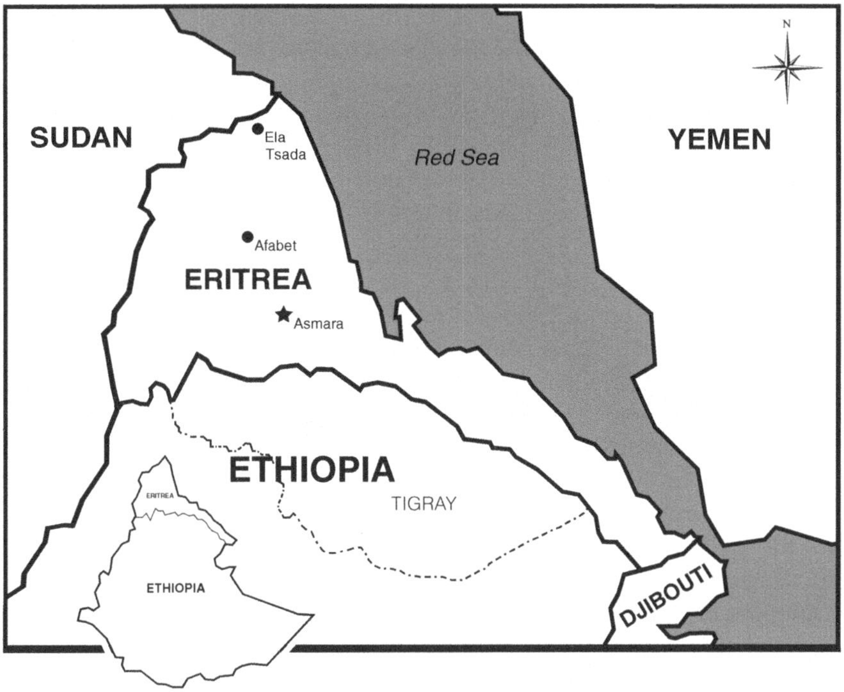

FIGURE 7.2 Eritrea and Ethiopia
SOURCE: University of Texas Libraries, http://www.lib.utexas.edu/maps/africa/eritrea_pol86.jpg.

The pro-independence parties split into four and then six competing groups in the late 1940s, and attempts at mergers and alliances failed as internal violence increased.[18] Such fragmentation and mixed messages allowed external actors like the Ethiopian monarch Haile Selassie to play factions against one another and successfully map their own desires onto many Eritreans. The United Nations voted for a federation between Ethiopia and Eritrea in 1952, even though many parts of Eritrea had never been under Ethiopian rule. Eritrean fragmentation had helped the nascent movement miss an opportunity for independence, not for the last time.

The Beginning of Armed Competition and Armed Struggle: 1960–1965

The lack of a robust, hegemonic national movement allowed Selassie to dismantle the federation during the 1950s and officially annex Eritrea as Ethiopia's 14th province in 1962. As the Eritrean flag was replaced by the Ethiopian in 1958, the Eritrean Liberation Movement (ELM) emerged to try to lead the national

[18] Iyob, *The Eritrean Struggle for Independence*, 72–73; Biziouras, "The Genesis of the Modern Eritrean Struggle."

movement. Formed by five Muslim exiles in Sudan who were influenced by the Communist Party there, the ELM founders sought to unite Eritreans through a secular message.[19] Cognizant of the previous failures of petitions and marches, the ELM initially planned to overthrow the regime in a coup, but it never came close to fruition. The clandestine nature of the organization—due in part to the 1954 banning of political parties—makes assessment of its strength difficult, but it is clear that it was the leading Eritrean nationalist actor in the early 1960s.[20]

In 1960 a challenger to the ELM's leadership arose in the form of the Eritrean Liberation Front (ELF). Founded in Cairo by exiles with ties to the Muslim League, the group was influenced by Arab nationalism and the ongoing revolution in Algeria. The competition between the organizations was clear from the very first shot, ironically fired by *shifta* chieftain Hamid Idris Awate and 13 fighters against police units on September 1, 1961. Both ELF and ELM claimed Awate as their own after his death a few months later, and the war of words helped expose the ELM and spark an Ethiopian crackdown that weakened the group.[21] The rising ELF challenger proceeded to launch attacks while criticizing the ELM leader for its "peaceful struggle."[22]

After the ELF passed the ELM as the new movement leader, the ELM let the ELF know that it was going to launch armed struggle against the Ethiopian regime in earnest in 1965.[23] The new challenger received an ultimatum in return, saying that it should unite with the ELF or face elimination. When the ELM sent 50 soldiers into Eritrea to fight against the Ethiopians anyway, they were ambushed at Ela Tsada, not by the Ethiopians but by the ELF, who killed many of the ELM fighters and disarmed the rest. The ELM disintegrated thereafter, and many of its members joined the ELF.[24] Iyob argues, "Ironically, in the end, the first Eritrean resistance movement, which has shown so much promise in its early days in 1958 due to its rejection of confessional and ideational rivalry, was mortally wounded by a rival group professing to share its goal of liberating Eritrea by armed struggle."[25] According to MST, there is nothing ironic about it: significant groups competing over power and position are

---

[19] T. H. Faddab, *Harakat al-Tahrir Iritiriya wa Masiratihya al-Tarihkiyya* (The Eritrean Liberation Movement and Its Historic Fate) (Cairo: Sharuf Press, 1994).

[20] Markakis claims that the ELM membership reached 40,000, although this is likely an overestimate. Nonetheless, there was no rival group with greater numbers. John Markakis, *National and Class Conflict in the Horn of Africa* (Cambridge: Cambridge University Press, 1987), 286.

[21] Markakis, *National and Class Conflict in the Horn of Africa*, 108.

[22] ELF, *Eritrea: The National Democratic Revolution versus Ethiopian Expansionism* (Beirut: ELF Foreign Information Centre, 1979), 30.

[23] By 1964, the ELF had gained Eritrean nationals from the Sudanese army, influxes of "peasants, workers, and students," foreign-trained fighters with Kalashnikovs, and some former ELM members (ELF, *Eritrea*, 31–32). The ELF claimed to have 250 fighters by 1963. ELF, *The Eritrean Revolution: 16 Years of Armed Struggle, September 1, 1961–September 1, 1977* (Beirut: ELF Foreign Information Centre, 1977), 36. Sabbe claims the same figure for the ELF in 1964. Uthman Salih Sabbe, *The Roots of Eritrean Disagreements and How to Solve Them*, (n.p., n.d.,1978), 41.

[24] David Pool, *From Guerrillas to Government: The Eritrean People's Liberation Front* (Oxford: James Currey, 2001), 62.

[25] Iyob, *The Eritrean Struggle for Independence*, 106.

prone to infighting not just *in spite of* but precisely *because* they share a common goal as well as a common base of support, spoils to win, and a movement to lead.

The Splintering of the ELF and the Rise of New Challengers: 1965–1973

Unfortunately for the movement, just as the ELF was eliminating its greatest internal competition from the field, its leaders decided to restructure their membership into a loosely united collection of autonomous groups rather than a single hegemonic organization to lead the struggle. The ELF had 500 to 1,000 fighters in 1965, a number that would continue to grow over the next few years.[26] Rather than attempt to mold these recruits into a cohesive organization with a single leadership that operated across Eritrea, the ELF divided the territory into four and later five zones, and "zone commanders continued to have full authority over their respective territories and armies."[27] There were no horizontal links between zonal groups, whose autonomous warlords had to procure their own weapons through separate and competing patronage networks.[28]

As such, the ELF in this period was truly a front of united groups or "mini-kingdoms" rather than a single cohesive organization that dominated the movement.[29] As the ELF itself admitted, "according to the zonal structure, the military commanders were given [a] free hand to engage themselves in unrevolutionary practices. Each zonal command recruit[ed] from its 'own' localities and entered contest with the others. Cooperation among the zones became virtually non-existent."[30] Furthermore, "on the external level, the front did not achieve any significant success .... No good propaganda work was carried out nor any clear-cut programme laid down for the internal and external activities of the organization."[31] The division hurt battlefield performance, as "the increasing success of the Ethiopian army in dealing with the Eritrean insurgency was also laid at the door of fragmented political and military structures" by ELF "reformists."[32] One former ELF member recalled, "Even in battles, you

---

[26] FO 371/183840, VA 1015/17, British Embassy, Addis Ababa, April 14, 1965; Roy Pateman, *Eritrea: Even the Stones Are Burning* (Trenton, NJ: Red Sea Press, 1998), 98.

[27] Iyob, *The Eritrean Struggle for Independence*, 112.

[28] Dan Connell, *Against All Odds: A Chronicle of the Eritrean Revolution* (Trenton, NJ: Red Sea Press, 1993), 76–77. For information on the balance of power among the zonal groups, see ELF, *Eritrea*, 34–40; Dan Connell, *Conversations with Eritrean Political Prisoners* (Trenton, NJ: Red Sea Press, 2005), 30–34. The patron of Zone 2, Idris Ghalaudios, competed with the patron of Zone 4, Uthman Sabbe, for Chinese support because he knew "it would affect their power base—the balance of power among divisions" (Connell, *Conversations with Eritrean Political Prisoners*, 45).

[29] The best evidence for this is that a loose alliance between just three of the five zonal groups was perceived as an *advance* toward greater cohesion, revealing how the ELF could not be considered a single organization previously (ELF, *Eritrea*, 34).

[30] Ibid., 33.

[31] Ibid., 32.

[32] Pool, *From Guerrillas to Government*, 54.

prefer to guard yourself from bullets that come through behind, rather than from the front."[33]

The fact that the ELF was not a single, cohesive organization became abundantly clear when it finally tried to become one in 1968–70: it failed. In the aftermath of the ELF's killing hundreds of Christian fighters recruited by those who wished to reform the front, competing attempts to merge the zonal groups—including the ELF's First National Congress in 1969—only created deeper cleavages.[34] Multiple factions formally split off from the ELF and formed their own nationalist armed groups, ending hopes of continued movement unity. The first group was the Popular Liberation Forces (PLF), which itself formed from two factions of ELF dissidents that united in July 1970.[35] From the outset, the PLF aimed to attract ELF fighters to its banner, and it was initially composed of a faction from Zone 4 and former ELF fighters from across Eritrea. A second organization of Christian Tigrinya speakers known as Selfi Natzinet, or the Ala group, emerged from the former Zone 5 of the ELF starting in 1969.[36] The Eritrean Liberation Forces, or Obel group, was formed in November 1970 from disaffected fighters of Zone 1 of the ELF.

MST correctly predicts the increase in violence, as "the growing splits within the Eritrean movement was a crucial factor in the increase in the number of actions, as rival factions competed for popular support."[37] The growing threat of an ELF crackdown against its challengers helped push them to unite, as the PLF, Ala group, and Obel group met in June 1970 and elected a joint political and military leadership. The strengthening alliance united their fighters with the significant funding of Uthman Sabbe's ELF–General Secretariat group (which had also split from ELF) at a meeting in Beirut in 1972. These groups still represented a united front rather than a single cohesive organization, as they agreed to dual autonomy and mutual noninterference. The balance of power among them was roughly embodied by the 57-member Gehteb executive committee formed in October 1972: 25 members from the Ala group, 21 from the PLF, and 11 from the Obel group.

The ELF failed to bring the competing alliance to heel, as all of its groups rejected the ELF's invitation to a national conference in 1971, which no doubt would have further cemented the ELF's leading position.[38] Although the ELF was the clear leader, it was not a dominant hegemon. The funding and arms from Sabbe's group ensured the ELF's challengers were better equipped but not yet more numerous. These realizations drove the ELF to declare war on the fledgling Eritrean People's Liberation Front (EPLF) in February 1972.[39]

---

[33] Connell, *Conversations with Eritrean Political Prisoners*, 33.

[34] Pool, *From Guerrillas to Government*, 55; Haggai Erlich, *The Struggle over Eritrea, 1962–1978: War and Revolution in the Horn of Africa* (Stanford, CA: Hoover Institution Press, 1983), 24.

[35] Pool, *From Guerrillas to Government*, 64.

[36] Ibid.

[37] Erlich, *The Struggle over Eritrea*, 28.

[38] Iyob, *The Eritrean Struggle for Independence*, 115.

[39] Pool, *From Guerrillas to Government*, 134.

"The Eritrean Field Cannot Bear More Than One Organization": 1973–1983

In an unintentional endorsement of Movement Structure Theory, the ELF proclaimed in 1971 and again in 1973 that the "Eritrean field cannot bear more than one organization and one leadership."[40] Although the ELF's argument that victory would arrive only after movement hegemony ultimately proved true, its main challenger disagreed over who that hegemon should be, fought with the ELF as the movement lost ground, and eventually assumed the dominant role the ELF envisioned for itself. For a decade before the EPLF became the hegemon, however, infighting between the groups ravaged Eritrea and led the movement to the brink of disaster.

The ELF initiated civil war in 1972 against its former allies, who merged to form the EPLF in 1973. Not only did the movement lose territory to the Ethiopian army amid the civil war, but its groups also lost significant numbers of fighters without changing the structure of the movement. Conflict between the ELF and EPLF ranged "from occasional skirmishes to several days of trench warfare fighting."[41] One observer noted, "The bulk of the fighting in the Eritrean countryside between February 1972 and October 1974 was between rival groups of Eritrean nationalists."[42] This observation is backed up by casualty figures: 3,000 dead from the civil war (100 deaths per month) compared to about 50 deaths per month in the Ethiopian army.[43] This level of movement losses was even more significant given that each group had fewer than 5,000 fighters at the time.[44]

The Ethiopians were happy to let the Eritreans do their work for them; they backed off and let the competing groups slug it out. Fighting against the Ethiopian military was so sporadic during this period that its officers used their time to plan a revolution of their own. It was this revolution that tossed the Eritrean national movement a life preserver as it consumed itself with infighting. Several earlier attempts to end the civil war failed, but a golden opportunity for the EPLF and ELF to enhance their positions at the expense of the Ethiopians—themselves now fragmented and consumed with infighting and consolidation—temporarily halted the civil war in November 1974, one month after the overthrow of Ethiopian emperor Haile Selassie.

In 1974–75 the ELF and EPLF jointly agreed to focus their efforts on the Ethiopians and the new ruling Coordinating Committee of military officers, generally known as the Derg. Unfortunately the fact that neither group was dominant meant that infighting continued to flare up even amid supposedly

---

40 Ibid., 70; Erlich, *The Struggle over Eritrea*, 30.

41 Pool, *From Guerrillas to Government*, 133.

42 Pateman, *Eritrea*, 132.

43 Erlich, *The Struggle over Eritrea*, 32; J. Bowyer Bell, "Endemic Insurgency and International Order: The Eritrean Experience," *Orbis* 18, no. 2 (1974): 442.

44 John Markakis, "The Nationalist Revolution in Eritrea," *Journal of Modern African Studies* 26, no. 1 (March 1988): 60; Pool, *From Guerrillas to Government*, 134–35; Woldemariam, "Why Rebels Collide," 184.

cooperative action, both before and after the ceasefire.[45] For example, as ELF and EPLF approached the capital city of Asmara for a joint attack against the Ethiopian forces, they kept fighting one another, including "an exceptionally bloody clash which lasted several days" just "eighteen kilometers from Asmara."[46]

Thankfully for the ELF and EPLF, the Derg's response to the Asmara assault played perfectly into their hands, as the reign of terror unleashed on the Eritrean civilian population (especially the youth) by the new Derg regime drove recruits to the insurgency as "thousands flocked to the fronts."[47] The ELF and EPLF both experienced a massive influx of 10,000 or more new fighters in 1974–75.[48] The ELF was still the leading group, but the EPLF was becoming a more robust challenger every day, as its increased activity "raised the profile of the EPLF and, allied with increased Ethiopian repression, enhanced recruitment."[49] The EPLF claimed 110 operations in 1975 in principal cities, including attacks on businesses, airports, and assassinations of Derg members.[50]

The ability of the ELF and EPLF to spend less time fighting each other and more time fighting the Ethiopians led to significant territorial gains from 1975 to 1978. By 1977 the national movement controlled the vast majority of Eritrea, and the ELF and EPLF had gained large numbers of fighters and captured a good deal of sophisticated weaponry.[51] However, the victories came in part because of the downfall of the Selassie government and civil war in Ethiopia, during which the Derg carried out multiple purges and fought new challengers to the regime amid their own fragmentation.[52] Just as the Derg began to solidify its position, a war with Somalia in the Ogaden further drained Ethiopian military strength from July 1977 to March 1978.

Despite all of these advantages, the Eritrean national movement was unable to secure independence because it remained fragmented. Members of the national movement collectively controlled most of the province (and would-be state), but the ELF and EPLF each controlled about 40 percent of it. Driven by organizational gains, the competing groups did not share captured territory or the authority over it, and they did not make a coordinated, concerted push for statehood.

Continued fragmentation in the movement hurt it diplomatically due to the lack of a single, clear message. Just as the EPLF tried to portray the Eritrean national movement as African and nonsectarian, the ELF portrayed it as Arab and Muslim. This alienated potential international backers and helped drive

---

[45] Awet Weldemichael, "The Eritrean Long March: The Strategic Withdrawal of the Eritrean People's Liberation Front (EPLF), 1978–1979," *Journal of Military History* 73, no. 4 (2009): 1234.

[46] Iyob, *The Eritrean Struggle for Independence*, 171.

[47] Pool, *From Guerrillas to Government*, 138.

[48] Woldemariam, "Why Rebels Collide," 114–15.

[49] Connell, *Against All Odds*, 43; Pool, *From Guerrillas to Government*, 138.

[50] Pool, *From Guerrillas to Government*, 138.

[51] Weldemichael claims that the two groups both had about 10 brigades of approximately 1,200 fighters in 1977, although the EPLF was turning members away while the ELF had to resort to conscription. Weldemichael, "The Eritrean Long March," 1238.

[52] Markakis, *National and Class Conflict in the Horn of Africa*, 240–44.

the United States, Israel, and others to line up behind Ethiopia, even after it was ruled by the Marxist Derg. The Derg was able to lure away state supporters of the Eritrean national movement—including South Yemen, Cuba, and Libya—by stressing the movement's fragmentation, which left it woefully unprepared for the coming Ethiopian counteroffensive.

Having defeated the Somalis in the Ogaden, destroyed many internal challengers, and gathered significant foreign support, the Derg launched a series of successful offensives in Eritrea in 1978–79, retaking vast tracts of territory from the ELF and EPLF. The Eritrean defense was far from coordinated. The ELF and EPLF not only fought with one another but also constantly accused each other of sabotage and retreats to hurt their nationalist rival, such as when the ELF unilaterally withdrew from the Sahel front on the EPLF's flank.[53] The recriminations and lack of cooperation led one observer to note a few years later that "Eritrean victory may realistically be excluded as a future possibility" because "the inhabitants of the peripheral coastal areas fell victim to disunity and decentralist tendencies resulting in military and political weakness."[54] The author had the reasoning right but the prediction wrong. He failed to recognize that in the aftermath of these setbacks, the cohesive EPLF would arise as a dominant hegemon that could marginalize internal challenges, gain international support, defeat the Derg on the battlefield, and, ultimately, secure the independence of an Eritrean state.

The EPLF overtook the ELF as the movement leader by 1977, when it held its first congress.[55] Unlike the ELF in the 1960s, the EPLF was not a loose coalition of autonomous organizations. The EPLF was a cohesive group, "differentiated from organizations operating in the same territory; autonomous; centralized; with internal structures coordinated with one another."[56] The EPLF had a clandestine party at its core (the Eritrean People's Revolutionary Party) and a clear leader from the outset, Isaias Afewerki, who led the group through its entire struggle and leads Eritrea to this day. The group actively worked to build an organization that smoothed over the ethnic and regional differences that plagued the ELF and other Eritrean groups, and so built a single, strong organization that was far less vulnerable to splits and was prepared to be a cohesive hegemon rather than a loosely allied front.

After the Ethiopian offensives failed to destroy the EPLF, the ELF turned down offers to merge into it and instead began to conduct negotiations with the Soviet Union to end the war on terms favorable to the ELF.[57] Unable to

[53] Iyob, *The Eritrean Struggle for Independence*, 121.
[54] Erlich, *The Struggle over Eritrea*, 119.
[55] Erlich explains that by 1977, "the more radical EPLF gained ascendance over the ELF as the strongest but definitely not the dominant factor in the movement" (Ibid., 18). The EPLF had 20,000 to 30,000 fighters by 1978, and the ELF had 10,000 to 15,000. Pateman, *Eritrea*, 135; Pool, *From Guerrillas to Government*, 145–46; Iyob, *The Eritrean Struggle for Independence*, 109.
[56] Pool, *From Guerrillas to Government*, xv.
[57] Iyob, *The Eritrean Struggle for Independence*, 120–21; Markakis, "The Nationalist Revolution in Eritrea," 66–67.

gain hegemony via bargaining and concerned about the ELF cutting a deal that cut them out, the EPLF sought to eliminate its Eritrean rival from the field. The EPLF attacked the ELF in August 1980, and its superior forces drove them over the Sudanese border by the following year. The EPLF's victory over the ELF came with an assist from the anti-Derg Tigray People's Liberation Front (TPLF), which itself became a hegemonic group within the anti-Derg Ethiopian insurgency.

Unlike the first civil war within the Eritrean national movement that was detrimental over the short and long term, the second civil war resulted in a major power shift that set the stage for movement victory. A large number of ELF fighters joined the EPLF in the aftermath of the conflict, and what was left of the ELF split apart in 1982 over religious and personal cleavages. By the early 1980s, the ELF was a "spent force."[58] Any question about the EPLF's dominance was removed by the late 1980s, as one of the ELF splinter groups (the ELF–Central Committee, or Sagem) joined the EPLF in 1987, followed by most of the rest of the Eritrean Democratic Movement in 1990.[59]

The Rise of a Hegemon and the Independence of Eritrea: 1983–1993

The EPLF immediately used its burgeoning hegemonic position to make diplomatic gains. While conducting secret negotiations with the Derg from September 1982 to April 1985, the EPLF began to change the narrative and international status of the Eritrean national movement. The EPLF successfully presented itself and the movement as multireligious, multiethnic, pro-African entities that were struggling against colonialism from a state that had not historically ruled it. The EPLF no longer had to contend with the ELF's diplomatic message, which often cast the Eritrean movement as purely Muslim and/or Arab nationalist and turned off African and Western supporters. This was especially problematic given the unwritten rule at the United Nations that "regional matters" like Eritrean independence must be brought up first by the regional organization (in this case the Organisation of African Unity). This meant that the Eritrean national movement needed to win over African states before getting a full international hearing.[60] The lack of a need to rhetorically outbid the

[58] Pool, *From Guerrillas to Government*, 146. Markakis claims that the ELF's active strength was one-quarter of the EPLF's 40,000 members by 1980, making the EPLF a weak hegemon, which would soon become more dominant (*National and Class Conflict in the Horn of Africa*, 248).

[59] As one member of the ELF-RC noted, "The departure of the Sagem group was a final military blow, as until then the ELF, though considerably weakened, still had a viable military force" (Pool, *From Guerrillas to Government*, 147); EPLF, *Political Report and National Democratic Programme: Adopted at the Second and Unity Congress of the Eritrean People's Liberation Front and the Eritrean Liberation Front (Central Leadership)*, Asmara, Eritrea, March 19, 1987; Iyob, *The Eritrean Struggle for Independence*, 121.

[60] A. M. Babu, "The Eritrean Question in the Context of African Conflicts and Superpower Rivalries," in *The Long Struggle of Eritrea for Independence and Constructive Peace*, by Lionel Cliffe and Basil Davidson (Trenton, NJ: Red Sea Press, 1988).

ELF meant that the EPLF's 1987 National Democratic Program lacked the anti-American rhetoric of the 1977 version, making a more favorable U.S. position toward Eritrea and Ethiopia more likely.

As for potentially divisive foreign influences, the EPLF benefited from having actively "sought to create an organization which was autonomous not only of Eritrean society but impenetrable by external forces."[61] The Eritrean national movement was now a seller's market for influence, not the buyer's market of the 1960s and 1970s. This allowed the EPLF to control state supporters rather than be controlled by them. Amid a significant famine in late 1984, the EPLF's aid arm distributed massive amounts of aid from foreign NGOs in Scandinavian countries while the Ethiopian government strategically denied food to the population.[62] With no other significant organizations to compete with in Eritrea, the EPLF acquired quasi-state status and growing international support. On the other hand, the EPLF was able to benefit from Ethiopia's fragmentation, as the group supported the TPLF and other insurgent organizations seeking to topple the Derg.

Diplomatic gains greased the skids for eventual international recognition, but the Eritrean national movement would win independence on the battlefield. The EPLF created brigades of three battalions in 1977 (each battalion had 400 to 500 fighters at full strength). In the 1980s, the group formed its first divisions consisting of three brigades, and it added tank battalions and heavy artillery units as it captured heavier weapons.[63] Free to engage directly with the Ethiopian army without having to worry about the ELF guarding or, more likely, abandoning or attacking its flanks, the EPLF turned back an Ethiopian offensive in 1982—killing tens of thousands of the over 100,000-strong attacking force—and won its first tank battle in the open plains in 1984.[64] This set the stage for the EPLF's momentous victory at Afabet in 1988, which spelled the end of Ethiopian control of Eritrea over the next three years. The EPLF defeated a 20,000-strong Ethiopian force and captured 50 tanks and three Soviet colonels in a triumph described by Africa scholar and eyewitness Basil Davidson as "one of the biggest ever scored by any liberation movement anywhere since Dien Bien Phu in 1954."[65]

By the end of 1988, the EPLF possessed over 200 tanks and armored vehicles, had a small navy, and was better equipped than all but six African state armies.[66] Unlike the periods of fragmentation with the ELF, the

[61] Pool, *From Guerrillas to Government*, 26. Pateman agrees that "the EPLF remains free from outside influence to a unique degree" (*Eritrea*, 112).
[62] Pool, *From Guerrillas to Government*, 155.
[63] Ibid., 151.
[64] EPLF member Christian Sabatier said in 1982, "For our part, we have never been so well prepared; never was morale so high. The fact that the ELF was no longer in the picture simplified things for the EPLF, as their behavior was always ambiguous and unreliable to the point of cooperating with the Ethiopians themselves at times." "Interview with Christian Sabatier," *Eritrea Information* 4, no. 2 (February 1982): 4.
[65] Yohannes, *Eritrea: A Pawn in World Politics*, 272.
[66] Pateman, *Eritrea*, 121.

number of Eritreans killed as a result of infighting was very low. By contrast, the EPLF claimed to have killed or captured 60,000 Ethiopian soldiers in 118 battles in 1988 alone. Hegemony paid off: even though the ratio between the Ethiopian forces and EPLF was around 4:1, the battlefield mortality ratio approached 10:1, respectively.[67]

The EPLF took Asmara in 1991 and was able to bargain from a position of strength with the international community and a new Ethiopian regime (dominated by an old ally, the TPLF) to set a referendum on independence. The referendum passed in 1993 with 99.8 percent in favor. Eritrea became a member of the United Nations, and the EPLF ensured its total success as the group transitioned to a ruling political party that dominates Eritrea to this day.

Analysis of Competing Arguments

All major histories of the Eritrean national movement written by observers and participants alike explicitly remark on the perils of fragmentation and implicitly note the benefits of hegemony.[68] When considered alongside the analysis provided in this chapter (summarized in Table 7.2), it is quite clear that the theory that fragmented movements are most successful and gain the most concessions does not hold up in the Eritrean case. On the contrary, periods of fragmentation were generally the least successful for the movement.

The argument that united movements are the most successful performs no better. The one period of unity (1965–70) saw no success, while the greatest victories came during hegemony, when subordinate groups were not allied with the EPLF in any case. Many observers at the time and scholars today note the back-and-forth splits of the ELF and EPLF and the "Will they, won't they?" negotiations for unity between the groups as significant changes in the structure of the movement likely to have a significant impact on group actions and outcome. I have shown that it is not whether or not significant groups ally with one another that matters, but rather whether one is removed from the field as a significant challenger, either through destruction, merger, or both.

The ELF tried to get the EPLF's predecessors to unite in the early 1970s and failed. The ELF tried to get the EPLF to sign a unity deal in 1975 and failed, while the EPLF tried to get the ELF to sign a unity deal in 1978–80 and failed. The groups actually signed a unity deal in 1977, but it had no impact on group behavior or movement outcome. In November 1980, an EPLF

[67] Pateman, *Eritrea*, 124.

[68] Iyob, *The Eritrean Struggle for Independence*, 108–9; Pool, *From Guerrillas to Government*, xiv; ELF, *The Eritrean Revolution*; EPLF, *Political Report and National Democratic Programme*; Sabbe, *The Roots of Eritrean Disagreements and How to Solve Them*.

member even said, "As far as the EPLF is concerned, the Unity Agreement is still alive," just as the EPLF was directly attacking the ELF to drive it out of Eritrea.[69]

Theories that measure fragmentation simply by counting the number of groups without gauging their relative power fare poorly. For example, Uthman Sabbe formed a new organization, the Eritrean Liberation Front–Popular Liberation Forces, which split from the EPLF, later joined the ELF, and recruited fighters away from each group. In response to the ELF reunification with Sabbe, a new group, called the Eritrean Democratic Movement (labeled *fallul,* or "anarchists," in Tigrinya), split off from the ELF to form their own organization, which later merged with the EPLF in 1977.[70] Ultimately these shifts of two subordinate groups and their few thousand fighters between the ELF and EPLF did not alter the balance of power in the movement or its success. Furthermore, the major victories of the hegemonic EPLF came while numerous smaller groups still existed. These merged into the EPLF only after victory, not before. As MST suggests, it was not the number of groups but rather the number of significant groups that mattered.

Theories that argue that the absolute or relative size of the movement drives success similarly fail to explain the Eritrean case. There were approximately 40,000 Eritrean fighters split between the ELF and EPLF in 1977, and approximately 40,000 EPLF fighters in the early 1980s, and yet the two periods had quite different strategic outcomes. There were more fighters in the Eritrean national movement than there were members in the Ethiopian army in 1975–77, but the movement did not succeed.[71] However, when the major battles were won against the Ethiopian army and independence was secured, the EPLF and the rest of the movement were outnumbered by 3 to 1 or 4 to 1.[72] Theories that focus on absolute and relative movement size rather than movement structure would predict the opposite outcomes.

Others might suggest that the key to the success of the Eritrean national movement was a change in the Ethiopian regime rather than the movement. In particular, the removal of the unfavorable Derg by the favorable TPLF-led regime could explain Eritrean independence. Of course, the Eritrean national movement had seen this play before. The unfavorable Selassie regime that had annexed Eritrea was overthrown in 1974 and replaced with the Derg, who claimed, "No nationality will dominate another." The Derg's first leader of Ethiopia (Gen. Aman Andom) had talked about greater Eritrean autonomy, and the group's Marxist ideology seemed more amenable to the anticolonial Eritrean cause. Soon after taking power, the Derg killed General Andom and brutally

[69] "Interview with Alamin Mohamed Said," *Eritrea Information* 2, no. 10 (November 1980): 4. Joint Supreme Political Leadership (EPLF and ELF), "Important Declaration from the Joint Political Leadership," Rome: Research and Information Centre on Eritrea, April 6, 1979.

[70] Pool, *From Guerrillas to Government*, 142.

[71] There were no more than 25,000 Ethiopian soldiers in Eritrea in 1975–77, but there were 38,500 to 43,000 Eritrean fighters by 1977 (Erlich, *The Struggle over Eritrea*, 16, 72).

[72] Pateman, *Eritrea*, 124, 127.

fought the fragmented Eritrean national movement to maintain union with Ethiopia.

Lest one forget, the TPLF and EPLF were not always allies; they had experienced a falling out in 1976 and again in 1985 over the fact that the TPLF made claims on Eritrean territory and was not clearly in support of Eritrean independence.[73] The groups later patched things up, but it is not as if they simply got along once the Derg was gone. The TPLF-led government worked hard to keep Eritrea in Ethiopia with economic incentives, and the EPLF had to use its control of Eritrea and the subsequent referendum to outwit and coerce their sometime allies. After independence, Eritrea and Ethiopia fought a brutal war over territory with tens of thousands of casualties from 1998 to 2000, with the former head of the EPLF and then president of Eritrea Isaias Afewerki squaring off against the former head of the TPLF and then Ethiopian prime minister Meles Zenawi.

If the history of the Eritrean national movement teaches us anything, it is that yesterday's (or even today's) alliances mean little in the face of self-interest. To the extent the TPLF wanted to cut a deal short of independence, the hegemony of the EPLF made it impossible. To the extent the TPLF would have wanted to crush the Eritrean national movement, the hegemony of the EPLF made it unlikely. And to the extent that the rise of the TPLF does help explain Eritrean success, the arrows first go the other way. In other words, the hegemony and success of the EPLF made the victory of the TPLF possible long before the TPLF could negotiate for Eritrean independence. Furthermore, the story of the TPLF's insurgency also fits MST, as that movement did not succeed until it, too, became hegemonic.[74]

Other scholars may look outside of Eritrea itself and suggest that the movement was bound to succeed due to two of the most significant international developments of the twentieth century: the wave of anti-European colonialism and the end of the Cold War. Neither explanation holds up to scrutiny. First, there was no European colonialism in Eritrea after 1952. If anything, it was African on African colonialism—the Ethiopians were the ones annexing and controlling Eritrea, not the British or Italians—and that did not have the same normative cost. Indeed, the Organisation of African Unity (along with the United Nations) supported Ethiopia's annexation due to the fear of secession and the precedent it might set for their own states.[75] Hegemony allowed the EPLF to shift the facts on the Eritrean ground and the narrative in the international air, as it defeated "Black Africa's most prestigious and well-equipped army" to become the *first* successful secession in postcolonial Africa.[76]

---

[73] Richard Trivelli, "Divided Histories, Opportunistic Alliances: Background Notes on the Ethiopian-Eritrean War," *Africa Spectrum* 33, no. 3 (January 1, 1998): 268–80.
[74] Pischedda, "Wars within Wars."
[75] Babu, "The Eritrean Question in the Context of African Conflicts and Superpower Rivalries."
[76] Iyob, *The Eritrean Struggle for Independence*, 2, 5.

Second, the fall of the Soviet Union simply does not explain Eritrean independence in timing or substance. The major victories of the EPLF came with the capture of Soviet officers on the battlefield in 1988, before the downfall of USSR. The Soviets sent $800 million worth of new weaponry in 1989, followed by three significant shipments of arms to Ethiopia in 1990 to try to prevent the collapse of the Derg regime.[77] Andargachew Tiruneh further notes, "The military supplies from the Soviet Union continued to trickle almost to the last days of the regime. Also, there was no report of shortage of weapons at all."[78] On the flip side of the Cold War, the United States had a long history of supporting Ethiopia for its military assets and links to Israeli security.[79] The Israelis themselves sent 200 military advisers in attempts to prop up the Derg regime in 1990, so external support did not collapse.[80]

U.S. Assistant Secretary of State Herman Cohen told the U.S. Congress that same year, "Ethiopia will be able to achieve a durable peace only by means of a negotiated, political solution. The outlines of that solution are not hard to see. Ethiopia must remain whole."[81] Cohen and the U.S. ultimately supported Eritrean independence, but only after the EPLF defeated Ethiopian forces on the battlefield and helped overthrow the Derg regime. Furthermore, changes in U.S. policy were in part a result of the hegemonic EPLF presenting a multireligious, pro-African message to change U.S. perceptions of the Eritrean national movement. EPLF General Secretary Afewerki made an official visit to the United States in 1989 while congressional staff toured Eritrean areas under EPLF control. The EPLF had previously been forbidden from entering the State Department, but were welcome to attend meetings starting in 1989.[82]

One cannot tell the full history of the Eritrean national movement without referencing small group splits and unity deals, the anti-Derg insurgency, colonialism, and the Cold War. However, the internal balance of power in the movement was the dominant factor in the actions of the groups and the outcome of their struggle.

---

77 Pateman, *Eritrea*, 236; Tekle Mariam Woldemikael, "Political Mobilization and Nationalist Movements: The Case of the Eritrean People's Liberation Front," *Africa Today* 38, no. 2 (June 1, 1991): 37.

78 Andargachew Tiruneh, *The Ethiopian Revolution 1974–1987: A Transformation from an Aristocratic to a Totalitarian Autocracy* (Cambridge: Cambridge University Press, 1993), 365.

79 Jeff Lefebvre, *Arms for the Horn: U.S. Security Policy in Ethiopia and Somalia, 1953–1991* (Pittsburgh: University of Pittsburgh Press, 1992).

80 Pateman, *Eritrea*, 236.

81 Iyob, *The Eritrean Struggle for Independence*, 44.

82 Tiruneh, *The Ethiopian Revolution*, 361.

CHAPTER 8

Is Technology the Answer?

The Limits of Combat Drones in Countering Insurgents

JAMES IGOE WALSH

CAN NEW WEAPONS TECHNOLOGIES make it easier to coerce insurgents and other violent nonstate actors? The key problems in countering insurgency are identifying the enemy while avoiding harm to civilians and protecting ground troops from surprise attacks. Unmanned aerial vehicles—better known as drones—would seem to be an ideal technological solution to these political-military problems. These aircraft can surveil potential targets for long periods and are armed with precision weapons. This should increase their ability to ensure that coercive force is directed at the intended adversary. The absence of an onboard crew reduces the costs of using force since the coercer no longer needs to worry about military casualties.

The United States increasingly relies on drones to target insurgent and terrorist groups around the world, in Pakistan, Yemen, Libya, Syria, Somalia, and Iraq, among others places. The objectives of these campaigns are to compel and deter insurgent and terrorist organizations. Drones are used to punish violent organizations by targeting their leaders and creating fear and uncertainty among their members. Drones also deter insurgents and terrorists from engaging in more violence, as well as to deter others from joining or supporting these movements.

While drones have attracted considerable attention, we still know relatively little about how effective they are as tools of compellence and deterrence. In particular, it is not clear how, if at all, drones differ from other technologies of violence, what experience with broadly similar technologies in past conflicts suggest will be the likely consequences of drone strikes, and what systematic analysis of the available evidence suggests about the effects of the drone campaigns. This chapter seeks to address these open questions by offering a survey of the state of knowledge concerning the efficacy of drones as instruments of coercion, particularly in the context of counterinsurgency operations.

Drone strikes are a form of selective violence, in which the attacker takes considerable care to distinguish combatant targets from noncombatants. Theory suggests that the more selective the application of violence is, the more effective it will be in punishing and deterring insurgent and terrorist organizations.[1] Yet there is not universal agreement on this point. Some conclude that even indiscriminate violence can be an effective strategy, while others suggest it frequently fails to achieve its objectives, as insurgents are strategic actors who change and adapt their internal organization to reduce their vulnerability to violence.[2]

The evidence from Pakistan suggests that insurgents have adapted to drone strikes in ways that are not conducive to the interests of the United States. Drone strikes are associated with subsequent terrorist attacks in Pakistan's urban areas, creating more political instability in this strategically important country. Insurgents are responding to drone strikes with their own acts of violence in an attempt to demonstrate to current and potential supporters that they can continue to bring the fight to the enemy. It also appears that while drones are less likely to cause civilian harm than other forms of violence employed in this theater, they have difficulty distinguishing between members of insurgent organizations that are hostile to the United States and its allies and those that are not. Inability to very carefully target drone strikes on particular militants appears to have pushed disparate insurgent organizations with distinct agendas to coalesce around the goal of responding to drone strikes with even more terrorist attacks.

Drones: Why They Are Different and Why They Might Work

Drones—more formally, unmanned aerial vehicles (UAVs)—are pilotless aircraft controlled by individuals located on the ground, often some distance from the area where the platform is operating. Drones come in many shapes and

[1] Stathis N. Kalyvas, *The Logic of Violence in Civil War* (New York: Cambridge University Press, 2006); T. David Mason and Dale A. Krane, "The Political Economy of Death Squads: Toward a Theory of the Impact of State-Sanctioned Terror," *International Studies Quarterly* 33 (1989): 175–98; Matthew A. Kocher, Thomas B. Pepinsky, and Stathis N. Kalyvas, "Aerial Bombing and Counterinsurgency in the Vietnam War," *American Journal of Political Science* 55 (2011): 201–18.

[2] Jason Lyall, "Does Indiscriminate Violence Incite Insurgent Attacks?: Evidence from Chechnya," *Journal of Conflict Resolution* 53 (2009): 331–62; R. Bhavnani, D. Miodownik, and H. J. Choi, "Violence and Control in Civil Conflict: Israel, the West Bank, and Gaza," *Comparative Politics* 44 (2011): 61; R. Bhavnani, D. Miodownik, and Hyun Jin Choi, "Three Two Tango: Territorial Control and Selective Violence in Israel, the West Bank, and Gaza," *Journal of Conflict Resolution*, 55 (2011):133–58; Yuri M. Zhukov, "An Epidemic Model of Violence and Public Support in Civil War," *Conflict Management and Peace Science* 30, no. 1 (2013): 24–52; Gonzalo Vargas, "Urban Irregular Warfare and Violence against Civilians: Evidence from a Colombian City," *Terrorism and Political Violence* 22 (2009): 110–32.

sizes and perform a variety of missions, including reconnaissance, intelligence collection, and combat. The focus here is on combat drones, such as the MQ-1 Predator and MQ-9 Reaper UAVs deployed in recent years by the United States. These drones are armed with precision-guided air-to-surface missiles and can transmit to their controllers intelligence collected from imagery, infrared, signals, and other types of sensors. Unarmed drones have been used by the United States for many years, but it is only within the past decade and a half that combat versions have been used to collect intelligence on and to target terrorists and insurgents. The first known use of an armed drone to strike at militants occurred in Yemen in late 2002, killing a senior Al Qaeda leader and five other men, including a U.S. citizen.[3]

How might the technologies utilized by combat drones change counterinsurgency outcomes? A key challenge in counterinsurgency campaigns is resolving the "identification problem" of distinguishing combatants from noncombatants. This is difficult because insurgents typically do not operate in large numbers in open terrain and often mix closely with the civilian population.[4] Drone strikes are intended to be a form of selective violence that targets bona fide insurgents while sparing noninsurgents from harm. Selective violence has the goals of undermining insurgent organizations' ability to plan and to engage in action, including political activities as well as acts of violence. It can exercise this effect both directly and indirectly. The direct, punishment effect is that it forces militants to change their activities in ways that make it difficult to engage in violence. Drone strikes kill leaders as well as rank-and-file members of terrorist organizations, destroy safe houses and equipment, force militants to rely on means of communication that cannot be easily intercepted but that are less efficient and reliable, lead them to change their locations frequently, and create mistrust of members of the organization suspected of providing intelligence to the United States or its proxies. All of these effects raise the costs to insurgents of engaging in violence.

In principle, selective violence also has indirect deterrent effects that can do long-term damage to the organization's capacity to sustain itself and deter current and future members from engaging in violence. Selective violence can deter potential recruits, who know that joining the insurgency will make them potential targets of drone strikes. Current members of the insurgency will face stronger incentives to leave or to defect to the government, since doing so may allow them to escape death or injury from a drone's missiles. Supporters of the movement who provide funds, safe haven, or intelligence may be dissuaded from doing so by the threat that they too may become the targets of selective violence. All of these effects will be reinforced if the campaign of selective

---

[3] Jonathan Masters, "Targeted Killings," *Council on Foreign Relations*, May 23, 2013, https://www.cfr.org/backgrounder/targeted-killings.

[4] Kalyvas, *The Logic of Violence in Civil War*; Jeff Goodwin, *No Other Way Out: States and Revolutionary Movements, 1945–1991* (Cambridge: Cambridge University Press, 2001); Mason and Krane, "The Political Economy of Death Squads"; Kocher et al., "Aerial Bombing and Counterinsurgency in the Vietnam War."

violence can be sustained over long periods of time, as the insurgency's loss of members and recruits will weaken its ability to achieve its aims and thus make it even less attractive for current and potential members.

Proponents hold that drones represent a *particularly* selective form of violence compared to the available alternatives. From this perspective, drone technology offers the promise of both punishing and deterring insurgent groups while minimizing risks to U.S. military forces and to civilians.[5] The reason is that drones combine multiple, complementary technologies into a single platform. Drones are armed with accurate missiles that can target individual vehicles, houses and other structures, and even particular rooms in a building. These precision-guided missiles are directed by intelligence collected in real time by the vehicle's sensors. Drones, freed from the constraints of the endurance of an onboard pilot, can loiter for long periods of time. This allows the operators of the drone to better identify their target before striking. It also allows the operator to ensure that any noncombatants in the target area can be identified in advance and that a strike can be called off or delayed if it is important to avoid civilian deaths.

These technological characteristics of armed drones could make them more effective than traditional air power delivered from manned aircraft. Their potential to collect intelligence and to accurately strike targets provides them with many of the advantages that ground forces offer in counterinsurgency operations. While all of these technologies and characteristics have existed independently of each other in the past, their combination allows drones to become the core element of a counterinsurgency campaign rather than an adjunct to operations conducted by ground forces. If drones can effectively play these roles in a counterinsurgency strategy, their use could reduce the need for large numbers of ground troops.

U.S. authorities emphasize that the precision allowed by drones marks an important advance over other technologies of violence available to the United States. The reason is that it maximizes the chance that insurgents will be killed, while also minimizing the likelihood that noncombatants will also be killed. Precision should make drones a particularly effective form of targeted killings that reduces any backlash against the United States resulting from civilian deaths. In the first official discussion of the drone strike program, a senior U.S. official emphasized:

> We only authorize a strike if we have a high degree of confidence that innocent civilians will not be injured or killed, except in the rarest of circumstances. The unprecedented advances we have made in technology provide us greater proximity to targets for a longer period of time, and as a result allow us to better understand what is happening in real time on the ground in ways that were

[5] Jason M. Brown, "To Bomb or Not to Bomb? Counterinsurgency, Airpower, and Dynamic Targeting," *Air and Space Power Journal* 21 (2007): 1–13; Norton Schwartz, "Airpower in Counterinsurgency and Stability Operations," *Prism* 22 (2011): 127–34.

previously impossible. We can be much more discriminating and we can make more informed judgments about factors that might contribute to collateral damage. I can tell you today that there have indeed been occasions when we have decided against conducting a strike in order to avoid the injury or death of innocent civilians[6]

The little publicly available research on this issue finds that drone strikes in Pakistan, the country that has experienced the most such attacks, are selective compared to other forms of violence. Avery Plaw and Matthew Fricker developed a data set of the victims of drone strikes in the region.[7] Their effort divides victims into three categories: militants, civilians, and those whose status cannot be determined. Based on a review of media reports, they measure the ratio of militants killed in drone strikes for every civilian that dies in such attacks. Using information from only media sources in Pakistan, they estimate that over 26 militants are killed for each confirmed civilian death. This ratio falls slightly to 19 militants per civilian killed if they draw on both Pakistani and international media sources. They then compare these ratios of militants and civilians killed by drone strikes with corresponding ratios for other types of armed conflict, including Pakistani military operations in the Federally Administered Tribal Areas and the Swat Valley, U.S. military operations in Pakistan that use types of force other than drones, targeted killings in the West Bank and Gaza Strip carried out by Israel between 2000 and 2008, and all conflicts in the world in the year 2000.

All of these types of force produce ratios that are lower than even the lowest estimates for the proportion of civilians killed per militant by drone strikes. This conclusion needs to be tempered by the fact that it is quite difficult to generate accurate counts of civilian and military victims during armed conflicts. But it also suggests that some of the controversy about the civilian deaths produced by drone strikes may be overstated. Instead of drones killing civilians indiscriminately, as some critics assume, the available data suggest that, *when compared to other types of force*, the proportion of civilian victims is at a lower or comparable level. Elsewhere Plaw and collaborators analyze how such ratios have evolved in the drone campaign in Pakistan. They find that the ratio of civilian to military deaths has dropped over time. This suggests that the drone pilots are getting better at distinguishing civilian from military targets and that the United States may be modifying its decisions to launch strikes from drones to minimize civilian casualties.[8]

---

[6] John O. Brennan, "The Ethics and Efficacy of the President's Counterterrorism Strategy," April 30, 2012, *Woodrow Wilson Center*, https://lawfare.s3-us-west-2.amazonaws.com/staging/s3fs-public/uploads/2012/04/WilsonCenterFinalPrepared1.pdf.

[7] Avery Plaw and M. S. Fricker, "Tracking the Predators: Evaluating the US Drone Campaign in Pakistan," *International Studies Perspectives* 13 (2012): 1–22. Note that their data only cover drone strikes through 2011.

[8] A. Plaw, M. S. Fricker, and B. G. Williams, "Practice Makes Perfect? The Changing Civilian Toll of CIA Drone Strikes in Pakistan," *Perspectives on Terrorism* 5 (2011): 51–69.

Stepping back from the Pakistan campaign, there is also evidence that selective violence in the form of targeted killings does undermine insurgencies more generally. Stathis N. Kalyvas's survey of the use of violence by the authorities in many insurgencies and civil wars concludes that selective violence degrades insurgent organizations.[9] The capture and trial of the leader of the Kurdish Workers Party in Turkey and the killing of the leader of the Shining Path insurgency in Peru both contributed to the decline of these insurgent organizations.[10] Two studies that systematically analyzed the effects of leadership decapitation—the use of selective violence (both killing and capturing) against senior members of insurgencies—on groups' subsequent behavior concluded that the strategy is effective. In the first, Patrick Johnston found that such targeted killings reduce the lethality and frequency of subsequent insurgent attacks. He also concluded that failed attempts at leadership decapitation do not increase the violence that insurgencies undertake, suggesting that the strategy has few negative consequences for states that use it.[11] In the second study, Bryan Price found that targeted killings substantially shorten the life spans of terrorist groups. He argued that organizational characteristics of terrorist groups, including their use of violence, clandestine structure, and focus on values, make such groups particularly susceptible to targeted killings.[12]

According to this line of reasoning, the technological characteristics of armed drones should make them quite effective at coercing insurgents. These characteristics also might reduce the political costs to the United States of engaging in coercion. If this is the case, we might expect that the development and deployment of armed drones could make the United States (or other actors with such weapons) more likely to initiate conflict. The fact that drones are pilotless means that their use does not endanger U.S. military personnel, potentially allowing their use in missions where the benefit of a successful attack is outweighed by the risk of harm to ground troops or pilots of manned strike aircraft. It may also mean that their use would generate less public opposition to the use of force.

A large body of research concludes that the deaths of U.S. military personnel in combat operations reduces the willingness of the U.S. public to support engagement in armed conflict.[13] There was a strong relationship between mounting U.S. casualties in Iraq and decline in public support for remaining

[9] Kalyvas, *The Logic of Violence in Civil War.*

[10] Audrey Cronin, *How Terrorism Ends: Understanding the Decline and Demise of Terrorist Campaigns* (Princeton, NJ: Princeton University Press, 2009).

[11] Patrick B. Johnston, "Does Decapitation Work? Assessing the Effectiveness of Leadership Targeting in Counterinsurgency Campaigns," *International Security* 36 (2012): 47–79.

[12] Bryan C. Price, "Targeting Top Terrorists: How Leadership Decapitation Contributes to Counterterrorism Targeting Top Terrorists," *International Security* 36 (2012): 9–46.

[13] Scott Sigmund Gartner, "The Multiple Effects of Casualties on Public Support for War: An Experimental Approach," *American Political Science Review* 102 (2008): 95–106; Harvey Sapolsky and Jeremy Shapiro, "Casualties, Technology, and America's Future Wars," *Parameters* 26 (1996): 119–27; John Mueller, *War, Presidents, and Public Opinion* (New York: Wiley, 1973).

engaged in the conflict, for example.[14] There is also evidence that individuals in the United States are more willing to support the use of force in the form of drone strikes compared to otherwise identical attacks that place military personnel at risk of harm.[15] Since drones reduce the likelihood of casualties, they may increase the freedom of political and military commanders to use drones in combat operations.

Remote operations such as drone strikes also minimize the footprint of U.S. military forces in foreign countries, who may be perceived as occupiers and the target of violence themselves and may insist on side payments from the United States in return for basing rights.[16] Most drone strikes that the United States has conducted outside of hot battlefields such as Iraq and Afghanistan have been covert, meaning that there is no official acknowledgment of U.S. participation. This makes it more difficult to reliably assign credit or blame for such strikes to the United States. It also means that drone strikes have been subject to far less scrutiny by the legislature, judiciary, and press than is true for traditional military operations. The comparatively low oversight costs of drones may make them a more attractive option for incumbent leaders, especially those facing polarized legislatures, as was the case for President Obama and the U.S. Congress.

Why Drones Might Not Work

At the same time, others hold that drones are unlikely to radically transform counterinsurgency. They contend that drones represent a quite modest change in their ability to coerce adversaries from past technologies of violence.[17] Drones may be less revolutionary than their advocates believe because their targets are strategic actors who organize themselves and their interactions with other insurgent movements so as to maximize their chance of surviving strikes. For example, documents captured from militants in Mali connected to Al Qaeda outline tactics that the group should or could use to avoid being targeted by drones, including changing location frequently, hiding under thick trees, and developing techniques for generating electronic signals that draw the drone away from the militants' location.[18] The fact that drones reduce the

---

[14] Matthew A. Baum and Tim Groeling, "Reality Asserts Itself: Public Opinion on Iraq and the Elasticity of Reality," *International Organization* 64 (2010): 443–79; C. V. Sirin, "Public Support for Military Interventions across Levels of Political Information and Stages of Intervention: The Case of the Iraq War," *Armed Forces & Society* 38 (2011): 252–72; W. A. Boettcher and M. D. Cobb, "Echoes of Vietnam? Casualty Framing and Public Perceptions of Success and Failure in Iraq," *Journal of Conflict Resolution* 50 (2006): 831–54.

[15] James Igoe Walsh, "Precision Weapons, Civilian Casualties, and Support for the Use of Force," *Political Psychology* 36 (2015): 507–23.

[16] Robert A. Pape and James K. Feldman, *Cutting the Fuse: The Explosion of Global Suicide Terrorism and How to Stop It* (Chicago: University of Chicago Press, 2010).

[17] "Flying under the Influence," *Foreign Policy*, July 20, 2012, https://foreignpolicy.com/2012/07/20/flying-under-the-influence/.

[18] Associated Press, "The Al Qaeda Papers: Drones," 2012, http://hosted.ap.org/specials/interactives/_international/_pdfs/al-qaida-papers-drones.pdf.

costs of initiating conflict could also backfire against the United States. Lower costs of coercion might push the United States to expand the range of conflicts in which it considers using force. Arguably we have already seen examples of this. The United States quickly ramped up its campaign of drone strikes in Pakistan, increasing the number of strikes from 36 in 2008 to 122 in 2010, while also expanding the drone campaign to Yemen, Libya, Iraq, and Syria. Such changes may also shift the domestic political calculus surrounding military action, making the public both more likely to support drone strikes than other forms of violence while at the same time undermining the credibility of threats to escalate further and/or to employ more direct, less surgical instruments of violence.

The Organization of Insurgency

Drone strikes are a form of targeted killings, defined as "the intentional killing of a specific civilian or unlawful combatant who cannot reasonably be apprehended, who is taking a direct part in hostilities, the targeting done at the direction of the state, in the context of an international or non-international armed conflict."[19] The most extensive and well-documented campaign of targeted killings is that conducted by Israel against Palestinian militant organizations. Israel has used missiles fired from drones and from helicopters, bombs dropped from fixed-wing aircraft, armed raids, and snipers to kill militants.[20] There is a small literature that assesses the effectiveness of these targeted killings. Researchers have collected open-source data about the occurrence of targeted killings, the outcome (such as the death of the targeted individual or others), and subsequent acts of violence by insurgent and terrorist groups. Findings are mixed; most of these studies conclude that targeted killings do not lead to a decline in subsequent terrorist attacks. Some find that targeted killings conducted by Israeli forces had no effect on subsequent attacks by Palestinian terrorists between 2000 and 2005.[21] An analysis focused on suicide terrorism in the Israeli-Palestinian conflict concludes that targeted killings are associated with fewer victims from suicide attacks and that high levels of targeted killings reduce Palestinian intentions to launch terrorist attacks.[22]

---

[19] Gary Solis, *The Law of Armed Conflict: International Humanitarian Law in War* (New York: Cambridge University Press, 2010), 528.

[20] Steven R. David, "Fatal Choices: Israel's Policy of Targeted Killing," 17 (2003): 111-126; Daniel Byman, "Do Targeted Killings Work?," *Foreign Affairs* 85 (2006): 95–111; Gal Luft, "The Logic of Israel's Targeted Killing," *Middle East Quarterly* 10 (2003): 3–13.

[21] David A. Jaeger and M. Daniele Paserman, "The Cycle of Violence? An Empirical Analysis of Fatalities in the Palestinian-Israeli Conflict," *American Economic Review*, 98 (2008): 1591–604; Mohammed M. Hafez and Joseph M. Hatfield, "Do Targeted Assassinations Work? A Multivariate Analysis of Israel's Controversial Tactic During Al-Aqsa Uprising," *Studies in Conflict & Terrorism* 29 (2006): 359–82.

[22] David A. Jaeger, "The Shape of Things to Come? On the Dynamics of Suicide Attacks and Targeted Killings," *Quarterly Journal of Political Science* 4 (2009): 315–42.

Why might such targeted killings be ineffective? Existing research on air power in war offers one answer. Robert Pape argues that air strikes directed at military targets and infrastructure—a strategy of denial—is more effective in coercing an opponent than is bombing civilian targets.[23] However, this effect depends on the target's military strategy: "Strategies that rely on large-scale mechanized operations are particularly vulnerable because they depend on massive logistic flows that make excellent targets for air attack. At the opposite end of the spectrum, guerrilla fighters are much less vulnerable to coercion because they need little logistical support."[24] Effective coercion of insurgents requires separating them from the population that provides them with support. This is difficult to achieve with air power alone, since the groups targeted for attack typically lack the logistical infrastructure, clear control of territory, and massed personnel that make a strategy of denial effective.[25] Pape's subsequent study of counterterrorism strategies concludes that targeted killings are not effective against terrorist groups that undertake suicide attack campaigns. Of the 13 groups in his study, only 1 was undermined by targeted killings.[26]

One way to separate insurgents from civilians, as discussed earlier, is to use force in ways that maximize harm to the former and minimize danger to the latter. From the perspective of the United States, the precision of drone strikes in achieving this battlefield objective is a key advantage of the technology. However, it is not clear that the civilians in areas where drones operate perceive them this way. Public opinion surveys in Pakistan that ask questions about drone strikes typically find large—in some cases overwhelming—opposition to their use. Citizens object that drones do in fact kill large numbers of civilians, create incentives for insurgents to launch attacks in response that target innocent Pakistanis, and violate the country's sovereignty. Conducting reliable public opinion surveys on sensitive issues in conflict-prone countries such as Pakistan is very difficult. A number of researchers suggest that simple readings of relevant surveys overstate the opposition to drone strikes. Nonetheless there is little evidence to date at the level of individual citizens that many are persuaded to see the drone campaign as a positive development or one that is likely to bring more stability to their country.[27]

Others connect the failure of selective violence to the organizational characteristics of insurgent groups. An important analysis of targeted killings

---

[23] Robert Pape, *Bombing to Win: Airpower and Coercion in War* (Ithaca, NY: Cornell University Press, 1996).
[24] Ibid., 8.
[25] Ibid., 31.
[26] Robert Pape, *Dying to Win: The Strategic Logic of Suicide Terrorism* (New York: Random House, 2005).
[27] C. Christine Fair, Karl Kaltenthaler, and William J Miller, "Pakistani Opposition to American Drone Strikes," *Political Research Quarterly* 129 (2014): 1–33; New America Foundation and Terror Free Tomorrow, *Public Opinion in Pakistan's Tribal Regions* (2010) http://www.terrorfreetomorrow.org/upimagestft/FATApoll1.pdf; Adeline Delavande and Basit Zafar, *How Deeply Held Are Anti-American Attitudes among Pakistani Youth? Evidence Using Experimental Variation in Information* (2012), https://papers.ssrn.com/sol3/papers.cfm?abstract_id=2043148.

aimed at top commanders of terrorist organizations—known as leadership decapitation—finds that they do contribute to the collapse of smaller and newer organizations that are not motivated by religious grievances.[28] Among the organizations that survived leadership decapitation, some subsequently engaged in fewer terrorist attacks, but others actually increased their use of violence. Larger and older groups have resources and time to develop organizational practices, such as succession plans and standard operating procedures that will allow them to survive the loss of key members. Many observers point out that even large terrorist groups, such as Al Qaeda, are careful to organize themselves into networks.[29] Rather than functioning as hierarchies in which leaders plan and organize attacks, they allow smaller cells of terrorists to operate on their own initiative. These cells might be better positioned to alter their behavior to avoid targeted strikes by, for example, not traveling in groups or remaining in the same location for extended periods of time. If this is the case, killing leaders should have a small or even no effect on the subsequent activities of the group. Network structures also limit how far the effects of selective violence diffuse within the insurgent organization. Wiping out the leader of one cell may have small effects on other cells because they are only loosely connected to each other.

Countering Coercion

Insurgent organizations targeted by U.S. drone strikes can respond in turn by attempting to coerce their coercer. Responding to drone attacks with more violence may convince the United States that the insurgency is resilient and that drone strikes are an ineffective strategy.[30]

One important difficulty with this strategy is that the insurgent organizations based in Pakistan have limited capacity for attacking the United States directly. Al Qaeda Central certainly is interested in attacking the homeland of the United States, and did so on a very large scale on September 11, 2001. But it has not managed to replicate such an attack since then. Some of its allies in Pakistan, especially the Haqqani network, are also targeted by drone strikes and have been able to retaliate against U.S. military forces in Afghanistan. But its other allies in Pakistan lack the means to engage in attacks against U.S. forces, and many are essentially insurgent movements associated with local warlords with few international connections.

---

[28] Jenna Jordan, "When Heads Roll: Assessing the Effectiveness of Leadership Decapitation," *Security Studies* 18 (2009): 719–55.

[29] Marc Sageman, *Understanding Terror Networks* (Philadelphia: University of Pennsylvania Press, 2004); Marc Sageman, *Leaderless Jihad: Terror Networks in the Twenty-first Century* (Philadelphia: University of Pennsylvania Press, 2008).

[30] For a version of this argument, see Thomas Schelling, *Arms and Influence* (New Haven, CT: Yale University Press, 1996). Evidence that air strikes are associated with more insurgent violence in Afghanistan is presented in Jason Lyall, *Bombing to Lose? Airpower and the Dynamics of Violence in Counterinsurgency Wars*, unpublished manuscript (2014).

Most of these groups can undertake attacks throughout Pakistan, however. This is an attractive target because the Pakistani government has long collaborated with the United States in its campaign of drone strikes by sharing intelligence on potential targets. Coercing the government to end this collaboration would make it more difficult for the United States to select targets for drone strikes. Attacks in Pakistan might also undermine the stability of the country's political institutions, which would also be costly for the United States, which worries about Pakistan's support for some insurgent groups, control of the country's nuclear arsenal, and potential conflicts between Pakistan and India. As discussed earlier, drone strikes have become increasingly unpopular and controversial in Pakistan, in part because they are seen as prompting insurgents to launch terrorist attacks in the country. Insurgents likely perceive their chances of pushing Pakistani authorities to withdraw their support for drone strikes as more likely to succeed than attempts to coerce the United States to stop engaging in such strikes.[31]

Who Are the Insurgents?

There may be another mechanism through which drone strikes and other forms of targeted killings influence insurgent violence. The idea that selective violence deters individuals from joining or supporting an insurgent movement assumes there is one cohesive insurgency. Quite frequently, however, insurgencies suffer from a great deal of fragmentation. More than one insurgent organization has used violence in almost half of all civil wars since 1989, for example.[32] Fragmented insurgencies have been defined as those with multiple organizations, weak institutional links among these organizations, and those with roughly equal distribution of power among their constituent organizations.[33]

Fragmentation makes it more difficult for the authorities to employ selective violence. The groups comprising fragmented insurgencies have different preferences regarding long-term goals, their strategies of violence, relations with the authorities, and other issues. The result is that "cooperation among factions of a single dissident group and among separate dissident organizations is rare."[34] In situations such as this, the authorities frequently prefer to direct their violence only against members of one or a few insurgent movements, while sparing members of other insurgent organizations. In Pakistan, for example, the United States has targeted insurgent organizations that

[31] Erik Gartzke and James Igoe Walsh, "The Drawbacks of Drones," unpublished manuscript (2017).
[32] Michael G. Findley and Peter J. Rudloff, "Combatant Fragmentation and the Dynamics of Civil War," *British Journal of Political Science* 42 (2012): 879–901.
[33] Kristin M. Bakke, Kathleen Gallagher Cunningham, and Lee J. M. Seymour, "A Plague of Initials: Fragmentation, Cohesion, and Infighting in Civil Wars," *Perspectives on Politics* 10 (2012): 265–83.
[34] Mark Lichbach, *The Rebel's Dilemma* (Ann Arbor: University of Michigan Press, 1995), 18.

engage in violence in Afghanistan but has avoided targeting militants favored by the Pakistani military.

This level of discrimination in targeting may be difficult to achieve because insurgencies are not regular armed forces. They typically do not wear uniforms, do not control well-defined areas of territory for long periods of time, seek to mask their communications and the identity of their supporters from outside scrutiny, and draw on the same population for recruits. In such circumstances, it may be practically impossible for the authorities to develop sufficiently accurate intelligence that allows them to determine the specific organizational affiliation of a suspected militant or small group of militants.

Drones, of course, can collect a great deal of intelligence about the location, movements, and communications of individuals, but this alone may not be sufficient to determine organizational affiliation among irregular forces. Human intelligence sources can supplement technical means of intelligence collection but may have personal incentives to incorrectly identify individuals as members of an insurgent organization targeted by the authorities.[35] The common insurgent tactic of hiding among the population can make it difficult for the authorities to solve the "identification problem" of distinguishing combatants and noncombatants.[36] Fragmentation creates a similar problem of determining if a particular militant is a member of an insurgent organization targeted for selective violence or belongs to another insurgent group against whom the government is not using force.

This means that anyone matching the characteristics of an insurgent could be the target of drone strikes, even if he or she is not a member of an insurgent organization the United States prefers to attack. From the perspective of the individual militant, this reduces the difference in the costs of being a member of an insurgent organization that the state opposes strongly and an insurgent group that does not attract such opposition. Indeed, in such a situation, the rewards from joining or allying with the insurgency most hostile to the authorities can be greater if it provides selective incentives that increase the chance of survival, such as safe havens, money or weapons, or intelligence about how to avoid being targeted by the state.[37] In such situations, then, selectively targeting militants from disparate organizations may lead them to coalesce to launch violent attacks on the state.

Evidence from quantitative data analysis suggests that these dynamics characterize drone strikes in Pakistan. Acts of violence by militants in the country appear to be aimed at countering U.S. coercion as well as a response to the fact that individuals associated with multiple militant groups are targeted by drone strikes. Strikes that kill civilians are not associated with subsequent increases in terrorist violence in the country. This is consistent with the argument that

---

35 Kalyvas, *The Logic of Violence in Civil War*.

36 Kocher et al., "Aerial Bombing and Counterinsurgency in the Vietnam War."

37 Stathis N. Kalyvas and Matthew A Kocher, "How 'Free' Is Free Riding in Civil Wars? Violence, Insurgency, and the Collective Action Problem," *World Politics* 59 (2007): 177–216.

drone strikes are sufficiently selective that they alone are not driving Pakistani citizens to lend more support to militants, at least in the short run. However, strikes that result in militant deaths do precede upticks in such violence, especially attacks on "soft" targets in major urban centers well away from the tribal areas, where the militants are targeted by drones.[38] Furthermore, the available data suggest that the organizational identity of many of the militants killed by drones cannot be reliably established, even by local reporters and nongovernmental organizations after the fact. This is consistent with the idea that the inability to systematically distinguish militants' organizational identity may be leading these organizations to more closely coordinate their subsequent attacks in Pakistan.

Furthermore, militant organizations that seek to weaken or overthrow the Pakistani government have used such strikes as a rallying cry with the goal of uniting under a single movement. Experts in the region suggest that the increased collaboration among insurgent groups is due, in part, to Pakistani military incursions into the Federally Administered Tribal Areas and U.S. drone strikes, in particular a drone strike in late 2006 that targeted Ayman al-Zawahiri of Al Qaeda but instead killed members of a local insurgent group.[39] This contributed to the formation of the Pakistan Taliban and reduced the fragmentation in the overall movement by institutionalizing ties among its constituent groups, leading to the sharing of information and the coordination of attacks in Pakistan.

Al Qaeda Central has played an important role in facilitating cooperation and providing benefits to other insurgent groups. It has used its sophisticated media relations arm to publicize justifications for attacks in Pakistan, provided allied groups with expertise on how to launch attacks, especially suicide attacks, and served as a mediator among these groups, especially when they experience conflict over leadership of the larger movement.[40]

The ramping up of the drone campaign, especially from 2008 through 2011, appears to have been associated with a reduction in the fragmentation of militant organizations in Pakistan and facilitated their cooperation during this period. The long-term consequences of this development remain unclear for at least two reasons. One is the decline in the frequency of drone strikes after 2011. This may weaken incentives for different militant organizations to continue to cooperate in targeting the Pakistani state. The second is the fact that it does not appear that one of the militant organizations constituting the Pakistan Taliban has achieved a hegemonic position within this umbrella

[38] Gartzke and Walsh, "Drawbacks of Drones."
[39] C. Christine Fair, "The Militant Challenge in Pakistan," *Asia Policy* 11 (2011): 105–37; Imtiaz Gul, *The Most Dangerous Place: Pakistan's Lawless Frontier* (New York: Penguin, 2012); Carlotta Gall and Sabrina Tavernise, "Pakistani Taliban Are Said to Expand Alliances," *New York Times*, May 6, 2010, http://www.nytimes.com/2010/05/07/world/asia/07pstan.html?ref=world.
[40] Gul, *The Most Dangerous Place*; Don Rassler and Vahid Brown, "Al-Qaeda's Pakistan Strategy," Combating Terrorism Center, U.S. Military Academy (2011), https://www.ctc.usma.edu/posts/al-qaida%E2%80%99s-pakistan-strategy.

organization. As Krause's chapter discusses, a hegemonic group can sustain intermilitant cooperation over the longer run. The absence of such a hegemon among militants in Pakistan suggests they may be unlikely to mount a sustained campaign to overthrow or greatly weaken the Pakistani state.

Task Expansion

Drone technology reduces the costs of military action. On the face of it, this is a good thing for the actor initiating conflict. But, as Todd Sechser explains in his contribution to this volume, lower costs also create incentives to engage in more risky actions and/or to expand the slate of missions drones are tasked to perform. For example, drone strikes in Pakistan and elsewhere were initially limited to individual leaders of militant organizations, such as Al Qaeda, that actively targeted the United States. However, it appears that drone targets have been expanded to include both lower-level militants as well as violent groups that target primarily the local authorities. The *New York Times* reports, "For at least two years in Pakistan, partly because of the C.I.A.'s success in decimating Al Qaeda's top ranks, most strikes have been directed at militants whose main battle is with the Pakistani authorities or who fight with the Taliban against American troops in Afghanistan. In Yemen, some strikes apparently launched by the United States killed militants who were preparing to attack Yemeni military forces."[41] Such an expansion of targets poses risks for the ability to effectively target members of militant organizations who aim their violence primarily against the United States. It is a good example of an attempt to implement transitive compellence, a concept developed in Keren Fraiman's chapter in this volume. Fraiman demonstrates that such coercion can be effective in altering the behavior of base states. In this case, however, the ability to coerce the militants directly with drones has made it more difficult to also push the Pakistani state to take more effective action.

Some governments that receive counterterrorism and counterinsurgency assistance have powerful incentives to exaggerate the threats they and the international community face from militants. Furthermore, actually eliminating the threat posed by such groups would undermine the rationale for foreign military and civilian funding and assistance. Such perverse incentives could lead host governments to carefully calibrate their own operations against such groups so that they do not become strong enough to overthrow the government or take control of large areas of national territory but remain powerful enough to pose some plausible threat.[42]

Such incentives could also lead host governments to attempt to influence the pattern and target of drone strikes in ways that privilege their own interests

---

[41] Scott Shane, "White House Presses for Drone Rule Book," *New York Times*, November 25, 2012, http://www.nytimes.com/2012/11/25/world/white-house-presses-for-drone-rule-book.html.

[42] David B. Carter and Andrew Boutton, "Fair Weather Allies: Terrorism and the Allocation of United States Foreign Aid," *Journal of Conflict Resolution* 58 (2014): 1144–73.

over the interests of those conducting drone strikes. Host governments, for example, might provide intelligence on the location and activities of militants they prefer to target, while providing less intelligence on militants that are of most interest to the United States.[43] Pakistan demanded that the United States direct drone strikes not only at insurgent groups closely affiliated with Al Qaeda or the Taliban but also at groups that the Pakistani authorities viewed as enemies. The United States subsequently collaborated with the Pakistani military and intelligence services in selecting some targets and informing their Pakistani counterparts of areas where they planned to launch strikes in the near future.[44]

An active campaign of drone strikes might also lead host governments to engage in "free riding" by taking less effective actions against militants with their own forces than they might otherwise. For instance, the United States frequently suggests that Pakistan should develop and implement a comprehensive counterinsurgency program including military force, effective police and judicial services, and economic development for areas in the northwest of the country. However, such a program would be both costly and risky for the Pakistani government and military. Drone strikes directed against militants in this area of the country might be seen by Pakistani leaders as a low-cost way to pressure insurgent organizations while avoiding the pitfalls associated with direct action.

Domestic Politics and the Credibility of Coercive Threats

Use of drones puts U.S. pilots and other service personnel out of harm's way. It also means that the occupation of foreign territory may not be necessary in order to wage some kinds of counterinsurgency campaigns. As discussed, there is some evidence that the U.S. public is more willing to support the use of force when it takes the form of drone strikes than of ground troops. A large body of research has shown that the public is more likely to oppose involvement in armed conflicts that involve U.S. military casualties or that involve issues of peripheral interest to the core national security goals of the country. Drones eliminate the possibility of such military casualties and, compared to ground forces, can be deployed relatively cheaply and easily to even minor conflicts. It is possible, then, that the U.S. public will be more willing to endorse drone strikes than they would other forms of armed conflict. Many critics

---

[43] James Igoe Walsh, *International Politics of Intelligence Sharing* (New York: Columbia University Press, 2010).

[44] Ashish Sen, "Pakistan Quietly Aids Drone Attacks," *Washington Times*, September 30, 2010, http://www.washingtontimes.com/news/2010/sep/30/pakistan-quietly-aids-drone-attacks/?page=all; Adam Entous, Siobhan Gorman, and Julian E. Barnes, "U.S. Tightens Drone Rules," *Wall Street Journal*, November 11, 2011; Adam Entous, Siobhan Gorman, and Evan Perez, "U.S. Unease over Drone Strikes: Obama Administration Charts Delicate Legal Path Defending Controversial Weapons," *Wall Street Journal*, September 26, 2012; Daniel Markey, *No Exit from Pakistan: America's Tortured Relationship with Islamabad* (New York: Cambridge University Press, 2013).

of drone strikes worry that these lower costs will create powerful incentives for the U.S. government to resort to drone strikes in the face of even minor challenges.[45]

These lower costs, though, might create political and military problems for the United States. One such problem is that political leaders might come to see drone strikes as a cheap way to mollify the public's demands that they "do something" about a foreign policy crisis. If this is the case, drones could be deployed in situations where their use alone is unlikely to alter the situation on the ground in the short run in ways that favor the United States. A good example is the initial U.S. reaction to the rapid rise of the Islamic State (ISIS) militant group in Syria and Iraq. The United States was quick to deploy drones (as well as manned attack aircraft) against ISIS when it threatened to engage in civilian massacres and to take over large parts of Iraq. As this campaign developed, the United States did deploy small numbers of ground troops to train and advise Iraqi forces. But the Obama administration made clear its intention to avoid involving those troops directly in combat operations.

Indeed, the reduced costs of conflict initiation that drones permit might also render threats to escalate less credible. An important element of effective coercion is convincing the adversary that one is willing to bear large costs in order to alter behavior. Such threats to escalate the costs of conflict are often not credible, in the sense that both states that are and states that are not willing to carry out such threats will issue them. Since drones impose fewer costs on the U.S. public, leaders may commit to their use in situations where the public and legislature are unwilling to support means of violence that might lead to military casualties, such as the introduction of ground troops. Adversaries that can correctly identify such situations have powerful incentives to try to ride out drone strikes in the knowledge that they do not face the risk of more direct combat if they do so.

Finally, the more widespread use of drone technology may begin to alter how Americans calculate the costs of war. As discussed, military casualties have long been a key driver of opposition to the use of force. By rendering such casualties impossible, drones may draw the public's and the media's attention to other undesirable aspects of military action. A likely candidate for greater attention is civilian casualties. The media pays far more attention to civilian harm that results from drone strikes in Pakistan or Yemen than the effects of U.S. military action on noncombatants in Afghanistan, for example. Surveys find that the public is more concerned about civilian harm when military casualties cannot occur because drones are employed. This suggests that, over time, heightened concern about civilian casualties may create a new constraint on the use of force.[46]

---

[45] Walsh, "Precision Weapons, Civilian Casualties, and Support for the Use of Force."

[46] Ibid.

Summary

Armed drones are a remarkable development in weapons technology. They combine multiple surveillance technologies with precision-guided munitions, allowing the United States to project selective violence over long distances while placing no U.S. personnel in harm's way. This technology seems well-suited to effective counterinsurgency operations, which, as a large body of scholarship and recent military doctrine suggests, are more effective when they employ force selectively in ways that reflect solid intelligence on and understanding of the targeted insurgent group and the population from which it seeks to draw support.

However, the evidence from the most sustained campaign to rely on drone strikes to deter and punish insurgent organizations in Pakistan suggests this technology has limited capacity to achieve these objectives and can create problems as well as solve them. Insurgencies are adaptive organizations that change their behavior in response to drone strikes in ways that render them ineffective or even counterproductive. Militants in Pakistan, for example, have responded to drone strikes with attacks on civilian targets in the country. This increased threat to Pakistan's urban areas creates more instability in the country. It may increase popular opposition to drone strikes (although we lack high-quality data demonstrating this link conclusively). More political violence in the core of the country creates a new problem for Pakistani police and military forces. This may have delayed their willingness to accede to U.S. demands that Pakistan use force in a more sustained way against militants in the tribal areas.

Drones also have implications for the use of and effectiveness of other instruments of coercion. A key concern is that they may lead to unbalanced counterinsurgency efforts that focus primarily on drone strikes and pull attention away from other tools. The fact that drones minimize military casualties reduces this cost of conflict onset. This may make political leaders more willing to resort to drones as a seemingly quick and easy solution to political-military problems and to neglect other tools that incur more costs but that may be more likely to succeed in the long run. There is considerable evidence that military force alone is unlikely to defeat insurgents,[47] suggesting that increasingly drone-centric counterinsurgency practices could produce few successes in future campaigns.

Despite these limitations, drone technology seems very likely to spread within the U.S. armed forces, the armed forces of other countries, and even to insurgent organizations. Better understanding the limits of armed drones for coercion may allow their use to be more effectively integrated with other types of armed force and tools of foreign and security policy.

---

[47] Seth Jones and Martin Libicki, *How Terrorist Groups End* (Santa Monica, CA: RAND, 2008).

PART IV | Domains and Instruments Other than Force

CHAPTER 9

Coercion through Cyberspace

The Stability-Instability Paradox Revisited

JON R. LINDSAY AND ERIK GARTZKE

THE INDISPENSABILITY AND VULNERABILITY of global information networks create serious challenges for global security. Critical infrastructure for banking, energy, transportation, and manufacturing increasingly relies on embedded computers connected to the Internet. Firms and citizens entrust their personal, medical, and financial data to distant servers in return for more convenient and efficient services. Military command and control depends on digital networks to connect pervasive surveillance to power projection capabilities. While interconnectivity and flexible functionality improves efficiency and control, it also facilitates new modes of crime, protest, espionage, and warfare. The U.S. Defense Department accordingly describes cyberspace as a new "war fighting domain" alongside the physical land, sea, air, and space domains.[1] Any military forces that drive, sail, fly, or orbit rely on computers for intelligence, communications, logistics, and administration; any intrusions that disrupt, confuse, or deceive these systems may undermine tactical performance, potentially with strategic consequences (i.e., forces may not get to the war in time or may not be able to target the enemy, and only the enemy, when they do). The cyber domain becomes attractive as a way to shape conflict in other domains, or to bypass military conflict altogether by exploiting civilian infrastructure for political or intelligence advantage.

Widespread belief that offense is easier than defense in cyberspace, that stronger states are increasingly vulnerable while weaker actors are increasingly empowered, and that the anonymity of cyber operations precludes effective deterrence leads many to argue that cyberspace brims with unprecedented, even revolutionary dangers.[2] Yet national security officials, defense firms,

[1] William J. Lynn III, "Defending a New Domain:. The Pentagon's New Cyberstrategy," *Foreign Affairs* (September/October 2010).

[2] Inter alia, Richard A. Clarke and Robert K. Knake, *Cyber War: The Next Threat to National Security and What to Do about It* (New York: Ecco, 2010); Joel Brenner, *America the Vulnerable: Inside the New*

media pundits, and a burgeoning private cybersecurity industry all have incentives to exaggerate the threat, while the extreme secrecy of cyber operations complicates sober assessment.[3] Critics of the cyber revolution argue that most actors lack the capacity to overcome significant barriers to weaponization in cyberspace, while those that have the capacity lack the motivation to use it, choosing instead to explore digital variations on traditional espionage and covert action.[4] Nevertheless, even if breathless scenarios of "digital Pearl Harbor" or "cyber 9/11" are overblown, cyberspace poses real challenges for international relations in theory and practice. As Austin Long argues in this volume, intelligence and coercion are increasingly linked, and cyberspace is increasingly valuable for intelligence. Recent events demonstrate that strategic actors are willing to use cyber operations as a tool of statecraft, even as the strategic results have proved ambiguous at best: Russian denial of service attacks and information operations in Estonia, Georgia, and Ukraine; relentless Chinese espionage and intrusive Internet censorship; U.S.-Israeli sabotage of Iranian nuclear enrichment infrastructure; Iranian retaliation against Saudi Aramco and U.S. banks; U.S. co-optation of major Internet firms for global signals intelligence collection revealed by Edward Snowden; criminal breaches of leading firms and government agencies exposing the private data of millions of citizens and government employees; North Korean harassment of Sony in Hollywood to protest a satirical movie; Russian active measures during the 2016 U.S. presidential election; and the list goes on.

To paraphrase Clausewitz, cyberwar is politics by other means. Understanding the dynamics, magnitude, and likelihood of aggression online requires an assessment of the operational requirements for staging various types of cyber operations, the strategic benefits actors hope to gain through them, and the risks of unintended consequences. In this chapter we lay out a typology of cyber operations that combines the logic of technological possibility with the logic of strategic utility. We distinguish a number of myths that assume cyber attacks can provide high rewards at low cost from more

---

Threat Matrix of Digital Espionage, Crime, and Warfare (New York: Penguin Press, 2011); Lucas Kello, "The Meaning of the Cyber Revolution: Perils to Theory and Statecraft," *International Security* 38 (2013): 7–40. For counterarguments to these three particular claims, see Jon R. Lindsay, "Stuxnet and the Limits of Cyber Warfare," *Security Studies* 22 (2013): 365–404.

[3] Myriam Dunn Cavelty, "Cyber-Terror—Looming Threat or Phantom Menace? The Framing of the US Cyber-Threat Debate," *Journal of Information Technology & Politics* 4 (2008): 19–36; Jerry Brito and Tate Watkins, "Loving the Cyber Bomb: The Dangers of Threat Inflation in Cybersecurity Policy," *Harvard National Security Journal* 3 (2011): 39–84; Sean Lawson, "Beyond Cyber-Doom: Assessing the Limits of Hypothetical Scenarios in the Framing of Cyber-Threats," *Journal of Information Technology & Politics* 10 (2013): 86–103.

[4] Thomas Rid, "Cyber War Will Not Take Place," *Journal of Strategic Studies* 35 (2012): 5–32; Adam P. Liff, "Cyberwar: A New 'Absolute Weapon'? The Proliferation of Cyberwarfare Capabilities and Interstate War," *Journal of Strategic Studies* 35 (2012): 401–28; Erik Gartzke, "The Myth of Cyberwar: Bringing War in Cyberspace Back Down to Earth," *International Security* 38 (2013): 41–73; Jon R. Lindsay, "The Impact of China on Cybersecurity: Fiction and Friction," *International Security* 39 (Winter 2014): 7–47; Brandon Valeriano and Ryan C. Maness, *Cyber War versus Cyber Realities: Cyber Conflict in the International System* (New York: Oxford University Press, 2015).

realistic options that deliver variable rewards at variable costs. There is no free lunch in cyberspace. As a result of technical and political constraints on secret operations that depend on interconnections between adversaries, the coercive potential of cyberspace is more limited than generally appreciated. Because voluntary connections to the Internet make cyber harms possible in the first place, aggressors must be careful not to provoke their victims to disconnect or erect barriers. The social and economic value of the Internet both expands and constrains the scope for minor aggression like espionage, covert influence, and symbolic protest. Moreover, the availability of military instruments beyond the cyber domain creates potential for retaliation for unacceptable harms. There are diminishing incentives to "go big" with cyberwarfare, even as an adjunct to battlefield operations, because victims have incentives to mount major investigations and shift domains to punish cyber aggression. Coercion has an important role to play in cyberspace, nonetheless, especially when exploited in conjunction with other forms of power, such as military force. We thus delineate the ways in which the cyber domain can be used alone or in conjunction with other domains for deterrence or compellence.

Strategic logic helps to explain the highly skewed distribution of cyber harms we observe historically. While information technology creates the *possibility* for harm, it is political and economic incentives that determine the *probability* of harm. Small-scale aggression online and computer crime are relatively appealing and thus more abundant; large-scale cyber attacks are more difficult and less desirable for initiators and thus far less likely to occur. This argument extends the logic of the "stability-instability paradox" pioneered in the 1960s. Mutually assured destruction may have restrained the superpowers from engaging in direct confrontations during the Cold War, but nuclear threats could not credibly prevent the exercise of proxy wars throughout the Third World. The mechanisms of restraint in the cyber domain are slightly different from those in the nuclear world insofar as actors look to maintain connectivity and avoid military retaliation or mutual Armageddon, but the results are similar: we see little to none of the most dangerous behavior but a great deal of provocative friction. It turns out that cyber revolutionaries and cyber skeptics are both partially correct: we should expect to see a lot more creative exploitation of global information infrastructure, but threat actors have strong incentives to restrain the severity of their exploitation.

The Power to Hurt Online

It is common to hear alarming claims about the magnitude of cyber threat activity such as that the U.S. Department of Defense is attacked 10 million times per day.[5] In reality most such "attacks" are routine automated port scans from cyber criminals trolling for low-hanging fruit. The majority of actual

[5] E.g., Zachary Fryer-Briggs, "U.S. Military Goes on Cyber Offensive," *Defense News*, March 24, 2012.

intrusions, including by nation-state intelligence agencies or "advanced persistent threats" (APTs), aim to steal data rather than disrupt systems. Cyber operations (also called "computer network operations") are conventionally divided into three functions: attack, exploitation, and defense.[6] Computer network exploitation seeks to preserve the illusion of normal functioning in the target system while illicitly stealing data and using system resources. Attack, by contrast, may cause servers to shut down, alter important data, or create malfunctions in computer-controlled industrial equipment. Computer network exploitation and attack are so closely related that U.S. doctrine considers them together, as offensive cyber operations (OCO). Both require the attacker to gain access to a target system through some combination of technical methods and malware (viruses, worms, Trojan horses, rootkits, etc.) that take advantage of design flaws or vulnerabilities, social engineering tricks to fool users into revealing sensitive data and passwords (phishing, baiting, water holing, candy drops, etc.), and a command and control network to coordinate the attack and obfuscate the attacker's identity. Only the malware payload differentiates exploitation from attack, which creates a challenge for the defender trying to differentiate an intelligence penetration from something more sinister.[7] Moreover, most disruptive attacks invariably require supporting exploitation for preparatory reconnaissance and performance feedback. Ambiguity about the purpose and severity of intrusions contributes to something of a siege mentality in popular accounts of cybersecurity.

Cyber defense includes all measures taken to protect networks from adversarial attack and exploitation: the use of physical boundaries, network firewalls, and intrusion detection systems; bureaucratic procedures to keep software patches and antivirus definitions up to date and to educate users about operational security (or cyber "hygiene"); active monitoring of network activity and investigation of suspicious activity; and coordination with law enforcement and intelligence entities before and after an attack.[8] U.S. doctrine differentiates defensive cyber operations that explicitly counter OCO from the routine maintenance of the Department of Defense Information Network, but there is a defensive aspect inherent in any positive use of cyberspace that depends on the confidentiality, integrity, and availability of user data. The witting or unwitting insider threat remains an organization's weakest link: users routinely disregard prophylactic advice or get fooled by creative phishing scams. Sophisticated intruders especially prize "zero day" vulnerabilities (engineering flaws that have not yet been patched by vendors)

---

[6] A good primer is William A. Owens, Kenneth W. Dam, and Herbert S. Lin, eds., *Technology, Policy, Law, and Ethics Regarding U.S. Acquisition and Use of Cyberattack Capabilities* (Washington, DC: National Academies Press, 2009). For U.S. doctrine see "Joint Publication 3-12 (R): Cyberspace Operations," Washington, DC, U.S. Joint Chiefs of Staff, February 5, 2013.

[7] Ben Buchanan, *The Cybersecurity Dilemma: Hacking, Trust, and Fear Between Nations* (New York: Oxford University Press, 2016).

[8] Ross Anderson, *Security Engineering: A Guide to Building Dependable Distributed Systems*, 2nd ed. (Indianapolis, IN: Wiley, 2008).

for eluding detection during infiltration and exploitation since they are unguarded by definition. The use of multiple precious zero days in a single cyber campaign (as in Olympic Games by the United States or the so-called Elderwood group in Beijing) is often indicative of a skilled and resourced state actor; a lucrative gray market has emerged to peddle zero days.[9] Cyber defense is often assumed to be relatively more difficult than attack or exploitation (i.e., cyberspace is supposedly "offense dominant"); however, it is not obvious that this is categorically true given the planning required for sophisticated penetrations and their vulnerability to quick remediation through patching or reconfiguration once compromised.[10]

The tactical contest in cyberspace, as in any other intelligence contest, is a battle of wits rather than brawn. OCO uses logical code rather than kinetic force to get into the target system, even as downstream effects of system malfunctions may result in physical damage. The hacker must find doors left open or con users into opening them; no amount of pounding on a closed door will cause it to open. As Martin Libicki rightly points out, "There is no forced entry in cyberspace."[11] All OCO depends on deception, and thus system developers and users become unwitting accomplices in their own exploitation. The ubiquity of deception in cyber operations also raises the possibility of using deception to reinforce defense and deter attacks.[12] An attacker who walks through an open door cannot be sure it does not lead to a trap. Defensive deception can undermine the attack through active counterintelligence measures like "honeypots" that draw intruders in for observation and quarantine, or even defensive counterattack (i.e., "active defense" or "hack back"). More complicated attacks are at greater risk of leaving behind clues for forensic investigations in technical artifacts or other behaviors exposed to intelligence collection, helping to attribute the identity of the intruder and, often more important, the nation-state sponsor.[13] More consequential attacks are also more likely to spur major investigations and create pressure to respond.[14] Attackers must exercise particular caution against resourced and resolved defenders.

---

[9] Kim Zetter, "How the Secretive Market for Zero-Day Exploits Works," *Slate*, July 24, 2015, http://www.slate.com/blogs/future_tense/2015/07/24/new_insights_into_zero_day_exploit_sales.html.
[10] Keir Lieber, "The Offense-Defense Balance and Cyber Warfare," in *Cyber Analogies*, ed. Emily O. Goldman and John Arquilla (Monterey, CA: Naval Postgraduate School, 2014), 96–107; Drew Herrick and Trey Herr, "Combating Complexity: Offensive Cyber Capabilities and Integrated Warfghting," Paper presented at the annual meetings of the International Studies Association, Atlanta, GA, 2016; Rebecca Slayton, "What Is the Cyber Offense-Defense Balance? Conceptions, Causes, and Assessment," *International Security* 41 (Winter 2016-2017): 72–109.
[11] Martin C Libicki, *Conquest in Cyberspace: National Security and Information Warfare* (New York: Cambridge University Press, 2007), 31.
[12] Erik Gartzke and Jon R. Lindsay, "Weaving Tangled Webs: Offense, Defense, and Deception in Cyberspace," *Security Studies* 24 (2015): 316–48.
[13] Thomas Rid and Ben Buchanan, "Attributing Cyber Attacks," *Journal of Strategic Studies* 38 (2015): 4–37.
[14] Jon R. Lindsay, "Tipping the Scales: The Attribution Problem and the Feasibility of Deterrence against Cyber Attack," *Journal of Cybersecurity* 1 (2015): 53–67.

Revolutionary Myths: Low Costs, High Rewards

In contemporary defense policy discourse there are three influential narratives of mounting cyber peril, corresponding roughly to the three operational modes of attack, exploitation, and defense. The most dangerous scenarios envision the *paralysis* of industrial control systems or military command and control through surprise attack by anonymous hackers. The imagined aggressor may be a revisionist state like China or Iran or a nonstate anarchist or terrorist empowered by the information revolution. A second narrative offers an alternative to the shock of sudden catastrophe, warning instead of the long term *erosion* of economic and military competitiveness drained away through persistent computer espionage. The relentless theft of vital secrets stored on corporate and government networks produces a "death by a thousand cuts" as states give their firms an unfair commercial advantage and equip their military forces with potent countermeasures to U.S. strengths. In both of these scenarios, commercial hacking tools and ubiquitous connectivity give weaker states and terrorists a potent means to exploit and attack the expanding surface of digitally dependent advanced industrial states. A third threat narrative concerns the transformation of Internet architecture to decisively benefit one political group at the expense of the other. At one extreme, the growth of flexible social media enables connected protesters to overwhelm and overthrow authoritarian regimes.[15] At the other extreme, authoritarian governments censor Internet content and reconfigure Internet governance to undermine the Internet's potential for innovation and freedom. State paranoia about the threats of paralysis and erosion thus leads to digital *lockout* or "the end of the Internet" as we know it.[16]

Threats of catastrophic attack, omniscient exploitation, and unassailable defense are myths because they imagine major rewards for little cost. The actual rewards of any given cyber campaign are rarely so great and the costs are rarely so trivial. Potential benefits of attack are discounted by uncertainty about the true value of the target to the adversary and the ability for the attacker to take advantage of it. Operative costs include the bureaucratic resources, development and testing requirements, human capital, and intelligence experience required to plan and run an effective covert cyber campaign. Setting aside the myths of low costs and high rewards (no free lunch), there are a variety of more realistic cyber operations with significant variation in their operative costs and benefits. A set of higher cost and, potentially, higher reward complements enhance the capabilities of stronger actors who can master them. A much larger set of low-cost, low-reward irritants are available to weaker actors or even solitary individuals, but they provide only a small marginal return on a small investment.

---

[15] Larry Diamond, "Liberation Technology," *Journal of Democracy* 21 (2010): 69–83.

[16] Jonathan L. Zittrain, "The Generative Internet," *Harvard Law Review* 119 (May 2006): 1974–2040.

TABLE 9.1 Types of Cyber Operation

CYBER OPERATION	REVOLUTIONARY MYTHS	OPERATIONAL COMPLEMENTS	MARGINAL IRRITANTS
Attack	Paralysis	Disruption	Hacktivism
Exploit	Erosion	Espionage	Fraud
Defend	Lockout	Control	Mobilization

Table 9.1 summarizes a typology of cyber harms across the three modes of attack, exploitation, and defense, from the mythic free-lunch varietals to more realistic complements and irritants. We use these terms to describe ideal type operations to focus attention on the relationship between costs and benefits, recognizing that many real-world activities going by the same names may blur these boundaries. We first describe the six types of operations we should expect to see from particular types of actors (i.e., complements and irritants) and then how they can be both used and limited through coercive strategies.

Complements: High Costs, (Potentially) High Payoffs

Operational complements are force multipliers. They amplify the power of actors who have enough resources and expertise to figure out how to manage the complexity and uncertainty of ambitious intrusions. They are less useful as stand-alone substitutes for material power, but they have the potential to augment the effectiveness of military or intelligence activity in other domains. Cyber *disruption* includes cyber attacks against industrial control systems (to include supervisory control and data acquisition subsystems) or military command and control systems (command, control, communications, computers, intelligence, surveillance, and reconnaissance [C4ISR]). The most famous historical example is the Stuxnet attack on Iran's nuclear program, used by the United States and Israel in conjunction with diplomatic, sanctions, and intelligence pressure as a covert alternative to air strikes. The sophisticated worm required considerable intelligence, preparation, and technical expertise, yet it caused only a temporary loss of Iranian enrichment efficiency; it emphatically was *not* designed to paralyze the Iranian program.[17] Russia's BlackEnergy attacks on Ukraine's power grid likewise occurred only after years of intelligence probes and caused only a six-hour disruption of electrical service.[18] Cyber attacks can potentially substitute for electronic warfare in the suppression or destruction of enemy air defenses, as reportedly used by Israel to facilitate a 2007 raid on a Syrian nuclear complex.[19] Similarly, Russian hackers coordinated cyber

[17] Lindsay, "Stuxnet and the Limits of Cyber Warfare."
[18] Kim Zetter, "Inside the Cunning, Unprecedented Hack of Ukraine's Power Grid," *Wired*, March 3, 2016.
[19] David A. Fulghum, "Why Syria's Air Defenses Failed to Detect Israelis," *Aviation Week, Ares Blog*, October 3, 2007. The cyber explanation has been disputed in this particular case, but the general concept is certainly feasible.

attacks against Georgian government websites and communications in conjunction with its land invasion of South Ossetia.[20] However, planning complications, intelligence gaps, and uncertainties about unintended consequences (e.g., encouraging the propagation of cyber weapons by establishing a precedent for their use) have led U.S. cyber planners to exercise restraint in considering cyber attacks against Libya and Syria.[21] Disruption can play a useful role in a combined cyber-military operation, but it takes significant organizational expertise and effort to integrate.

Less cost-intensive but hardly inexpensive, cyber *espionage* is the use of computer network exploitation to access the secrets of an economic competitor or political adversary (or to use similar tradecraft for covert influence, or what the Russians describe as active measures, shading into the category of hacktivism below). Espionage has the potential to alter the balance of power over time, but realizing this advantage in the form of competitive products or effective countermeasures requires an actor to leverage complementary strengths. Chinese APT campaigns have received great notoriety penetrating Western firms, governments, and nongovernmental organizations, stealing far more data than Chinese human intelligence ever managed alone. Yet the theft of secret data is only the first step in converting espionage into competitive advantage to produce, in the words of Gen. Keith Alexander, former director of the National Security Agency (NSA), "the greatest transfer of wealth in history." Cyber spies must extract valuable "needles" from a petabyte-scale "haystack" of junk data and then successfully disseminate the take to customers who can make sense of and absorb the stolen data into production or decision processes. While China has invested large sums in improving its capacity to absorb foreign technology, it is still playing catchup to Western innovation.[22]

To capture the positive network effects and efficiency gains that information technology makes possible,[23] networks must be defended against intrusion and misuse. Cyber *control* is neither cheap nor absolute. Indeed, to the degree that disruption and espionage are possible (or hacktivism, fraud, or mobilization, for that matter), perfect control (lockout) is not. This claim is generally uncontroversial, as cyber defense is widely held to involve difficult coordination problems in an offense-dominant medium. Some aspects of cyber defense have private goods characteristics, such as firewall and intrusion detection systems protecting the owner's network perimeter, but cybersecurity is also beset

[20] R. J. Deibert, R. Rohozinski, and M. Crete-Nishihata, "Cyclones in Cyberspace: Information Shaping and Denial in the 2008 Russia-Georgia War," *Security Dialogue* 43 (2012): 3–24.
[21] Ellen Nakashima, "U.S. Accelerating Cyberweapon Research," *Washington Post*, March 18, 2012; David E. Sanger, "Syria War Stirs New U.S. Debate on Cyberattacks," *New York Times*, February 24, 2014.
[22] Jon R. Lindsay and Tai Ming Cheung, "From Exploitation to Innovation: Acquisition, Absorption, and Application," in *China and Cybersecurity: Espionage, Strategy, and Politics in the Digital Domain*, ed. Jon R. Lindsay, Tai Ming Cheung, and Derek S Reveron (New York: Oxford University Press, 2015).
[23] Erik Brynjolfsson and Adam Saunders, *Wired for Innovation: How Information Technology Is Reshaping the Economy* (Cambridge, MA: MIT Press, 2010).

by public goods problems.[24] Examples include users who opt not to patch their systems and end up hosting botnets that attack other users and software vendors who neglect the development of security features in the rush to get their products to market. Meanwhile, offensive cyber threats may change their signatures faster than defenders can keep up.[25] Even authoritarian governments cannot achieve absolute advantage in the arms race with technologically savvy dissidents, at least as long as those states also desire digital access to international economic transactions. Yet weak dissidents face even greater challenges assuring control of their social networks, since regime actors can use not only espionage but also more draconian enforcement measures against them. The relationship between Internet control, innovation, and freedom is too complicated to analyze further in this chapter, but that very complexity makes either version of lockout an unlikely possibility.[26]

Irritants: Low Costs, Low Payoffs

Operational complements can make the strong even stronger, if coordinated with other sources of strength. Contrary to conventional wisdom about the asymmetric nature of cyberwarfare, operational complements tend to advantage nation-state actors, especially Great Powers with institutional resources who can overcome planning and intelligence challenges and price in the risk of failure. Marginal irritants, by contrast, are widely affordable for all types of actors, weak or strong, and they can be employed with lower risk of adverse consequences. The risks are low because those who have the power to intervene to stop or punish irritant behavior often do not have the motivation to do so. While irritants are often illegal under domestic statutes, law enforcement authorities often do not launch sufficiently aggressive investigations, for want of resources or authorization, to discover and sanction the perpetrators. Irritant attackers can thus hide safely behind their digital anonymity, whereas the use of offensive complements described earlier would provoke a more concerted investigation and response. By the same token, the expected rewards are low.

The vast majority of empirically observable cyber attacks can be grouped into the category of *hacktivism*, which includes distributed denial of service (DDoS) attacks that knock servers offline, website defacements, defamation, and other forms of online protest. An early example of hacktivism as defined here is the barrage of DDoS attacks and defacement from Russian nationalists that wracked Estonia in 2007 following the removal of a Soviet memorial in

---

[24] Ross Anderson and Tyler Moore, "The Economics of Information Security," *Science* 314 (October 27, 2006): 610–13; Paul Rosenzweig, *Cyber Warfare: How Conflicts in Cyberspace Are Challenging America and Changing the World* (Santa Barbara, CA: Praeger, 2013).

[25] Dale Peterson, "Offensive Cyber Weapons: Construction, Development, and Employment," *Journal of Strategic Studies* 36 (2013): 120–24.

[26] Ronald Deibert et al., eds., *Access Contested: Security, Identity, and Resistance in Asian Cyberspace Information Revolution and Global Politics* (Cambridge, MA: MIT Press, 2012); Sarah McKune, "'Foreign Hostile Forces': The Human Rights Dimension of China's Cyber Campaigns," in Lindsay et al., *China and Cybersecurity*.

Tallinn. Similar activity from Chinese nationalists is also common in China's periodic tensions with Taiwan and Japan. The anarchist collective Anonymous has embarrassed several firms and government agencies by illicitly acquiring and then publicly posting (doxing) confidential data. Colloquially *hacktivism* is sometimes used to cover what we call mobilization in our typology (i.e., when hacktivists seek to encourage one another and create support for a cause). The same technical methods used for criminal exploitation or what we categorize as fraud can also be considered hacktivism if conducted for the purposes of defamation or political influence rather than financial gain (e.g., when hackers steal and expose confidential information, a practice known as doxing, after the manner of WikiLeaks). Hacktivist techniques might also be combined with OCO disruption, as in North Korea's attack on Sony, which destroyed hard drives and released embarrassing internal memos, an episode that attempted but ultimately failed to prevent the release of a satirical comedy, exemplifying the limitations of anonymous cyber coercion.[27] Hacktivist attacks can grab headlines and be embarrassing or financially costly to those they target, but they usually subside within a few news cycles. At the technical level, mitigation techniques for things like DDoS are readily available. DDoS and defacements have become prominent during almost any period of political tension as a form of nationalist protest, and there is often much ambiguity behind whether government actors or nationalist citizens are responsible, a plausible deniability that can aid either hacktivists seeking to avoid punishment or targets that are not motivated enough to punish them. The Russian campaign targeting the 2016 U.S. election was perhaps the most blatant employment of hacktivist techniques to date, combining cyber espionage, doxing, and propaganda in a large scale coordinated campaign (highlighting the ability to combine operations in our typology). Yet even here the results were ambiguous given many other unusual aspects of the 2016 season.[28]

Cyber *mobilization* is the use of social media to coordinate protest activity online and on the ground. We categorize this as a mode of defense because dissidents seek to use social media as designed to realize its positive network benefits. Recent large-scale political protest movements associated with the Arab Spring and Ukrainian EuroMaidan leveraged social media to mobilize and organize protesters.[29] However, whatever success they enjoyed owed more to the tenacity of the protestors, their physical presence in numbers, and the restraint of government security forces. The limits of mobilization were highlighted in the abortive Iranian "Green Revolution" of 2009 and the Chinese "Jasmine Revolution" of 2010, where government security forces exploited the

[27] Stephan Haggard and Jon R. Lindsay, "North Korea and the Sony Hack: Exporting Instability through Cyberspace," *AsiaPacific Issues* (Honolulu: EastWest Center, May 2015).

[28] Joshua Rovner et al., "Russia and the 2016 U.S. Presidential Election," ISSF Policy Roundtable 1–7, *H-Diplo*, (March 26, 2017), https://networks.h-net.org/node/28443/discussions/173096/issf-policy-roundtable-1-7-russia-and-2016-us-presidential.

[29] Diamond, "Liberation Technology."

use of social media to identify and punish protesters.[30] The defenses of mobilization are weak because software products must be distributed wholesale to interconnected users with uneven technical skills. State-sponsored attackers can exploit this vulnerability; for example, the Chinese state sought to provide spyware to protesters in Hong Kong in 2014.[31] Mobilization can also take on virulent or socially dysfunctional forms such as cyber bullying and its industrial-scale Chinese analogue known as "human flesh search," a virtual lynch mob defaming corrupt officials, disgraced celebrities, and unfortunate citizens alike.[32]

Financially motivated computer crime or *fraud* accounts for the overwhelming empirical manifestation of cyber insecurity. There is a complex, segmented, global market for cybercrime divided into interdependent advertising, theft and fraud, and technical support rackets. This underground ecosystem also supports more sophisticated OCO complements by providing malware and compromised hosts to facilitate intrusion. However, APTs that conduct targeted espionage require much more skill and effort per target and assume greater risk. Unlike APTs, retail cybercrime is untargeted and scales more easily to exploit millions of potential victims since it only has to be successful a fraction of a percent of the time to be profitable. Underground revenues total hundreds of billions of dollars annually, although the vast majority of cyber criminals actually make very little money because of rampant dishonesty in the underground economy and nontrivial law enforcement risks. Even spectacular compromises of millions of credit card accounts do not readily translate into handy profits because translating that data into a usable monetary instrument is difficult.[33]

To sum up, cyber attack, exploitation, and defensive operations can be employed as costly complements to enhance other advantages an experienced and resourced actor might have, or as inexpensive irritants for minor gain. Myths of grave harms are based on an unrealistic assessment of the operational barriers and strategic risks involved. For the most part our discussion so far has focused on the ways in which cyber means can provide some direct benefit to adjust the balance of power, however marginally, via offensive or defensive cyber operations support to military operations, intelligence collection, information system control, symbolic protest, political mobilization,

[30] Evgeny Morozov, *The Net Delusion: The Dark Side of Internet Freedom*, reprint ed. (New York: Public Affairs, 2011).
[31] Shannon Tiezzi, "China's Cyber War against Hong Kong Protestors," *Diplomat*, October 1, 2014, http://thediplomat.com/2014/10/chinas-cyber-war-against-hong-kong-protestors/.
[32] Saul Levmore and Martha C. Nussbaum, eds., *The Offensive Internet: Speech, Privacy, and Reputation* (Cambridge, MA: Harvard University Press, 2011).
[33] Kirill Levchenko et al., "Click Trajectories: End-to-End Analysis of the Spam Value Chain," in *Proceedings of the 2011 IEEE Symposium on Security and Privacy*, SP '11 (Washington, DC: IEEE Computer Society, 2011), 431–46; Ross Anderson et al., "Measuring the Cost of Cybercrime," in *The Economics of Information Security and Privacy*, ed. Rainer Böhme (Berlin: Springer-Verlag, 2013), 265–300; Cormac Herley, "When Does Targeting Make Sense for an Attacker?," *IEEE Security & Privacy* 11 (2013): 89–92; Jianwe Zhuge et al., "Investigating the Chinese Online Underground Economy," in Lindsay et al., *China and Cybersecurity*.

financial gain, and more. Some mention of deterrent threats (or their absence) has been unavoidable even in our discussion of cyber harms thus far, such as the unwillingness of law enforcement to pursue all irritants and the willingness of strong actors to employ disruptive complements when backed up by other capabilities. We now turn from harmful means to coercive ends, and from the power to hurt to the power to persuade.

Cyber Coercion

As Robert Art and Kelly M. Greenhill point out in their chapter in this volume, coercion is different from pure harm, even though coercing may require causing some harm in the process of creating credible threats of more harm. Harm pure and simple (brute force), aims to change the balance of capabilities between adversaries in the present, while coercion uses harm or threats of harm to influence an adversary's decision-making in the future. Coercion is a signaling process that attempts to link particular behaviors to unpleasant consequences in the mind of the opponent. It targets the willingness of the opponent to endure suffering or comply with demands and can include *deterrence,* to prevent something from happening, or *compellence,* to cause something to happen, as well as more complicated forms of signaling that we will not address in this chapter.

The future-directedness of all forms of coercion seems to create a problem in cyberspace. How can an adversary be made to understand a credible threat of future harm via network connection and yet voluntarily maintain the connections on which that future harm depends? As mentioned earlier, cyber intrusions depend on deception because logical, massless code cannot kinetically force its way through anything. If software vulnerabilities are highlighted by an explicit threat to exploit them unless the target complies with a demand, then the target can patch or otherwise neutralize the threat. Therefore, if attackers rely on the difficulty of attribution to protect themselves, they cannot easily make credible coercive demands that would reveal their identity and methods. Moreover, if bad intelligence or buggy malware in the threatened cyber attack causes unexpectedly high or low damage when exercised, then the punishment may have little resemblance to the threat. Vague threats from anonymous sources lack credibility, fail to precisely specify the action proscribed or demanded, and offer little reassurance that the coercer will withhold punishment if the target complies. Furthermore, a necessary reliance on deception and ambiguity creates considerable potential for the misperception of coercive signals.[34]

Nevertheless, cyber operations are not completely devoid of coercive potential, even if they are more limited compared to traditional means of aggression. Cyber operations can be employed in some circumstances for deterrence and compellence, especially if expectations for success are limited or coercers are

[34] Gartzke, "The Myth of Cyberwar."

TABLE 9.2 Cyber Coercion

	DETERRENCE	COMPELLENCE
Cyberspace	Detection Denial Deception	Latency Extortion Seduction
Cross-Domain	Retaliation Disconnection	Escalation Protection

satisfied with ambiguous results. The most promising coercive cyber tools are complements (rather than irritants) because they have the potential to impose higher costs in conjunction with other (noncyber) tools. Table 9.2 summarizes strategies for coercion using cyber means along (within-domain) and in conjunction with other means (cross-domain).

Cyber Deterrence

The difficulty of attributing responsibility for cyber attacks is widely thought to undermine the credibility of retaliatory threats and thus cyber deterrence in general.[35] However, these assumptions are not categorically true across the entire range of cyber operations. Pervasive surveillance or the threat of detection can augment general deterrence. Public investment in cyber defense can improve deterrence by denial. Defensive deception can improve both punishment and denial strategies.

Insofar as cyber operations are particularly well suited for intelligence, they should also be expected to enhance the intelligence dimensions of coercion, discussed by Long in this volume. A reputation for skill at surveillance by any means can dissuade targets from planning and executing harmful operations. Intelligence collection can provide the direct benefit of targeting data, and it can help, potentially, to shift the balance of power over time by transferring knowledge and evening the playing field (with all the caveats regarding absorption mentioned earlier). Moreover, the fact or fear of surveillance can also encourage paranoia and force a target to adopt onerous security measures. Extensive signals intelligence monitoring of underground groups forces many of them to rely on couriers who are slower, more expensive, and less efficient than mobile phones. Battlefield targets that adopt debilitating "emissions control" postures effectively commit "EMCON suicide." Paranoia that detection will be followed by swift precision strikes or law enforcement action may cause targets to forgo misbehavior altogether. Likewise, citizens subject

[35] For extensive discussions see Martin C. Libicki, *Cyberdeterrence and Cyberwar* (Santa Monica, CA: RAND, 2009); National Research Council, ed., *Proceedings of a Workshop on Deterring Cyberattacks: Informing Strategies and Developing Options for U.S. Policy* (Washington, DC: National Academies Press, 2010).

to continuous monitoring via public cameras and Internet surveillance tend to internalize obedience to the state or at least curtail observably deviant behavior. Pervasive cyber espionage may be undesirable from a civil liberties perspective but may be effective for suppressive coercion.

Deterrence by *detection* works when a potential cyber attacker fears that the probability of detection is high and is concerned about the consequences of getting caught; detection provides the option for targeted retaliation. While attribution is not strictly needed for punishment (think of a minefield or retributive razing of a village), prompt detection and convincing attribution does lower the costs and thus the credibility of punishment.[36] Credibility here is enhanced by cultivating a reputation for skilled cyber exploitation, which in turn improves the credibility of threats of punishment by whatever means, cyber or cross-domain. While Snowden's leakage of top-secret NSA documents certainly compromised technical intelligence sources, it also (inadvertently) helped the United States to advertise the technical skill of the NSA. This leak was credible because it was also costly in terms of lost sources and, potentially, lost market share for U.S. firms wittingly or unwittingly collaborating with the NSA. Michel Foucault introduced the metaphor of the panopticon to describe how pervasive state surveillance deters social deviance; likewise, the state cyber panopticon offers some general deterrent that dissuades some challenges from materializing in the first place.[37] Once immediate challenges do emerge, this benefit is much diminished.

A reputation for skilled cyber defense, above and beyond the ability simply to detect threats, enhances deterrence by *denial*. Cyber defense can block, parry, or redirect intrusions. Public knowledge of the robustness of defense makes attackers worry that their efforts might be futile, even dangerous. Defensive aptitude can be signaled through costly investment in cyber intelligence, law enforcement, and regulatory agencies and the advertisement of success in detecting and thwarting attacks. Creation of U.S. Cyber Command to defend military networks, major exercises like the Cyber Storm series, and budgetary investment in training and capabilities all provide signals of U.S. commitment to the defense of its warfighting networks. It is not necessary for all intrusions to be prevented. In the case of Chinese APTs, the public disclosure of Chinese tradecraft and government responsibility heightens the suspicion future Chinese intruders must face when trying to hide or deny their involvement in espionage. Indeed, Chinese APT activity paused and reconfigured following the February 2013 exposé by cybersecurity firm Mandiant, which identified a specific Chinese military unit in Shanghai involved in the exploitation of 141 English-speaking targets worldwide via a variety of lapses in Chinese tradecraft (e.g., operator reuse of names and emails, command and control

[36] Lindsay, "Tipping the Scales."
[37] Michel Foucault, *Discipline and Punish: The Birth of the Prison*, trans. Alan Sheridan (New York: Random House, 1977).

servers located in China, operators checking personal Facebook accounts from their attack infrastructure, etc.).[38]

Deception is an underappreciated strategy that is particularly promising for network protection. Ruses, honeypots, digital bait, data obfuscation, and more aggressive counterintelligence techniques have already been employed by security engineers. Deception can confuse, delay, misdirect, or even harm the attacker, for instance by enabling the exfiltration of harmful malware to infect the attacker's home networks. Whereas pure deterrent strategies punish intrusion and pure denial strategies impede it, deception actually encourages intrusion, but then turns it against the intruder. For this reason, deception is rightly considered a distinct protective strategy, even though in practice it operates to reinforce defense or deterrence by punishment or denial. While deception has always been available and has been practiced in the past, the growth in complexity of information technology from the telegraph to the Internet has made deception more possible and useful than ever before. The supposed offense dominance of cyberspace is actually a result of the increased potential for deception, especially for less sophisticated gambits, but defenders can use deception too. There are clearly some operational and legal challenges associated with cyber deception and all forms of active defense. Credible deception is difficult, so, as with control complements generally, the advantage in deception usually goes to the stronger and/or better organized actor.[39]

The traditional distinction between punishment and denial is muddied for forms of cyber defense that involve counterattack and deception against the intruder. U.S. officials have begun to announce that the cyber attribution problem is not as daunting as once believed and that attackers will be met with a decisive response in cyberspace or elsewhere.[40] A reputation for skill at cyber operations is useful not only for the deterrence of cyber attacks (because of the risk of detection and punishment or of denial) but also for more general coercion, if they augment the effectiveness of other threats or undermine the target's confidence in defending against them. So far the United States has demonstrated the greatest capacity for and willingness to use cyber operations through its Olympic Games program, which allegedly produced the Stuxnet attack on Iran. Unfortunately this same case highlights the deterrent limitations of cyber punishment, as Iran continued to enrich uranium and even accelerated the modernization and relocation of its program after 2010 while also pursuing its own offensive cyber program.[41]

---

[38] Mandiant, "APT1: Exposing One of China's Cyber Espionage Units," White Paper, *FireEye* (February 2013), https://www.fireeye.com/content/dam/fireeye-www/services/pdfs/mandiant-apt1-report.pdf; Mandiant, "M-Trends 2014 Annual Threat Report: Beyond the Breach," *FireEye* (April 2014), https://www2.fireeye.com/fireeye-mandiant-m-trends-report.html.

[39] Gartzke and Lindsay, "Weaving Tangled Webs."

[40] Elisabeth Bumiller and Thom Shanker, "Panetta Warns of Dire Threat of Cyberattack on U.S.," *New York Times*, October 11, 2012.

[41] Christopher Bronk and Eneken Tikk-Ringas, "The Cyber Attack on Saudi Aramco," *Survival* 55 (April 3, 2013): 81–96; Lindsay, "Stuxnet and the Limits of Cyber Warfare."

There is no reason for threats of punishment or *retaliation* to be limited to cyber actions. In fact, the most important bounds on the severity of cyber aggression probably have nothing to do with the technology of cyberspace. Victims of aggression can and likely will look to responses not only in kind but also through whatever other means they possess, ranging from conventional military retaliation to irregular warfare and covert subversion, trade and financial sanctions. The problem of attribution is often thought to preclude the ability to retaliate, but as mentioned, this problem is overstated for any serious attack. The question for an aggressor contemplating truly serious cyber harm is not whether but how the victim will retaliate. The only exception would be for the attacker to launch a cyber attack so devastating that it effectively paralyzes all ability for the target to retaliate, but as we argued earlier, such paralysis is a myth for operational reasons alone—a splendid first cyber strike is simply too complex and full of uncertainties to reliably deliver its results—let alone the risks of cross-domain retaliation. If the victim retains significant options in other domains where the attacker's ability to resist is slight, then the attacker has strong incentives to avoid provoking a response in those domains. Even if the target is asymmetrically more dependent on the Internet, making a disruptive cyber attack seem like an attractive possibility, advanced industrial countries are for the same reason more likely to have other advanced military and economic options available where the asymmetries do not favor the attacker. Serious attacks invite serious responses, which need not be in kind.

Perhaps the simplest form of cross-domain response to cyber threats is to forgo the use of the cyber domain altogether. While it is hard if not impossible to limit exposure to nuclear weapons and even a determined conventional assault, the risk of cyber attack can be completely eliminated by *disconnection* from digital networks. The Internet is an artificial environment, and connection to it is voluntary. Individuals, organizations, and states retain the ability to unplug completely, limit their online transactions, or erect various technical and organizational barriers to connection. Obviously disconnection is not very feasible commercially, socially, and militarily today, but this is more of an indicator of how great the benefits of interconnection are compared to the perceived risks. If the risks were perceived as extreme, then firms and states could go back to making a living as they did before 1991 (when the World Wide Web came to be). This is a cross-domain threat because it entails exiting the cyber domain to some degree to engage in more traditional economic and military transactions. The threat of disconnection follows from the more general logic of international institutions, where contracts must be self-enforcing.[42] On the Internet as in institutions, ties among egoistic actors under anarchy must be mutually beneficial. If the Internet is a bad deal for actors, they can throw up boundaries or exit cyberspace altogether. The threat of voluntary disconnection is especially relevant for repeated interactions, or repeated exploitation,

[42] Kenneth A. Oye, ed., *Cooperation under Anarchy* (Princeton, NJ: Princeton University Press, 1986).

rather than a one-shot "bolt from the blue" cyber attack, which is better countered with cross-domain retaliation. The threat of disconnection is implicit in the voluntary nature of connection to the Internet, and the potential loss of the ability to make future attacks exercises a deterrent effect on attacks in the present. An aggressor who does not want to lose access to cyber complements for espionage and disruption it has invested so much in developing will show restraint in their employment. This does not mean that coercion cannot take place online, but dependence on mutual interconnection bounds coercion by excess value. One implication is that the countries that can be most coerced on the Internet will be those that have the most to lose by leaving it.

Detection—leveraging cyberspace as a panopticon—removes the cloak of anonymity cyber attackers depend on and facilitates retaliation. Denial—a reputation for effective defense—counters attackers who believe they can, nonetheless, maintain their tactical covertness. Deception—using attackers' strengths in stealth against them—reinforces both punishments and denial. Importantly, all three of these strategies are useful for the entire range of cyber operations, complements as well as irritants, although for many irritants the effort for protection may not be worthwhile. By contrast, the other two cross-domain strategies—retaliating by any means necessary and disconnecting from the threat altogether—are aimed more at deterring high-impact aggression (operational complements in our typology) or keeping aggression confined more toward the lower (irritant) end of the spectrum. This gives rise to a cyber analogue of the stability-instability paradox.

Cyber Compellence

Schelling and others have argued that compellence is harder than deterrence. Deterrence dissuades, while compellence persuades. Deterrence stops something in motion, while compellence starts something at rest. Deterrence need only signal "Don't cross this line," while compellence must signal "Move across this line, and only so far." If the United States threatens or conducts a cruise missile attack against a state believed to be harboring a suspected leader of Al Qaeda (i.e., using the base state coercion strategy described by Keren Fraiman in this volume), the goal is to get the target to extradite the Al Qaeda leader. Would a nonlethal cyber attack or threat of attack be able to accomplish the same thing? When would coercion work because of cyber means but not because of something else? Is there any target that cyber tools have particular power to compel? If cyber deterrence is thought to be difficult, surely cyber compellence should be more difficult still.

The biggest obstacle to cyber coercion is the difficulty of credible signaling about potential harm when it depends on secrecy to be harmful. Advertised cyber threats that are specific enough to be credible can be neutralized through patching, reconfiguration, or other countermeasures. Sacrifice of the anonymity on which offensive deception depends exposes the cyber attacker to retaliation. Coercive cyber threats thus tend to be more generalized, which undercuts their effectiveness in targeted or crisis situations. The effectiveness of deterrence by deception (the cyber panopticon) depends more on generalized concerns that an intelligence service might be reading email or snooping around networks than any immediate threat of detection. This form of deterrence is especially effective when employed by a strong state with a sophisticated digital surveillance system. A compellent analogue is the generalized threat of escalation from cyber exploitation to disruptive attack. Detection carries the latent possibility of punishment, and exploitation the latent possibility of attack.

Escalation *latency* is not a specific threat of harm but more of a generalized paranoia that "our networks are already so penetrated that resistance is useless!" If intelligence intrusions into vital systems are detected, the target cannot be sure that the same intrusion might be used to activate or deliver a more dangerous payload. The potential for escalation from exploitation to attack is latent most of the time in reality, yet the inherent ambiguity about purpose and scale encourages some paranoia: What if the networks on which our prosperity and strength depend were turned against us? What if defense against societal paralysis is as fruitless as defense against cybercrime? What if all it takes is a change of mind by the adversary to convert probes into destruction? Technological, intelligence, and operational constraints in fact render the fungibility of technique from exploitation to attack less of a realistic concern than often feared (because engineering destruction on command requires significant additional expertise and testing) or restrict it only to large actors with resources and experience to make disruptive complements work. Nonetheless, the prospect of ongoing technological innovation and falling barriers of entry to cyber attack tempt many observers to take this dormant potential seriously. Since this fear rests on a misperception—escalation is operationally nontrivial; victims of network disruption often find alternatives; and both sides will learn these points as the crisis drags on—cyber latency is not very reliable for compellence on its own. But anything that creates fear can be at least a little bit useful in a broader gambit; again cyber appears useful as a complement to, not a substitute for, other means of coercion.

Specific and credible coercive signaling is more feasible in the realm of irritant cybercrime beneath the threshold of state-sanctioned retaliation. There exist *extortion* scams that use ransomware to disable a computer or lock out access to data unless the victim pays into an account that the anonymous attacker can access.[43] This strategy uses the threat of disconnection in a compellent rather than a deterrent role. (Extortion is also analogous to denial as both threaten failure of the target's cyber operations, the failure of normal operations, or the failure of an attack.) Cyber blackmail is useful only at small scales where the ransom is less than the reconstitution cost of the embargoed system or the cost of contacting law enforcement. It thus can be most effective against victims who themselves might be on the wrong side of the law,

---

[43] Ian Urbina, "Hackers Find New Ways to Breach Computer Security," *New York Times*, June 21, 2014.

for instance, a threat to embargo a bookie's books or computers that support an illegal racetrack. Authoritarian states can also use threats of disconnection from the Internet to cow media outlets and muzzle dissidents. Attempts to cut off a population from the Internet altogether, for example in Egypt during the Arab Spring or in China during the Xinjiang unrest of 2009, bleed into the category of control rather than coercion, although expectations that a "kill switch" might be thrown could have a slight persuasive effect on dissidents (who would surely worry more about riot police if it came to that). One can conjure up scenarios wherein a cyber attack causes costly malfunctions but for some reason audience costs prevent the victim from publicly admitting to the damage or the mechanism. Joel Brenner imagines a scenario in which China blackmails a U.S. president by knocking out large sections of the U.S. power grid that only China can repair through its monopoly on a particular type of generator, but only if the United States recalls a carrier strike group en route to Taiwan.[44] Importantly, all such examples of cyber extortion can work only when the victims are weak or lack alternatives or recourse for some reason. Brenner's scenario would almost certainly backfire on the Chinese.

We discussed how deception can enhance deterrence by punishing intruders who steal baited data or attack honeypot systems. Deception can also enhance compellence by making the desired action appear more attractive to the target than it actually is. The strategic essence of deception is persuading an adversary to voluntarily take action that is not, ultimately, in its interest. Compellent deception can be described as *seduction*. It is the bread and butter of commonplace Internet fraud and one of the charms of the Nigerian princess who needs your help to recover lottery winnings held by an alien hovering over London. Cyber seduction might also be useful for sending bogus orders to enemy troops in the field instructing them to retreat or stow their weapons, or to lure enemy commanders into an ambush. Importantly, as with other cyber complements, the window of vulnerability created by a seductive ruse is useful only if the seducer plans to exploit it in the terrestrial domain.

OCO can be used in conjunction with other forms of military force—for example, disabling early warning or command and control networks in support of an air campaign—to make a threatened intervention seem more potent, if an actor is inclined to threaten military action. That is, a hostile adversary armed with cyber weapons in addition to tanks, fighters, and missiles might appear more able to overcome defenses and thus be better able to issue compellent threats. Likewise, a preparatory cyber campaign to destabilize communications or carry out deception operations could signal a willingness to employ more meaningful forms of aggression in a process of cross-domain *escalation*. Certainly the presence of aggression online helps to cultivate an air of crisis, which could be useful for strategies of risk or brinksmanship. Something like this seems to have happened in Ukraine in 2014, when cyber

---

[44] Brenner, *America the Vulnerable*, chapter 7.

attacks accompanied the incursion of Russian commandos to take Crimea without resistance, while mechanized Russian forces mobilized and exercised on the border.[45] Another route to coercion involves outbursts of DDoS attacks and website defacement by civilians to cultivate an air of crisis and provide elites with a diplomatic argument that their hands are tied by popular nationalism. The hands-tying argument loses credibility if the state has demonstrated an ability in tamp-down online outbursts at will, as China has. Importantly, all of these mechanisms depend on the coercer having the ability to escalate beyond the cyber domain, leveraging the fear of substantive military assault. Cyber aggression is used to signal the risk or potency of cross-domain escalation.

Cyber defense can likewise enhance the credibility of coercive military threats. If a coercer has and is known to have robust cyber *protection*, then the target will have less faith in preempting or defending against the threatened punishment. Conversely, a coercer who lacks adequate cyber defenses is like the proverbial stone-thrower in a glass house. Threats will lack credibility if exercising them means assured retaliation, in this case a cyber counterattack on military C4ISR that delays or degrades the ability to carry out the promised punishment. But if cyber defense can be assured, then it is easier—or at least less hard—to project military power in the service of coercive diplomacy.[46] The protection of computer networks is thus an important complement to the issuance of cross-domain threats that depend on them. Protection is the inverse of disconnection, seeking to persuade the target that cyber systems will not be unplugged.

To sum up, latency exploits the ambiguity between cyber exploitation and attack to create fears of harmful punishment if the target doesn't comply with demands. Extortion denies the target's use of cyber resources for blackmail purposes. Seduction uses deceptive techniques to lure the target into a position where compellent punishment and denial will be more effective. Escalation uses cyber aggression to signal a risk of more punishing consequences in other domains. Protection of cyber assets improves the credibility of military threats in other domains. This whole discussion shows how closely related deterrence and compellence are. Deterrence can facilitate aggression by blocking counterattack. This may be especially the case for cyber operations, particularly for strong nations like the United States that can use the deterrent threat of military retaliation to cover the employment of offensive cyber tools. As with all forms of coercion, cyber compellence appears to be more complicated than deterrence, even as they share many constraints and signals. For both deterrence and compellence, cyber coercion is most effective when employed as a complementary adjunct with capabilities to hurt in other domains. The

[45] David E. Sanger and Steven Erlanger, "Suspicion Falls on Russia as 'Snake' Cyberattacks Target Ukraine's Government," *New York Times*, March 8, 2014.

[46] Michael Fortmann and Stefanie von Hlatky, "The Revolution in Military Affairs: Impact of Emerging Technologies on Deterrence," in *Complex Deterrence: Strategy in the Global Age*, ed. T. V. Paul, Patrick M. Morgan, and James J. Wirtz (Chicago: University of Chicago Press, 2009), 304–20.

capacity of cyber to operate as a substitute is highly constrained and effective mostly for aggression of the irritant class.

Misperception

No discussion of coercion would be complete without some attention to the psychological dimension. After all, coercion seeks to influence the mind of the opponent by generating credible signals of future costs and benefits associated with taking (avoiding) certain behavior. These signals can be missed, garbled, or misinterpreted. If, as we argue, cyberspace is a domain that is especially conducive to deception, then misperception is liable to be a major problem.[47] Cyber operations characterized by secrecy and ambiguity often lack the clarity associated with, say, a military invasion of territory. This secrecy and duplicity inherent in cyber operations make it easy to misinterpret signals, if indeed it is possible to signal at all. There is an emerging consensus in political science that uncertainty is a major—if not the major—cause of war.[48] Uncertainty in the cyber domain makes it unstable, especially at the low end, even as improved knowledge of the likely costs of war in other domains places a bound on conflict at the higher end. Cyber operations are most useful in an intelligence role, and they can potentially convey information about interests (including the willingness to escalate) without actual fighting. Deliberate collection and pervasive leaks all enhance transparency, which should make conflict less likely. Furthermore, cyberspace is a human construct of commonly embraced and mutually beneficial protocols—interoperability is the condition for the possibility of cyber operations—so states collaborate in making Internet infrastructure more stable and reliable.[49] At the same time, the secrecy of cyber operations, their complexity, and the asymmetry of access to high-quality intelligence may only exacerbate problems of uncertainty.

Misperception has the potential to cause inadvertent escalation. In a crisis combining secret OCO with threats to act in other military domains, adversaries may end up inflicting and accepting greater costs than they would have been willing to pay at the start of the crisis. For example, the use of cyber attacks to degrade an opponent's strategic command and control systems, either as part of a coercive risk strategy or to facilitate limited conventional strikes, could put the opponent into a "use it or lose it" situation.[50] The dangers

[47] Rose McDermott, "Decision Making under Uncertainty," in *Proceedings of a Workshop on Deterring Cyberattacks: Informing Strategies and Developing Options for U.S. Policy*, ed. National Research Council (Washington, DC: National Academies Press, 2010), 227–42.

[48] James D. Fearon, "Rationalist Explanations for War," *International Organization* 49 (1995): 379–414; Erik Gartzke, "War Is in the Error Term," *International Organization* 53 (1999): 567–87; Jeffrey M. Kaplow and Erik Gartzke, "Knowing Unknowns: The Effect of Uncertainty in Interstate Conflict," paper presented at the 56th annual convention of the International Studies Association, New Orleans, 2015.

[49] Lindsay, "The Impact of China on Cybersecurity"; Daniel W. Drezner, "The Global Governance of the Internet: Bringing the State Back In," *Political Science Quarterly* 119 (2004): 477–98.

[50] Barry R. Posen, *Inadvertent Escalation: Conventional War and Nuclear Risks* (Ithaca, NY: Cornell University Press, 1991).

of inadvertent escalation through the cyber domain are thought to be particularly salient in a U.S.-China conflict scenario due to the dangerous combination of U.S. preferences for aggressive C4ISR counterforce operations, the consolidation of nuclear and strategic missile forces in the PLA Rocket Force, Chinese and U.S. convictions that cyberwarfare must be used preemptively, and nationalist pressures in both states to retaliate for costly losses.[51]

Escalatory danger is theoretically most stark when the instability of the cyber domain (a result of ambiguity and deception) is combined with the relative stability of the nuclear domain (a result of the transparently horrific costs of nuclear war). OCO penetration of nuclear command and control could lead one side to run greater risks during a brinksmanship contest in the knowledge that the other side's capabilities are degraded, while the other side remains resolved to resist in false confidence that its nuclear deterrent remains intact. The counterforce advantage of OCO depends on its secrecy and thus cannot be revealed, but this erodes the signaling advantages of nuclear weapons that must be revealed. This tension between "winning" and "warning" recurs in many instances of cross-domain deterrence but is dangerously extreme in the cyber-nuclear combination.[52] Fortunately such a crisis is also extremely unlikely (although, unfortunately, slightly less unlikely than during the Cold War).

The Stability-Instability Paradox in Cyberspace

In a half-century of Internet history we have seen far more cyber espionage and crime than disruption and warfare, and more marginal irritants than operational complements. The attacks that do occur are usually minor and reversible, like website defacement and service denial, rather than serious and destructive, like attacks on industrial control systems. The distribution of actual harms inflicted through cyber operations reflects a lot of minor aggressions and very little of anything major.

This trend is partly explained by barriers to entry. We distinguished irritant from complement cyber harms based on the low costs (and low rewards) of the former and the higher resource and effort requirements (and potentially higher rewards) of the latter. Anyone can get into cybercrime. It is a highly differentiated market to facilitate easy entry and exchange. By the same token, it's hard for most cybercriminals to make much money. High-end espionage is more complicated because it focuses on particular targets and heterogeneous networks rather than indiscriminate predation on homogeneous assets. Even successful intrusions do not translate into successful absorption and application; thus fears of erosion of competitive advantage are largely mythical.

---

[51] David C. Gompert and Martin Libicki, "Cyber Warfare and Sino-American Crisis Instability," *Survival* 56 (2014): 7–22; Avery Goldstein, "First Things First: The Pressing Danger of Crisis Instability in U.S.-China Relations," *International Security* 37 (2013): 49–89.

[52] Erik Gartzke and Jon R. Lindsay, "Thermonuclear Cyberwar," *Journal of Cybersecurity* 3 (2017): 37-48.

Cyberwarfare (disruption) is more complicated still and, for now, is mainly only a nation-state competency. It is possible to imagine sophisticated nonstate groups overcoming the technical, organizational, and intelligence hurdles to conduct seriously disruptive attacks, even as systemic paralysis remains out of reach for all. No one can take anonymity for granted if the offense is serious. Moreover, all digitally savvy actors, including terrorists, are more likely to find the Internet useful in an adjunct role supporting other types of operations rather than as a vector for staging a major attack.[53] Apart from the inherent complexity of attack planning, defenders also tend to invest more effort protecting high-reward targets than low-reward targets, which further exacerbates the differential barriers to entry.

Operational costs are only half the story, however. Deterrence also helps to explain the distribution of cyber aggression. Restraint is built into strategic interaction in cyberspace, under most conditions. OCO as a direct harm (i.e., brute force to change the balance of power) is likely to stay beneath the threshold at which the harm inflicted relative to the benefits of connection is great enough to trigger disconnection. The exception is certain situations where pervasive surveillance is used to compel miscreants to avoid using the Internet altogether, thus realizing some benefit from their disconnection. Usually, however, political economic actors want to continue to be able to use the Internet productively even as they cheat at the margins of mutual agreement about the benefits of connectivity. Cyber attack as a direct harm will likewise be contained to situations where the disruption of computation is minor enough so as not to trigger cross-domain retaliation for serious loss of life or incapacitation of critical infrastructure, or in situations where cyber disruption provides a tactical window of opportunity for a broader combined arms military operation. Cyber options are attractive as substitutes for force only when they are calibrated to enable the attacker to realize some benefit without the exposure to risks that the use of force usually involves. Limited cyber attacks are most appealing to those who have the capacity to conduct them when aggressors are deterred from using more violent measures.

The combination of cross-domain deterrence and voluntary connection to the Internet gives rise to a variant of the classic stability-instability paradox. In Glenn Snyder's original articulation, mutually assured destruction could deter nuclear war but was not credible for, and might even encourage, limited conventional or proxy conflict.[54] According to Robert Jervis, "to the extent that the military balance is stable at the level of all-out nuclear war, it will become less stable at lower levels of violence."[55] Cyber capacity is a poor substitute for nuclear weapons, myths of paralysis notwithstanding, yet there is a similar

---

[53] David C. Benson, "Why the Internet Is Not Increasing Terrorism," *Security Studies* 23 (2014): 293–328.

[54] Glenn H. Snyder, *Deterrence and Defense: Toward a Theory of National Security* (Princeton, NJ: Princeton University Press, 1961).

[55] Robert Jervis, *The Illogic of American Nuclear Strategy* (Ithaca, NY: Cornell University Press, 1984), 31.

logic constraining the distributions of harms that are possible from information technology. To extend this logic to the cyber domain, a variety of deterrent mechanisms contain the most disruptive types of cyber attacks yet fail to contain, and even enable, a wide variety of online espionage, subversion, symbolic protest, and criminal predation. In cyberspace we observe a rather stable damage contest (i.e., no paralysis and only limited disruption) but a very unstable intelligence-counterintelligence contest (lots of espionage and fraud vying with efforts at control and mobilization). Thus the actors that have the ability to carry out highly destructive cyber attacks (mainly state actors for now) lack the motivation to attack. Yet these same actors as well as many others have both the ability and the motivation to inflict irritant aggression with little fear of suffering consequences. By and large, cyber options fill out the lower end of the conflict spectrum, where deterrence is not as credible or reliable. The very few cases of physically disruptive cyber attack we do observe—mainly powerful states conducting covert action, subversive propaganda, or battlefield support operations against militarily weaker opponents—have notably involved stronger actors who not only have the capacity to plan and conduct a sophisticated attack but also have the ability to deter retaliation against their use of OCO.

The cyber variant of the stability-instability paradox has a slightly different logic, however. In the nuclear realm, actors cannot disconnect from the threatened harm, and this is what makes the threatened destruction both mutual and assured. When there are many missiles with many warheads, the chance of intercepting them on the ground through a disarming counterforce strike or in the air through ballistic missile defense with any confidence is depressingly small. Not so in cyberspace, where connection to the Internet and acceptance of connections through it is voluntary. Attackers thus rely on deception to exploit vulnerabilities and ensure they can access their targets. However, offensive deception can fail in the fog of cyberwar, and defenders can be deceptive as well; both are more likely with high-reward targets, where cross-domain deterrence is also more credible. The need to preserve Internet connections to facilitate ongoing and future deception as well as the need to preserve stealth to avoid the consequences of getting caught imposes discipline on attackers.

Actors cannot enjoy the substantial benefits of interconnection without accepting some risk of exploitation and attack. Perfect defense (Internet lockout) with advantage accruing exclusively to one political group or another is not feasible. Moreover, because cyber harms share similar techniques, the observed abundance of exploitation represents a latent potential for attack. The latent escalatory potential of even minor irritants leads to rampant fears of unrestrained catastrophe, to be sure. Yet this latent potential is difficult to harness for targeted coercion because the threat is self-effacing. Declared cyber threats that highlight the target's vulnerability to exploitation are readily mitigated. Instead, the ineradicable threat of cyber catastrophe, so long as the Internet continues to be useful, creates a general if diffuse deterrent effect among all parties that value their connection to the Internet. No one who wants to make money on the Internet really wants to have a cyberwar that ruins the domain for everyone.

Large powers like the United States are highly dependent on the Internet but also highly skilled at inflicting harm through a variety of means. Poor powers across the digital divide may have a smaller digital attack surface, while medium powers may have vulnerability but lack a range of forces to deter attacks. This might imply a curvature to the utility of cyber coercion. Strong and capable countries are vulnerable to cyber harm but can deter through other military instruments. Poor states are not vulnerable. It may be the prosperous small or digitally developing who are in the most trouble, since they cannot credibly deter and are highly dependent on the Internet. The cases of Estonia and Ukraine are suggestive. The information revolution is often thought to be a boon to nonstate actors, and indeed it is, but mainly in the irritant class of cyber operations. Moreover, the increasing ubiquity and sophistication of information technologies can be expected to have something of a democratizing effect on intelligence and counterintelligence techniques whereby firms and citizens will have access to and be concerned about the types of things that were historically the purview of obscure state intelligence organs. However, it would be a mistake to use the increasing ferment of low-intensity information contests to infer the shape of higher intensity activity. On the contrary, the traditional logic of war will continue to dominate the expression of cyber aggression.

Because threatened Internet harms depend on voluntary connections in the first place, and as many actors have alternative means to inflict (cross-domain) harm in retaliation, the coercive utility of cyberspace is actually somewhat limited. At the same time an ever increasing variety of irritants and more temperamental operational complements becomes available for political interaction. The "net" result is that opponents have strong incentives to impose costs via the Internet but also to keep those costs low enough to preserve interconnection and avoid retaliation. Therefore, contests in damage will remain relatively stable, while contests in intelligence will be increasingly unstable. The human-built world is becoming more complex, to be sure, but it is not necessarily more dangerous. As long as it is desirable to connect to the Internet tomorrow, there will be only limited harm via the Internet today.

CHAPTER 10

Migration as a Coercive Weapon

New Evidence from the Middle East

KELLY M. GREENHILL

This is like a little bomb. It goes "tick, tick, tick," and we have to handle it.
—KRISTALINA GEORGIEVA, *then European Commissioner for Humanitarian Aid and Civil Protection, on the 2011 Libyan refugee crisis*

IN 2015 ALONE, MORE than one million refugees and migrants entered the European Union (EU) through unregulated channels in the midst of the continent's greatest migration emergency since the end of World War II.[1] In the months that followed, Britain would vote to exit the EU (the so-called Brexit), in no small part due to mounting concerns about unrestricted population movements within and into the EU. Other member states would also express grave concerns about the consequences of a "seemingly unending flow" of displaced people into Europe, and right-wing populist parties would grow in strength and numbers in many of them. Even before the Brexit vote, Donald Tusk, president of the European Council, even warned that, if not brought under control, the migration crisis could spell "doom" for the EU.[2]

---

[1] Some material herein is drawn and reprinted from Kelly M. Greenhill, "Understanding the Coercive Power of Mass Migrations," in *Weapons of Mass Migration: Forced Displacement, Coercion and Foreign Policy* (Ithaca, NY: Cornell Studies in Security Affairs, 2010). Used by permission of the publisher, Cornell University Press. Georgieva is quoted in Joshua Chaffin, "EU Warns of Libya Refugee Crisis," *Financial Times*, March 10, 2011, online. I thank Robert Art and Peter Krause for valuable feedback and suggestions.

[2] "No Rest for Migrant-Weary Europe in 2016 as Desperate Refugees Flood Continent," *CNBC*, January 2, 2016, www.cnbc.com/2016/01/02/migrant-weary-europe-to-get-hit-with-new-wave.html; Natalia Banulescu-Bogdan, "Top 10 of 2016 – Issue #5: As Publics Fear Loss of National Identity, Far-Right Populist Movements Gain Strength," *Migration Policy Institute*, December 13, 2016; http://www.migrationpolicy.org/article/top-10-2016-%E2%80%93-issue-5-publics-fear-loss-national-identity-far-right-populist-movements-gain; Tusk quoted in "We're Facing Destruction, EU Chief Warns," *TheTimes*, September 24, 2015.

Responding to mounting fears and anxiety, in late March 2016, ambassadors from then 28 EU member states concluded what was supposed to be a secret deal to curtail further in-migration with leaders of eight countries in the Horn of Africa. In exchange for a promise to help stanch unregulated flows of people into Europe, the EU agreed to provide about $50 million in monetary and in-kind aid and equipment over three years. The EU-Horn of Africa deal followed closely on the heels of a far more broadly publicized and widely criticized agreement between the EU and Turkey, which was concluded, as one observer put it, "with EU policymakers' backs seemingly against the wall, and in an atmosphere of palpable panic."[3] In exchange for permitting Greece to return to Turkey all irregular migrants arriving after March 20, the EU agreed to assist the regime of President Recep Tayyip Erdogan in meeting the mounting burden of hosting approximately three million refugees via provision of more than 6 billion Euros in aid and increased resettlement of Syrian refugees residing in Turkey.[4] The EU also agreed to accelerate visa liberalization for Turkish nationals and to "reenergize" previously moribund talks on Turkish EU membership, both of which Turkey had been seeking for years without success.[5] Conclusion of the March 2016 EU-Turkey deal—like its predecessor in November 2015—followed directly from a series of threats issued by Turkish officials that effectively amounted to "We're tired of waiting. Either concede to our array of demands or face the migration-related consequences of failing to do so."[6]

While European concessions to Turkey generated an unusual quantity of press coverage, coercive bargains effected using this kind of non-military, migration-driven "people pressure" are neither new nor unusual. Indeed, exercises in coercive engineered migration (CEM) have been attempted at least once a year on average since the advent of the 1951 Refugee Convention alone.[7] This kind of coercion has been undertaken by dozens of discrete challengers against at least as many disparate targets. Such episodes include both war and peacetime use, by both state and nonstate actors, in the service of objectives as

---

[3] Elizabeth Collett, "The Paradox of the EU-Turkey Deal," *Migration Policy Institute*, March 2016, http://www.migrationpolicy.org/news/paradox-eu-turkey-refugee-deal.

[4] European Council, "EU-Turkey Statement," March 18, 2016, http://www.consilium.europa.eu/en/press/press-releases/2016/03/18-eu-turkey-statement/.

[5] Kelly M. Greenhill, "Open Arms behind Barred Doors: Fear, Hypocrisy and Policy Schizophrenia in the European Migration Crisis," *European Law Journal* 22 (May 2016): 279–94; D. Robinson and A. Barker, "EU and Turkey Agree Deal to Return Migrants," *Financial Times*, March 18, 2016. Whether the EU will fulfill its promises to Turkey remains an open question as of this writing. See, for instance, Safik Timur and Rod Nordland, "Erdogan Threatens to Let Migrant Flood into Europe Resume," *New York Times*, November 25, 2016.

[6] See again Greenhill, "Open Arms"; "Turkish President Threatens to Send Millions of Syrian Refugees to EU," *The Guardian*, February 11, 2016; Agence France-Presse, "Turkey Threatens to Back Out of EU Migrant Deal over Visas," *France24.com*, April 19, 2016.

[7] For an accounting of all confirmed and suggestive cases from 1951 to 2015, see Greenhill, *Weapons of Mass Migration*; Kelly M. Greenhill, "When Virtues Become Vulnerabilities: The Achilles' Heel of Migration Social Policy," in *Handbook of Migration and Social Policy*, ed. Gary Freeman and Nikola Mirilovic (Cheltenham: Edward Elgar, 2016).

diverse as financial assistance on one end of the spectrum to full-scale military invasion and regime change on the other.

Moreover, in nearly three-quarters of the identified cases, coercers have succeeded in achieving at least some of their objectives. This is an impressive rate of success, considering that the U.S. record on coercive diplomacy success lies somewhere between 19 and 37.5 percent.[8] Given these favorable odds, there are real incentives—particularly, but not exclusively, for relatively weak state and nonstate actors who either lack effective recourse to more traditional methods of persuasion—to create new and manipulate extant migration crises, at least in part in order to influence the behavior of (potential) recipient states. Indeed, although the aims and specific tactics employed vary, the vast majority of thus far documented cases (81 percent) have been cases of asymmetric coercion of relatively strong states by relatively weak state and non-state actors, and in about 70 percent of these cases, the targets have been liberal democracies.[9] In the cases where more powerful and more capable actors have been the coercers rather than the targets, coercers (be they democrats or autocrats) have sought objectives deemed either too dangerous or costly to pursue using military means.[10]

Despite the fact that this brand of unconventional coercion is a relatively common phenomenon in international politics, it remains underreported, and its influence generally underappreciated. The summer 2013 issue of the journal *International Security* provides a powerful case in point. The issue features two articles, one by Alan Kuperman and one by Aidan Hehir, on Operation Odyssey Dawn, the 2011 EU-NATO Libyan intervention, and its ostensibly humanitarian causes and consequences—in particular, the hypothesized influence of the so-called Responsibility to Protect (R2P).[11] However, although the Libyan uprising and subsequent civil war produced on the order of 800,000 refugees and many hundreds of thousands of internally displaced persons—and, at one time, at least theoretically threatened to generate more than a million more—neither article discusses the refugee-related aspect of the crisis or its R2P-related implications.

---

[8] Estimated rates of success are as follows: Blechman and Kaplan (1978): 19 percent; George and Simons (1994): 29 percent; Art and Cronin (2003): 31 percent; and Sechser (2007): 37.5 percent. See Barry M. Blechman and Stephen S. Kaplan, *Force Without War: U.S. Armed Forces as a Political Instrument* (Washington, DC: Brookings Institution, 1978); Alexander L. George and George Simons, eds., *The Limits of Coercive Diplomacy*, 2nd ed. (Boulder: Westview Press, 1994); Robert J. Art and Patrick Cronin, eds. *The United States and Coercive Diplomacy* (Washington, DC: US Institute of Peace, 2003); Todd S. Sechser, "Winning without a Fight: Power, Reputation, and Compellent Threats in International Crises" (Ph.D. dissertation, Stanford University 2007)

[9] Though weak relative to their targets, perpetrators are generally strong relative to their victims.

[10] Examples include the United States against the North Vietnamese in 1954–55 and against North Korea in the early 2000s and the Russian Federation against some of its central Asian neighbors in early 2014.

[11] Alan Kuperman, "A Model Humanitarian Intervention? Reassessing NATO's Libya Campaign" and Aidan Hehir, "The Permanence of Inconsistency: Libya, the Security Council, and the Responsibility to Protect," both in *International Security* 38 (Summer 2013), http://www.mitpressjournals.org/toc/isec/38/1.

Indeed, the word *refugee* appears in one of the articles only in reference to the migration crisis in Mali, which the author (Kuperman) rightly notes was a negative second-order effect of the NATO-led intervention. Hehir mentions refugees only twice: once with reference to the fact that the 1994 U.S.-led Haitian intervention was undertaken to stanch a burgeoning flow of boatpeople to the United States, and in passing, in acknowledgment that concerns about North Africans flooding into Europe *might* have been one of the myriad factors that influenced French president Nicolas Sarkozy's decision to attack Libya.

Whatever one's position on the role of R2P as a factor in the decision to intervene and ultimately to depose Libyan president Muammar Gaddafi, failing to take into account the role Gaddafi's threats to "turn Europe black" played in the European decision to intervene helps foster distorted and misleading understandings of both the causes and the consequences of the Libyan operation. Such misapprehensions impede our ability to draw accurate and actionable lessons from the case as they pertain to the theory and practice of coercion. They also obscure the significant and wide-ranging implications of the Libyan cases for the protection for those fleeing violence and persecution more generally, as the EU's halting, disjoined and belated response to its migration crisis makes clear.[12]

This chapter aims to help address this consequential oversight in two ways. First, to enhance general understanding of the frequency and political importance of migration-driven coercion, I briefly present the theory I first introduced in *Weapons of Mass Migration* and then offer a new test of the theory by applying it to Libyan cases that transpired subsequent to the book's publication. Second, I examine how CEM was exercised by the Gaddafi regime and how and why EU and NATO target states responded as they did. I demonstrate that Gaddafi engaged in a multistage attempt (i.e., compellence, followed by attempted deterrence, followed by compellence) to influence select EU and NATO member states' behavior through the use of migration-driven coercion. Already visible fissures between front-line states about how to respond to unrest in Libya and the EU's (and select member states') salutary responses to Gaddafi's previous—similar, if less extravagant—threats gave the Libyan leader reason to believe he might succeed. After deterrence failed, however, Gaddafi persisted in trying to cultivate discord within the EU and to cultivate fear of a massive influx within front-line states, particularly Italy.[13]

While not critical test cases for CEM theory, the Libyan-EU coercive episodes examined in this chapter are significant and highly illustrative ones for the study of coercion for several reasons. First, they dramatically demonstrate how exercises in coercion can hide in plain sight. In conjunction

[12] See, for instance, Greenhill, "Open Arms"; Franziska Brantner, "The Libyan Context of the Migration Crisis," *European Council on Foreign Relations* (May 2015); http://www.ecfr.eu/article/commentary_the_libyan_context_of_the_migration_crisis3040.

[13] In some respects, the 2011 Libya case bears some striking similiarities to another multistage case of CEM that also resulted in NATO military action, the 1998-99 Kosovo conflict. See chapter 3 in Greenhill, *Weapons of Mass Migration* for details.

with the insights offered in other chapters in this volume, this fact alone should cause us to reexamine how we evaluate the relative virtues and vices of coercive tools (e.g., kinetic vs. nonmilitary) and the strategies (e.g., denial vs. punishment) that undergird them. Second, like other chapters in this section of the volume, Gaddafi's serial successful use of CEM from 2004 to 2010 further demonstrates how efficacious nonmilitary instruments of coercion can be, especially for weak actors aiming to "punch above their weight" in international politics. Finally, the Libya cases reveal within a single country context the myriad of political, economic, and military objectives a challenger who employs this unconventional instrument may seek (as well as achieve).

The Weaponization of Migration

As defined by Robert Art and myself in chapter 1 of this volume, coercion is, loosely speaking, the ability to get an actor to do something he or she would prefer not to do. By extension, coercive engineered migrations are cross-border population movements that are deliberately created or manipulated in order to induce (involuntary) political, military, and/or economic concessions from a target state or states.[14] The instruments employed to effect CEM are myriad and diverse. They run the gamut from compulsory to permissive, from the employment of hostile threats and the use of military force, the offer of positive inducements and provision of financial incentives, to the straightforward opening of normally sealed borders.

CEM is frequently, but not always, undertaken in the context of outflows strategically generated for other reasons, including but not limited to the seizure of territory and resources, the removal of politically, socially, or economically threatening groups, and the acquisition of military advantage (e.g., in counterinsurgency operations). In fact, coercive engineered migration represents just one subset of a broader class of events that rely on the creation and exploitation of in- and out-migrations as means to political and military ends, that is, "strategic engineered migration." It is likely at least in part as a consequence of its embedded nature that CEM's prevalence and significance have long been underappreciated.

CEM further tends to be self-camouflaging for two other mutually reinforcing reasons. First, states that have been successfully targeted in the past are often reluctant to advertise that fact, even within their own foreign policy establishments. After all, what leader wants to voluntarily admit having been forced to offer concessions to actors who are commonly portrayed in the media and public fora not as formidable adversaries but rather as foes worthy of derision? Second, some coercers issue their threats and demands only privately. However, the relative invisibility of CEM does not make it

[14] Greenhill, *Weapons of Mass Migration*, 12–13.

any less real or consequential for either its victims or its targets. It also does not make it any less effective as a nonmilitary alternative to traditional, kinetically-focused coercion.

Why CEM?

Why would relatively weak actors resort to the creation and exploitation of unnatural disasters as a method of influence? In many policy arenas, weak actors view crisis generation as a necessary precursor to negotiations with more powerful counterparts, who, as Sechser, Downes, and Haun observe in their chapters in this volume, tend to both overestimate their own capabilities to coerce and underestimate or dismiss outright the resolve of their weaker counterparts. Crisis generation can serve as an asymmetric instrument of influence, as it represents one of the few areas in which weaker actors may possess relative strength vis-à-vis their targets—and, in the case of migration crises, also vis-à-vis their even weaker victims. After intentionally generating crises—or threatening to do so—coercers can offer to make them disappear (or not to follow through on their threats) in exchange for military, financial, or political payoffs. Strong actors, previously unwilling to even talk to, much less negotiate with, weaker counterparts will often abruptly temper or reverse positions in the face of clear and present crises, opening up bargaining space where previously there was none.[15]

Specifically, crisis generation can help level the playing field, enhance weak actors' credibility, increase the potency of their threats, and thereby improve their coercive capabilities in several ways. First, migration crises may permit weak challengers to inflict punishment on targets disproportionate to the costs of compliance. Although targets may be understandably reluctant to concede ex ante, quite often demands that were unacceptable at the outset may begin to appear nominal compared with the costs of managing sustained, large-scale outflows into the indefinite future. Consider that, unlike a bombing sortie—which may be profoundly damaging but is perforce finite—a migration crisis can be, to borrow a well-known phrase, "a gift that keeps on giving." Second, because in-kind retaliation is rarely an option for targets—many of which are advanced liberal democracies—challengers may achieve a kind of highly credible escalation dominance over their targets. For instance, launching a war to counter a migration crisis is an option in certain circumstances, but often the expected costs associated with escalation to that level exceed the expected costs of conceding to challengers' demands in whole or in part. Likewise, if the challenger is already internationally isolated, the methods short of war that powerful states may employ in response may be slow-acting—for example, sanctions—and thus inappropriate as a method of countercoercion during a crisis, as Drezner notes in this volume.

[15] See, for instance, Scott Snyder, Negotiating on the Edge: North Korean Negotiating Behavior (Washington, DC: US Institute of Peace, 1999), 71.

How, When, and Why Does CEM Succeed and Fail?

Operationally speaking, CEM is a "coercion by punishment" strategy. Challengers aim to create domestic conflict and/or public dissatisfaction within the target in an attempt to convince its leadership to concede to the challenger's demands rather than incur the anticipated (domestic and/or international) political costs of resistance.[16] As is the case with terrorism and strategic bombing, and also punishment strategies, the principal targets (namely, states) tend not to be synonymous with the principal victims (the displaced themselves).

There are two distinct but not mutually exclusive pathways by which CEM can be effected using punishment strategies; loosely speaking, they might be thought of as "capacity swamping" and "political agitating." Simply put, swamping focuses on manipulating the *ability* of targets to accept, accommodate, or assimilate a given group of migrants or refugees, while agitating focuses on manipulating the *willingness* of targets to do so. In both swamping and agitating, coercion is effectively a dynamic, two-level game in which target responses on the international level to threats issued or actions taken by challengers tend to be driven by simultaneous (or subsequent) actions taken by actors within the target state.[17] Somewhat paradoxically, evidence suggests the *objective dangers* posed to targets tend to be greater in the case of swamping, but the *probability of coercive success* tends to be greater in the case of agitating.

In the developing world, coercive attempts most often focus on swamping and comprise threats to severely tax or overwhelm a target's physical and/or economic capacity to cope with an influx—thereby effectively debilitating it—if it fails to concede to the coercer's demands. Capacity swamping can also be an effective strategy in the developed world, or "the West," broadly defined. This is particularly true if the incipient crisis is large and sudden since even highly industrialized states need time to gear up to effectively deal with disasters, be they natural or manmade. The ongoing European migration emergency represents one such example and helps explain the efficacy of Turkish threats (and the alacrity and nature of the concessions made) in the fall of 2015 and spring of 2016.[18] That said, advanced industrial societies tend to have greater resources to bring to bear in a crisis, making credible threats to overwhelm their physical ability to cope harder—if far from impossible—to accomplish.

In the developed world, therefore, political agitating often supplants capacity swamping as the lynchpin of coercion. Challengers on the international level seek to influence target behavior on the domestic level by engaging in a

[16] "The hope is that the government will concede or the population will revolt." Robert Pape, *Bombing to Win: Air Power and Coercion in War* (Ithaca, NY: Cornell University Press, 1996), 21.

[17] Robert Putnam, "Diplomacy and Domestic Politics: The Logic of Two-Level Games," *International Organization* 42 (1988): 427–60.

[18] See, for instance, Kelly M. Greenhill, "The Weaponization of Migration," in *The World of Geo-Economics: An Essay Collection*, ed. Mark Leonard (London: European Council on Foreign Relations, 2016).

kind of norms-enhanced political blackmail that relies on *exploiting* and *exacerbating* what Robert Putnam has called the "heterogeneity" of political and social interests within polities.[19] Exploitation of heterogeneity within Western states is possible because population influxes, such as those created in migration and refugee crises, tend to engender diverse and highly divisive responses within the societies expected to bear the brunt of their consequences. Like immigration and refugee policy more generally, real and threatened migration crises tend to split societies into (at least) two mutually exclusive and often highly mobilized groups: the pro-refugee/migrant camp and anti-refugee/migrant camp.

What it means to be pro- or anti-refugee/migrant will perforce vary across targets and across crises. Depending on circumstances, pro-refugee/migrant camps may call for relatively limited, short-term responses, such as accepting financial responsibility for settling the migrant or refugee group in a third country or far more significant—even permanent—commitments, like offering asylum or citizenship. Conversely, anti-refugee/migrant groups may demand that requests for financial assistance be rejected or, more radically, that migrants be interdicted and refugees refused asylum or even, in extreme cases, forcibly repatriated. The bottom line is that because targets cannot simultaneous satisfy demands to both "accept" and "reject" a given group of migrants or refugees, leaders facing highly mobilized and highly polarized interests on both sides of the divide can find themselves on the horns of a real dilemma—in which it is impossible to satisfy the demands of one camp without alienating the other. Thus it is not heterogeneity per se that makes targets vulnerable. Instead, political agitating strategies can succeed due to the fact that these competing groups tend to have mutually incompatible interests that they may be strongly committed to defending, coupled with the fact that target leaderships may have compelling political, legal, and/or moral reasons to avoid running afoul of either of them. As journalist and activist Marco Scalvini aptly put it in the middle of the 2011 Libyan crisis, "The anxiety over a refugee invasion from Africa reveals the contradictions present in Europe today, where, on the one hand, the moral imperative of universal emancipation is proclaimed, but on the other, policies and practice continue the trend of refusing a safe haven to the very refugees they have helped to create."[20] Under such conditions, leaders may face strong domestic incentives to concede to coercers' international-level demands—particularly if doing so can make real or potential migration crises cease or disappear, thereby freeing target leaderships from the proverbial trap between a rock and a hard place.

In societies marked by a heterogeneity of interests and unevenly distributed costs and benefits associated with mass migrations, situations in which only one (or the other) camp mobilizes in the face of a crisis will be the exception

---

[19] Putnam, "The Logic of Two-Level Games."

[20] Marco Scalvini, "Humanitarian Wars and Rejected Refugees," *OpenDemocracy*, April 17, 2011, http://www.opendemocracy.net/marco-scalvini/humanitarian-wars-and-rejected-refugees.

rather than the rule. Moreover, would-be coercers often not only seek to exploit extant heterogeneity but also aim to increase target vulnerability over time by acting in ways designed to directly or indirectly catalyze greater mobilization, heighten the degree of polarization between groups, and thereby reduce the available policy options open to targets. Challengers can do so by increasing the size, scale, and scope of an existing outflow, shifting its character—for instance, adding more members of either "undesirable" or particularly sympathetic groups, making escalatory threats, or simply directly lobbying members of pro- and anti- groups.

In short, challengers aim to influence targets by force majeure, a choice dictated by overwhelming circumstances. Targets always have a choice, of course, but one that is skewed if they believe the consequences of noncompliance will be a denial of future choice.[21] This is not to suggest that concession is cost-free, only that in the face of a threatened or mounting crisis the anticipation of future pain and escalating costs must be weighed against the costs and opportunities associated with ending a crisis immediately through concession.

Consequently, targets will be most vulnerable not when their publics and/or elites are unified but rather when there is widespread (and intense) disagreement about the way to respond to an incipient or ongoing crisis: when there are highly concentrated interests in favor of the refugee/migrant group and highly concentrated interests opposed to the same group. Conversely, when neither camp is mobilized and opinion is less polarized, targets will be least vulnerable, and coercion is least likely to succeed. Likewise, in cases where only the anti-camp is mobilized, targets should also be relatively less vulnerable because the option of interdiction, border closure, or simple rejection should be easier to implement. This last scenario is effectively what transpired in Europe in the spring of 2011 and explains why Gaddafi's final attempt at CEM failed. There was simply no significant public appetite for accepting, even on a temporary basis, large numbers of North Africans, many of whom would be expected to attempt to remain in Western Europe even after the unrest and conflict(s) plaguing the region abated.

Evidence of Coercion?

Before turning to our examination of Libya, it is worth highlighting how one can know if an actual or anticipated migration event represents a bona fide case of CEM. Specifically, three distinct questions must be answered in the affirmative: Was the (threatened) outflow largely controlled by the principals? Was it strategic? Was it coercive? Thus a case makes the cut if, and only if, there is evidence of (1) orchestration and/or overt control over the size, timing, and destination of a real or imminently threatened population movement;

[21] Lawrence Freedman, "Strategic Coercion," in *Strategic Coercion: Concepts and Cases*, ed. Lawrence Freedman (New York: Oxford University Press, 1998), 29.

(2) strategic motivation—that is, that the outflow was created or threatened in the service of identifiable and articulated interests and objectives; and (3) perception of coercive intent, expressed by the would-be coercer and recognized by the coercee(s). These are strict criteria, and many real and threatened migrations do not meet them.

The Case of Libya, 2004–2011: Four Successes and One Dramatic and Fatal Failure

Between 2004 and 2011 Gaddafi engaged in multiple discrete exercises in CEM—in 2004, 2006, 2007–8, 2010, and 2011. With the exception of the final episode, which was a dramatic failure of both deterrence and compellence, Gaddafi's other attempts were noteworthy successes that collectively provided Libya with what observers have described as a "constant flow of money, equipment, and technology." It was surely because of his successful track record that Gaddafi hubristically believed his threats to flood Europe in 2011 would engender a similar response from European leaders. The EU had been repeatedly coerced, as one commentator put it, with "ruthless effectiveness" by Gaddafi, who was "a shrewd and cynical manipulator of Europe's immigration obsessions." However, before 2011, the costs of concession likely still seemed low, at least relative to the domestic political consequences of a flood of North African migrants into Europe.[22] By outsourcing its border controls to a dictatorship that was not a signatory to the Refugee Convention, the EU was able to prevent asylum seekers from reaching its shores, while continuing to proclaim its commitment to the principle of refugee protection. (Indeed, according to Italian officials, Libya intercepted and detained more than 2.5 million asylum seekers between 2006 and 2011.[23]) As detailed below, Gaddafi engaged in a series of coercive bargaining exercises whose appeasement-like outcomes favored the Libyan leader, while also providing some short-term benefits to the coercees, until the costs of continued concession appeared to begin to exceed those of bringing his lengthy reign to an end.

A Series of Successes

In October 2004, EU foreign ministers met and agreed to lift all remaining sanctions on the one-time international pariah state. This array of sanctions, including a comprehensive arms embargo, had been in place since the 1980s, enacted in response to several high-profile Libyan-sponsored terrorist attacks within Western Europe. This dramatic policy shift was not driven by Libya's decision to disband its weapons of mass destruction program, its public

[22] Matthew Carr, "How Libya Kept Migrants Out of EU—At Any Cost," *The Week*, April 5, 2011. http://www.theweek.co.uk/politics/6515/how-libya-kept-migrants-out-eu-any-cost#ixzz2OILrmoXq.
[23] "600 Believed Dead in Libya Refugee Boat Sinking," *Associated Press*, May 10, 2011.

repudiation of terrorism, or even its acceptance of responsibility for the bombing of Pan Am 103 over Lockerbie, Scotland.[24] Rather, EU sanctions were explicitly lifted in exchange for a Libyan promise to help stop North African migrants and asylum seekers from crossing the Mediterranean onto European soil.[25] The EU decision to lift sanctions came after months of pressure from Italy, which had threatened to lift sanctions unilaterally if the EU failed to do so after over 9,700 migrants arrived on Italian shores in 2004 alone (see Figure 10.1).[26] After previously threatening it would "no longer act as Europe's coast guard" were sanctions not lifted, Libya also received promises of significant annual financial assistance from the European Commission; soon thereafter outflows largely ceased.[27]

Then, in August 2006, the number of migrants drowned and intercepted between Libya and Italy again began to mount. Italian officials voiced suspicions that Gaddafi was engineering the outflow to extort further financial concessions. Consistent with this claim, Gaddafi soon publicly declared, "We will ask Europe to pay 10 billion Euros per year if it really wants to stop migration . . . . Europeans who do not want to take the immigrants in should either emigrate to America or pay Libya to keep its [*sic*] borders closed."[28] The EU again blinked. Although the monetary transfers this time around were more modest than in 2004, Gaddafi extracted additional assistance worth millions of euros in the form of in-kind aid and equipment (such as boats) that could be used for a variety of activities beyond migration enforcement.[29]

In December 2007, whether because of a private threat or as a preemptive gesture to forestall one, Italy and Libya concluded another bilateral deal, with full EU support.[30] A follow-on "Partnership Treaty" was signed the following summer, which included a $5 billion compensation package, conditional upon Libya's reinforcing its commitment to contain illegal immigration. Subsequently, Gaddafi rounded up asylum seekers trying to reach Italy via

---

[24] Although, to be clear, these all helped make the EU decision easier to sell domestically and internationally.

[25] *Afrol News*, November 3, 2004; "Immigration: EU to Assist Libya," *AKI* (Italy), June 3, 2005; (Report from the) "Third European Parliament/Libya Interparliamentary Meeting," Tripoli, April 2005, http://www.europarl.europa.eu/cmsdata/40858/att_20090513ATT55732-4791712908714818 74.pdf.

[26] Italy concluded a separate bilateral deal with Libya in August 2004, which Italy refused to make public despite requests from the European Parliament, the UN Human Rights Committee, and NGOs, including Human Rights Watch. Human Rights Watch, *Stemming the Flow* 18 (September 2006); https://www.hrw.org/reports/2006/libya0906/libya0906web.pdf.

[27] "EU Lifts Arms Embargo on Libya for Refugee Deal," *AfrolNews*, October 11, 2004; http://afrol.com/articles/14503; Graham Bowley, "European Union Agrees to Lift Arms Embargo on Libya," *International Herald Tribune*, October 11, 2004; http://www.nytimes.com/2004/10/11/international/europe/europe-union-agrees-to-lift-arms-embargo-on-libya.html.

[28] "African Immigrants: Gaddafi's Price Has Gone Up," *Brussels Journal*, September 13, 2006. The Commission reportedly paid Libya €2 billion in 2005 alone.

[29] "African Immigrants: Gaddafi's Price Has Gone Up"; Paolo Cuttitta, "The Case of the Italian Southern Sea Borders: Cooperation across the Mediterranean?," in *Immigration Flows and the Management of the EU's Southern Maritime Borders*, ed. Gemma Pinyol (Barcelona: Cidob, 2008).

[30] Details remain sketchy as of this writing.

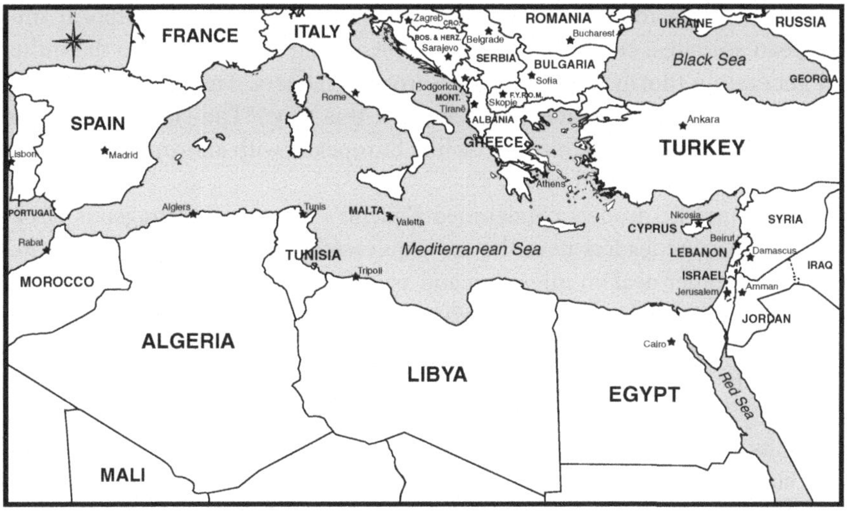

FIGURE 10.1 Map of Libya and the Mediterranean Basin
SOURCE: Adapted from "Map of North Africa and the Middle East," University of Texas Libraries, http://www.lib.utexas.edu/maps/middle_east_and_asia/n_africa_mid_east_pol_95.jpg.

Libya and put many in camps.[31] Although widely criticized by refugee rights groups, the agreement reduced the number of migrants arriving in Italy from 36,000 in 2008 to 4,300 in 2010.[32]

Then, in autumn 2010, Gaddafi once again upped the ante by publicly threatening to "turn Europe black" unless paid several billion euros.[33] Gaddafi declared that "unless his demands were met, Europe ran the risk of becoming another Africa . . . . Tomorrow Europe might no longer be European and even black as there are millions who want to come in . . . . We don't know if Europe will remain an advanced and cohesive continent, or if it will be destroyed, as happened with the barbarian invasions."[34] Playing directly into the fears of European politicians, Gaddafi added, "What will be the reaction of the white Christian Europeans to this mass of hungry, uneducated Africans?"[35] He made plain his understanding that European front-line states could not simply expel or refuse to admit all those moving across the Mediterranean: some were legitimate asylum seekers; some could claim to be; and all had the right to

[31] "Sunk: More Boats, More Drownings—And Suspicions about Libya's Role," *Economist*, August 24, 2006; Sara Hamood, "EU-Libya Cooperation on Migration: A Raw Deal for Refugees and Migrants?," *Journal of Refugee Studies* 21 (2008): 19–42.
[32] "600 Believed Dead."
[33] Gregor Noll and Mariagiulia Giufre, "EU Migration Control: Made by Gaddafi?," *OpenDemocracy*, February 25, 2011, online.
[34] Nick Squires, "Gaddafi: Europe Will 'Turn Black.' Unless EU Pays Libya £4bn a Year," *Telegraph*, August 31, 2010.
[35] Nick Pisa, "'Pay Me £4bn a Year and I'll Stop Europe from Turning Black': Col. Gaddafi Demands EU Cash to Stop Immigration via Libya," *Daily Mail*, August 31, 2010.

have their claims adjudicated. In the meanwhile, many might disappear into European societies, creating fear and unrest among those hostile to the influx and generating thorny dilemmas for European leaders. The commentator Ed West hyperbolically described the situation this way: "The sight of Africans crossing the Mediterranean *en masse* fills Europeans with an impending sense of civilizational doom and dread."[36]

While some EU leaders condemned Gaddafi's threats as "outrageous blackmail," these same leaders nevertheless acquiesced to his demands, and the EU sealed yet another deal on migration and asylum that was to result in payments of more than €50 million over three years.[37] A joint memorandum of understanding on immigration was also issued, whereby the EU agreed to provide technical assistance to Libya as well as to resettle an indeterminate number of refugees within Libya in EU member states.[38] The EU further agreed to assist Libya in reinforcing its southern border and in enhancing its maritime patrolling capacities. To be sure, Gaddafi extracted less than the billions he had demanded. Moreover, EU officials' public accusations that they were being blackmailed demonstrate that tolerance for Gaddafi's recidivism was wearing thin.[39] Still, thereafter flows slowed to a relative trickle until the outbreak of what became known as the Arab Spring.[40]

A Fatal Failure

When unrest and protests spread to Libya in February 2011, Gaddafi tried to employ CEM against the EU yet again, this time with ultimately fatal results. His multiple previous successes surely gave him reason to think he would again prevail. However, his assessment of his prospects for success suffered from a "failure of imagination" for four reasons. First, he failed to take into account that there might actually be a limit to EU leaders' tolerance for his CEM-related recidivism. Second, he failed to recognize that EU leaders might conclude that a mass influx from North Africa might transpire—albeit not in an orchestrated way—whether or not the Libyan rebellion succeeded. Third, Gaddafi failed to anticipate that some EU leaders might—as they actually did—seize on his threats to target Libyan civilians who were supporting the insurgents as a rationale for military action.[41] Fourth, he failed to recognized

---

[36] Ed West, "Gaddafi Floods Europe with Refugees: This is Beginning to Feel Like the Fall of Rome," *Guardian*, April 8, 2011.

[37] Noll and Giufre, "EU Migration Control."

[38] Bjarte Vandvik, "The EU's Dubious Refugee Deal: The EU Is Paying Libya to Deal with Refugees Seeking a New Life in Europe," *Guardian*, October 20, 2010.

[39] A French government official and two NATO officials from other member countries have also intimated as much.

[40] Ian Traynor, "EU Keen to Strike Deal with Muammar Gaddafi on Immigration: Commission Chiefs to Hold Talks with Libya over Gaddafi's Demand for €5bn a Year to Stop Europe Turning 'Black,'" *Guardian*, September 1, 2010.

[41] To be clear, this does not preclude the possibility that said leaders might also have been in earnest about protecting vulnerable Libyans, only that it was, on its own, not a sufficient condition/ or

that his unpopularity within the Middle East and North Africa and poor historical reputation outside of it would create permissive conditions that allowed for mobilization of international support in favor of military action against him. (The fact that there was a weak but motivated rebel army fighting within Libya certainly did not hurt either.) Taken together, and coupled with long-standing European hostility toward North Africans seeking to enter Europe by sea, these four factors proved decisive.

Skeptics might argue that the outflow from Libya in the spring and early summer of 2011 was simply an unintended consequence of the uprising and the NATO bombing that followed; this is to say, they might doubt that the (threatened) crisis was engineered and manipulated for strategic reasons and/or that it was designed to be coercive. However, as the discussion that follows will make clear, that coercion was Gaddafi's intention—and that his intentions were understood by EU leaders—is borne out by four strands of evidence: (1) the existence of explicit and credible (if exaggerated) threats, (2) the timing and pattern of outflows, (3) the complexion of the migrant/refugee population moving across the Mediterranean, and (4) the behavior and discourse of target state leaders.

(Credible) Threats and the Timing and Pattern of Outflows That Followed Them

A First Attempt at Compellence Coupled with Deterrent Threats

There can be little doubt that Gaddafi sought to influence European behavior. His threats were myriad and unambiguous. In the earliest days of the uprising, in February 2011, the Libyan leader summoned EU ministers to Tripoli and issued an ultimatum: "Stop supporting the protestors, or I'll suspend cooperation on migration, and Europe will be facing a human flood from North Africa."[42] Several weeks later, Gaddafi gave an interview in which he warned, "The regime here in Libya is fine. It is stable. I want to make myself understood: if one threatens [Libya], if one seeks to destabilize [Libya], there will be chaos, Bin Laden, armed factions. That is what will happen. You will have immigration. Thousands of people will invade Europe from Libya. And there will no longer be anyone to stop them. Bin Laden will base himself in North Africa and will leave Mullah Omar in Afghanistan and Pakistan. You will have Bin Laden at your door step."[43]

---

motivation for intervention. "Gaddafi Tells Rebel City, Benghazi, 'We Will Show No Mercy,'" *Reuters*, March 17, 2011.

[42] "EU Sends Small Team to Help Italy with North African Migrants," *EU Observer*, February 21, 2011. See also Kelly M. Greenhill, "Using Refugees as Weapons," *New York Times*, op-ed, April 20, 2011, online.

[43] "Kadhafi: 'J'en Appelle à la France,'" *Journal du Dimanche*, March 6, 2011, http://www.lejdd.fr/International/Afrique/Actualite/Exclusif-L-interview-integrale-accordee-par-Mouammar-Kadhafi-au-JDD-278745?from=cover.

Gaddafi followed up this initial threat in early March—just after more than 1,000 migrants landed on the tiny Italian island of Lampedusa in just 12 hours[44]—declaring that he could "turn the entire the entire Mediterranean into a battlefield [by launching demographic bombs at Europe]."[45] To remove any ambiguity about his weapon of choice, he added that if the EU failed to comply with his demands, "thousands of people from Libya will invade Europe. [If I am gone], there will be no one to stop them any more."[46]

Switching Tack and Narrowing the Target Set

Once it became clear that Gaddafi's generalized threats against the EU were not going to work—as evidenced, for instance, by the fact that deliberations on the parameters of the Libyan no-fly zone then in effect moved ahead despite his threats—he switched tack and issued somewhat more subtle, bilateral threats directly against Italy, the country most likely to face the most significant and direct effects of a mass outflow. "Let's hope Italy keeps out of this initiative," Foreign Minister Khaled Kaaim told the Italian news agency ANSA, just as the UN Security Council was voting. "We are certain Italy has Libya's integrity and the protection of the population at heart. Let's hope that it doesn't consent to the use of its bases."[47] In bilateral communications between the Libyan and Italian governments, the consequences of the Libyan military following through on Gaddafi's threats were also reiterated.[48] To this point, there had been no significant population movements across the Mediterranean toward Europe.[49]

At the same time, at least in part to demonstrate Libya's ability and resolve to control cross-border movements, the size of outflows to neighboring countries suddenly plummeted. Consistent with a risk strategy, after an extended period when 10,000 to 15,000 were crossing into Tunisia on a daily basis, on March 4 the UN High Commissioner for Refugees (UNHCR) reported that heavily armed pro-regime forces had begun manning the Libyan side of the border with Tunisia, and daily movements slowed to fewer than 2,000 per day.[50]

---

44 Palesh Ghosh, "EU officials fear waves of illegal immigrants from Africa if Gaddafi falls," *International Business Times*, February 21, 2011; http://www.ibtimes.com/eu-officials-fear-waves-illegal-immigrants-africa-if-gaddafi-falls-269233.

45 "Kadhafi: 'J'en Appelle à la France'," See also Soeren Kern, "Why France Was So Keen to Attack Libya," International Policy Council, *Gatestone Institute.org*, March 23, 2011; https://www.gatestoneinstitute.org/1983/france-libya-attack.

46 "Kadhafi: 'J'en appelle à la France' "; Kern, "Why France Was So Keen."

47 "EU Ministers Reject Italian Request for Help with Feared Libyan 'Exodus,' " *DW News*, February 24, 2011, http://www.dw.de/eu-ministers-reject-italian-request-for-help-with-feared-libyan-exodus/a-14872918.

48 Frank Jordans, "UN Says Close to 600 May Be Dead on Migrant Ship from Libya," *Associated Press*, May 10, 2011.

49 "EU Ministers Reject Italian Request for Help with Feared Libyan 'Exodus.' "

50 This observation was corroborated by UN officials who observed steep declines in refugee registrations and evidence of border closure. See "Libya Revolt as it Happened: Friday," *BBCNews*, March 4, 2011; http://news.bbc.co.uk/2/hi/africa/9414812.stm; Barney Henderson, "Libya Protests: As it Happened March 4," *Telegraph*, March 4, 2011; http://www.telegraph.co.uk/news/worldnews/africaandindianocean/libya/8365654/Libya-protests-as-it-happened-March-4.html.

With few in frontline states keen to welcome those fleeing and many overtly hostile—polling data revealed that 67 percent of Italians thought immigration from the Middle East and North Africa was a "bad thing" for their country, while 83 percent agreed "we should restrict and control entry into our country more than we do now"[51]—Libyan threats and signals failed to have the desired effects. Instead of bowing to Gaddafi's demands, Italy offered up use of its military bases at Aviano, Naples, and Puglia in addition to two bases on Sicily and one on Sardinia. It also froze $10 billion in Libyan assets.[52]

This gesture represented a dramatic about-face for the Italians, as Prime Minister Silvio Berlusconi and his advisers worked assiduously to maintain good relations with the Libyans for as long as the Italian government viewed it diplomatically possible. For instance, when Libyans first took to the streets and violence erupted, Berlusconi did not follow other world leaders in condemning the Libyan leader and suggesting he exercise restraint; instead, Berlusconi maintained that he did not wish to "bother" Gaddafi. At that time, Foreign Minister Franco Frattini declared, "We are following very closely the situation. Italy as you know is the closest neighbor, both of Tunisia and Libya, so we are extremely concerned about the repercussions on the migratory situation in the southern Mediterranean."[53] In short, the Italians sought to at least appear neutral in the early weeks of the crisis, seemingly in the hope that Libya's domestic political crisis might dissipate or otherwise be resolved before Gaddafi decided to follow through on his threats. However, once it became clear that such a resolution was unlikely and an outflow might result irrespective of their diplomatic stance, the Italians changed tack.

In stark contrast to declarations made just days and weeks before, in early March, Minister Frattini declared, "We know for sure that the stronger the military pressure . . . the more difficult it will be for the regime to organize flows of refugees toward Europe as a means of reprisal." Frattini further acknowledged that the Italians feared what might happen if Gaddafi fell in an unmanaged way: "We know what to expect when the Libyan national system falls . . . a wave at least 10 times larger than what we faced when Albania fell [in 1997]."[54] For his part, the federal secretary of the nationalist Northern League, Umberto Bossi, threatened to dump the problem on other EU countries: "If they arrive we'll send them to France and Germany."[55]

---

[51] See, e.g., Juliana Menasce Horowitz, "Widespread Anti-Immigrant Sentiment in Italy," *Pew Research Global Attitudes Project*, January 12, 2010, http://www.pewglobal.org/2010/01/12/widespread-anti-immigrant-sentiment-in-italy/.
[52] Barbie Nadeau, "Italy's Refugee Camp Horror," *Daily Beast*, March 21, 2011, http://www.thedailybeast.com/articles/2011/03/21/italys-libyan-refugee-camp-horror.html.
[53] Quoted in Deepa Babbington, "Berlusconi Under Fire for Not 'Disturbing Gaddafi,'" *Reuters*, February 20, 2011.
[54] "Close to 600 May Be Dead on Migrant Ship," *Associated Press*, May 10, 2011; "Libya Migrants Seemingly Encouraged to Flee," *Associated Press*, May 17, 2011.
[55] Nick Squires, "Libya: Italy Fears 300,000 Refugees," *Telegraph*, February 23, 2011.

Failed Deterrence Begets Countercompellence

Once NATO commenced its bombing campaign, Operation Odyssey Dawn, on March 19, Gaddafi's forces abandoned attempts to thwart people smuggling by private nonstate actors and also began actively encouraging and facilitating flows themselves. In short, the Libyans began making good on their threats. Libyan government spokesman Moussa Ibrahim announced that the regime would no longer prevent boats full with African migrants from leaving for Europe: "There will be illegal immigration. It is a very lucrative business and the government had taken action against it, but it cannot any more. Libyans are involved, we are not stopping it."[56] (This rhetoric strikingly echoes that of the Milosevic regime's response to NATO air strikes in Kosovo in 1999.)[57] Libyan officials further declared that this decision was taken "in protest of the NATO air strikes." For his part, Prime Minister Al-Baghdadi Ali al-Mahmoudi indicated that he "could see no reason to stop the flows, because doing so would serve the interests of NATO member states bombing Libya."[58]

Consistent with these threats, the UN reported that boats started leaving Libya for Europe in earnest on March 24, the same day NATO took over military operations. Likewise, just hours after Italy said it would lend airfields to any NATO-led UN-sanctioned military effort, a ferry from Tripoli carrying 1,800 men (but no women and children) tried to dock in Lampedusa. It was turned away, reportedly because, according to Interior Minister Roberto Maroni, the Italians had "intelligence about some of the passengers" and could not "be sure there [we]re no terrorists on board."[59]

The following day, two boats bypassed Lampedusa and limped into the port of Catania on the Sicilian island, and four more boats arrived in Lampedusa. The Italian coast guard reported "many more" on the horizon. Further reports began to emerge of North Africans being individually selected—with a marked preference for young men, presumably viewed as particularly threatening to Europeans (viz. the ferry incident above)—and forcibly put to sea.

Chief UNHCR spokesperson Melissa Fleming indicated receiving reports that the Libyan army was organizing and directing the exodus and that when some migrants had initially "refused to board a ship they believed to be dangerously overcrowded, Libyan soldiers fired their guns into the air to force people to go on board."[60] Some soldiers reportedly gave "navigational instructions to random passengers before towing the ship(s) to open waters."[61] The International Organization for Migration likewise testified that some of those

---

[56] Nick Squires and Damien McElroy, "Libya to Unleash Wave of Migrants on Europe," *Telegraph*, April 7, 2011.

[57] Greenhill, *Weapons of Mass Migration*, chapter 3.

[58] Martin Chulov and Simon Tisdall, "Libyan Regime Accused of Exploiting Boat People," *Guardian*, May 11, 2011; "Libya Official Admits Migrant Ships Being Allowed to Sail as Protest against NATO," *Guardian*, May 11, 2011.

[59] Nadeau, "Italy's Refugee Camp Horror."

[60] Nadeau, "Italy's Refugee Camp Horror."

[61] Barbie Nadeau, "Exodus," *Newsweek*, June 12, 2011.

arriving on Lampedusa and in Malta said they had been forced onto boats at gunpoint by Libyan soldiers.[62] Others told journalists "they had being forced onto inflatables with dozens of others before being dispatched from Tripoli's port."[63] Some of those landing on Lampedusa reported that their passage had been free, whereas under normal circumstances smugglers would demand $1,000 for the crossing.[64]

In this same time frame, several thousand North Africans arrived on Malta, prompting the Maltese Green Party to publicly acknowledge that Gaddafi was using migration flows to pressure the EU.[65] Antonio Guterres, then UN High Commissioner for Refugees, was slightly less blunt in his assessment, suggesting, "There are elements to make us think that at least some of the actors involved in what's happening today in western parts of Libya may be attempting to use this weapon of forcing people to move into Europe."[66] UNHCR spokeswoman Sybella Wilkes acknowledged, "We know that the people running the boats are smugglers. But obviously you cannot have over 2,000 people leaving in a few short days without the government knowing and allowing it . . . [and] the port of Tripoli is under government control."[67]

Once airstrikes commenced, flows to Lampedusa jumped to several thousand per day over a three-day period—from a previous average of about 200 per day since the start of the Arab Spring—and outflows continued apace until rebels overran Tripoli.[68] Although the numbers of migrants and refugees who reached Western Europe were nominal compared to the numbers sheltering in the countries neighboring Libya, by late March nearly 400 boats loaded with illegal immigrants had reached Italy, and the population of North African migrants on Lampedusa was significantly larger than the number of Italian residents. The island's desperate mayor declared, "Lampedusa cannot be transformed into a refugee camp just a few weeks before the summer tourist season begins. You are giving us a death sentence."[69] What was happening was a combination of attempted capacity swamping on the local level and political agitating farther afield. By the time Gaddafi's forces were ousted from Tripoli, about 50,000 refugees had arrived on Lampedusa. Maroni declared a state of emergency and formally requested from the EU £84 million to deal with extra arrivals as well as resettlement in other parts of Europe.[70] Lest there be any remaining doubt that the Libyans were controlling and manipulating outflows,

---

[62] Len Cendrowicz, "Sorry, We're Closed: Amid Migrant Fears, Europe Could Bring Back Border Controls," *Time*, May 4, 2011.

[63] William Wheeler and Ayman Oghanna, "After Liberation, Nowhere to Run," *New York Times*, October 30, 2011.

[64] Cendrowicz, "Sorry, We're Closed."

[65] Carr, "How Libya Kept Migrants out of EU."

[66] "Libya May Be Using Migrants as Weapon Against EU-UN," *Reuters*, May 11, 2011.

[67] Jordans, "UN Says Close to 600 May Be Dead."

[68] "The Tiny Italian Fishing Island Which Now Has MORE Migrants Fleeing Tunisia and Libya than Inhabitants," *Daily Mail Online*, March 29, 2011.

[69] Nadeau, "Italy's Refugee Camp Horror."

[70] "Libya: US Calls on Europe to 'Open Its Borders' to Migrants," *Channel 4 News*, February 24, 2011, online.

note that no boats left Libyan ports between Gaddafi's ouster and the end of the conflict in October, despite the fact that the bombing campaign continued until the end.[71]

European Responses

Did the Europeans feel coerced? Indeed. Gaddafi's threats were taken seriously and, unsurprisingly, with greatest trepidation by the leaders of the country likely to bear the brunt of an influx. Italy's Frattini, for instance, feared "a wave of 200,000 to 300,000 immigrants. [Although even these are just] estimates, and on the low side. It is a Biblical exodus. It's a problem that no Italian should underestimate." Interior Minister Roberto Maroni told his EU counterparts in Brussels that up to 1.5 million refugees could flee Libya. Calling the feared movement "an invasion . . . that would bring any country to its knees," Maroni declared, "What's happening in the Mediterranean is a problem for Europe and the world. We have never seen an emergency of this scale." Maroni also acknowledged the direct connection between Italian behavior and the Libyan response, declaring that "Gaddafi's threats toward Italy for its role in the NATO-led mission" were "materializing in the flows of migrants after the bombing began."[72]

Leaders of countries farther afield were equally cognizant of what Gaddafi was threatening. European Affairs Minister Werner Hoyer of Germany declared the EU would "not allow itself to be blackmailed." Foreign Minister Steven Vanackere of Belgium admitted that while the Libyan threat made "many people nervous," others were simply "furious," declaring Gaddafi's threat to use demographic bombs against Europe "a Mafia extortion racket."[73] France's Europe minister Laurent Wauquiez—speaking for a country only slightly less geographically vulnerable than Italy—asserted, "There should not be any state blackmail," but at the same time also declared that the influx was a "real risk for Europe that must not be underestimated."[74] Another European diplomat, speaking anonymously, conceded, "If Gaddafi uses this weapon, he can create a lot of problems for Europe."[75] And, as the *New York Times* reported in an interview conducted in the midst of the NATO campaign with Ian Lesser, a senior transatlantic fellow at the German Marshall Fund, the Libya

[71] "Europe Braced for Immigrant Influx as Chaos Reigned," *Sydney Morning Herald*, September 5, 2011.

[72] Jordans, "UN Says Close to 600 May Be Dead."

[73] Ayman Khalil, "Germany, France, Belgium Condemn Violence in Libya," *Global Arab Network*, February 21, 2011; http://www.english.globalarabnetwork.com/201102219938/Libya-Politics/germany-france-belgium-condemn-violence-in-libya.html; "EU Should Not Target Gaddafi Personally," *FlandersNews.BE.com*, February 21, 2011; http://deredactie.be/cm/vrtnieuws.english/News/1.967917; Soeren Kern, "Why France Was So Keen to Attack Libya," *Gatestone Institute*, March 23, 2011; https://www.gatestoneinstitute.org/1983/france-libya-attack.

[74] Colin Randall, "Europe Braces for Tidal Wave of Refugees from across Mediterranean," *NationalAE*, February 24, 2011.

[75] Guy Dinmore and Joshua Chaffin, "Libya Accused of Forcing Migrants to Flee," *Financial Times*, May 9, 2011.

intervention and the subsequent influx of immigrants are "an extraordinary series of tests on very different fronts for European cohesion and European strategy, and the result is clearly very mixed. The migration piece of this is in some way the toughest. There, the measures are very direct; there's a direct connection to public opinion and daily politics."[76]

Within EU member states, incentives were strong to make the crisis disappear. In France, President Sarkozy was contending with the growing popularity of the hard-right National Front, known for its pronounced anti-immigrant stance. As foreign policy analyst Soeren Kern quipped, "So what explains Sarkozy's about-face vis-à-vis Libya? His sudden support for the anti-Gaddafi rebels can be attributed to two main factors: opinion polls and the closely related issue of Muslim immigration . . . . [Marine] Le Pen has single-handedly catapulted the twin issues of Muslim immigration and French national identity to the top of the French political agenda. In recent weeks, Le Pen has been a permanent fixture on prime-time television to discuss the threat to France of a wave of immigrants from Libya."[77] Similar fears were also shaping politics in Germany as well as other EU countries, and of course Berlusconi's center-right coalition hinged on the staunchly anti-migrant Northern League. Catherine de Wenden, director of research at the Center for International Studies and Research at Sciences Po, observed, "In this renationalization of European countries, and the rise of xenophobia, governments are very careful toward new migration flows . . . . At the same time, this is contradictory with liberal European models."[78] Indeed, such contradictions reflect the essence of what can make the political agitation pathway such an effective cross-domain coercive strategy. Had circumstances within in the spring of 2011 resembled those that had existed in the years leading up to the uprising, Gaddafi's final attempt at CEM might well have succeeded.

At the same time, some European leaders had concluded that they might "be damned if they did cave into Gaddafi's threats and damned if they did not," for if the rebellion in Libya succeeded, mass migration across the Mediterranean might still result. This was because, even before the first Arab Spring protests broke out in Tunisia, significant numbers of North Africans had indicated strong interest in migrating or moving to Europe. In an October 2010 Gallup poll, for instance, more than 25 percent of those surveyed in Algeria, Tunisia, Egypt, Morocco, and Libya reported that they desired to migrate permanently, while 35 percent of Libyans and 28 percent of North Africans overall reported that they would like to migrate either temporarily or permanently. Of all of those polled, more than 33 percent reported that Western Europe was their destination of choice.[79] Journalist Daniel Korski observed, "European

---

[76] Rachel Donadio, "Fears about Immigrants Deepen Divisions in Europe," *New York Times*, April 12, 2011.

[77] Kern, "Why France Was So Keen to Attack Libya."

[78] Kern, "Why France Was So Keen to Attack Libya."

[79] Neli Esipova and Julie Ray, "One in Four in North Africa Desired to Migrate before Unrest," *Gallup*, April 29, 2011, www.gallup.com/poll/147344/one-four-north-africa-desired-migrate-unrest.aspx.

governments may talk about democracy and practically every European leader has enjoyed a walk through the banner-clad Tahrir Square. But when they return home, shake the sand off their trousers and start thinking of their voters, their thoughts quickly turn to managing the flow of illegal immigrants who dream of a better life in Europe . . . . The rest is rhetoric."[80] Scalvino was blunter still, declaring, "We have to acknowledge how much the logic of humanitarian intervention is actually limited to self-interest. At this point, Italy and France are playing an obscene ping-pong match, the result of which is the wholesale rejection of new refugees."[81]

None of this precludes the possibility that European military action was driven in part by concerns about what Gaddafi might do to his people. However, policymakers were at least as concerned about what might happen if those people decided to flee to Europe and what the domestic political consequences might be for these same leaders in such an eventuality. Consider, for instance, that whereas asylum applications in Italy had actually fallen to 8,200 in 2010 from a peak of 30,300 in 2008, this decline was offset by increases elsewhere in Europe, especially in Germany (49 percent), Sweden (32 percent), Denmark (30 percent), Belgium, (16 percent), and France (13 percent).[82] None of these countries was eager to welcome more.

Why Did Gaddafi's Gambit Fail?

Although EU leaders were clearly growing impatient with Gaddafi and had tired of his episodic threats "to turn Europe black" long before unrest erupted in early 2011, his previous exercises in CEM were viewed by most, if certainly not all, as insufficient grounds for military intervention. Indeed, as one NATO representative put it, "it was not even something we realistically contemplated."[83] However, after Gaddafi simultaneously threatened to do grievous harm to a portion of his own population and to "turn the entire Mediterranean into a battlefield" by "flooding Europe with migrants," the calculus within some member states changed definitively: not only would further coercion not succeed, but Gaddafi would also have to go.[84] Thus it was Gaddafi's own increasingly outrageous threats to unleash chaos domestically and internationally that, along with domestic and regional uprisings, precipitated moves to overthrow him and created international political support for that course of action.

In the end, however, the feared "human tsunami," as Berlusconi called it, never materialized. This was surely due in part to the fact that once NATO

[80] Daniel Korski, "Europe's North Africa Policy Drowns in a Flood of Migrants," *Guardian*, May 10, 2011.
[81] Scalvini, "Humanitarian Wars and Rejected Refugees.".
[82] "Asylum Claims Drop to Nearly Half the Level of 2001—UN," *Reuters*, March 28, 2011.
[83] Interview with author, Cambridge, MA, November 2012.
[84] See, e.g., Hugh Roberts, "Who Said Gaddafi Had to Go?," *London Review of Books* 33 (November 2011): 8–18.

bombing escalated and the rebels started receiving weapons and other forms of external assistance, escalating the size and scope of the insurgency, Libyan government forces had less time and fewer opportunities to set people to sea. Even so, these outflows were still controlled and manipulated by government officials until August 2011, when the rebels, with NATO assistance, drove Gaddafi and his remaining forces out of Tripoli. After that time, no additional boats loaded with migrants or asylum seekers landed in Italy until the end of the conflict in October.[85]

At least as significant is the fact that the EU, with NATO assistance, responded to the threat of a mass influx by positioning helicopters, speedboats, and war ships in theater and by deploying a rapid-reaction force to the Libyan and Tunisian coasts to conduct maritime patrols designed to impede or forestall the flight of North Africans to Europe.[86] Moreover, many of those who were intercepted by NATO and European forces were declared economic migrants rather than asylum seekers and summarily repatriated back to North Africa. Some number also drowned before reaching Europe.[87] All of these factors combined ensured that the true size of the displacement crisis remained invisible to most European publics and thus failed to generate the kind of pro- and anti-group mobilization upon which most exercises of successful CEMs rely.[88]

Furthermore, whereas the displaced populations in Libya's neighboring countries were more mixed in terms of age and gender, those being sent to southern Europe were disproportionately comprised of young men. Libyan forces rightly assumed this would make the groups arriving in Europe seem more threatening. However, this strategy proved a double-edged sword, because it also inhibited mobilization of a significant countervailing group who supported protection of and refuge for the displaced, which too helped undermine CEM success in this case.[89]

Conclusions and Implications

Given the benefit of hindsight and the ultimate outcome in the fall of 2011, Gaddafi's resort to CEM in response to European support of Libyan domestic dissent and antigovernment protests may appear foolhardy at best. However,

---

[85] "Europe Braced for Immigrant Influx as Chaos Reigned." Frontex reported a significant drop in the number of crossings on the central Mediterranean route (CMR) for the third quarter of 2011. After the National Transitional Council gained control of Tripoli, flows of migrants from Libya stopped abruptly.

[86] Richard Jozwiak, "Europe Braces for Tide of North African Refugees," *Radio Free Europe*, April 6, 2011, online.

[87] Collee Barry, "Migrant: Many Ships Failed to Aid Libyan Refugees," *CNSNews*, May 14, 2011, online.

[88] See, for instance, Chris Ulack, "The Arab Spring's Looming Refugee Crisis," *Foreign Policy*, June 23, 2011, online. For a discussion of the role of simultaneous pro- and anti-migrant mobilization, see Greenhill, *Weapons of Mass Migration*, chapters 2–5 and appendix.

[89] This does not mean there was no support for those fleeing, only that it was the group had few supporters relative to historically more popular groups.

as many observers would concede, by late February 2011 Gaddafi had few attractive policy options from which to choose. He was an international as well as a regional pariah, particularly among influential heads of state such as the Saudi royal family.[90] Facing both a mounting insurgency by rebels within and pressure from some of the most powerful members of the world's most powerful military alliance. Under these circumstances, countercoercion via CEM probably appeared a worthwhile gamble, particularly given that Gaddafi had effected it against EU member states with relative ease multiple times before.

For the Europeans' part, faced with the unattractive alternative of conceding to Gaddafi's demands (and possibly still confronting a massive influx) and handed a legitimate rationale to intervene by the Libyan leader himself, pursuing regime change not surprisingly also seemed like a good gamble. Here again Gaddafi is not unique. In many circles, the impulse to attempt to stop potential outflows at their source—often via a change in regime leadership—has been pronounced on both sides of the ideological and power spectrums. Before concluding that regime change is some kind of silver bullet, however, it is worth remembering, as Downes notes in this volume, that such enterprises can be costly and the outcomes uncertain, as recent experiences in Iraq, Afghanistan, and even Libya make abundantly clear. Overthrowing a tyrant does not necessarily beget liberal democracy or mean an end to engineered outflows. Indeed, even in the best-case scenario, the overthrow of a sitting dictator and an increase in economic development may actually increase emigration from that state, at least in the short run, and what we have witnessed in recent years represents anything but such a best-case scenario.[91]

More important still, regime change may not even eliminate the threat of CEM. If the compelling incentives are in place and targets ripe, this tool may remain attractive, especially for actors with little to lose and much to gain. Consider, for instance, that on November 2, 2015, Jamal Zubia, spokesman for the National Salvation Government of Libya's General National Congress—one of the two rival governments currently vying for power—issued a not terribly veiled threat against the EU: if not offered official diplomatic recognition and financial assistance by Brussels, it might actively assist migrants and asylum seekers in their bids to reach Europe. Explicitly citing the example of the deposed leader—and apparently undeterred by his fate—Zubia quipped, "Gaddafi did this threat and brought Europe to its knees . . . . It is a strategic threat, yes, but I would not rule out us doing it one day."[92] In light of

---

[90] Alex J. Bellamy and Paul D. Williams, "The New Politics of Protection? Côte d'Ivoire, Libya and the Responsibility to Protect," *International Affairs* 87 (July 2001): 833.

[91] This tendency, known as a "migration hump," reflects the fact that economic development tends to disrupt traditional economic relationships and traditionally noncompetitive sectors and also provides prospective emigrants with the economic means to emigrate.

[92] In an interview with the *Telegraph*, Zubia emphasized that although his Tripoli-based faction was not planning to follow through on its threat imminently, it might in future. Colin Freeman, "Libya Warns It Could Flood Europe with Migrants If EU Does Not Recognize New Self-Declared Government," *Telegraph*, November 2, 2015.

subsequent developments on both sides of the Mediterranean—including further unrest in the Middle East and North Africa on one side of the Sea and discussion of the potential collapse of the Schengen Accords, and even of the EU more broadly, on the other—such threats seem anything but idle and the sagacity of the decision to unseat Gaddafi anything but obvious.

CHAPTER 11 | The Strategy of Coercive Isolation

TIMOTHY W. CRAWFORD

IF, AS FREDRICK THE GREAT said, "Diplomacy without arms is like music without instruments," arms without diplomacy is apolitical force: the anathema of strategy. The strategy of coercive isolation plays out through diplomacy; it may therefore be deemed an "other than force" kind of coercion, as it has been in this volume's scheme. But in such diplomacy's logic resides a pure expression of coercion: the attempt to use fear of force to control political outcomes. To isolate an adversary when threats of violence are salient *is* a military threat.[1] A foundational understanding of force's role in international politics underpins this argument: states "conduct [their] affairs in the brooding shadow of violence"; any policy to make a state more vulnerable to violence is a kind of "armed coercion."[2]

In the study of coercion there has been a curious disinterest in that diplomacy which seeks to cause or reinforce the adversary's isolation. So intuitive is it that such diplomacy matters that the way it does has eluded careful thought. The essential idea—that such diplomacy can coerce by increasing expectations of escalating costs—has not been clearly framed. Leading coercion studies recognize that isolating a target is important but conceive it as a background condition for success. Thus, for Alexander George and William Simons the extent to which the adversary "is supported diplomatically and militarily by allies" is a "contextual variable": coercing a target backed by allies is "more complex and sometimes more difficult" than coercing an isolated target.[3]

[1] I thank the Princeton Research Program in International Security for the opportunity to present my first attempt to develop these ideas and the S. Rajanatnam School of International Studies' Working Paper series for helping me to advance them in an earlier version of this paper.
[2] Kenneth Waltz, *Theory of International Politics* (New York: Random House, 1979), 103; Robert Osgood and Robert Tucker, *Force, Order and Justice* (Baltimore: Johns Hopkins University Press, 1967), 3.
[3] Alexander George and William Simons, ed., *The Limits of Coercive Diplomacy*, 2nd ed. (Boulder, CO: Westview Press 1994), 273.

Similarly, Robert Art and Patrick Cronin observe that if the coercer lacks adequate support for its policy, "its actions could easily be undermined or frustrated" by others.[4] Having a situation in which others do not bolster the target is therefore an important "prerequisite" for success.[5] This way of thinking makes the target's isolation an exogenous condition rather than one that operates and can be manipulated as a mechanism of coercion as crises unfold.

But diplomacy that raises an opponent's expected cost of fighting by shrinking its alignment network *is* coercion. In a crisis, the ability to coerce often turns on actions or developments that shift the opponents' expected payoffs of war, reducing the costs for the coercer and increasing them for the target.[6] Alignment shifts that deprive the opponent of expected support can impose costs on it—by increasing its risks—in alarming ways.[7] And if opponents understand that they are more vulnerable to force when they are isolated, then the *process* of losing expected support, or failing to secure it, will generate coercive pressure.

Basic principles and dynamics of realist foreign policy analysis are at work here. A country's ambitions tend to expand and contract with its power.[8] Alliances are an important part of national power and condition countries' choices in big ways. When strong allies are available, states are more likely to resist a threatening foe than accommodate it.[9] Similarly, a country's ambitions expand and contract with the gain and loss of allies, and allies can embolden each other by increasing their partners' expectations of support, and restrain each other by decreasing them. Coercive isolation (CI) seeks to reverse the moral hazard of an opponent's alliance ties, restraining or pressuring the opponent by reducing its expectations of allied support.[10]

Coercion theories that focus on the dyadic axis of confrontation—such as those developed in part II of this volume—can miss this outside game. The game, however, generates not only crises (e.g., when a weak party, expecting outside support, refuses to compromise with a much more powerful

---

[4] Robert Art and Patrick Cronin, eds., *The United States and Coercive Diplomacy* (Washington, DC: USIP Press, 2003), 371–72. This is also a central theme of research on economic sanctions: see Drezner in this volume.

[5] Art and Cronin, *United States and Coercive Diplomacy*, 372.

[6] Branislav Slantchev, *Military Threats: The Costs of Coercion and the Price of Peace* (Cambridge, UK: Cambridge University Press 2011).

[7] On risks as costs, see David A. Baldwin, *Power and International Relations: A Conceptual Approach* (Princeton, NJ: Princeton University Press, 2016), 185.

[8] Robert Gilpin, *War and Change in World Politics* (Princeton, NJ: Princeton University Press, 1981), 22–23.

[9] Stephen Walt, *Origins of Alliances* (Ithaca, NY: Cornell University Press, 1987), 30.

[10] Glenn H. Snyder, *Alliance Politics* (Ithaca, NY: Cornell University Press 1997); Timothy W. Crawford, *Pivotal Deterrence: Third Party Statecraft and the Pursuit of Peace* (Ithaca, NY: Cornell University Press, 2003); Timothy W. Crawford and Alan J. Kuperman, eds., *Gambling on Humanitarian Intervention: Moral Hazard, Rebellion and Civil War* (New York: Routledge, 2006); Brett V. Benson, *Constructing International Security: Alliances, Deterrence, and Moral Hazard* (Cambridge: Cambridge University Press, 2012).

opponent) but also their outcomes.[11] When powerful states set out to coerce much weaker opponents, they are often surprised their foes do not fold easily.[12] One reason may be that the coercer does not consider the target's expectations of external support or misjudges them because the target's expectations do not match their own; either way, the coercer does not act effectively to reduce those expectations.[13] For both policymakers and analysts of coercion, the perspective developed here is pertinent: many of the things states may wish to do through coercive diplomacy involve targets that are not isolated but must be for coercion to work. Consider the problem of coercive regime change, examined in Downes's chapter in this volume. To get a government, like the one in Syria, to relinquish power, one may need to detach it from a powerful patron like Russia.[14] To get a country like Iran to curtail its nuclear program, one may need to do so as well.[15] The same principle applies to attempts to coerce terrorist groups or their state sponsors, which are explored in Fraiman's chapter.[16]

Model and Coercion Scenarios

Alignments

The CI model highlights the specific coercive effect of diplomacy that reduces a target's expectations of support in a fight. For coercive isolation, alignments—patterns of states' "expectations . . . about whether they will be supported or opposed by other states" in future military conflicts—are the primary objects of attack.[17]

Risk versus Denial Effects

CI generates *denial* and *risk* effects.[18] Denial directly eliminates resources the target can use to prepare and practice military defense, and thus leads it to curtail its plans.[19] By detaching its patron, one can thus impose on the target an immediate loss of power to resist; for example, if the patron withdraws

---

[11] If the adversaries' initial perceptions of the balance of capabilities between them don't change in a confrontation (as will likely be true when asymmetries are large), but alignment expectations move sharply in the coercer's favor, then the shift probably explains the target's capitulation.
[12] On these puzzling failures of asymmetric coercion and other potential explanations, see the chapters in this volume by Sechser, Haun, and Downes.
[13] On the need to have good intelligence about a target's understanding of its capabilities to resist coercion (which may include expected outside support), see Long in this volume.
[14] See Downes in this volume.
[15] For a different perspective on coercive bargaining over nuclear development, see Volpe in this volume.
[16] See Fraiman in this volume.
[17] Snyder, *Alliance Politics,* 6.
[18] Robert Pape, "Coercion and Military Strategy: Why Denial Works and Punishment Doesn't," *Journal of Strategic Studies* 15 (December 1992): 423–75; Art and Cronin, *United States and Coercive Diplomacy*, 362–63.
[19] On denial, see Art and Greenhill in this volume.

forces from the target's territory that would have been used for defense. *Risk* effects are more psychological and central to the model. They shape the target's intentions—and willingness to run risks—insofar as they are conditioned by expectations about future levels of support. Denial and risk effects overlap and interact. But the coercive "leverage" of CI comes from the target's *anticipation* of escalating punishment, unmitigated by outside support.[20] The target's increased vulnerability to future force is thus an imposition of costs that weakens its ambitions and resolve.

Primary and Secondary Targets of Influence

CI involves triangular, second-order influence. In order to coerce the primary target (PT) the coercer influences secondary targets (ST) who shape the primary target's expectations of support and behavior.[21] Thus, in the chain of influence the ST comes first and the PT comes second. A necessary condition for success against the PT is some measure of success with the ST.[22] As argued elsewhere, the approach to the ST (unless the ST is very weak or likely to abandon the target anyway) usually emphasizes accommodation and rewards.[23] While the coercive isolation model does not preclude the option of bullying the PT and the ST simultaneously,[24] the cases in this chapter mostly conform to the "confront PT and accommodate ST" pattern.

Depth of Isolation: The ST's Alignment Change and the PT's Expectations

The model posits that change in the ST's alignment puts coercive pressure on the PT. But *risk* effects stem from the degree to which the ST's position changes relative to the PT's expectations of and dependence on allied backing. The strength of risk effects is thus a function of (1) the PT's initial expectations and valuation of ST's support, (2) the degree of the ST's subsequent divergence from the initial baseline, and (3) the PT's altered expectations due to ST's shift. In simple terms, the ST's alignment can change from a supporting position to one of neutrality or, going further, to one of positive support for the coercer's policy. The PT will confront the greatest risk effects when an ST it expected and needed to be an ally instead becomes an active opponent. But

---

[20] On coercion "via risk" see Art and Greenhill in this volume; Robert Pape, "The Strategic Logic of Suicide Terrorism," *American Political Science Review* 97 (August 2003): 346–47.

[21] For a related triangular dynamic, see Fraiman's concept of "transitive compellence" in this volume. Also see Daniel Byman and Matthew Waxman, *The Dynamics of Coercion* (Cambridge: Cambridge University Press, 2002), 82–83.

[22] This implies that coercive isolation attempts might "work" by isolating the PT—imposing costs and risks on it—but fail to cause compliance.

[23] Timothy W. Crawford, "Preventing Enemy Coalitions: How Wedge Strategies Shape Power Politics," *International Security* 35 (Spring 2011): 155–89.

[24] Yasuhiro Izumikawa, "To Coerce or Reward? Theorizing Wedge Strategies in Alliance Politics," *Security Studies* 22 (2013): 498–531.

TABLE 11.1 A Model of Coercive Isolation

Change in ST's Alignment Needed to Coerce PT	Neutralize ST	Realign ST
Strategic Logic	If PT's initial calculus depends on active ST support, then it will comply if it loses ST's support.	If PT's initial calculus depends on ST's neutrality, then it will comply if the ST is aligned against it.

lesser alignment swings can also deliver a coercive punch. If the PT is initially counting on the ST's active support, then neutralizing the ST will set it back. If, however, the PT initially discounted the likelihood or value of active ST support, then neutralizing the ST will do little. The implication for analysts: to explain the success or failure of a coercive isolation attempt, one must try to ascertain the target's initial pattern of expectations (see Table 11.1).

This suggests a useful point of analytical leverage. The low end of CI risk effects start with neutralizing an ST that the PT expects to be a supporter. If this can be shown to cause targets to comply with coercer demands in scenarios that are hard to succeed in, then the model captures an important facet of coercion.

Coercion Scenarios: Blackmail and Compellence

Coercion studies often distinguish between deterrence and compellence. Because reinforcing existing behavior is easier than changing it, it is generally thought to be easier to deter than to compel.[25] In this sense, one may presume that CI is more likely to work for deterrence than for compellence. Within the latter category there are really two kinds of coercion to consider.[26] The first, blackmail, is proactive: it tries to impel the target to initiate an action, to undertake some new course it otherwise would not. The second—now, more restrictively, called compellence—is reactive: it tries to impel the target to stop doing what it would otherwise keep doing.

The best cases for demonstrating significant effects of coercive isolation are the harder cases of blackmail and compellence, where success means changing the target's behavior in a marked way. If we can show that minimal forms of coercive isolation pressure worked in these more challenging scenarios, we may infer that it is even more likely to work in the more plentiful and less challenging deterrence scenarios.[27] Moreover, because successful CI means

[25] On the distinction between deterrence and compellence, and the difficulty of the latter, see Art and Greenhill in this volume.

[26] Peter Viggo Jakobsen, "Coercive Diplomacy," in *Contemporary Security Studies*, ed. Alan Collins (Oxford: Oxford University Press, 2013), 235–55.

[27] See Jack Levy, "Case Studies: Types, Designs, and Logics of Inference," *Conflict Management and Peace Science* 25 (February 2008): 1–18.

changing the target's behavior in a marked way, the posited effect of CI *and* the process leading to it will be more observable. The six cases discussed below involve either blackmail or compellence scenarios.

Conducive Conditions and Case Studies

To build policy-relevant insights, coercive diplomacy studies move from abstract theory to contingent generalizations about conditions conducive to success.[28] Three such propositions follow.

First, *the more the PT depends on the ST's support, the more likely it will comply with the coercer's demands when deprived of that support.* "Depends" means two things here: the PT considers the level of the ST's support it expects to be necessary for risking military confrontation with the coercer; the PT cannot turn elsewhere for such support—substitutes are scarce. The more the PT is confined in such conditions, the easier it will be to make it comply by neutralizing the ST. For the policymaker attempting CI, a realistic estimate of PT's expectations about ST's support, and the level of such support that it considers necessary to sustain or advance its position, is therefore critical.

Second, *the more valuable (and credible) the rewards the coercer can offer the ST, the more able the coercer will be to isolate the PT and make it comply.* "Valuable" refers to how *useful* the rewards are to the ST and how *hard it would be* for the ST to otherwise obtain them (again, substitutes are scarce). For credibility, what matters is that the coercer can convince the ST that rewards promised (as opposed to those given up front) will be delivered if the ST alters its relations with the PT as desired, even if the PT does not comply with the coercer's demands. Making the rewards to ST contingent on PT's compliance may sound like a good way to avoid being bamboozled, but doing so gives the PT a veto—in the form of noncompliance—over the relations between the coercer and the ST. So a credible policy of inducements toward the ST will be one that the PT cannot nullify through either counterconcessions to the ST or noncompliance.

Third, *the better the coercer and its allies coordinate their policies vis-à-vis PT and STs, the more likely the PT will be to comply.*[29] Coordination can matter in a variety of ways. Well-coordinated allied diplomacy can help the coercer to divide the PT from its supporters, either through threats to punish those supporters or promises that reinforce the coercer's reward power. Allies' diplomacy may also bolster the coercer's threats by signaling to the PT that they will not restrain the coercer. By the same token, poorly coordinated allied diplomacy can subvert the coercer's efforts. The coercer's allies—if they are opposed to conciliating the ST—may dilute the quality or subvert the credibility of the

---

[28] Alexander George, *Bridging the Gap: Theory and Practice in Foreign Policy* (Washington, DC: USIP Press, 1993), 120–25.

[29] See also Art and Cronin, *United States and Coercive Diplomacy*, 371.

coercer's promises. They may also weaken the PT's perception of the costs and risks of increased isolation by acting in ways that suggest they might try to restrain the coercer or, worse, that they may open up "substitute" channels of relations with the PT that counteract its constricted alignment.

Of the six cases that follow, four are successes (two of blackmail and two of compellence) and two failures (one of each). Several things are accomplished with these cases. First, all six illustrate how rewards played a role in the coercer's diplomatic isolation of the ST (Proposition 2). Second, the four success cases show how the coercer's diplomacy —which caused and revealed the neutralization of the PT's expected support—was an important *proximate* cause of the target's compliance. Each of these also shows the PT's dependence on ST support to be conducive to success (Proposition 1). Third, two success cases also demonstrate how coordination between the coercer and its allies contribute to success (Proposition 3). Fourth, the case of failed blackmail shows how the PT's initial lack of dependence upon the ST's support doomed the policy, even though the ST was effectively neutralized (Proposition 1). Fifth, the case of failed compellence illustrates how the emergence of a substitute for the ST's support—after the ST had been effectively neutralized—caused the policy to fail (Proposition 1).

Blackmail Cases

In the ideal blackmail scenario, the PT is trying to maintain a position, for example, a claim to territory, an occupation, a military capability, a form of government, or a relationship with other actors. Its policy hangs on this calculation: it can defy threats as long as it gets expected ST support. The coercer induces the ST to withhold or withdraw support. The PT then complies with the coercer's demands in order to avoid the risk of fighting in its isolated position.

Japan and China, 1915

In January 1915, Japan issued "twenty-one demands" to China, calling for it to concede legal control over territory and economic assets and activities in Shantung, southern Manchuria, eastern Mongolia, Fujian province, and elsewhere. The demands were assembled in five groups (I, II, III, IV, V). Group I concerned Japan's position in Shantung, where it had just expelled and taken over the German concession in Tsingtao. These aimed to strengthen Japan's legal claim to inherit and extend the concession and to prevent China from giving any other power concessions there. Group II focused on deepening Japan's predominant position in southern Manchuria and eastern Mongolia, extending its leases on ports and railways, and expanding the rights of Japanese nationals to live, own property, and conduct business there. Group III aimed to establish Sino-Japanese joint control over the Hanyeping mines and exclude other foreign interests from mining in the area. Group IV demanded that China not cede or lease seaports on its coast to any other power. Group V demands reached furthest into China's internal governance and foreign relations and would, if agreed to, have "made China a Japanese protectorate."[30] They ranged from insisting that China use Japanese as political, economic, and military advisers to the creation of a joint police force, the requirement that China consult with Japan before arranging foreign loans for other industrial or transport projects, and a call for new Japan-run railroad projects in parts of China in the British sphere of interests.

From the outset, Japanese leaders understood the Group V demands—the most provocative—as "wishes" not imperative to obtain. But they did not say this to the Chinese or the other powers when the latter pressed Tokyo to disclose its demands. Though Japan eventually dropped Group V, its negotiating tactics alarmed others about its long-range goals. Nevertheless, when China resisted Japan's demands and the confrontation escalated, powers that could have stepped in did not. Denied the expected support, China capitulated. Japan was in a strong position to promote China's isolation. The war left the Entente allies badly needing Japan's help. This enabled Japan to sideline them.

China's Dependence on Britain, France, and Russia

China depended on outside powers—Britain and Russia especially—to shield it from Japanese ambitions. China's president, Yuan Shikai, relied on Fabian tactics to blunt Japan's demands. He first stalled and began leaking Japan's demands to the press and British and American officials "to win foreign support for his attempts to resist Japanese aggression."[31] When the formal negotiations began on February 2, "any hope [Tokyo] had entertained of bringing them to a rapid and secret conclusion had to be given up." A source near Yuan reported that Chinese leaders were expecting European intervention to prevent Japan from resorting to force. Japan's ambitions in China did conflict with other powers' interests, and Britain and Russia had before been played off against Japan to check it. But over time it grew clear that neither European powers nor the United States would step in. China's ambassador to Japan advised Yuan in early May to accede to Japan's final proposal, which was then backed by an ultimatum, because "China, left to herself, could not resist Japanese forces; the outcome of the unequal contest would be worse than submission to the demands." On May 9 China capitulated to nearly all of the Group I–IV demands because it "could not resist [Japan's] terms without outside support."[32]

---

[30] Madeleine Chi, *China Diplomacy, 1914–1918* (Cambridge, MA: Harvard East Asian Monographs, 1970), 32.
[31] Chi, *China Diplomacy*, 41; Ian Nish, *Alliance in Decline* (London: Athalone Press, 1972), 153.
[32] Thomas E. La Fargue, *China and the World War* (Palo Alto, CA: Stanford University Press, 1937) 55, 42, 55; Nish, *Alliance in Decline*, 155.

Japan's Diplomacy and Inducements

The war placed demands on the Entente that helped Japan to isolate China. Japan capitalized on three. The first was the general need for cohesion. For Britain and France, keeping the Entente united became a war aim in itself.[33] In January 1915 Germany had initiated secret negotiations with Japan, seeking a separate peace that would break the Entente. In April 1915, as the China crisis escalated, Tokyo revealed to Britain its secret talks with Germany but did not terminate them. On May 3 the British foreign minister Edward Grey asked Japan to disclose them to France and Russia and to inform Germany that Japan was bound by its Entente commitment not to seek a separate peace.[34] The timing of Britain's requests was not coincidental: it was reminding its allies of the need to keep Japan's loyalty when Japan was about to give an ultimatum to China. After the May 7 ultimatum, Britain, France, and Russia were careful not to undercut Japan's coercive diplomacy.

Second, Russia desperately needed war material, and Japan could provide it. In the first year of the war, Russia suffered from colossal weapons shortages. Its early 1915 offensives and massive defeats starting in May magnified the problem and the urgency of Russian efforts to overcome it.[35] In this context, Japanese supplies were seen as critical to its ability to stay in the fight.[36] This was an explicit factor in Russia's decision, as Russia's Foreign Minister, Sergei Sazanov, put it to the Japanese ambassador, "not [to] interfere in the twenty-one demands."[37]

Third, the allies wanted Japan to increase its commitment to the Entente in other formal and material ways. Russia wanted Japan to go beyond its Anglo-Japanese alliance commitments and embrace the Entente's London Agreements of November 1914. This, Russia hoped, would ensure more Japanese aid to Russia's war effort. France similarly hoped for Japanese troops on the Western Front. Japan played off these hopes.

The Negotiations and the Role of the European Powers

Japan's negotiations with China went through two stages. The first, formal talks that started on February 2, deadlocked on April 17. The second culminated in the May 3 ultimatum and China's capitulation. Japan's ability to neutralize the Powers was revealed in both stages of the negotiations.

---

[33] Mira Rapp-Hooper, "Ambivalent Albion, Ambitious Ally: Britain's Decision for No Separate Peace in 1914," *Security Studies* 23 (November 2014): 814–44.
[34] F. W. Ikle, "Japanese-German Peace Negotiations during World War I," *American Historical Review* 71 (1965): 62–76.
[35] William C. Fuller, "The Eastern Front," in *The Great War and the Twentieth Century*, ed. Jay Winter, Geoffrey Parker, and Mary Habeck (New Haven, CT: Yale University Press 2000), 40.
[36] Peter A. Berton, "The Secret Russo-Japanese Alliance of 1916" (Ph.D. dissertation, Columbia University, 1956), 90–95.
[37] Berton, "Secret Russo-Japanese Alliance," 90.

In its first counterproposal, China indicated that it was willing to negotiate on Groups I–III, but not on IV or V. Even on the points deemed negotiable, however, China's positions tended to defeat Japan's objectives.[38] In early March, Japan hinted at force if China did not make serious concessions. Japan boosted its troop strength on its bases in China (within treaty limits). This produced movement. By late March, China accepted most of Groups I and II. It had accepted that Japan would inherit Germany's "economic rights and preferred position" in Shangtung and bent to many of Japan's demands for deepening and extending Japan's control in Manchuria; softened its refusal to admit linkage between arrangements in Manchuria and arrangements in Mongolia (by suggesting that a parallel approach was possible if Japan dropped the Group V demands); and agreed to permit a joint-control arrangement for the Hanyehping Company.[39] Nevertheless, there remained outstanding disagreements on important points. Japan wanted more.

The European powers held back. In late February, at Grey's urging, Japan disclosed to Russia, France, and the United States an abridged version of its demands: "None of [them] questioned the propriety of the Japanese demands."[40] In Grey's view, Britain's "proper course [was] to lie low" and give "the Chinese no hint of support." Russia too did not raise objections. In a private note to Japan on March 13, the United States criticized several of Japan's Group V demands. But it amounted to a "frank admission that the United States would not influence China in opposing Japan."[41]

After negotiations deadlocked on April 17, Japan decided to threaten force explicitly. It presented somewhat moderated demands on April 26. After China's defiant reply, Japan's May 7 ultimatum demanded unconditional acceptance within 48 hours (but also dropped the Group V "wishes"). China once more sought outside support. President Woodrow Wilson released a statement declaring that the United States would not surrender any of its rights with China and that there would be no "abatement of [U.S.] interests in the welfare and progress of China."[42] Washington also sent diplomatic messages to Tokyo and Beijing, encouraging them to continue negotiating with patience and peaceful means. A historian notes that the United States then "was the only power which the Chinese government could hope to play off against Japan. In this crucial test it was fully demonstrated that the United States could not be depended upon to go beyond a friendly protest, and that only in protection of her own treaty rights."[43]

China's isolation was reinforced by Wilson's request to other powers to join a formal appeal to Japan and China to negotiate peacefully. Grey said no, on the grounds that Britain had already privately communicated a similar message to

[38] La Fargue, *China and the World War*, 56

[39] Chi, *China Diplomacy*, 43; La Fargue, *China and the World War*, 60–61.

[40] Chi, *China Diplomacy*, 41.

[41] Nish, *Alliance in Decline*, 154; Chi, *China Diplomacy*, 38–39, 46.

[42] La Fargue, *China and the World War*, 72–73; Chi, *China Diplomacy*, 55.

[43] La Fargue, *China and the World War*, 77.

Japan; China would likely fold since Japan had dropped the Group V demands. In fact, Britain told China to fold. On May 5 the British ambassador in Beijing told Yuan's private secretary, "It would be folly for China to count on the prospect of any assistance from British subjects." On May 7, when China's ambassador in London asked Grey directly what Britain's position was, Grey replied that he "saw no prospect of any interference in the dispute between China and Japan." On May 8, just before the ultimatum expired, the British ambassador in Beijing warned Yuan that he needed to give "an absolutely unconditional acceptance." Similar warnings came from France and Russia.[44] The Chinese cabinet agreed on May 8 to all of Japan's April 26 demarche.

The scale of Japan's coercive isolation victory is explained by the conditions highlighted in our framework. China was dependent upon the support of European powers, and vulnerable without it. The war put Japan in a strong position to induce the outside powers not to interfere; the benefits Japan could offer them were both valuable and hard to replace. This created a nearly automatic level of coordination with the parties that could have otherwise undermined its policy.

China and Vietnam, 1988–1989

With Soviet support, Vietnam invaded Cambodia in 1975 and toppled the Khmer Rouge regime (backed by China) and replaced it with a proxy government. China retaliated with a border war against Vietnam and declared that it would maintain a militarized border and a state of war as long as Vietnamese forces stayed in Cambodia.[45] Hanoi countered that it would not withdraw from Cambodia unless the Chinese threat was first lifted. This set the benchmark for gauging the success of China's coercive diplomacy: if Vietnam pulled its forces out of Cambodia under Chinese military pressure, Beijing's policy worked.

Vietnam's Dependence on the USSR

Until the late 1980s, Vietnam's position was reinforced by Soviet military and political support. Under Gorbachev things began to change. The USSR sought better relations with its Great Power competitors. China seized the opportunity to isolate Vietnam.

China's Diplomacy and Soviet Reactions

China linked normalization of Sino-Soviet relations to Soviet pressure on Vietnam to retreat from Cambodia. The Soviets responded in two ways, both "consistent with Beijing's preferences." First, Moscow overrode Hanoi's refusal to allow the Khmer Rouge any role in a Cambodian political settlement.

[44] Chi, *China Diplomacy*, 56–58.

[45] Robert S. Ross, *Chinese Security Policy: Structure, Power and Politics* (New York: Routledge, 2009) 123.

Knowing that China insisted on a place for the Khmer Rouge in the settlement process, the Soviets pushed Hanoi to concede the point. When the Vietnamese balked, Moscow "bypassed Hanoi to deal directly with the Phnom Penh government." Hanoi then caved.[46]

Second, the Soviets retracted support from Vietnam in a way that pressured it to enact a full withdrawal from Cambodia. When fighting between China and Vietnam broke out in the South China Sea in March 1988, Moscow "maintained near total silence" at Vietnam's attempt to contest China's move to occupy the Spratly Islands, which was crushed. Two months later Hanoi signaled that it would withdraw half of its 100,000--man force deployed in Cambodia. In December 1988, China agreed to a Sino-Soviet summit in 1989 that would pave the way for full normalization of relations. But Premiere Deng Xiao-ping stipulated that a full Vietnamese withdrawal from Cambodia would have to be worked out before Beijing would make a final commitment to participate. In early 1989, amid a broader retrenchment in the region, Moscow pulled out its fighter and bomber aircraft deployed in Vietnam and began reducing its naval presence at Cam Rahn Bay. As Robert Ross notes, "without Soviet military support, the risk to Vietnam of continuing its occupation of Cambodia and alienating China grew considerably as China showed less restraint in challenging Vietnamese policy."[47]

Vietnam's Retreat from Cambodia

Just ahead of the May 1989 Sino-Soviet summit, Hanoi announced that it would pull out the rest of its forces from Cambodia within six months without any preconditions.[48] Even as Soviet military aid to Vietnam sharply declined, China maintained military pressure on the border with Vietnam. The melting away of Soviet support drove Vietnam to give up its position in Cambodia. Vietnam's heavy dependence on Soviet support was thus revealed by its reactions to the loss of it. For China, detaching the Soviet Union from its protégés in Hanoi was sufficient to force Vietnam into compliance.

Germany, Britain, and France, 1939

Hitler went to considerable lengths to woo Moscow into the Nazi-Soviet Pact of August 1939.[49] He did so because he expected the shock of Soviet reversal to quash Britain's and France's efforts to organize resistance in Eastern Europe and prompt them to abandon their commitments to Poland. This thinking is

---

[46] Ross, *Chinese Security Policy*, 124; Nicholas Khoo, *Collateral Damage: Sino-Soviet Rivalry and the Termination of the Sino-Vietnamese Alliance* (New York: Columbia University Press, 2011), 149, 150.
[47] Ross, *Chinese Security Policy*, 123.
[48] Khoo, *Collateral Damage*,150–51.
[49] Crawford, "Preventing Enemy Coalitions," 183–85; Timothy W. Crawford, "Powers of Division: From the Anti-Comintern to the Nazi-Soviet and Japanese-Soviet Pacts," in *The Challenge of Grand Strategy: The Great Powers and the Broken Balance between the World Wars*, ed. Jeffrey Taliaferro, Norrin Ripsman, and Steven Lobell (Cambridge: Cambridge University Press, 2012), 259–62.

captured, for example, in the diary of Ernst Von Weizacker, state secretary in Ribbentrop's Foreign Office, which noted on July 30, 1939, that if the Anglo-Franco-Soviet negotiations failed, "the depression" among the Allies "would be so great that we could permit ourselves everything [all things] against Poland."[50] Thus George Kennan concludes the Germans "interpreted the negotiations which the French and British had been conducting so openly all summer with the Soviet Government to mean that Britain and France, unless assured of Russian help, would never dare to oppose a German attack on Poland."[51]

Why German policy—despite its success in neutralizing the USSR—failed to deter Anglo-Franco intervention is the critical question. The logic of the model points to a simple answer supported by the historical sequence. In theory, for blackmail by neutralization to work, the PT(s) must value the ST's support to the point that they would not, in its absence, take and hold the position in question. Yet when Britain unilaterally committed to defend Poland on March 31, 1939, its political leaders still "largely downplayed the value of Soviet military strength" and were constrained by ideological biases that reinforced their view of the Soviet Union as an unattractive potential ally.[52] Indeed, at the time, British and French officials saw the Polish guarantee as an *alternative* to seeking an alliance with Moscow.[53] It was only in late May that Chamberlain and his cabinet were persuaded to reverse this view by new military assessments of the value of Soviet support for Britain's Eastern Front and blockade strategy.[54] *Then* they decided to join France in pursuing an alliance with the USSR.

The British and French committed to defending Poland without placing a high value on Soviet support. When Hitler eliminated that support, he delivered a painful shock to the allies and dashed their plans for organizing an Eastern Front. But he did not remove Soviet support that London and Paris had initially calculated was necessary. His attempt to coerce Britain and France into abandoning their Polish commitments failed because Britain and France had not counted on much Soviet support in the first place.

Compellence Cases

In the ideal CI-compellence scenario, the PT has already initiated use of force or committed to some other action that the coercer wants to halt and/or reverse. The PT's decision to initiate or commit was informed by the expectation that it would be supported by ST—and thus to some extent insulated from

---

[50] Ernst Von Weizsacker, *Die Weizsacker-Papiere 1933–1950*, ed. Leonidas E. Hill (Frankfurt: Propylaen Verlag, 1974), 157.
[51] George Kennan, *Russian and the West under Lenin and Stalin* (New York: Penguin, 1961), 309.
[52] Talbot Imlay, *Facing the Second World War* (Oxford: Oxford University Press, 2003), 98; Mark Haas, *The Ideological Origins of Great Power Politics* (Ithaca, NY: Cornell University Press, 2005), 135.
[53] Robert Manne, "The British Decision for Alliance with Russia, 1939," *Journal of Contemporary History* 9 (1974): 11–13.
[54] Imlay, *Facing the Second World War*, 44–46, 98–99; Manne, "British Decision," 24–26.

the costs of punishment it might suffer for maintaining that action or position. The coercer's goal here is to expand the PT's perception of vulnerability to retaliation by reducing its expectations of ST's support, and in this way forcing the PT to cease its behavior.

Austria-Hungary and Serbia, 1908

In July 1908, the Russian and Austrian foreign ministers secretly agreed to a bargain: Austria could formally annex the Ottoman territories of Bosnia-Herzegovina that it de facto controlled; Russia's warships would gain access to the Mediterranean via the Turkish straits. Jointly they would press these revisions to the 1878 Treaty of Berlin upon the Concert. The Bosnian Annexation crisis began in early October, when that bargain came unglued. Austria moved unilaterally when political instability in Constantinople created an opening to act. Its October 7 announcement that it would annex Bosnian territory was timed to immediately follow a Bulgarian declaration of independence, which also infringed the Berlin Treaty and Ottoman sovereignty. When Russia tried to get its part of the deal accepted as compensation for Austria's move, Britain opposed it. It held that no changes to the Berlin Treaty were acceptable without Concert consent. When Britain and Russia called jointly for a Concert meeting to mediate Austria's annexation, Britain refused to put Russia's bid for the Straits on the agenda.

The sharpest challenge to Vienna's bid came from Serbia, which had long sought to liberate Bosnia and join it to a larger Serb state. With Russia's encouragement, it lodged formal protests, mobilized and expanded its army, called for Concert-guaranteed autonomy for Bosnia, and demanded an Adriatic port from Austria as compensation. Turkey was also an initial opponent of the annexation: it supported Russia and Britain's call for the Concert conference to work out compensation for Serbia and Turkey.

Austria refused to accept any conference mediation, nor would it give autonomy to Bosnia or territorial compensation to Serbia. It insisted that unqualified acceptance of its annexation had to come from all concerned before any Concert formalities.[55] Moreover, it laid counterthreats and demands on Serbia, which became the primary target of Austrian compellence. Austria demanded that Serbia agree to the annexation of Bosnia, renounce demands for compensation, reverse mobilization, cut the size of its army, and do this in a declaration that essentially accepted subordination to Vienna.

Serbia's Dependence on European Support

Militarily, Serbia was dwarfed by Austria. It needed allied support to back its demands for compensation, and to defy Austria's counterdemands it had to keep it. Serbia banked on assistance from Russia, Britain, and Turkey. All three

[55] G. Gooch, *History of Modern Europe, 1878–1919* (New York: Henry Holt, 1922) 416.

refused, at first, to recognize Austria's annexation absent a Concert conference to arrange compensations, and Russia and Britain explicitly lobbied for compensations for Serbia. Russia, though militarily weak and unready for conflict, was focused on supporting its Slav protégé. Britain, though unwilling to go to war in support of Serbia, was inclined to support Russia's stance diplomatically. For Austria, the key to successfully coercing Serbia lay in getting those powers to tell Serbia they would not support it militarily.

Austrian Diplomacy and Inducements

Austria first moved against Serbia's support network by accommodating Turkey—the party directly harmed by the annexation. When it annexed Bosnia, Vienna at the same time returned the Sanjak concession to Constantinople. With this sop to Turkey came expectations of further compensation. So even though Turkey initially withheld recognition of the annexation and imposed a boycott on Austrian goods—as leverage to ensure Austrian compensation—Turkey rejected Serbia's offer to form an alliance and actively cooperate in resisting Austria's move.[56] Austro-Turk negotiations over financial compensation dragged on for several months, but in January 1909, when tensions with Serbia and Russia escalated sharply, Austria decided to pay the cash price (2.5 million Turkish lire) required to gain Constantinople's recognition of the annexation.[57] Austria then insisted that with Turkey's consent to annexation, other, less interested powers should fall in line. Russia and Britain were the remaining secondary targets of Austria's CI policy. But in accommodating Turkey, Austria had addressed Britain's specific interest in protecting its Turkish protégé from predation. Austria also quickly agreed to pay London for British property taken in the annexation. These things clarified the situation because Britain was not willing to go to war over Russia's wish to back Serbia. So the real key to isolating Serbia—and thus exposing it to the full force of Austrian coercion—was to convince Russia to withdraw its support. This proved easy to do. Russia was simply too weak to defend Serbia against Austria.[58]

Coordination with German Diplomacy

Austria benefited from the well-coordinated policy of its German ally. Berlin made it clear throughout the crisis that it fully supported Austria and used its wider influence to "hold the ring" and thereby promote Austria's isolation strategy. Thus in early February 1909, it induced French noninvolvement by endorsing a deal to recognize French primacy in Morocco, which Paris had sought since 1907. And when Germany declared it would not participate

[56] Bernadotte Schmitt, *The Annexation of Bosnia 1908–1909* (New York: Howard Fertig, 1970), 111; Gooch, *History of Modern Europe*, 418.
[57] Schmitt, *Annexation of Bosnia*, 117–19.
[58] Schmitt, *Annexation of Bosnia*, 161–62.

in a conference unacceptable to Austria, France signaled to Russia that Serbia's demands were "difficult to justify" and unlikely to be realized and that France would not support Russia in a fight over Serbia. Britain, while insisting the Concert should have a say in the solution, signaled to Russia that it would not fight for Serbian compensation, then it withdrew even its "diplomatic support of the Serbian pretensions, and [it] advised Russia to do likewise."[59]

Resolution and Serbia's Capitulation

At the end of February, the Russian government formally urged Serbia to drop its demands for territorial compensation. Serbia did so on March 10, asserting that it would let the Concert decide a settlement (that it hoped would yield financial recompense such as Turkey had gotten). This was unacceptable to Vienna: Serbia's declaration evaded the demand that it disarm, and its bid for a Concert settlement defied Austria's insistence that the issue was strictly a bilateral one. Austria demanded that Serbia directly acknowledge that the Austro-Turk agreement had fully settled the annexation matter and renounce all "earlier claims . . . based on the annexation."[60] It also demanded that Serbia directly and concretely communicate its intentions to be a peaceful and loyal neighbor, or else Vienna would have to take action against Serb military preparations. If Belgrade did those things, then Austria would welcome efforts to renew an Austro-Serb trade treaty.

By early March, Russia's leaders were advising Belgrade to completely renounce all claims, "economic as well as political." Yet on March 14 Belgrade sent a direct reply to Vienna that virtually ignored the substance of Austria's demands, dwelling instead on the process of trade treaty negotiation. Vienna rejected it as "entirely unsatisfactory," and the other powers shared that view. Austria stepped up military preparations and signaled that it would soon act if Serbia did not comply. At this point, Britain began to negotiate—over Belgrade's head—on the terms of a much more conciliatory Serb reply, which the Powers, expecting Austria to accept, would pressure Belgrade to give.[61]

On March 17, Germany offered Russia a formula: Austria could invite the Powers each, through an exchange of notes with Vienna, to recognize the Austro-Turk settlement; such all-around recognition would then confer Concert sanction on the alteration of the Treaty of Berlin, if not obviating the need for a conference, then making it possible to hold one on Austria's terms. Russia balked. Germany poured on the pressure. On March 22 it requested a prompt and explicit confirmation that, separate from and prior to any conference negotiation, Russia would formally recognize Austria's annexation. Without this, Germany would do nothing to restrain Austria. Russia complied, and Serbia's

[59] Schmitt, *Annexation of Bosnia*, 160, 158.
[60] Schmitt, *Annexation of Bosnia*, 163–64, 171, 175, 180.
[61] Schmitt, *Annexation of Bosnia*, 176, 182–85.

isolation was nearly complete: "In the absence of Russian support it would have been mere folly for Serbia to precipitate an open conflict with [Austria]."[62]

All that remained was Britain's desire that the annexation be baptized by a Concert agreement that gave Serbia some face-saving concessions. Thus in late March, Britain negotiated with Austria over the terms of Serbian capitulation while Austria prepared to attack. The final settlement that Serbia soon accepted did moderate Austria's demands for Serbia's political subordination, but it entailed Serbia's acceptance of Austria's annexation (without any compensation) and compliance with the demands to shrink the Serbian army. Isolation of Serbia had made Austria's threats of force credible and effective. Russia's weakness meant that Austria did not have to reward it to isolate Serbia; for that, threats from Austria's ally Germany sufficed.

USSR and Japan, 1939

In 1938 and 1939, the Soviets and Japanese fought along the Mongolia-Manchuria borders. Japan's army instigated the confrontations, but in the last, at Kalkhin Gol in late August 1939, Moscow struck preemptively. An estimated 45,000 Japanese and 17,000 Soviet fatalities resulted. After May 1939 border incursions, Molotov had warned that Moscow's patience had run out: in the Supreme Soviet he declared that it would no longer "tolerate any provocations on its frontiers on the part of Japanese-Manchurian military units." When Moscow launched its August riposte, it signaled to Tokyo that it sought normalization of relations and a nonaggression pact, which would amount to acceptance of Soviet border claims.[63] In sum, Soviet objectives were to stop Japan's encroachment in the border areas and to compel it to accept the lines Moscow claimed.

Japan's Expectations of German Support

Japan initiated its challenges with rising expectations of German military partnership. During the summer of 1939, Tokyo negotiated with Germany to turn the Anti-Comintern Pact into a military alliance directed against the USSR.[64] In mid-July, Japan's leaders firmly decided to enter such an alliance. As the Polish crisis deepened, the Japanese army's escalation against Soviet borders was encouraged by anticipated German pressure on the USSR.

Soviet Accommodation with Germany

Moscow's part in the Nazi-Soviet Pact is usually seen as a response to the German threat in Europe, buck-passing to Britain and France. But Russia was

---

[62] Gooch, *History of Modern Europe*, 420; Schmitt, *Annexation of Bosnia*, 187, 194–96; Rene Albrecht-Carrie, *A Diplomatic History of Europe Since the Congress of Vienna* (New York: Harper and Row 1973), 267.

[63] Jonathan Haslam, *The Soviet Union and the Threat from the East, 1933–41* (Pittsburgh: University of Pittsburgh Press 1992), 130, 136.

[64] Haslam, *The Soviet Union and the Threat from the East*, 131, 133.

motivated to isolate Japan and pressure it to come to terms. The Soviet talks with Germany in the summer of 1939 "were guided in no small measure" by the "concern to outflank the Japanese diplomatically . . . . Certainly, Soviet concern to solve the Japanese problem played its part in causing Stalin [to decide] in favor of a deal with Germany."[65]

Just as the climactic Far East battle began on August 20, Stalin and Hitler cut the deal. Tokyo was completely surprised.[66] The betrayal sank in as the Soviets rolled to victory on August 31. "As a result of [that] victory and the non-aggression pact, the balance of power between Russia and Japan shifted decisively to Soviet advantage. This gave the Russians new leverage in negotiations with the Japanese."[67] "The Japanese army's crushing defeat" combined with the shock of "the Soviet-German non-aggression pact," writes Boris Slavinsky, "change[d] Japan's war plans, compelling it to strive for reconciliation with the USSR."[68] How important was the shock of the Pact compared to the shock of the military defeat in forcing Japan to change its posture? Consider this counterfactual: What would Japan have done after Khalkhin Gol if Germany and the USSR had gone to war in September 1939? Almost certainly Japan would have returned to the offensive against Soviet borders. An immediate consequence of the Pact was the fall of the Japanese government.[69] The successor (Abe) government was chastened; it promptly communicated to Moscow that it wanted a ceasefire and to work toward a larger accommodation.[70] That policy led ultimately to the April 1941 Japanese-Soviet neutrality pact.[71] The compellent effects of coercive isolation were immediate and far-reaching.

Japan and China, 1941

The Nazi-Soviet Pact also gave Moscow more freedom to concentrate on strengthening Chiang Kai-shek's forces in China. Tokyo immediately grasped this, adopting a new policy for winning the war in China that hinged on improving relations with the USSR.[72] By isolating Chiang, Japan hoped to compel a settlement. In 1939 the USSR was the Kuomintang's principal patron. In June a new trade agreement had led to a major upswing in Soviet aid. The next month, Prince Konoe Fumimaro received a policy paper that

---

65 Haslam, *The Soviet Union and the Threat from the East*, 133–34.
66 Ikuhiku Hata, "The Japanese-Soviet Confrontation," in *Deterrent Diplomacy: Japan, Germany, and the USSR, 1935–1940*, ed. James W. Morley (New York: Columbia University Press, 1976), 177.
67 Haslam, *Soviet Union and the Threat from the East*, 135
68 Boris Slavinsky, *The Japanese-Soviet Neutrality Pact: A Diplomatic History, 1941–1945* (New York: Routledge Curzon, 2004), 16.
69 Chihiro Hosoya, "The Tripartite Pact," in Morley, *Deterrent Diplomacy*, 193.
70 Haslam, *Soviet Union and the Threat from the East*, 136.
71 Chihiro Hosoya, "The Japanese-Soviet Neutrality Pact," in *The Fateful Choice: Japan's Advance into Southeast Asia, 1939–41*, ed. James W. Morley (New York: Columbia University Press, 1980); Crawford, "Powers of Division," 265–71.
72 Hosoya, "The Japanese-Soviet Neutrality Pact," 18.

argued for quickly improving relations with the USSR: if the Soviet "pillar" beneath Chiang's regime were removed, there was "a definite possibility that in less than half a year the [China] incident could be completely brought to an end." That advice was ignored then. But six months later, after cabinet reshuffles, the Japanese Army General Staff, "concerned with the settlement of the Sino-Japanese war, came forward as the driving force toward Japanese-Soviet cooperation."[73]

China's Dependence on Soviet Support

Chiang's initial decision for war with Japan wagered that Soviet support would make victory possible. His "overall strategic concept" recognized that "China's armed forces could not defeat those of Japan . . . . It was the Soviet Union . . . which provided Chiang with the hope of direct foreign military intervention."[74] The August 1937 Sino-Soviet nonaggression treaty was the first of several signals of strong Soviet support and potential intervention in favor of the Kuomintang. Even after Stalin's unwillingness to intervene directly became evident, Moscow continued to provide "very substantial material and political assistance" that sustained the Kuomintang through mid-1941.[75] Particularly significant was the Soviet Union's "training and equipping of the Nationalist air force."[76]

Japanese Diplomacy and Inducements

Britain and France were also, to a lesser degree, propping up the Kuomintang through Burma and French Indochina. After Nazi victories in summer 1940 made it easier to squeeze these supply lines, Japan's military saw new avenues to victory in China.[77] In July the Army Ministry and General Staff agreed on a statement of basic national policy that set forth as one of its main objectives "settl[ing] the China incident as quickly as possible." "To bring about the [Kuomintang's] prompt submission," Japan would "make special efforts to block acts of assistance [to it] by third powers"; the first would be to "rapidly improve relations with Soviet Russia."[78] That month Japan's ambassador to the Soviet Union gave Molotov a draft proposal for a neutrality agreement.[79] Japan also got Britain to agree to close down the Burma Road for three months and the Vichy regime to allow Japan to occupy northern Indochina. All that

---

[73] Hosoya, "Japanese-Soviet Neutrality Pact," 23, 32–33.
[74] John Garver, "Chiang Kai-shek's Quest for Soviet Entry into the Sino-Japanese War," *Political Science Quarterly* 102 (1987): 296–97.
[75] Garver, "Chiang Kai-shek's Quest," 299, 306–9, 315.
[76] George Lensen, *The Strange Neutrality: Soviet-Japanese Relations during the Second World War, 1941–1945* (Tallahassee, FL: Diplomatic Press 1972), 93.
[77] Hosoya, "Japanese-Soviet Neutrality Pact," 32–33.
[78] Ibid., 208.
[79] Hata, "Japanese-Soviet Confrontation," 175.

remained was to close the gap with the USSR—and Chiang's last remaining lifeline.

In late July 1940, a new cabinet was formed; the foreign minister, Matsuoka Yosuke, would execute the isolation strategy. Six months of hard bargaining followed. Moscow pressed for significant economic concessions as a prerequisite for a political deal, but Molotov signaled that if Japan was forthcoming, "the issue of Soviet aid to China can also be solved in the negotiations." When the Tripartite Pact was forged in September 1940, Japan secured Germany's pledge to "do all in its power to promote friendly understanding [between Japan and the USSR]."[80] For several more months this remained German policy.

In early 1941 Matsuoka approached Molotov with a proposal that he hoped would succeed with Germany's help. Japan would give back northern Sakhalin in exchange for a five-year supply of Soviet oil and Soviet agreement to "cease aid to Chiang Kai-shek," among other things. But German-Soviet relations had by then soured.[81] Berlin disapproved of Matsuoka's plan. Hitler warned him, "You cannot report to your Emperor that a conflict between Germany and the Soviet Union is impossible."[82] By then "Matsuoka must have realized . . . that German-Soviet relations had deteriorated beyond redemption."[83]

Yet Matsuoka did not heed German counsel. Instead, he gave Moscow a more aggressive proposal. The Soviets rejected it; Japan would have to "liquidate" its northern Sakhalin concession as part of any neutrality deal. But Molotov also proposed that the USSR and Japan should agree to respect not only each other's territorial integrity but that of their protégés in Manchukuo and the Mongolian People's Republic too. This was an offer to diplomatically recognize Manchukuo, at Chungking's expense.[84] On April 12 Matsuoka accepted the deal on those basic terms: the Japan-Soviet Neutrality Agreement was announced on April 14, 1941. For Japan, dividing Russia from China was "the central question" in the negotiations: "It was precisely because of the need to resolve the 'China incident' that Matsuoka came to Moscow and sought conciliation with the Kremlin, so that it would cease helping Chiang Kai-shek." As Matsuoka's personal secretary later put it, "By negotiating with the Soviets we hoped to stop Soviet help to China, and by doing so deal Chiang a strong blow."[85]

Why Japan's Policy Failed

Japan's coercive isolation strategy failed, but not because Soviet support for Chungking continued unabated. In mid-1941 "all Soviet volunteers were

---

[80] Hosoya, "Japanese-Soviet Neutrality Pact," 44, 46, 51.
[81] Ibid., 66; James E. McSherry, *Stalin, Hitler and Europe*, (Arlington, Virginia: Open Door Press, 1970), vol. 2, chapter 2.
[82] Lensen, *Strange Neutrality*, 17.
[83] Hosoya, "Japanese-Soviet Neutrality Pact," 80.
[84] Ibid., 77.
[85] Slavinsky, *Japanese-Soviet Neutrality Pact*, 53, 52.

recalled from China, and supply of military power to that country practically ceased."[86] The reason Japan's strategy failed corresponds to the proposition concerning the PT's dependence on the ST: as Soviet support to China decreased, a major substitute for that support arose. In 1940 "the United States began stepping up its support for China."[87] Days after the Japanese-Soviet neutrality deal was announced, "to boost Chinese morale and resistance to Japan, the United States government announced a $50 million loan to Chungking."[88] After mid-1941 "the United States took over the task of providing China with the equipment and technical training necessary to resist the Japanese invaders."[89]

Implications for the Study and Practice of Coercive Diplomacy

Coercion theory has long emphasized the importance of establishing the credibility of threats through "costly signals" and "commitment devices." Yet the recognized inventory of credibility-boosting techniques is quite limited. Strategic theorists tend to focus on "what amounts to numerous variants of two general ways" to create commitments that are costly to break, both involving the use of reputation costs.[90] The first arises from domestic audience costs and the second from international audience costs of breaking pledges. Such theorizing captures a narrow range of credibility signals. The most important contribution of coercive isolation theory, then, is to describe a kind of concrete political action that lends credibility to coercive threats because it is costly (because concessions are used to isolate a target) and because it reduces the coercer's direct costs of fighting and increases them for the target. The theory explains how, in practical terms, such action can coerce, by showing the target—in a way that is easy to perceive—the coercer's increased ability to use force on advantageous terms. To appreciate the credibility of that threat, the target does not need to decipher the coercer's domestic audience cost calculus or its wider reputational concerns. It merely needs to see that it is isolated.

A maxim of coercive diplomacy is that success often requires coupling "carrots" (positive inducements) with "sticks" to promote compliance.[91] Giving inducements *to the target* is what people usually have in mind. By contrast, this study has stressed that coercive isolation often entails using inducements to sway the target's potential supporters. Indeed, the latter are perhaps the more important carrot consumers. Statecraft theorists have drawn our attention to a cost asymmetry between threats and promises. Threats are cheap when they work and costly when they fail. Promises are costly when they work and cheap

[86] Slavinsky, *Japanese-Soviet Neutrality Pact*, 60.
[87] Garver, "Chiang Kai-shek's Quest," 316.
[88] Hosoya, "Japanese-Soviet Neutrality Pact," 85.
[89] Lensen, *Strange Neutrality*, 32.
[90] Slantchev, *Military Threats*, 47.
[91] See Art and Greenhill, this volume.

when they fail.[92] This schema implies that when coercive threats succeed, the target's compliance comes at little cost to the coercer. But there is an accounting trick at work here, if the inducement costs incurred to isolate the adversary are kept off the books. Putting them back onto the coercion ledger gives a more politically realistic perspective on the likely costliness of successful coercion. Thus, as U.S. policymakers came to appreciate, to make real progress in coercive diplomacy against Iran's nuclear program, it was necessary to accommodate Russia, Tehran's major supporter, in other areas. China too will find that there is no free lunch when it comes to coercive diplomacy against its smaller neighbors: maximizing coercive influence over one will require making costly compromises with others (and especially the United States).

Strategic theorists also stress the importance of assurances in coercive diplomacy; these are promises—implicit or explicit—to not impose punishment or to stop imposing it if the target complies.[93] Here we come up against a significant limit to the utility of isolation as a discrete strategy of coercive pressure. If increasing a target's isolation is itself a way of imposing costs, it is not a kind of damage that is likely to be undone. Indeed, the more likely result of successful isolation—especially if it is achieved by realigning the secondary target—is that the political costs to the target will continue to accumulate as its weakened position invites further demands. To push the implications of this point further, recall that, as James Davis puts it, "for a threat to prove effective . . . the corresponding assurance must appear credible and *within the control* of the [coercer]."[94] This suggests two things that may work against the efficacy of the overall policy. First, what increases the credibility of the threat to punish the target (its isolation) also makes it easier for the coercer to renege on the assurance to withhold or stop punishment if the target complies. The constellation of forces that might constrain the coercer to fulfill assurances and limit its subsequent demands has been contracted, and the situation is unlikely to reset back to the initial alignment pattern. Second, even if the coercer wished to reduce the target's isolation after having increased it, it may have little control over this if positive feedback kicks in, and the decay of relations between the target and its supporters takes on a dynamic of its own.[95]

These observations have an important implication for the kind of objectives to which CI may be ill suited. Thus, for example, coercive isolation diplomacy to prevent nuclear proliferation may be counterproductive if insecurity is driving a target state's pursuit of nuclear weapons. Allies, as we know, are a key substitute for self-defense capabilities, and a CI policy that permanently damages a target's alliance ties will deepen the insecurity that makes a nuclear

---

[92] Thomas Schelling, *The Strategy of Conflict* (Oxford: Oxford University Press, 1963), 177; David Baldwin, *Paradoxes of Power* (New York: Blackwell, 1989), 69–71; James Davis, *Threats and Promises* (Baltimore: Johns Hopkins University Press, 2000), 16.

[93] See Art and Greenhill, this volume.

[94] Davis, *Threats and Promises*, 12.

[95] Robert Jervis, *System Effects: Complexity in Political and Social Life* (Princeton, NJ: Princeton University Press, 1997), 147–65.

deterrent so attractive to it. CI may also be counterproductive as an instrument of regime change if weakening the target's alliance support leads to internal changes that usher in more reckless or hostile leaders. CI works best against a target with a government securely in power that will prefer to comply rather than risk fighting when it is isolated, or against a target whose isolation will tend to bring a more compliant government to power.

CHAPTER 12

Economic Sanctions in Theory and Practice

How Smart Are They?

DANIEL W. DREZNER

WHILE ECONOMIC SANCTIONS HAVE often been the forgotten stepchild of international relations scholarship, they have experienced a policy renaissance in recent years.[1] Within the academy, the use of force is at the center of international relations scholarship; the study of sanctions has often been at the margins. In the policy world, policymakers used to disdain economic sanctions,[2] but attitudes have changed in the twenty-first century. Honed during the global war on terror, sanctions now enjoy plenty of bipartisan support in the United States. Juan Zarate, a deputy national security adviser in the George W. Bush administration, argues that the United States can use sanctions "to confront its most critical national security threats."[3] Assistant Treasury Secretary Danny Glaser bragged to *Newsweek* in early 2014 that financial sanctions are "at the center of our national security."[4]

It is therefore interesting and surprising to note that—from the sanctioning country's perspective, at least—the gap between policymakers and scholars on sanctions is extremely narrow. Indeed, despite persistent laments

[1] Some material in this chapter is drawn and reprinted from "Sanctions Sometimes Smart," *International Studies Review* 13 (2011): 155–66, by Daniel Drezner. Used by permission of the publisher, Taylor and Francis. All of the recent literature on sanctions is written from the sender's perspective. While there is plenty of scholarship arguing that sanctions are an ineffective policy tool, to my knowledge there is little to no work that focuses on how to subvert or weaken sanctions from the target's perspective.

[2] Richard Haass, "Sanctioning Madness," *Foreign Affairs* 76 (1997): 74-95; Richard Cheney, "Defending Liberty in a Global Economy," in *Economic Casualties*, ed. Solveig Singleton and Daniel T. Griswold (Washington, DC: Cato Institute, 1999).

[3] Juan Zarate, *Treasury's War: The Unleashing of a New Era of Financial Warfare* (New York: PublicAffairs, 2013).

[4] Quoted in Leah McGrath Goodman and Lynnley Browning, "The Art of Financial Warfare," *Newsweek*, April 24, 2014.

about the need to bridge the gap between the scholarly and policymaking communities, in the sanctions literature that gap has been fully bridged.[5] The overwhelming focus of the scholarly literature on economic sanctions has been on whether they "work" as opposed to pure theory development.[6] As scholarship has moved into more fine-grained analysis of the sanctions instrument, practitioners of economic statecraft have been informed by theory, and vice versa.

As scholars have observed the negative externalities of comprehensive trade sanctions, they have advocated for smart sanctions.[7] Ostensibly, smart or targeted sanctions are the precision-guided munitions of economic statecraft. They are designed to hurt elites and key supporters of the targeted regime, while imposing minimal hardship on the sanctioned country's mass public. By altering the material incentives of powerful supporters, the argument runs, these supporters will eventually pressure the targeted government into making concessions. The history of targeted sanctions as a policy tool is, in many ways, a rare success story of fruitful collaboration among scholars, policymakers and diplomats. The smart sanctions approach has been accepted as an example of best practices in both the United Nations and the United States.

This chapter examines the state of the literature on economic sanctions, with a particular emphasis on the targeted sanctions approach. How and why did the smart sanctions approach successfully permeate the foreign policy community? Has this innovation yielded a better approach to the use of economic sanctions? In many ways, smart sanctions represent a classic example of Kingdon's model of policy innovation.[8] In his work on agenda-setting, Kingdon suggests three "streams" that feed into policy creation: problem recognition, the development of policy alternatives, and the sating of key principals' political incentives. All three of these streams come into play in looking at the development of the smart sanctions framework.

This chapter contends that the development of smart sanctions has solved many of the political problems that prior efforts at comprehensive trade sanctions created. In many ways, these sanctions are smarter. Nevertheless, there is no systematic evidence that smart sanctions will yield better policy results

---

[5] Alexander L. George, *Bridging the Gap: Theory and Practice in Foreign Policy* (Washington, DC: U.S. Institute of Peace Press, 1993); Stephen M. Walt, "The Relationship between Theory and Policy in International Relations," *Annual Review of Political Science* 8 (2005): 23–48.

[6] David Baldwin, "The Sanctions Debate and the Logic of Choice," *International Security* 24 (1999–2000): 80–107; Jonathan Kirshner, "Economic Sanctions: The State of the Art," *Security Studies* 11 (2002): 160–79; David M. Rowe, "Economic Sanctions and International Security," in *International Studies Encyclopedia*, ed. Robert A. Denemark (Oxford:Blackwell, 2010).

[7] Thomas Weiss, "Sanctions as a Foreign Policy Tool: Weighing Humanitarian Impulses," *Journal of Peace Research* 36 (1999): 499–509; David Cortright and George A. Lopez, eds., *Smart Sanctions: Targeting Economic Statecraft* (New York: Rowman and Littlefield, 2002); David Cortright and George Lopez, *Sanctions and the Search for Security: Challenges to UN Action* (Boulder, CO: Lynne Reiner, 2002); Michael Brzoska, "From Dumb to Smart? Recent Reforms of UN Sanctions," *Global Governance* 9 (2003): 519–35; Peter Wallensteen and Carina Staibano, eds., *International Sanctions: Between War and Words in the International System* (London: Routledge, 2005).

[8] John Kingdon, *Agendas, Alternatives, and Public Policies* (Boston: Addison-Wesley, 1984).

vis-à-vis the targeted country. Consistent with what Art and Greenhill (this volume) observe is true of coercion more generally, when smart sanctions work, they work because they impose significant costs on the target economy. It thus behooves policymakers and scholars to look beyond targeted sanctions to examine the conditions under which different kinds of economic statecraft should be deployed.

This chapter is divided into five sections. The next section briefly reviews the history of the economic statecraft literature prior to the introduction of targeted sanctions. As will be seen, there have always been contentious debates about other dimensions of economic sanctions, and the lack of consensus might have been one reason for the failure of this literature to permeate the policy discourse. The third section looks at the evolution of targeted sanctions in theory and practice. It explains why smart sanctions emerged as a useful focal point for the integration of scholarship and practice in this area, and how it solved the political problems raised by the sanctioning of Iraq. The fourth section evaluates the use of smart sanctions as a policy tool based on the scholarly literature. The final section summarizes and concludes with suggestions for future study of economic statecraft.

The Literature

The modern scholarly literature on economic sanctions can be divided into three eras, all revolving around the question of whether sanctions "worked" as a policy tool.[9] The pre-1985 era generated a strong consensus that economic sanctions were a largely ineffective tool of statecraft. As David Baldwin observed, "The two most salient characteristics of the literature on economic statecraft are scarcity and the nearly universal tendency to denigrate the utility of such tools of foreign policy."[10] Indeed, it is not hard to find pessimistic conclusions about the utility of economic coercion during this period.[11] With a few

[9] "Modern" refers to research after 1945. During the interwar era, scholars were more confident about the power of economic coercion. See Hirschman (1945) for the most obvious example, and Daoudi and Dajani (1983) for a review of the literature of that time. Albert O. Hirschman, *National Power and the Structure of Foreign Trade* (Berkeley: University of California Press, 1945); Mohammed S. Daoudi and Munther S. Dajani, *Economic Sanctions: Ideals and Experience* (Boston: Routledge and Kegan Paul, 1983).

[10] David Allen Baldwin, *Economic Statecraft* (Princeton, NJ: Princeton University Press, 1985), 51.

[11] Fredrik Hoffmann, "The Functions of Economic Sanctions: A Comparative Analysis," *Journal of Peace Research* 2 (1967): 154; Johan Galtung, "On the Effects of International Economic Sanctions, with Special Reference to Rhodesia," *World Politics* 19 (1967): 409; Peter Wallensteen, "Characteristics of Economic Sanctions," *Journal of Peace Research* 5 (1968): 249–50; Henry Bienen and Robert Gilpin, "Economic Sanctions as a Response to Terrorism," *Journal of Strategic Studies* 3 (1980): 89; Otto Wolff van Amerongen, "Economic Sanctions as a Foreign Policy Tool?," *International Security* 5 (1980): 165; James A. Blessing, "The Suspension of Foreign Aid: A Macro-Analysis," *Polity* 13 (1981): 533; Robin Renwick, *Economic Sanctions* (Cambridge, MA: Center for International Affairs, 1981), 85; Thomas Willett and Mehrdad Jalalighajar, "U.S. Trade Policy and National Security," *Cato Journal* 3 (1983): 718.

exceptions, these studies reached an impressionistic conclusion after focusing on a few high-profile cases.[12]

In 1985 two books introduced the next stage in the sanctions debate by questioning the conclusion that sanctions never worked. Baldwin's *Economic Statecraft* used a "social power" framework to suggest a reappraisal of sanctions. He suggested that the definition of success or failure needed to be widened.[13] Even if sanctions did not succeed in altering the objectionable policies of the target country, they might succeed in other political and policy tasks, including deterring like-minded states from pursuing policies akin to those of the target state.[14] Baldwin further argued that the utility of sanctions always had to be compared to the alternatives; claiming that sanctions often do not work is irrelevant if other policy instruments, like coercive bombing, work just as poorly.[15] In the same year, Hufbauer Schott, and Elliott published the first effort to collect a large-N data set of the use of economic sanctions.[16] They coded events data on the sanctions outcomes as well as a welter of independent variables. The headline figure from their effort was that sanctions succeeded 34 percent of the time. While this is not an overwhelming success rate, it was definitely higher than the scholarly consensus to date would have predicted.

These two publications altered perceptions about the utility of economic sanctions, and soon after, the end of the Cold War led to an explosion in the use of sanctions. The United Nations Security Council voted for economic sanctions 12 times in the 1990s; between 1945 and 1990, the UN had only employed sanctions twice.[17] According to Hufbauer and colleagues, there were nearly as many sanctions episodes after the Cold War as there were during the first 90 years of the twentieth century.[18]

The shift in practice led to a resurgence in sanctions scholarship. The literature proceeded in two directions. The first track was a high-profile debate over the validity of the Hufbauer, Schott, and Elliott (HSE) data set. Pape

---

[12] Galtung, "On the Effects of International Economic Sanctions"; Anna Schreiber, "Economic Coercion as an Instrument of Foreign Policy: U.S. Economic Measures against Cuba and the Dominican Republic," *World Politics* 25 (1973): 387–413; Donald Losman, *International Economic Sanctions: The Cases of Cuba, Israel and Rhodesia* (Albuquerque: University of New Mexico Press, 1979); Margaret P. Doxey, *Economic Sanctions and International Enforcement* (London: Macmillan, 1980). For the exceptions, see Klaus Knorr, *The Power of Nations: The Political Economy of International Relations* (New York: Basic Books, 1975).

[13] Baldwin, *Economic Statecraft.*

[14] See also James Lindsay, "Trade Sanctions as Policy Instruments: A Re-examination." *International Studies Quarterly* 30 (1986): 153–73.

[15] Robert Pape, *Bombing to Win: Air Power and Coercion in War* (Ithaca, NY: Cornell University Press, 1996).

[16] Gary Hufbauer, Jeffrey Schott, and Kimberly Elliott, *Economic Sanctions Reconsidered* (Washington, DC: Institute for International Economics, 1985). Their data set has been updated several times since their first effort.

[17] David Cortright and George Lopez, *The Sanctions Decade: Assessing UN Strategies for the 1990s* (Boulder, CO: Lynne Reiner, 2000).

[18] Gary Hufbauer, Jeffrey Schott, Kimberly Elliott, and Barbara Oegg, *Economic Sanctions Reconsidered,* 3rd ed. (Washington, DC: Institute for International Economics, 2007).

reexamined the HSE data set and argued that the success rate was much lower than the authors claimed: approximately 5 percent.[19] This in turn provoked a series of inconclusive exchanges.[20] The debate was not terribly productive in advancing scholarly understanding of economic sanctions.[21] Rowe concluded, "These taxonomical debates have come at great cost. On the one hand, they have not contributed to the accumulation of knowledge about economic sanctions. The Pape–Elliott–Baldwin exchanges of 1997–2000 occupied a substantial number of pages of one of the leading journals of international politics, yet did little to advance knowledge of sanctions significantly beyond where it stood in 1985."[22] In large part this was because of incommensurate definitions of *sanctions* and *success*. Pape's definition of both of these terms was far more stringent than the rest of the literature, which takes partial concessions into account.[23]

The second track moved away from the question of *whether* sanctions worked to the question of *the conditions* under which sanctions would be likely to succeed. Multiple paths were pursued to get at this answer.[24] Game-theoretic approaches looked more carefully at the strategic interactions involved in coercion attempts.[25] Scholars in this approach used different assumptions regarding the informational environment and how sender demands are articulated but reached the same deductive conclusion: coercion episodes that are likely to succeed should end before economic sanctions are ever imposed. Both Norruddin and Drezner tested this hypothesis using existing sanctions data

---

[19] Robert Pape, "Why Economic Sanctions Do Not Work," *International Security* 22 (1997): 90–136.

[20] David Baldwin and Robert Pape, "Evaluating Economic Sanctions," *International Security* 23 (1998): 189–98; Kimberly Elliott, "The Sanctions Glass: Half Full or Completely Empty?," *International Security* 23 (1998): 50–65; Robert Pape, "Why Economic Sanctions Still Do Not Work," *International Security* 23 (1998): 66–77; Baldwin, "The Sanctions Debate and the Logic of Choice."

[21] One important exception is Pape's observation that HSE had lumped together cases of economic sanctions with strategic embargoes and examples of economic warfare. See Michael Mastanduno, *Economic Containment: COCOM and the Politics of East-West Trade* (Ithaca: Cornell University Press, 1992) on the conceptual distinctions between these terms.

[22] Rowe, "Economic Sanctions and International Security," (online).

[23] Pape, "Why Economic Sanctions Do Not Work," 97.

[24] Because this essay is largely devoted to how scholarship informs policy, research that focuses on the causes of sanctions *imposition* rather than *outcome* is elided. See Drury, A. Cooper. 2005. *Economic Sanctions and Presidential Decisions: Models of Political Rationality* (New York: Palgrave MacMillan, 2005); and Fiona McGillivray and Allan Stam, "Political Institutions, Coercive Diplomacy, and the Duration of Economic Sanctions," *Journal of Conflict Resolution* 48 (2005): 154-172.

[25] R. Harrison Wagner, "Economic Interdependence, Bargaining Power, and Political Influence," *International Organization* 42 (1988): 461–83; George Tsebelis, "Are Sanctions Effective? A Game-Theoretic Analysis," *Journal of Conflict Resolution* 34 (1990): 3–28; Daniel Drezner, *The Sanctions Paradox: Economic Statecraft and International Relations* (Cambridge, UK: Cambridge University Press, 1999); Alastair Smith, "The Success and Use of Economic Sanctions," *International Interactions* 21 (1996): 229–45; T. Clifton Morgan and Annie C. Miers, "When Threats Succeed: A Formal Model of the Threat and Use of Economic Sanctions," paper presented at the annual meeting of the American Political Science Association, Atlanta, GA, September 2, 1999; Dean Lacy and Emerson Niou, "A Theory of Economic Sanctions and Issue Linkage: The Role of Preferences, Information, and Threats," *Journal of Politics* 66 (2004): 25–42; Valentin Krustev, "Strategic Demands, Credible Threats, and Economic Coercion Outcomes," *International Studies Quarterly* 54 (2010): 147–74.

sets and reached findings that backed up the strategic logic.[26] Sanctions likely to succeed are also likely to end at the threat stage.[27] Therefore the observed cases of sanctions should be biased toward less successful outcomes.

Another vein of research looked at "sanctions and" issues, that is, the relationship between the use of economic coercion and the use of other tools of statecraft. Lektzian and Sprecher examined the relationship between sanctions and the use of force.[28] They concluded that sanctions are often used as a signal for the sender's willingness to use military coercion. The problem is that sanctions are such a poor measure of credibility that they function as a weak signal because most sanctions are not costly to the sender country. It is therefore unsurprising that Lektzian and Sprecher found that the use of sanctions *increases* the probability of a subsequent use of force. Thyne concluded that sanctions imposition by third parties had no appreciable effect on the prevention of civil wars.[29]

Other research has focused on the relationship between sanctions and inducements.[30] Drezner observed that while carrots are more likely to yield target concessions, they are a relative rarity in world politics.[31] There are multiple reasons for this phenomenon, including the fear of moral hazard; sender states are wary of acquiring a reputation for proffering carrots in response to target misbehavior. As a result, the use of incentives is often sequenced after the use of economic coercion. Hafner-Burton and Montgomery compared the use of sanctions with preferential trade agreements.[32] Institutionalists posit that PTAs would act as a brake on the uses of economic coercion. They find that mutual membership in a PTA has no effect on the use of economic coercion.

One of the basic working assumptions behind sanctions was that multilateral cooperation should increase the likelihood of success.[33] Multiple tests of the HSE data, however, revealed that cooperation was negatively correlated with success.[34] This counterintuitive finding led to more sophisticated tests

[26] Irfan Nooruddin, "Modeling Selection Bias in Studies of Sanctions Efficacy," *International Interactions* 28 (2002): 59–75; Daniel W. Drezner, "The Hidden Hand of Economic Coercion," *International Organization* 57 (2003): 643–59.

[27] There are counterexamples, such as the Sino-American relationship. See, for instance, A. Cooper Drury and Yitan Li, "U.S. Economic Sanction Threats Against China: Failing to Leverage Better Human Rights," *Foreign Policy Analysis* 2 (2006): 307-24.

[28] David Lektzian and Christopher Sprecher, "Sanctions, Signals and Militarized Conflict," *American Journal of Political Science* 51 (2007): 415–31.

[29] Clayton Thyne, "Cheap Signals with Costly Consequences: The Effect of Interstate Relations on Civil War," *Journal of Conflict Resolution* 50 (2006): 937–61.

[30] David Cortright, ed., *The Price of Peace: Incentives and International Conflict Prevention* (Lanham, MD: Rowman and Littlefield, 1997); Richard Haass and Meghan O'Sullivan, eds., *Honey and Vinegar: Incentives, Sanctions, and Foreign Policy* (Washington, DC: Brookings, 2000).

[31] Daniel W. Drezner, "The Trouble with Carrots: Transaction Costs, Conflict Expectations, and Economic Inducements," *Security Studies* 9 (1999–2000): 188–218.

[32] Emilie Hafner-Burton and Alex Montgomery, "Power or Plenty: How Do International Trade Institutions Affect Economic Sanctions?," *Journal of Conflict Resolution* 52 (2008): 213–42.

[33] Lisa L. Martin, *Coercive Cooperation: Explaining Multilateral Economic Sanctions* (Princeton, NJ: Princeton University Press, 1992).

[34] Gary Hufbauer, Jeffrey Schott, and Kimberly Elliott, *Economic Sanctions Reconsidered*, 2nd ed. (Washington: Institute for International Economics, 1990); Peter A. G. Van Bergeijk, *Economic Diplomacy, Trade and Commercial Policy: Positive and Negative Sanctions in a New World Order*

on the data. Drury and Drezner found that cooperation was significantly *more* effective if an international institution supported the sanctions; without institutional support, multilateral sanctions were less effective.[35] Multiple reasons have been proffered for the role that international governmental organizations play in augmenting the effect of sanctions. Drezner argues that institutions serve a reassurance function, preventing states from backsliding on prior promises of cooperation.[36] Bapat and Morgan test these theories and conclude that the value-added of intergovernmental organizations is that they foster a structure-induced equilibrium, enabling all participating senders to agree on specific demands vis-à-vis the target.[37]

Other work took the raw data from the HSE and ran ever more sophisticated econometric tests to tease out robust correlations between key independent variables and the sanctions outcome. Dashti-Gibson, Davis, and Radcliff focused on the costs to the target country of sanctions imposition.[38] Similarly, Morgan and Schwebach and Ang and Peksen found that sanctions were more likely to succeed if the target's costs outweighed the salience of the issue under dispute.[39] Drezner argued that the expectations of future conflict between the sender and target was a crucial variable.[40] The more conflict expected in the future, the more reluctant the target government would be in making concessions in the present. Hart argued that sanctions were more likely to be successful if the sender country was a democracy because of the ability to tie one's hands through democratic institutions.[41]

Combined, these results are suggestive. Economic coercion appears to work better at the threat stage than at the imposition stage. On the whole, sanctions appear to be more likely to produce concessions when the target's costs of sanctions imposition are significant, when the sender's costs are minimal, when the issue under dispute is of low salience to the target country, when the sender and target are closely allied, when an international institution endorses the sanctions, and when the target state is a democracy. The robustness of these results to alternative specifications and data sets is somewhat unclear,

---

(Brookfield, VT: Edward Elgar, 1994); Shane Bonetti, "The Analysis and Interpretation of Economic Sanctions," *Journal of Economic Studies* 24 (1997): 324–48; Drezner, *The Sanctions Paradox.*

35 A. Cooper Drury, "Revisiting *Economic Sanctions Reconsidered*," *Journal of Peace Research* 35 (1998): 497–509; Daniel W. Drezner, "Bargaining, Enforcement, and Multilateral Sanctions: When Is Cooperation Counterproductive?," *International Organization* 54 (2000): 73–102.

36 Drezner, "Bargaining, Enforcement, and Multilateral Sanctions."

37 Navin Bapat and T. Clifton Morgan, "Multilateral versus Unilateral Sanctions Reconsidered: A Test Using New Data," *International Studies Quarterly* 53 (2009): 1075–94.

38 Jaleh Dashti-Gibson, Patricia Davis, and Benjamin Radcliff, "On the Determinants of the Success of Economic Sanctions: An Empirical Analysis," *American Journal of Political Science* 41 (1997): 608–18.

39 T. Clifton Morgan and Valerie Schwebach, "Fools Suffer Gladly: The Use of Economic Sanctions in International Crises," *International Studies Quarterly* 41 (1997): 27–50; Adrian U-Jin Ang and Dursun Peksen, "When Do Economic Sanctions Work? Asymmetric Perceptions, Issue Salience, and Outcomes," *Political Research Quarterly* 60 (2007): 135–45.

40 Drezner, *The Sanctions Paradox.*

41 Robert Hart, "Democracy and the Successful Use of Economic Sanctions," *Political Research Quarterly* 53 (2000): 267–84.

however. Perhaps the most symbolic article of this vein is Cooper Drury's effort to replicate the conclusions reached by Hufbauer, Schott, and Elliott.[42] He finds that the strong bivariate relationships posited in the initial study fade away when tested at the multivariate level. The only effect that retains statistical significance is the significance of institutionalized cooperation. Combined, the pseudo-R^2 is remarkably low in capturing the variation in sanctions outcomes.

This does not mean that the other hypothesized relationships are necessarily insignificant. In almost all of the statistical work, the cost of sanctions to the target country is positively and significantly correlated with successful outcomes. With the addition of post-Cold War data to the HSE data set, updates and additions to the Hufbauer, Schott, Elliott, and Oegg data set, and the development of the Threat and Imposition of Economic Sanctions data set, the opportunity exists for further testing.[43] However, the failure of many hypothesized relationships to retain their statistical significance in the face of different specifications and different sets of control variables is suggestive. For policymakers, the kind of advice that follows from these findings would appear to be highly contingent. Until and unless more robust relationships can be developed from these data sets, it is highly unlikely that the policy recommendations that flow from this vein of scholarship will permeate the corridors of power.

The Birth of Smart Sanctions

The origins of smart sanctions lie in the comprehensive UN sanctions imposed at the end of the Cold War.[44] In the first half of the 1990s, the UN Security Council (UNSC) imposed comprehensive or near-comprehensive sanctions on Iraq, Haiti, and the former Yugoslavia. It is worth observing that all three sanctions episodes generated at least moderate concessions. Saddam Hussein was forced to abandon his weapons of mass destruction program.[45] The Haitian military dictatorship eventually conceded power to Jean-Bertrand Aristide—though the threat of U.S. military force driven by concerns about the ongoing Haitian boatpeople crisis in the United States had a greater role to play in that concession.[46] The combination of sanctions and coercive bombing

[42] Drury, "Revisiting *Economic Sanctions Reconsidered*"; Hufbauer et al., *Economic Sanctions Reconsidered*, 2nd ed.

[43] T. Clifton Morgan, Navin Bapat, and Valentin Krustev, "The Threat and Imposition of Economic Sanctions, 1971–2000," *Conflict Management and Peace Science* 26 (2009): 92–110.

[44] Thomas Weiss et al., eds., *Political Gain and Civilian Pain: Humanitarian Impacts of Economic Sanctions* (New York: Rowman & Littlefield, 1997); Cortright and Lopez, *The Sanctions Decade*; Cortright and Lopez, *Smart Sanctions*; Cortright and Lopez, *Sanctions and the Search for Security*.

[45] David Cortright and George Lopez, "Containing Iraq: Sanctions Worked," *Foreign Affairs* 83 (2004): 90-103.

[46] Charlotte Werleigh, "The Use of Sanctions in Haiti: Assessing the Economic Realties," in *Economic Sanctions: Panacea or Peacebuilding in a Post–Cold War World?*, ed. David Cortright and George Lopez (Boulder, CO: Westview Press, 1995). See Kelly M. Greenhill's chapter in this volume for a discussion of the role fears of migration crises play in motivating state behavior, including the threat and use of

eventually brought an end to Greater Serbia and the fall of Slobodan Milosevic. Obviously, military statecraft was also used in all three cases, but Rogers argued that economic sanctions played a crucial supporting role in determining the outcomes.[47]

Despite the modest policy successes, these cases were judged to be failures in the eyes of most policy analysts—particularly Iraq. Measured in terms of cost, these sanctions were by far the most comprehensive in history.[48] The comprehensive trade embargo was truly crippling in its economic and humanitarian effects.[49] O'Sullivan estimated that Iraq lost between $175 billion and $250 billion in possible oil revenues from the sanctions. (On this issue, see also Phil Haun's chapter in this volume.) The price for a family's food supply for a month increased 250-fold over the first five years of the sanctions regime.[50] Garfield estimated that the sanctions caused a minimum of 100,000 and up to 227,000 excess deaths among young children from August 1991 through March 1998.[51] Mueller and Mueller concluded, "Economic sanctions may well have been a necessary cause of the deaths of more people in Iraq than have been slain by all so-called weapons of mass destruction throughout history."[52]

The Iraq sanctions created three significant and overlapping political problems for the proponents of economic statecraft as a foreign policy tool, and the Iraq embargo created three major headaches for politicians and policymakers. First, they did not seem to work. When they were initially imposed, most policymakers believed that Saddam would be the victim of a coup in short order. Instead, he was defiant in his refusal to acquiesce to Security Council demands on weapons inspections. As previously noted, it is true that the sanctions were quite effective in denying Saddam the ability to develop weapons of mass destruction. During the 1990s, however, the Iraqi government threw up one obstruction after another to make life difficult for UN weapons instructors. The sanctions worked in practice, but the perception was that they failed to yield anything of value. From a social science perspective, the perceived failure of the Iraq case seemed damning. The Iraq sanctions were an extreme outlier in terms of cost to the target; Iraq's GDP was cut roughly in half. If sanctions

---

military force, and Alexander Downes's chapter for further discussion of the junta's decision to step aside in 1994.

[47] Beth Rogers, "Using Economic Sanctions to Control Regional Conflicts," *Security Studies* 5 (1996): 43–72.

[48] Hufbauer et al., *Economic Sanctions Reconsidered*, 2nd ed.; Weiss et al., *Political Gain and Civilian Pain*; Weiss, "Sanctions as a Foreign Policy Tool."

[49] Eric Hoskins, "Humanitarian Impacts of Sanctions and War in Iraq," in Weiss et al., *Political Gain and Civilian Pain*; Abbas Alnasrawi, "Iraq: Economic Sanctions and Consequences, 1990–2000," *Third World Quarterly* 22 (2001): 205–18.

[50] Hoskins, "Humanitarian Impacts of Sanctions and War in Iraq."

[51] Richard Garfield, *Morbidity and Mortality among Iraqi Children from 1990 through 1998: Assessing the Impact of the Gulf War and Economic Sanctions, Relief Web*, March 1999, http://reliefweb.int/sites/reliefweb.int/files/resources/A2E2603E5DC88A4685256825005F211D-garfie17.pdf.

[52] John Mueller and Karl Mueller, "Sanctions of Mass Destruction," *Foreign Affairs* 78 (1999): 51.

this costly failed to yield concessions, then the entire sanctions enterprise could be called into doubt.

While not appearing to work, the political blame for Iraq's humanitarian disaster was placed squarely on the United States and the United Nations. As Brzoska observes, "Baghdad was quite successful in blaming the UN for the humanitarian crisis in Iraq, both within the country and worldwide."[53] As the main backer of the United Nations sanctions initiative, and the country most adamant in trying to force out its leader, responsibility fell on the United States. The United States and the United Kingdom stoutly resisted pressures to alter the sanctions regime from the other permanent members of the UNSC during the 1990s.[54] Madeleine Albright, the U.S. ambassador to the United Nations at the time, provided the defining sound bite for this culpability in May 1996. In a *60 Minutes* interview, she said that even if the sanctions had killed half a million Iraqi children, "the price is worth it."[55]

The final policy problem was the link between sanctions and the spread of corruption, as the UN's Oil-for-Food scandal made clear. Sanctions and black market activity go together. By punishing ordinary market activity, sanctions give entrepreneurs a strong incentive to take the criminal route, and they usually earn higher than usual profits in the bargain. As Peter Andreas has demonstrated, trade sanctions encourage the creation of organized crime syndicates and transnational smuggling networks.[56] Sanctions therefore do not just weaken the rule of law in the target country; they weaken the rule of law in bordering countries and monitoring organizations as well. The corruption has a path-dependent quality, persisting long after sanctions have been lifted. For example, according to Transparency International's 2009 Corruption Perceptions Index, the five most corrupt countries in the world were subject to trade sanctions in the 1990s.

The humanitarian and political costs that emanated from the Iraq sanctions caused a great deal of consternation in political circles. Humanitarian groups ranging from the Red Cross to Human Rights Watch questioned the ethics of comprehensive trade sanctions. In 1995 UN Secretary-General Boutros Boutros-Ghali labeled sanctions a "blunt instrument" and asked "whether suffering inflicted on vulnerable groups in the target country is a legitimate means of exerting pressure on political leaders whose behavior is unlikely to

---

[53] Brzoska, "From Dumb to Smart?," 520. It should be remembered that five years passed before Saddam Hussein allowed the Oil-for-Food program to help feed the Iraqi population. See Meghan O'Sullivan, *Shrewd Sanctions: Statecraft and State Sponsors of Terrorism* (Washington, DC: Brookings Institution Press, 2003).

[54] Intriguingly, upon taking office, the Bush administration tried to shift the Iraq embargo to a "smart sanctions" framework. After the September 11 attacks, however, that initiative was overtaken by events.

[55] The clip can be accessed at "Madeleine Albright: 60 Minutes," *YouTube*, http://www.youtube.com/watch?v=FbIX1CP9qr4.

[56] Peter Andreas, "Criminalizing Consequences of Sanctions: Embargo Busting and Its Legacy," *International Studies Quarterly* 49 (2005): 335–60.

be affected by the plight of their subjects."[57] Beyond the anguish caused by the humanitarian costs, powerful actors within the UNSC became implacably opposed to any new comprehensive sanctions. Given these political problems, UN officials began casting about for solutions to the problem.

The failure of sanctions to yield immediate results in Iraq also caused the scholarly work on economic sanctions to shift in new directions. Most of the academic research cited in the previous section treated senders and targets as rational unitary actors. Little attention was paid to the causal mechanisms through which sanctions were supposed to lead the target government into acquiescing. The Iraq case suggested that more effort should be paid to the causal logic by which sanctions were supposed to work.

At this juncture, scholarship emerged that opened up the black box of the target state. Intriguingly, research emanating from wildly disparate theoretical and methodological perspectives came to the same conclusion about the effect of comprehensive sanctions: they disproportionately hurt politically weak groups and benefited target regime sympathizers. Kaempfer and Lowenberg and Kaempfer, Lowenberg, and Mertens used a public choice framework to argue that sanctions had distributional effects on interest groups within the target country.[58] If the sanctions enriched—or could be manipulated to enrich—key supporters of the target regime, then the aggregate cost of the sanctions would have minimal impact on the target government. Kirshner proposed a microfoundations approach, arguing that, "instead of considering how those sanctions hurt the target state, this approach emphasizes how groups within the target are affected differently, and how these consequences change with the form of statecraft chosen."[59] He concluded that financial sanctions—aid cutoffs, asset freezes, and monetary pressures—were more likely to pressure key supporters of the target regime than broad-based trade sanctions. Buck, Gallant, and Nossal used a feminist approach to argue that the costs of trade sanctions are disproportionately imposed on women, who are often the most powerless political actors in the target country.[60] David Rowe's research on the effects of the sanctions regime on the Rhodesian government demonstrated how the target regime could manipulate the effects of sanctions to reward supporters and weaken opponents of the government.[61]

---

[57] Darren Hawkins and Joshua Lloyd, "Questioning Comprehensive Sanctions: The Birth of a Norm," *Journal of Human Rights* 2 (2003): 444.

[58] William Kaempfer and Anton Lowenberg, "The Theory of International Economic Sanctions: A Public Choice Approach," *American Economic Review* 78 (1988): 786–93; William Kaempfer and Anton Lowenberg, *International Economic Sanctions: A Public Choice Perspective* (Boulder, CO: Westview Press, 1992); William Kaempfer, Anton Lowenberg, and William Mertens, "International Economic Sanctions against a Dictator," *Economics and Politics* 16 (2004): 29–51.

[59] Jonathan Kirshner, "The Microfoundations of Economic Sanctions," *Security Studies* 6 (1997): 33.

[60] Lori Buck, Nicole Gallant, and Kim Richard Nossal, "Sanctions as a Gendered Instrument of Statecraft: The Case of Iraq," *Review of International Studies* 24 (1998): 69–84.

[61] David M. Rowe, *Manipulating the Market: Understanding Economic Sanctions, Institutional Change, and the Political Unity of White Rhodesia* (Ann Arbor: University of Michigan Press, 2001).

In the past decade, the emphasis of sanctions research has focused primarily on the political economy of authoritarian countries. As Allen observes, more than 78 percent of sanctions were imposed on nondemocratic target states.[62] At the same time, Wintrobe and Bueno de Mesquita et al. developed political economy models that could explain the domestic incentives for nondemocratic leaders.[63] In these regimes, leaders had an incentive to create private, excludable goods for supporters. Comprehensive sanctions created the opportunity for target governments to allocate rent-seeking opportunities to those supporters. This policy response would, if anything, increase an authoritarian regime's grip on power. Relying on this theoretical framework, a number of sanctions scholars argued that broad-based economic sanctions would have a minimal effect on authoritarian targets.[64] Smart sanctions that hurt key elites, on the other hand, would have a better chance of success without hurting the target country's mass public.

This research trend dovetailed nicely with the evolution in policymaking on sanctions.[65] Smart sanctions could raise the target regime's costs of noncompliance while avoiding the collateral damage that comes with comprehensive trade embargoes. The most prominent countrywide examples included financial sanctions, asset freezes, travel bans, restrictions on luxury goods, and arms embargoes. Furthermore, instead of sanctioning an entire country, smart sanctions advocates advocated the targeting of individuals or restrictions on corporations or holding companies associated with the target government's leadership. Targeted sanctions would hamper the ability of leaders to offer crucial supporters rent-seeking opportunities.

Smart sanctions seemed the perfect policy compromise between the Security Council members. Russia, China, and France grew frustrated by their inability to alter the sanctions regime once the initial measures were approved. At the same time, the United States and the United Kingdom wanted to keep sanctions in the policy tool kit. For recalcitrant members of the Security Council, smart sanctions offered the opportunity to cooperate with the hegemonic actor in the international system. At the same time, smart sanctions would not impose excessive humanitarian costs or threaten lucrative trading relationships with

[62] Susan Hannah Allen, "Political Institutions and Constrained Response to Economic Sanctions," *Foreign Policy Analysis* 4 (2008): 269.

[63] Ronald Wintrobe, "The Tinpot and the Totalitarian: An Economic Theory of Dictatorship," *American Political Science Review* 84 (1990): 849–72; Bruce Bueno de Mesquita et al., "An Institutional Explanation of the Democratic Peace," *American Political Science Review* 93 (1999): 791–807; Bruce Bueno de Mesquita et al., *The Logic of Political Survival* (Cambridge, MA: MIT Press, 2003).

[64] Risa Brooks, "Sanctions and Regime Type: What Works, and When?," *Security Studies* 11 (2002): 1–50; David Lektzian and Mark Souva, "An Institutional Theory of Sanctions Onset and Success," *Journal of Conflict Resolution* 31 (2007): 848–71; Susan Hannah Allen, "The Determinants of Economic Sanctions Success and Failure," *International Interactions* 31 (2005): 117–38; Allen, "Political Institutions and Constrained Response"; Susan Hannah Allen, "The Domestic Political Costs of Economic Sanctions," *Journal of Conflict Resolution* 52 (2008): 916–44.

[65] Cortright and Lopez, *Smart Sanctions*; Cortright and Lopez, *Sanctions and the Search for Security*; Brzoska, "From Dumb to Smart?"

target countries. For the United States and the United Kingdom, the targeted sanctions framework seemed like a more precise policy tool.

Advocates of targeted sanctions were also adroit in their rhetorical tropes. "Smart sanctions" sounds better than the alternative; one British policymaker acknowledged that the label did generate official support.[66] Furthermore, advocates of smart sanctions contrasted their theoretical model of how sanctions worked in the target country with the "naïve theory" of sanctions that assumed greater costs equaled greater concessions.[67] The obvious implication was that sanctions scholarship that assumed states to be unitary actors were less sophisticated than work that allowed second image variables to play a causal role.

A two-track process emerged to improve the use of targeted sanctions. Within the UN machinery, an ongoing series of sanctions committees were formed to monitor and assess the effect of different Security Council resolutions authorizing sanctions. These committees had little enforcement power and therefore acted only as a minimal deterrent against private actors engaging in sanctions-busting activity. These committees succeeded, however, in explicitly naming and shaming countries that were violating existing sanctions resolutions.[68] Given the powerful norms of diplomatic comity at the United Nations, this move in and of itself represented a significant break from past practices in Turtle Bay.

Outside the Security Council, a series of conferences were convened to figure out how to improve the implementation of sanctions. In 1998 the Swiss government convened the Interlaken Process, a rolling series of meetings designed to improve the practice of financial sanctions. The Interlaken Process brought together government officials, private sector experts, and academics to hammer out the technicalities of imposing sanctions. In 2001 the Swiss contracted sanctions experts at Brown University's Watson Institute for International Studies to prepare a "how-to" sanctions manual, including a model Security Council resolution for future cases.[69] The German government followed up Interlaken with the Bonn-Berlin Process to focus exclusively on arms embargoes and travel sanctions. The Swedish government subsequently convened the Stockholm Process to improve the sanctions machinery at the United Nations. Uppsala University's Department of Peace and Conflict Research provided significant expertise for the Stockholm Process. These processes led to significant buy-in from United Nations members. They also demonstrated the tight linkage between scholars and policymakers on this issue. Scholars and other experts participated in all three of these processes.

Bipartisan support for targeted sanctions also emerged in the United States—particularly for financial sanctions. The Clinton administration

---

[66] Daniel W. Drezner, "Off Target," *New Republic*, May 31, 2010.

[67] Brzoska, "From Dumb to Smart?," 520.

[68] Ibid.

[69] Thomas Biersteker et al., "Consensus from the Bottom Up? Assessing the Influence of the Sanctions Reform Process," in *International Sanctions: Between War and Words in the International System*, ed. Peter Wallensteen and Carina Staibano (London: Routledge, 2005), 17.

embraced the idea as part of the Treasury Department's initiative to combat financial abuse.[70] Financial countermeasures were developed to punish states and jurisdictions with lax anti–money laundering statutes. These acts of financial statecraft proved surprisingly effective in forcing target countries to alter their policies.[71] Because the United States is the epicenter of global finance, international bankers needed access to U.S. capital markets to conduct international transactions. An advisory warning from the Treasury Department was sufficient to get foreign bankers to stop doing business with terrorist entities for fear of losing access to U.S. banking services. After the September 11 terrorist attacks, the Bush administration also embraced the smart sanctions initiative.[72]

By 2010 both the United Nations and the United States had internalized the idea of targeted sanctions. The United Nations has not implemented comprehensive sanctions for the past 15 years. Biersteker and his coauthors argue that the sanctions reform effort had a manifest impact on the ways the UNSC authorized economic coercion.[73] They, along with Foot, observe that concerns about the humanitarian and human rights effects of sanctions increased the degree of due process within existing UN sanctions committees over the past decade.[74] Even the 1267 Committee, authorized to sanction individuals working with Al Qaeda, grew more sensitive to minimizing the humanitarian impact of the sanctions. Hawkins and Lloyd argue, "A new norm against comprehensive sanctions has become part of the shared understanding among states."[75]

The bipartisan consensus within the U.S. foreign policy community in favor of targeted sanctions has also grown over time. Rose Gottemoeller, now Deputy Secretary General of NATO, concluded in early 2008 that smart sanctions "had been honed through the 'war on terror,' and sanctions are hitting their targets among corrupt elites more often."[76] Zarate argued that the tools of financial statecraft "provide the United States and its allies the best source of diplomatic leverage to affect regimes' behavior and calculus."[77] Loeffler concludes, "It is hard to imagine any serious foreign policy issue down the line in which financial tools would not be or should not

---

70 William F. Wechsler, "Follow the Money," *Foreign Affairs* 80 (2001): 40–57.

71 Daniel W. Drezner, *All Politics Is Global: Explaining International Regulatory Regimes* (Princeton, NJ: Princeton University Press, 2007), 142–45.

72 Juan Zarate, "Harnessing the Financial Furies: Smart Financial Power and National Security," *Washington Quarterly* 32 (2009): 43–59.

73 Biersteker et al., "Consensus from the Bottom Up?"

74 Ibid.; Rosemary Foot, "The United Nations, Counter Terrorism and Human Rights: Institutional Adaptation and Embedded Ideas," *Human Rights Quarterly* 29 (2007): 489–514. For a review of the legal due process issues raised by the sanctioning of individuals in the UN Security Council, see Andrea Bianchi, "Assessing the Effectiveness of the UN Security Council's Anti-terrorism Measures: The Quest for Legitimacy and Cohesion," *European Journal of International Law* 17 (2007): 881–919.

75 Hawkins and Lloyd, "Questioning Comprehensive Sanctions," 441.

76 Rose Gottemoeller, "The Evolution of Sanctions in Practice and Theory," *Survival* 49 (2008): 109.

77 Zarate, "Harnessing the Financial Furies," 55.

be considered as part of a comprehensive strategy."[78] U.S. policy journals are replete with essays arguing in favor of financial statecraft as the best policy lever available to the United States.[79] Smart sanctions appear to be one of those rare initiatives in which one can use the terms *United Nations, academics,* and *success* in the same sentence.

Assessing Smart Sanctions

There are two ways to evaluate the performance of the smart sanctions framework in world politics. First, have targeted sanctions accomplished their stated goal in improving target state compliance? Second, have smart sanctions ameliorated the humanitarian impact and corruption that comprehensive sanctions create?

The preliminary evidence suggests a mixed track record for targeted sanctions. After reviewing United Nations sanctions during the 1990s, Cortright and Lopez noted, "The obvious conclusion is that comprehensive sanctions are more effective than targeted or selective measures. Where economic and social impact have been greatest, political effects have also been most significant."[80] Elliott arrived at a similar conclusion: "With the exception of Libya, the results of UN targeted sanctions have been disappointing."[81] In their review essay, Tostensen and Bull concluded, "The optimism expressed in some academic circles and among decision makers at national and international levels appears largely unjustified."[82] At a 2010 International Studies Association panel on the topic, many of the scholarly architects of the smart sanctions approach agreed that, compared to comprehensive sanctions, policy results had been mixed at best.

To be sure, there are case studies that demonstrate the utility of targeted sanctions. The exemplar case is the pressure put on Libya to renounce its weapons of mass destruction programs. That episode, however, also shows the limits of targeted sanctions. A welter of different policy tools was used to get Libya to alter course, including backchannel negotiations, the Proliferation Security Initiative, and the unspoken threat of invasion after Operation Iraqi Freedom. It was the combination of these policy tools, along with Muammar Gaddafi's quixotic nature, that led to Libya's acquiescence.[83]

---

78 Rachel Loeffler, "Bank Shots: How the Financial System Can Isolate Rogues," *Foreign Affairs* 88 (2009): 110.

79 Gary Hufbauer and Barbara Oegg, "Targeted Sanctions: A Policy Alternative," *Law and Policy in International Business* 32 (2000): 11–20; Paul Bracken, "Financial Warfare," *Orbis* 51 (2007): 685–96; Jodi Liss, "Making Monetary Mischief," *World Policy Journal* 24 (2007): 29–38; Sue E. Eckert, "The Use of Financial Measures to Promote Security," *Journal of International Affairs* 62 (2008): 103–11.

80 Cortright and Lopez, *Smart Sanctions;* Cortright and Lopez, *Sanctions and the Search for Security*, 8.

81 Kimberly Elliott, "Analyzing the Effects of Targeted Sanctions," in Cortright and Lopez, *Smart Sanctions*, 171.

82 Arne Tostenson and Beate Bull, "Are Smart Sanctions Feasible?," *World Politics* 54 (2002): 402.

83 Bruce Jentleson and Christopher Whytock, "Who 'Won' Libya? The Force-Diplomacy Debate and Its Implications for Theory and Policy," *International Security* 30 (2005): 47–86. See also Greenhill's chapter in this volume.

There have been more extensive investigations into the two most common forms of targeted sanctions, arms embargoes and financial statecraft.[84] The results have been underwhelming. Tierney evaluated arms embargoes in civil wars across five criteria for success, including their symbolic impact. He concluded, "Much of the impact of UN arms embargoes in civil wars can be summarized as irrelevance or malevolence."[85] Fruchart et al. reached a similar conclusion.[86] Brzoska offered a slightly more hopeful assessment. He pointed to clear successes, such as the 1993–2003 arms embargo of Angola. He also argued that there has been an increasing amount of effectiveness over time in halting the transfer of weapons to armed combatants.[87] Qualifying this result as a "success," however, is problematic. As Damrosch and Tierney observed, arms embargoes can have malevolent distributional effects. They reward the actor possessing the largest cache of weapons ex ante.[88] Brzoska also acknowledged that, over time, arms embargoes have been less successful in altering the behavior of target countries, working less than 8 percent of the time. Paradoxically, however, sender country satisfaction with arms embargoes has increased.

The literature on financial statecraft is slightly more upbeat. Hufbauer, Schott, and Elliott originally found in bivariate tests that financial sanctions had a better track record of success than trade sanctions.[89] Shagabutdinova and Berejikian replicated that finding in multivariate tests, while also discovering that financial sanctions are both more effective and of shorter duration than trade sanctions.[90] These results are based on pre-1990 episodes, however, and principally involve aid cutoffs; it is far from clear whether these results would carry over into modern financial sanctions.[91] There is evidence that financial sanctions have been useful in coercing countries into changing their anti–money laundering rules.[92] It is not clear whether financial statecraft can be as successful on issues more highly valued by the target regime, however.[93] Steil and Litan surveyed recent efforts by the United States to use capital market access to force policy changes in Sudan, Russia, and China.[94] They found

[84] The literature assessing travel bans is much more sparse. Cortright and Lopez provide a mixed assessment.

[85] Dominic Tierney, "Irrelevant or Malevolent? UN Arms Embargoes in Civil Wars," *Review of International Studies* 31 (2005): 661.

[86] Damien Fruchart et al., *United Nations Arms Embargoes: Their Impact on Arms Flows and Target Behavior* (Stockholm: SIPRI, 2007).

[87] Michael Brzoska, "Measuring the Effectiveness of Arms Embargoes," *Peace Economics, Peace Science and Public Policy* 14 (2008): 1-34.

[88] Lori Fisler Damrosch, "The Collective Enforcement of International Norms through Economic Sanctions," *Ethics and International Affairs* 8 (1994): 59–75; Tierney, "Irrelevant or Malevolent?"

[89] Hufbauer et al., *Economic Sanctions Reconsidered*, 2nd ed.

[90] Ella Shagabutdinova and Jeffrey Berejikian, "Deploying Sanctions While Protecting Human Rights: Are Humanitarian 'Smart' Sanctions Effective?," *Journal of Human Rights* 6 (2007): 59–74.

[91] These results also suffer from omitted variable bias. Aid flows are strongly correlated with alliance relationships, which Shagabutdinova and Berejikian did not include in their regression analysis.

[92] Beth Simmons, "The International Politics of Harmonization: The Case of Capital Market Regulation," *International Organization* 55 (2001): 589–620; Drezner, *All Politics Is Global.*

[93] Ang and Peksen, "When Do Economic Sanctions Work?"

[94] Benn Steil and Robert Litan, *Financial Statecraft* (New Haven, CT: Yale University Press, 2006), 77.

that all the targeted entities were able to find alternative sources of financing at minimal cost, concluding, "Rarely has so powerful a force been harnessed by so many interests with such passion to so little effect." A collaborative effort to examine efforts at monetary statecraft reached a similar conclusion: "Among the central findings of our study are the substantial impediments to the efficient exercise of monetary power as a deliberate instrument of economic statecraft. . . . The tools of monetary statecraft . . . are often too blunt to be effective when they would most be desired and too diffuse to be directed at particular targets without incurring substantial damage."[95]

The evidence suggests that financial sanctions have hurt both the Iranian and the North Korean economies.[96] The case of Iran is particularly instructive. One former Iranian official admitted in late 2008 that the UN sanctions had increased the price of imports anywhere from 10 to 30 percent.[97] It was the post-2008 sanctions that really mattered, however. In 2010 the UN Security Council voted to impose a fourth round of economic sanctions on Iran in response to that country's refusal to cooperate with the International Atomic Energy Agency. The United States and European Union announced their intent to impose additional financial sanctions.

The financial restrictions were so comprehensive that the Society for Worldwide Interbank Financial Telecommunication ended all transactions with Iranian banks named in the sanctions. Iran was effectively cut off from twenty-first-century finance. The European Union also implemented an embargo on Iranian oil beginning in 2012. By 2013 the sanctions had clearly proven to be more crippling than most experts thought. Iran's oil export revenues were cut in half between 2010 and 2012; overall oil production was at its lowest levels in 25 years. Compared to its peer group of oil exporters, Iran's economy deteriorated after 2010, with relatively anemic growth, higher inflation, a rapidly depreciating currency, and less than $20 billion in liquid hard currency reserves.[98] In the fall of 2013, Iran's president Hassan Rouhani publicly acknowledged that the effect of sanctions on the Iranian economy was severe and required quick negotiations to settle the nuclear question.[99] The Iran case highlights the potency of economic sanctions but also suggests that financial sanctions work best when they generate real economic costs to the target economy—and when they are married to sectoral sanctions as well.

Recent research on the impact of economic coercion in the target country, on the other hand, has largely backed up the humanitarian arguments in

---

[95] David M. Andrews, ed., *International Monetary Power* (Ithaca, NY: Cornell University Press, 2006), 25.
[96] Eckert, "The Use of Financial Measures to Promote Security"; Loeffler, "Bank Shots."
[97] Suzanne Maloney, "Sanctioning Iran: If Only It Were So Simple," *Washington Quarterly* 33 (2010): 139.
[98] U.S. Government Accountability Office, "U.S. and International Sanctions Have Adversely Affected the Iranian Economy," GAO Report-13-326, accessed October 25, 2013.
[99] See, for example, Thomas Erdbrink, "Iran Staggers as Sanctions Hit Economy," *New York Times*, September 30, 2013.

favor of smart sanctions. Wood examined the effect of economic sanctions on state repression using data from 1976 to 2001.[100] He found that comprehensive sanctions were likely to increase repression in authoritarian countries. Peksen and Drury found in bivariate tests that the implementation of sanctions triggers drops in democracy and human rights scores in target governments.[101] Peksen also showed that sanctions lead to a decline in the physical integrity rights of individuals in target countries.[102] He further found that the decline in those rights was greater if comprehensive sanctions were imposed rather than targeted sanctions.

These results suggest that, all else being equal, targeted sanctions are a superior policy tool. However, not all else is equal. Paradoxically, there are a number of conditions under which comprehensive sanctions appear to be better at ameliorating suffering in the target country. All of the sanctions literature of the past decade agrees that if the target state is a democracy, comprehensive sanctions are more likely to trigger quick concessions.[103] The goal of the sanctions episode also matters. If the sender's aim is regime change, then sanctions that impose larger costs have a greater likelihood of success.[104] Marinov found that sanctions of any stripe tended to reduce the staying power of the target government; military action, in contrast, increased the duration of the government in power.[105] Major and McGannargue suggested that there might be instances when sanctioning the "innocent bystanders" in the target country will be more likely to produce target concessions.[106] Most intriguingly, comprehensive sanctions were most useful in bringing about a quicker end to civil wars. Both Gershenson and Escribà-Folch found that comprehensive embargoes were more effective than targeted sanctions at ending intrastate conflicts.[107] Moreover, as some have argued, many target states can compensate themselves for the costs of targeted sanctions through taxation, confiscation, redistribution, and other policy tools, passing the cost of sanctions onto the regime's opponents or the population as a whole; thus one might argue that

---

[100] Reed Wood, "'A Hand upon the Throat of the Nation': Economic Sanctions and State Repression, 1976–2001," *International Studies Quarterly* 52 (2008): 489–513.
[101] Durson Peksen and A. Cooper Drury, "Economic Sanctions and Political Repression: Assessing the Impact of Coercive Diplomacy," *Human Rights Review* 10 (2009): 393–411.
[102] Dursun Peksen, "Better or Worse? The Effect of Economic Sanctions on Human Rights," *Journal of Peace Research* 46 (2009): 59–77.
[103] Brooks, "Sanctions and Regime Type"; Lektzian and Souva, "An Institutional Theory of Sanctions Onset and Success"; Allen, "The Domestic Political Costs of Economic Sanctions."
[104] Jaleh Dashti-Gibson, Patricia Davis, and Benjamin Radcliff, "On the Determinants of the Success of Economic Sanctions: An Empirical Analysis," *American Journal of Political Science* 41 (1997): 608–18.
[105] Nikolay Marinov, "Do Economic Sanctions Destabilize Country Leaders?," *American Journal of Political Science* 49 (2005): 564–76.
[106] Solomon Major and Anthony J. McGann, "Caught in the Crossfire: 'Innocent Bystanders' as Optimal Targets of Economic Sanctions," *Journal of Conflict Resolution* 49 (2005): 337–59.
[107] Dmitriy Gershenson, "Sanctions and Civil Conflict," *Economica* 69 (2002): 185–206; Abel Escribà-Folch, "Economic Sanctions and the Duration of Civil Conflicts," *Journal of Peace Research* 47 (2010): 129–41.

smart sanctions are something of an illusion because ultimately there cannot really be sanctions that inflict pain solely on leaders.[108]

Summary

For decades, economic statecraft was thought to be a backwater in international relations scholarship. Since the mid-1990s, however, there has been a remarkable symbiosis between the scholarly and policy communities on the subject. The political and humanitarian disaster of the Iraq sanctions episode led policymakers to search for innovations in the implementation of economic statecraft. At the same time, researchers began to focus on the precise causal mechanisms through which sanctions were supposed to compel change in the target's behavior. Smart sanctions were the resulting alchemy between the scholarly and policymaking communities.

Any assessment of targeted sanctions at this juncture must be labeled preliminary. States and international organizations only started moving down the learning curve on implementing sanctions in the past decade.[109] Further work is clearly needed. Nevertheless, the evidence to date suggests that smart sanctions are no better at generating concessions from the target state. They do, however, appear to solve several political problems for sender countries. Because they are billed as minimizing humanitarian and human rights concerns, they receive only muted criticism from global civil society.[110] Because they do not impede significant trade flows, smart sanctions can be imposed indefinitely at minimal cost. They clearly solve the political problem of "doing something" in the face of target state misbehavior. They do not solve the policy problem of coercing the target state into changing its policies.

One methodological problem with the older generation of sanctions scholarship was the tendency to extrapolate general propositions from high-profile cases.[111] It is worth pondering whether the research on targeted sanctions suffers from a similar problem. Targeted sanctions were designed in response to Iraq—but Iraq was an extreme outlier on multiple dimensions. In the sanctions universe, the most common outcome is for sanctions to be lifted within a year's time; sanctions on Iraq lasted more than 13 years. Most sanctions have a modest impact on the target country's GDP of less than 2 percent.[112] Iraq's economy was cut in half. Smart sanctions were designed to limit the economic

---

[108] See, for example, Jean-Marc Blanchard and Norrin Ripsman, *Economic Statecraft and Foreign Policy: Sanctions, Incentives and Target State Calculations* (London: Routledge, 2013); Peter Feaver and Eric Lorber, "The Sanctions Myth," *National Interest*, June 15, 2015.

[109] Cortright and Lopez, *Sanctions and the Search for Security*.

[110] Matthew Craven, "Humanitarianism and the Quest for Smarter Sanctions," *European Journal of International Law* 13 (2002): 43–61.

[111] David Collier and James Mahoney, "Insights and Pitfalls: Selection Bias in Qualitative Research," *World Politics* 49 (1996): 56–91; Drezner, *The Sanctions Paradox*.

[112] Hufbauer et al., *Economic Sanctions Reconsidered*, 2nd ed.

damage that sanctions can impose, but most economic sanctions *already* have limited effects.

Future research in this area should focus on two areas. First, more rigorous empirical work is needed on the relative effect of smart sanctions versus more comprehensive sanctions. There are now a sufficient number of smart sanctions cases for statistical analysis. The long-term impact of smart sanctions is worthy of further study, to see whether their effects are different from sanctions that include a trade component. Second, and more important, the statecraft literature needs to pay greater attention to the burgeoning work on politics in authoritarian countries. As Allen observes, the overwhelming majority of sanctions targets are nondemocratic polities.[113] The general assumption behind recent sanctions scholarship is that authoritarian leaders are better able to resist economic pressure than democratic states. Clearly, however, authoritarian leaders have domestic constraints that affect their behavior in international crises.[114] Different types of authoritarian countries have different kinds of domestic constraints. A greater theoretical and empirical focus on authoritarian politics would inform both the theory and the practice of economic statecraft and, in the process, illuminate the inner workings of nondemocratic governments.

---

[113] Allen, "The Domestic Political Costs of Economic Sanctions."

[114] Abel Escribà-Folch, "Economic Growth and Potential Punishment under Dictatorship," *Kyklos* 60 (2007): 187–210; Jessica Weeks, "Autocratic Audience Costs: Regime Type and Signaling Resolve," *International Organization* 62 (2008): 35–64.

CHAPTER 13

Prices or Power Politics?

When and Why States Coercively Compete over Resources

JONATHAN N. MARKOWITZ

HISTORICALLY, THE COMPETITION OVER the governance of resources and their distribution has been a principal driver of the Great Game in international politics. Today the Great Game is not in the mountains of the Hindu Kush but on the bottom of the ocean floor. A revolution in deep-sea drilling technology combined with unprecedented climatological change has exposed previously inaccessible energy reserves around the globe, and some states have projected military power to coercively compete over these potentially massive stores of resources.

Yet resource wars are rare.[1] Most states are content to rely on markets and to allow prices, not power politics, to determine the division of global resources. While this has led some researchers to contend that competition over resources is obsolete,[2] it would be incorrect to suggest that coercion has no role in the division and governance of resources. For nearly 40 years, the United States has projected military force to deter threats to the free flow of Middle East oil,[3] and recent jockeying over maritime seabed resources in the East and South China Sea, Arctic Ocean, and eastern Mediterranean shows that coercive behavior is not a uniquely American activity.

---

[1] Nils Petter Gleditsch, "Armed Conflict and the Environment: A Critique of the Literature," *Journal of Peace Research* 35 (1998): 381–400; David G Victor, "What Resource Wars?," *National Interest* 92 (2007) : 48-55; Jeff Colgan, *Petro-Aggression: When Oil Causes War* (Cambridge: Cambridge University Press, 2013).

[2] Danielle F. S. Cohen and Jonathan Kirshner, "The Cult of Energy Insecurity and Great Power Rivalry across the Pacific," in *The Nexus of Economics, Security, and International Relations in East Asia*, ed. Avery Goldstein and Edward Mansfield (Palo Alto, CA: Stanford University Press, 2012).

[3] Eugene Gholz and Daryl Press, "Protecting the Prize: Oil and the US National Interest," *Security Studies* 19 (2010): 453–85.

These empirical patterns suggest two puzzles. First, if global resource markets are the most efficient means for states to ensure access to resources, why are some states still employing coercive diplomacy? Second, why are some states coercively competing over the direct control of these resources, while others are focused on deterring threats to open-access resource markets? These are not mutually exclusive objectives, as states can pursue and have historically pursued both; however, we do not know why some states have a stronger *interest* in pursuing one objective over another.

We need a more nuanced explanation of when and why states employ coercion to compete over the control and governance of resources. Nothing in liberal or realist arguments suggests that state preferences for securing resources should vary *across states*, leaving a gap in our understanding of which states are most likely to engage in militarized resource competition. Filling this gap is critical for officials who must anticipate *how* states like Russia and China will behave and *where* resource competition is most likely to threaten regional stability. The theory developed here aims to fill this gap and, in doing so, contributes to this volume's greater mission of improving our understanding of the causes and effects of coercion.

I argue that the domestic political institutions and economic interests of the state determine its preferences and that the more a state relies on resource rents to generate income, the stronger its preference to control stocks of resources as a source of power, profits, and patronage. The domestic political institutions of the state condition the impact of resource dependence on the state's foreign policy. Democracy restrains and autocracy liberates the rent-seeking incentives of the state, but irrespective of institutions, the more resource-dependent a state is, the stronger its preference will be to seek resource rents. In sum, the central theoretical claim developed in this chapter is that a state's preference for control of resource rents is a function of both the representativeness of its domestic political institutions and the degree to which it is reliant on resource rents as a source of income.

The core contribution of this chapter is to develop a theory of why some states have a stronger preference to employ coercive diplomacy to control resources. While most of the chapters in the volume focus on the *effect* of coercive force, my work focuses on the *causes* of coercion. Understanding the causes of coercion is critical for scholars who are attempting to understand the effects of various coercive tools.[4] As Downes notes in this volume, without understanding why some states opt into employing coercion, scholars will be more likely to arrive at biased estimates of the effectiveness of various coercive tools.

For example, Art and Greenhill note that one of the critical factors behind deterrence failure is a highly motivated challenger and that it is difficult for policymakers to anticipate which interests challengers will be highly motivated to pursue. I introduce such a theory of state preferences or why some states are

[4] See chapters by Downes, Drezner, and Greenhill in this volume.

highly motivated to pursue certain interests, such as resources and territory, while others are not, focusing on the critical issue of resources.

Furthermore, like many of the other chapters in this volume, my theory speaks directly to ongoing policy debates.[5] Specifically, the theory developed here improves our understanding of the dynamics of cross-domain deterrence.[6] Whereas Gartzke and Lindsay illuminate the domain of cyber, my theory is especially relevant for policymakers who seek to deter conflict over resources in relevant maritime domains, such as the Arctic and South China Sea. My theory suggests that the states most motivated to engage in coercive diplomacy will be those states that are most economically dependent on resources rents to generate income.

Prices or Power Politics?

When do states choose to use military coercion to compete over the division of and access to resources? Broadly speaking, there are two ways to determine the global allocation of scarce resources: prices and power politics.[7] In an open market economy, resources are largely allocated by prices determined by global supply and demand. Alternatively, resources can be divided by power politics when states compete over resources through coercive bargaining.

I am interested in explaining whether states use coercion to pursue *exclusionary foreign policies,* designed to gain direct control of resource stocks, or *open foreign policies,* designed to ensure that the division of resources is determined by international law and prices. Each state's preference for seeking direct control of resource reserves or protecting open access to resource markets is dependent on the role that resources play in generating wealth and security for the state and its supporters.[8] Resources play two major roles in terms of generating wealth and security for states. First, resources serve as inputs to the economic productivity and military power required to secure the state and its interests. Second, stocks of resources represent future flows of rents that can be redistributed to political supporters.

In his influential book, *The Prize,* Daniel Yergin describes the history of the competition over oil.[9] In an homage to Yergin, Gholz and Press outline the U.S. strategy for "protecting the prize," which, for Washington, represents access to Middle Eastern energy markets and low and stable energy prices.[10]

---

[5] See chapters by Drezner, Haun, Crawford, Gartzke and Lindsay, Greenhill, and Walsh in this volume.

[6] See also the chapters by Gartzke and Lindsay, Greenhill, and Krause in this volume.

[7] David A. Lake, "The Challenge: The Domestic Determinants of International Rivalry between the U.S. and China," *International Studies Review,* forthcoming.

[8] I use the term *state* to represent the collection of individuals that govern the state, and I consider *state, government,* and *regime* equivalent. I use these terms rather than *leader* to distinguish my explanation from those that use attributes of individual leaders to explain foreign policy behavior.

[9] Daniel Yergin, *The Prize: The Epic Quest for Oil, Money, and Power* (New York: Simon & Schuster, 1992).

[10] Gholz and Press, "Protecting the Prize."

However, for other states, energy resources represent a different prize: rents that can be captured through conquest. Why do states sometimes view the prize as a fountain of rents, while others see it as an input to produce goods and services?

States' domestic political institutions and economic interests determine this difference in views. The more dependent a state is on rents as a source of wealth, the more it will view resources through the prism of rents. States that view resources this way will have a stronger preference to *directly control* resources to capture the greatest share of the rents. In contrast, the more a state relies on the production of goods and services to generate wealth, the more it will view resources through the prism of inputs. These states will be most concerned with ensuring *access* to resources. States may ensure access by directly controlling resources; however, it is often more costly than purchasing them on the open market.[11] While economic interests influence the set of goods that the state will pursue, their political institutions determine who in society enjoys the goods.

Competing Theories of Resource Competition and Governance

Some scholars have suggested that war is obsolete and that military coercion has no role in the competition for resources.[12] These beliefs do not reflect our current reality, where states surrounding the South China Sea and Arctic Ocean antagonize one another over maritime resources and the United States has pursued a policy in the Middle East based on the premise that they need to *prevent* military coercion over oil resources.

It has been argued, particularly by those writing on energy security, that *who* controls energy reserves is relatively unimportant, as any actor will need to sell resources on an international market to profit.[13] This is true from the standpoint of access to energy; in today's market, those that are prepared to pay will have access. However, this perspective assumes that open global energy markets exist, markets that are themselves a product of international political choices. More important, although actors who control resources must sell them to profit, control allows them to determine *who* gets to capture these profits.

Much of the literature in international politics, particularly in the realist or mercantilist tradition, has focused on the competition over resources as a

[11] There may be times, such as during military crises, when markets become so vulnerable that states prefer direct control over resources, even if it's costlier. However, the costs associated with conquest generally make it cheaper to purchase inputs than appropriate them. See Stephen G. Brooks, "Economic Actors' Lobbying Influence on the Prospects for War and Peace," *International Organization* 67 (2013): 863-888.

[12] John Mueller, *Retreat from Doomsday: The Obsolescence of Major War* (New York: Basic Books, 1989); Cohen and Kirshner, "The Cult of Energy Insecurity and Great Power Rivalry across the Pacific."

[13] Gholz and Press, "Protecting the Prize," 461.

struggle over inputs to power or security.[14] Insofar as security is a public good and ensuring access to resources is part of maximizing the security of the state, all governments will have a strong interest in securing access to resources.

In contrast, the comparative politics literature on the resource curse has largely viewed resource competition as a struggle between domestic political factions over the control of resource rents. These factions seek control of the state so they may redistribute rents to their political supporters.[15] Building on the insights of comparative politics research on the resource curse, Jeff Colgan demonstrates that oil-dependent petrostates, particularly those with revolutionary leaders, are prone to pursuing aggressive foreign policies.[16] Following in Colgan's footsteps, I use previous work on the rentier state to explain states' foreign policy choices. However, I differ from Colgan in that my theory explains the foreign policy preferences of all states, not just petrostates. Additionally, I explain how resource dependence alters the type of foreign policy objectives states pursue beyond their overall willingness to use aggression.

Why States Coercively Compete over Resources

I begin by outlining variation in my dependent variable: a state's choice of foreign policy. Open foreign policies are designed to facilitate access to resources by securing sea lanes and ensuring the free flow of resources onto global markets. An alternative method of generating benefits is to produce rents by limiting economic competition, known in the economics literature as rent-seeking.[17] Rent-seeking is the pursuit of super-normal profits made by limiting economic competition rather than producing a superior product or service; in perfect economic competition, there are no rents. Exclusionary foreign policies are designed to limit economic competition and secure rents. States can choose to pursue exclusionary foreign policies by projecting military power to coercively bargain over or conquer stocks of resources, gaining control of future flows of rents.[18] Alternatively, states can seek rents by pursuing a mercantilist policy of limiting access to resource markets, thus producing monopoly or

[14] See Eric J. Hamilton and Brian C. Rathbun, "Scarce Differences: Toward a Material and Systemic Foundation for Offensive and Defensive Realism," *Security Studies* 22 (2013): 436–465; Hans J. Morgenthau, *Politics among Nations: The Struggle for Power and Peace* (New York: Knopf, 1948); Stephen D. Krasner, *Defending the National Interest: Raw Materials Investments and US Foreign Policy* (Princeton, NJ: Princeton University Press, 1978).

[15] Macartan Humphreys, "Natural Resources, Conflict, and Conflict Resolution: Uncovering the Mechanisms," *Journal of Conflict Resolution* 49 (2005): 508–37; Paul Collier and Anke Hoeffler, "Testing the Neocon Agenda: Democracy in Resource-Rich Societies," *European Economic Review* 53 (2009): 293–308.

[16] Colgan, *Petro-Aggression*.

[17] Gordon Tullock, "Rent Seeking as a Zero-Sum Game," in *Toward a Theory of the Rent-Seeking Society*, ed. James M. Buchanan, Robert D. Tollison, and Gordon Tullock (College Station: Texas A&M University Press, 1980).

[18] Frederic C. Lane, *Profits from Power: Readings in Protection Rent and Violence-Controlling Enterprises* (Albany: SUNY Press, 1979), 15.

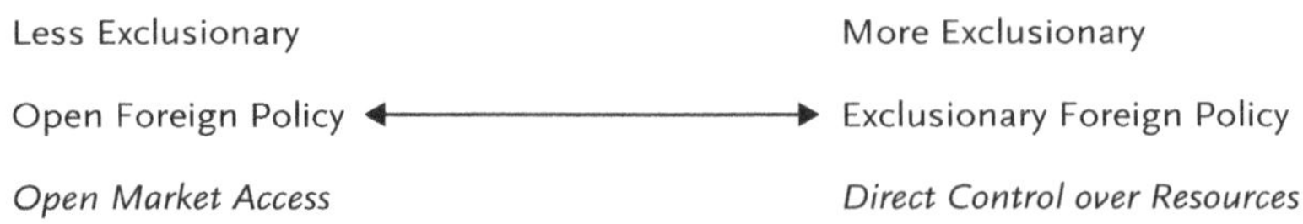

FIGURE 13.1 The Exclusionary Policy Continuum

oligopoly rents. This chapter focuses on explaining variation in the strength of states' preferences to directly control stocks of resources; however, the theory I've developed can also explain why states choose mercantilist foreign policies.

Broadly speaking, my theory is designed to explain why states employ coercion to secure resources via open or exclusionary foreign policies.[19] All policies fall somewhere along a continuum, with open and exclusionary foreign policies representing ideal types. This is illustrated in Figure 13.1.

Explaining Exclusionary Policy Preferences

I argue that states possess stronger preferences to pursue more exclusionary foreign policies when at least one of two conditions hold: (1) the state has autocratic political institutions; (2) the state has land-oriented economic interests. States that meet either of these conditions will be more likely to employ coercion to pursue exclusionary foreign policies because they will enjoy greater gains from doing so.

My theory is built on three core assumptions:

1. Those who govern the state seek to remain in power.
2. In order to remain in power, they must maintain the support of their domestic political coalitions.[20]
3. The individuals in the coalitions seek to maximize their consumptions of goods.

From these assumptions, I derive the following proposition: States use coercion to secure goods for their domestic political supporters.[21] The set of goods they wish to pursue represents their foreign policy interests.

My central claim is that states' foreign policy interests are driven by the characteristics of their domestic political coalitions. These characteristics are determined by two variables: the state's domestic political institutions, which determine the degree to which the coalition is representative of societal

[19] I borrow the concept of open and exclusionary foreign policies from Leo J. Blanken, *Rational Empires: Institutional Incentives and Imperial Expansion* (Chicago: University of Chicago Press, 2012).
[20] A coalition is a group of individuals whom the state relies upon to stay in power.
[21] Bruce Bueno de Mesquita et al., *The Logic of Political Survival* (Cambridge, MA: MIT Press, 2003).

interests, and the economic interests of the coalition members, which are influenced by their sources of income. The representativeness of the coalition is theoretically continuous; however, for simplicity, I refer to them as either broad or narrow. Following work in comparative politics on the effect of domestic political institutions on the distribution of goods, less representative coalitions (autocracies) will seek to narrowly distribute goods to the members of their small governing coalition.[22] Conversely, states with more representative coalitions (democracies) will prefer to broadly distribute goods.[23]

Beyond the representativeness of the coalition, it is also critical to understand the actors in the coalition and what their interests may be.[24] In terms of economic interests, there are two ideal types of coalitions: coalitions that are totally dependent on trade in manufactured goods and services, which I will call production-oriented coalitions, and coalitions that are dependent on extracting wealth derived from the control of land, which I will call land-oriented coalitions.

States that rely on revenues from the control of land should be more likely to use coercion to secure territory and resources. In contrast, states that rely on manufactured goods and services should be less interested in securing direct control of resources and more interested in ensuring access to resource markets. But why can't states that rely on extracting wealth from land substitute and invest in manufactured goods and services? They can, but it is costly for three reasons: *entrenched interests*, the *costs of substitution*, and *political benefits* associated with resource wealth. Each of these mechanisms makes it more difficult for states to diversify their governing coalition.

Groups become *entrenched interests* by creating rules and institutions that solidify their hold on power, limit the profitability and influence of the political opposition, and increase their own profits. They then reinvest the profits gleaned from their investments into securing additional political influence, further strengthening their control of the state.

Governments and members of their coalitions also face *costs of substitution*. Production-oriented coalitions prefer policies that increase returns in their own sector of the economy: intellectual property rights, universities, and investment in basic research and development. In contrast, land-oriented coalitions will invest in building the infrastructure required to extract resources and bring them to market—pipelines, refineries, liquefied natural gas terminals—and underinvest in infrastructure needed for production of other goods and

---

[22] Phillip Roeder, *Red Sunset: The Failure of Soviet Politics* (Princeton, NJ: Princeton University Press, 1993); Susan L. Shirk, *The Political Logic of Economic Reform in China* (Berkeley: University of California Press, 1993).

[23] David A. Lake and Matthew A. Baum, "The Invisible Hand of Democracy: Political Control and the Provision of Public Services," *Comparative Political Studies* 34 (2001): 587–621; Matthew A. Baum and David A. Lake, "The Political Economy of Growth: Democracy and Human Capital," *American Journal of Political Science* 47 (2003): 333–347; Bueno de Mesquita et al., *The Logic of Political Survival.*

[24] Jessica Weeks, "Strongmen and Straw Men: Authoritarian Regimes and the Initiation of International Conflict," *American Political Science Review* 106 (2012): 326–47.

services.[25] Underdevelopment increases costs of substitute investments for two reasons: first, because of high fixed costs (i.e., investment in infrastructure and education); second, because there are high opportunity costs associated with the time until returns are realized.

For an illustration, consider Russia's recent difficulties in building its own Silicon Valley.[26] Having spent years underinvesting in education, basic research, and development, Russia cannot quickly shift to generating innovation in science and technology. Infrastructure and human capital must be built in order for a country to derive wealth from manufacturing and services, a very costly activity in the short and medium term.

The third and final mechanism concerns the *political benefits* associated with land rents. Land rents may be more attractive to autocracies for several reasons: first, many autocracies lack the capacity to effectively tax their citizens; second, land rents are appropriable goods and can be controlled through coercion; and third, land rents can be targeted to supporters and denied to opponents.[27] This suggests that autocratic, land-oriented states disproportionately benefit from resource rents.

Deriving States' Interests from Ideal Types

I combine the representativeness and economic interests of the state's coalition to generate a typology that explains variation in states' foreign policy interests. Deriving states' interests from the characteristics of their coalitions allows for more precise inferences and facilitates more accurate predictions about policy choices.

I characterize all coalitions as being broad or narrow and production-oriented or land-oriented. I operationalize coalition size using the polity measure of democracy. States that are below a 6 have a narrow coalition, and those above a 6 have a broad coalition, according to my coding.[28] I operationalize land-oriented economic interests by measuring the percentage of state GDP derived from resource rents. States with resource rents above 10 percent of GDP are considered land-oriented, whereas states below this threshold are production-oriented. My approach borrows from previous work that has used

[25] Kenneth L. Sokoloff and Stanley L. Engerman, "History Lessons: Institutions, Factors Endowments, and Paths of Development in the New World," *Journal of Economic Perspectives* 14 (2000): 217–32. On oil rents retarding service sector development, see Nimah Mazaheri, *Oil Booms and Business Busts: Why Resource Wealth Hurts Entrepreneurs* (Oxford: Oxford University Press, 2016).
[26] "Can Russia Create a New Silicon Valley?," *Economist*, July 14, 2012.
[27] "Can Russia Create a New Silicon Valley?"; Daron Acemoglu and James A. Robinson, *Why Nations Fail: The Origins of Power, Prosperity and Poverty* (New York: Crown, 2012); Stephen Brooks, *Producing Security: Multinational Corporations, Globalization, and the Changing Calculus of Conflict* (Princeton, NJ: Princeton University Press, 2005).
[28] Monty Marshall, Keith Jaggers, and Ted R. Gurr, "Polity IV Project: Political Regime Characteristics and Transitions 1800–2010 Dataset Users' Manual," Center for Systemic Peace, www.systemicpeace.org/polity/polity4.htm.

TABLE 13.1 Ideal State Types

	NARROW COALITION	BROAD COALITION
Land-Oriented	Predatory states	Stakeholder states
Production-Oriented	Opportunistic states	Liberal states

TABLE 13.2 Ideal State Types and Predictions of Foreign Policy Behavior

STATE TYPE	LIKELIHOOD OF EMPLOYING COERCION
Liberal	Least likely
Stakeholder	More likely
Opportunistic	More likely
Predatory	Most likely

similar indicators to capture the degree to which a state is a petro- or rentier state.[29]

Combining representativeness and economic interests, there are four ideal types of coalitions and corresponding state types: liberal, stakeholder, opportunistic, and predatory (see Table 13.1). Table 13.2 previews my theoretical predictions regarding which state types will most likely employ coercion to pursue an exclusionary foreign policy. Liberal states should be the least likely to do so, with stakeholder and opportunistic states being more likely, and predatory states being the most likely. I explain the logic behind the state types and why their domestic political coalitions incentivize them to pursue different foreign policies.

Predatory States: Narrow Land-Oriented Coalitions

Narrow coalitions comprising individuals with land-oriented economic interests produce predatory states. *Predatory* denotes their preferred method of maintaining power: extracting land rents and redistributing them to a narrow elite.[30] Like all labels used here, it is *not* intended to confer normative value, nor does it describe their foreign policy behavior. Although predatory states have stronger incentives to pursue territory, it is because of the characteristics of their coalitions, not because they are inherently aggressive.

Because predatory states depend on a small number of political supporters who rely on land to generate wealth, they have strong incentives to pursue additional territory. Appropriating territory allows predatory states to extract

---

[29] Jeff Colgan, "Oil and Revolutionary Governments: Fuel for International Conflict," *International Organization* 64 (2010): 661; Collier and Hoeffler, "Testing the Neocon Agenda."

[30] Thad Dunning, "Resource Dependence, Economic Performance, and Political Stability," *Journal of Conflict Resolution* 49 (2005): 451–82.

and redistribute goods to their supporters and buy off their opposition. Thus I expect predatory states to pursue exclusionary foreign policies.

Putin's Russia, Saddam's Iraq, and Gaddafi's Libya are examples of autocratic petrostates where physical control of territory is or was key to keeping the regime in power. There is empirical evidence to suggest petrostates are more *willing* to act as the aggressor in militarized interstate disputes and are more likely to engage in conflict than non-petrostates.[31] The Iran-Iraq War, Iraq's annexation of Kuwait, and Russia's recent behavior in the Arctic are all examples of predatory states employing coercion to gain control over territory.[32]

The foregoing discussion implies the following hypothesis:

> H1: Predatory states will be the most likely to use coercion to pursue exclusionary policies.

Liberal States: Broad Production-Oriented Coalitions

Coalitions that are broad and production-oriented give rise to liberal states, which should pursue policies that secure access to resources and broadly benefit their societies. To continue the oil example, ensuring the free flow of oil (access) to resource markets keeps prices lower than if they were market-restricted. The citizens of production-oriented states benefit because it keeps the price of inputs lower, lowering the cost of both production and consumer goods.

One example of a liberal state pursuing these policies is the United States. Historically, as the United States moved from a land-based economy to one that was dependent on industry and services, its government shifted the type of investments it made. In domestic and economic policy, this meant focusing on intellectual property rights, universities, and public education. In foreign policy, instead of focusing on the control of territory, the United States focused on facilitating *its citizens'* economic interests, pursuing secure sea lanes and access to markets. Ensuring market access can encompass many foreign policy behaviors, from lowering trade barriers to ensuring that no actor uses military power to threaten markets.

For states that wish to maintain access to resource markets, military coercion is principally useful for deterring actors that seek to limit access. For example, from 1945 to 1971, Britain, a liberal state, maintained a military presence in the Middle East to deter other states from limiting its access to oil.[33]

---

[31] Colgan, *Petro-Aggression*, 8.

[32] For more on Russia in the Arctic, see Jonathan N. Markowitz, "When and Why States Project Power" (Ph.D. dissertation, University of California, San Diego, 2014), chapter 4.

[33] Joshua Rovner and Caitlin Talmadge, "Hegemony, Force Posture, and the Provision of Public Goods: The Once and Future Role of Outside Powers in Securing Persian Gulf Oil," *Security Studies* 23 (2014): 568.

In January 1980, the United States adopted a similar policy through the Carter Doctrine, threatening the use of military force to deter threats to the free movement of Middle East oil.[34] The United States has projected military power into the Middle East for over 40 years, but it has rarely sought to directly control the land rents, despite their enormous value.

Although I expect liberal states will generally facilitate access to resource markets, this does not mean they will not sometimes pursue exclusionary policies. However, on balance, liberal states should be more restrained because the characteristics of their coalitions make such policies costly: production-oriented states are generally more economically interdependent, and therefore their interests are more sensitive to retaliation from other states.[35] Additionally, liberal states should be more restrained in seeking rents at society's expense because democratic institutions lower the cost of punishing the government for pursuing suboptimal policies.

The previous discussion implies Hypothesis 2:

H2: Liberal states will be the least likely to pursue exclusionary policies.

Stakeholder States: Broad Land-Oriented Coalitions

Broad coalitions with land-oriented economic interests produce stakeholder states. These states extract rents from territory and broadly distribute them. The citizens of these states are essentially stakeholders in governing the state's resources and enjoy dividends from the resource rents, which are broadly redistributed to society in the form of public-regarded goods, such as education, health care, and infrastructure.

An illustrative example of the stakeholder type is Norway. Norway's economy is relatively dependent on resources, as resource rents represent 12 to 14 percent of its GDP. However, Norway has invested its wealth in public education, research and development, healthcare, and a generous social safety net for its citizens; it has also created the world's largest sovereign wealth fund to ensure that its citizens will continue to enjoy these benefits long after it has exhausted its natural resources reserves.

Because stakeholder states generate wealth from resource extraction, I expect them to have a stronger incentive to secure additional stocks of resources than liberal states have. This may explain why Norway has focused much of its foreign policy on expanding its maritime territorial boundaries. This policy has been so successful that today it controls an exclusive economic

---

[34] Rovner and Talmadge, "Hegemony, Force Posture, and the Provision of Public Goods." Also see Gholz and Press, "Protecting the Prize."

[35] See Drezner's chapter in this volume.

zone (EEZ; and resources beneath) seven times larger than the state of Norway itself.[36]

Although stakeholder states have a stronger preference than liberal states to coercively compete over resource rents, I expect them to have a weaker preference to do so than predatory states, because resource rents captured through coercion are broadly distributed. Citizens in stakeholder states can also punish the government if the rents captured are not larger than the costs associated with pursuing exclusionary foreign policies.

The implication is that stakeholder states should have a weaker incentive than predatory states to pursue exclusive policies. Stakeholder states will employ coercion to compete over resource rents when the expected gains are large enough to compensate their large, land-oriented coalitions.

This leads to the following hypothesis:

> H3: Stakeholder states are more likely than liberal states to use coercion to pursue exclusionary policies, but less likely than predatory states.

Opportunistic States: Narrow Production-Oriented Coalitions

Narrow coalitions dependent on manufactured goods and services produce opportunistic states. The state distributes goods among a narrow elite, and economic interests of the individuals in the coalition motivate the government to ensure access to resources in a manner that captures rents for narrow interests or firms in the coalition. Opportunistic states view resources as both an input for their production-oriented economies and a way to generate rents for the elite.

I expect an opportunistic state to pursue a policy of resource mercantilism, seeking preferential access to foreign markets and excluding others from making these investments.

For example, opportunistic states might secure access to resources by encouraging state-backed firms to extract resources in regions with high risk and high return. This allows investors in state-backed firms to capture the returns, while society at large pays the costs if the investments are appropriated.[37]

An illustrative example is China. China's coalition is narrow and production-oriented, and it pursues mercantilist foreign policies in Africa and Central Asia designed to secure access to resources for individual Chinese companies.[38]

---

[36] Norwegian Ministry of Foreign Affairs, "The High North Visions and Strategies," (2011), 13, https://www.regjeringen.no/en/dokumenter/high_north_visions_strategies/id664906.

[37] Weiyi Shi, "Rent Capture, Moral Hazard, and Risk-Taking Abroad: Evidence from Chinese Outbound Direct Investments," working paper (University of California, San Diego, 2014).

[38] Erica Downs, "The Fact and Fiction of Sino-African Energy Relations," *China Security* 3 (2007): 42–68; Deborah Brautigam and Tang Xiaoyang, "African Shenzhen: China's Special Economic Zones in Africa," *Journal of Modern African Studies* 49 (2011): 34.

China has also employed coercion to compete over the direct control of resource rents in the South and East China Sea.

As in China, opportunistic states seek rents because they can socialize the costs while concentrating the benefits. For this reason, I expect opportunistic states to engage in exclusionary foreign policies more often than liberal states do. However, because of their production-oriented coalitions, opportunistic states should be less willing than predatory states to pursue exclusionary policies because they are better able to generate wealth from production. This does not mean that opportunistic states will be less rent-seeking than predatory states, but rather that they are less willing to seek rents through the direct control of resources.

The previous discussion allows us to derive Hypothesis 4:

> H4: Opportunistic states are more likely than liberal states to use coercion to pursue exclusionary polices, but less likely than predatory states.

Expected versus Observed Outcomes: Comparing My Predictions with Colgan's

Although there is not sufficient space for an appropriate test of my theory against all its competitors, I briefly illustrate how my claims compare to those of Colgan. I begin by demonstrating how my theory addresses shortcomings associated with Colgan's explanation.

Colgan's pioneering work, *Petro-Aggression: When Oil Causes War*, explores the relationship among oil wealth, revolutionary leaders, and aggressive foreign policy behavior. He writes, "If states are simply fighting over access to oil, it is not clear why the states that are already oil rich should be so aggressive."[39] His answer is that revolutionary leaders are more likely to have aggressive preferences and that oil makes states more powerful and reduces accountability, making it easier for leaders to engage in aggression. This is a powerful explanation and one that has advanced the study of the effect of resource wealth on conflict.

However, the explanation has several limitations. First, it is not clear why leaders *want* to be aggressive, other than that revolutionary leaders are more risk-acceptant. They may take on greater risk for some reward, but what is the reward? Generally, aggression is used to further some objective of the state. Colgan essentially assumes that revolutionary leaders have aggressive preferences, but he is unclear about what leaders want to obtain with their aggression. Second, by Colgan's definition, the United States is a highly aggressive state, but his theory cannot explain why, as it is neither a revolutionary state

[39] Colgan, *Petro-Aggression*, 3.

nor a petrostate.[40] Third, Colgan cannot explain why states like Russia, which is a petrostate but does not have a revolutionary leader, have chosen to pursue an aggressive foreign policy. These problems stem from the inability of Colgan's theory to explain the foreign policy objectives that states seek to pursue using aggression.

My theory can address these shortcomings. By using resource rents to explain why some states have more aggressive foreign policy preferences, I demonstrate why Colgan's puzzle is not a puzzle at all: resource-dependent states are not interested in fighting over access to oil but rather to secure control over additional stores of resource rent. Additionally, democratic non-petrostates like the United States project power to the Middle East to deter and defend against threats that might dramatically increase the price of oil. My theory is capable of explaining why states employ coercion to pursue different objectives, not just why they are more or less aggressive generally. I am able to do this because my framework allows me to deduce states' interests from the characteristics of their coalitions and make strong predictions about their foreign policy objectives, regardless of whether they are petro- or revolutionary states.

Competing Predictions

Both my theory and Colgan's theory have implications for policymakers who want to know where resource competition is likely to occur and how rising powers are likely to behave with regard to resources. My theory predicts that the Middle East will continue to be rife with coercive competition over resource rents, as the region is populated by a number of predatory states: Iran, Saudi Arabia, Iraq, Egypt, and the United Arab Emirates. These governments are extremely dependent on oil as a source of wealth, with resource rents making up between a quarter and a half of many states' total GDP. Most of the leaders of these states are beholden to small coalitions and need to keep them loyal with profits extracted from the oil and gas that lie beneath the desert sand.

In the Middle East, more than anywhere in the world, wealth is still derived from the physical control of territory, and perhaps more important, it can be appropriated by military force. These conditions explain why Middle Eastern states invest heavily in building military capabilities to protect their wealth from both domestic and international challengers.

In contrast to Colgan, I predict that Middle Eastern states will continue to coercively compete over oil long after individuals associated with revolutions have passed away. The Iranian Revolution occurred over forty years ago, and yet Iran continues to invest in power projection capabilities via both conventional means, such as its ballistic missile program, and unconventional means,

[40] Colgan defines petrostates as those whose oil rents exceed 10 percent of GDP; U.S. oil rents equal less than one percent of GDP in 2012, the last year for which data are available. See "Oil Rents (% of GDP)," World Bank, http://data.worldbank.org/indicator/NY.GDP.PETR.RT.ZS.

such as its support of paramilitary groups and its nuclear weapons program. Although we may rarely observe actual wars over territory, as occurred during the 1980s between Iran and Iraq, it does not mean that states are not engaging in military competition, either through conventional means, such as arming, or unconventional means, such as backing factions in civil conflicts in Syria or Iraq.[41]

The preference of the predatory states in the region is to maximize resource rents, and the appropriable nature of those rents drives the level of geopolitical competition higher.[42] This explains why Saudi Arabia, a state that never had a revolutionary government, spends more on defense as a percentage of GDP than any other state except Oman, another Middle Eastern predatory state, and South Sudan, an African predatory state involved in a conflict over oil.[43] Excluding China, Saudi Arabia is the state with the greatest increase in defense spending from 2004 to 2013. These expenditures represent not just domestic repressive capabilities but also expensive power projection assets, including Riyadh's $30 billion purchase of F-15SA air superiority and strike aircraft in 2011.[44]

The Middle East is not the only region where powerful predatory states will coercively compete over the division of resource rents. Russia is the world's most powerful predatory state, with a GDP that grew from $340 billion to over $2.1 trillion in the past decade. Russia's autocratic political institutions and land-oriented economic interests give it a stronger preference to pursue exclusionary policies. Its projection of power to compete over Arctic seabed resources and its recent annexation of Crimea are illustrative of its exclusionary impulses. It has plunged its newfound wealth into modernizing its military and acquiring greater power projection capabilities, as Moscow has more than doubled its defense spending in recent years.[45]

I once again contrast with Colgan, whose theory suggests that Russia should not be more aggressive than the average petrostate, given that Vladimir Putin is not a revolutionary leader; Russia has behaved exactly as my theory predicts. As a predatory state, it has a stronger preference to coercively compete over territory, as it is a source of goods that can be redistributed to the elite. The real prize in annexing Crimea may be the offshore reserves of oil and gas that exist in the Black Sea. This offshore area is three times larger than Crimea and

---

[41] Emma Ashford, "The Foreign Policy of Oil-Exporting States" (Ph.D. dissertation, University of Virginia, 2014), chapter 5.

[42] In equilibrium, we are unlikely to observe wars because states in this region understand each other's predatory preferences and have invested heavily in deterring territorial aggrandizement. The United States has also made it clear that it will not tolerate one state dominating Middle East energy reserves. The absence of war does not mean that relations are peaceful or noncompetitive.

[43] "Military Expenditure (% of GDP)," World Bank, http://data.worldbank.org/indicator/MS.MIL.XPND.GD.ZS?order=wbapi_data_value_2012+wbapi_data_value+wbapi_data_value-last&sort=desc.

[44] Devin Dwyer, "White House, Saudi Arabia Sign $30B F-15 Deal," *ABC News*, December 29, 2011, http://abcnews.go.com/blogs/politics/2011/12/white-house-saudi-arabia-sign-30b-f-15-deal/.

[45] "Arms and the Man: The Countries Spending the Most on Their Military," *Economist*, April 15, 2014, http://www.economist.com/blogs/graphicdetail/2014/04/daily-chart-9.

has allowed Russia to claim an additional 36,000 square miles of EEZ. More important, prior to the annexation, it had been the focus of energy exploration by Exxon, Royal Dutch Shell, and other companies, with some experts estimating that the reserves could be as large as those in the North Sea. Russian companies had also taken an interest in exploring the Black Sea, but the Russian area was not considered as promising as the area within Ukraine's EEZ.

Geologists have suggested that the annexation of Crimea gives Russia control of the most valuable oil reserves in the Black Sea,[46] though it is too early to assess the size of the reserves or what the returns will be. Russia's annexation of Crimea may prove costly, and it may even be a net loss to Russia's citizens, but as long as ex ante Russian leaders believed it would benefit the ruling elite, Moscow's behavior is consistent with my theoretical expectations.

Colgan and I also differ on how we expect states like China to behave. China is not a petrostate or governed by a revolutionary leader, and therefore, according to Colgan's theory, it should be no more aggressive than liberal democratic states. In contrast, my theory suggests that China's autocratic political institutions incentivize it to pursue goods that will benefit a small ruling elite. This gives China a stronger preference for pursuing exclusionary foreign policies. However, China also has a production-oriented economy and is heavily dependent on access to foreign energy as an input to the production of goods and services. Therefore I expect China to secure access to resources while simultaneously generating rents for a narrow elite.

China's preference to pursue exclusionary policies is illustrated by its recent behavior in the East and South China Sea. These policies are often veiled by energy security or nationalism but have the potential to generate rents for a narrow elite through appropriating control of undersea resource reserves.[47] This might explain why China has been willing to project power and burn political capital to secure control of resources reserves that are not large enough to solve its demands for foreign energy supplies.

Summary

I began this chapter with two puzzles: Why do some states use coercion to secure access to or control over resources rather than rely on markets? Why are some states more interested in securing open-market access as opposed to direct control over resources? My theory suggests that the answer to the first question is that states employ coercion because they believe other actors may

---

[46] William J. Broad, "In Taking Crimea, Putin Gains a Sea of Fuel Reserves," *New York Times*, May 18, 2014, http://www.nytimes.com/2014/05/18/world/europe/in-taking-crimea-putin-gains-a-sea-of-fuel-reserves.html?hp&_r=0.

[47] Ian Storey, "China's Bilateral and Multilateral Diplomacy in the South China Sea," in *Cooperation from Strength: The United States, China and South China Sea*, ed. Patrick M. Cronin (Washington, DC: Center for a New American Security, 2012); Jeff Himmelman, "A Game of Shark and Minnow," *New York Times*, October 27, 2013, http://www.nytimes.com/newsgraphics/2013/10/27/south-china-sea/.

interfere with markets. Indeed, military competition over the direct control of resource reserves has historically disrupted energy markets, limiting access to resources.

This brings us to the second part of the puzzle: Why do some states prefer to compete over control of rather than access to resource rents? The more autocratic and economically dependent on resource rents a state is, the stronger its interest will be in controlling additional resource reserves. In contrast, the more democratic and economically dependent on the production of goods and services a state is, the more interested it will be in securing access to resources as a source of inputs.

This answer follows from my theory of foreign policy, which suggests that states will employ coercion to secure goods and that the set of goods they are interested in will be conditioned by the characteristics of their governing coalitions. The proposition that liberal states are more likely to pursue open foreign policies may seem like an obvious one, but what is less obvious is what makes states liberal in the first place. Some have suggested that this is a story that is purely about regime type. However, theories that focus on regime type alone cannot explain why so few democracies chose to pursue open foreign policies in the nineteenth and early twentieth century. Conversely, theories that focus on whether states are capitalist or trading states cannot explain why some, such as China, choose to pursue exclusionary foreign policies. By incorporating both regime type and economic structure, my theory is able to explain why some democracies will be more interested in controlling territory and why some trading states will still prefer to pursue exclusionary foreign policies.

My theory contributes to this volume's core mission of enriching our understanding of coercion and international politics in two ways: it allows us to identify ex ante different types of coalitions and their corresponding interests, and we can now predict which states should have a stronger interest in employing coercive diplomacy before they act on those interests. This is an improvement over existing theories that incorporate either domestic coalitions or ideal types to predict state behavior. Empirical tests will be the arbiter of whether my theory or its competitors can better explain state behavior. In other work, I take the first steps toward assessing my theory against its competitors with a set of quantitative and qualitative tests.[48]

---

[48] Jonathan N. Markowitz and Christopher J. Fariss, "Power, Proximity, and Democracy: Geopolitical Competition in the International System," *Journal of Peace Research*, forthcoming; Jonathan N. Markowitz, "Arctic Shock: Utilizing Climate Change to Test Theories of Resource Competition," paper presented at the annual meeting of the American Political Science Association, Washington, DC, August 28–31, 2014.

PART V | Nuclear Coercion

CHAPTER 14

Deliberate Escalation

Nuclear Strategies to Deter or to Stop Conventional Attacks

JASEN J. CASTILLO

IN JANUARY 2016 IRAN and the P5+1 countries (United States, United Kingdom, France, Russia, China, and Germany) implemented the Joint Comprehensive Plan of Action, which seeks to prevent Iran from developing a nuclear weapons program. In exchange for an end to crippling sanctions, Iran agreed to physical constraints and verification provisions that hamper its ability to produce the fissile material required for nuclear weapons over the next 10 to 15 years.[1] For now, the agreement has tempered anxieties over an Iranian nuclear program. These worries focus on how an ambitious—often characterized as reckless—regime in Tehran could use nuclear weapons to dominate the Middle East. An Iranian bomb could also convince neighboring states to acquire nuclear arsenals of their own.[2] In particular, the prospect of Iran acquiring nuclear weapons highlights a growing strategic problem for the United States: opponents seeking nuclear capabilities to offset U.S. superiority in conventional capabilities. Iran's quest for nuclear weapons could reflect several motives, but shielding itself from regime change by the U.S. military surely plays a central role.[3]

As the number of nuclear-armed states increases, the ability of the United States to project power into a region could become more difficult.[4] Not only will the United States need to consider the conventional balance when planning for

---

[1] For an overview of the agreement, see Gary Samore, *The Iran Nuclear Deal: A Definitive Guide* (Cambridge, MA: Belfer Center for Science and International Security, August 2015).

[2] A representative view is Eric S. Edelman, Andrew F. Krepinevich, and Evan Braden Montgomery, "Dangers of a Nuclear Iran: The Limits of Containment," *Foreign Affairs* 90 (January 2011): 66–82.

[3] Scott D. Sagan, "Why Do States Build Nuclear Weapons? Three Models in Search of a Bomb," *International Security* 21 (Winter 1996–97): 54–86.

[4] Outlining the difficulties posed by a nuclear-armed regional power is Barry Posen, "U.S. Security Policy in a Nuclear-Armed World (Or: What If Iraq Had Had Nuclear Weapons?)," *Security Studies* 6 (Spring 1997): 1–31.

regional intervention, but it will also need to evaluate the balance of nuclear forces. Any U.S. effort to defend its friends and allies, therefore, must begin by asking how and under what conditions these potential nuclear-armed adversaries might use their nuclear weapons in a conflict. Specifically, policymakers and military planners must consider how these possible opponents could use nuclear weapons to deter U.S. intervention, how these weapons could affect stability, and how escalation could take place during a conflict.

To better understand these problems, this chapter addresses the following questions: What strategies could nuclear weapon states—outside of the U.S. security umbrella—adopt to deter conventional attacks? If deterrence fails, how would they use nuclear weapons to compel an attacker to back down? If nuclear use occurs, can combatants control further escalation?

These questions should interest policymakers and scholars trying to understand how states outside the U.S. security umbrella might use nuclear weapons in their defense planning. Already the ranks of nuclear weapons states not afforded protection from the United States include Russia, China, India, Pakistan, and North Korea. Because their ranks might grow in the future, policymakers and scholars need a framework to explore the full range of nuclear strategies these states could adopt for deterrence and, if necessary, defense. This information could also shed light on the choices they make about nuclear command and control arrangements, both day-to-day as well as during a crisis. In a crisis, these nuclear powers could decide to improve the survivability of their nuclear forces by dispersing them and by pre-delegating use authority to local commanders. Although these measures increase the odds that a country's nuclear forces will survive a disarming attack, they also increase the chances of accidental use and theft.[5]

To address these questions, this chapter presents a framework for understanding the potential deterrence and defense strategies of nuclear powers outside of the U.S. security umbrella. Building on what has been learned about compellence and deterrence since the Cold War, the framework outlines potential strategies, shows the conditions under which countries could adopt them, and unpacks the implications for the control of escalation if nuclear use occurs. Based on a few simple assumptions, the framework outlines the likely strategic choices of nuclear powers by examining the capabilities available to them and the international military threats they face. The framework provides a baseline for analysts to assess the deterrence strategies of nuclear powers, a subject suffering from very little reliable data. Baselines are starting points. Although a variety of factors likely influence the deterrence strategies of nuclear powers, it seems reasonable to start with their security environment as a first cut to understanding this puzzle.

[5] See the description of the 2001–02 crisis between India and Pakistan in Steve Coll, "The Stand-Off: How Jihadi Groups Helped Provoke the Twenty-First Century's First Nuclear Crisis," *New Yorker*, February 13 2006, http://www.newyorker.com/archive/2006/02/13/060213fa_fact_coll.

By necessity, this type of analysis is more theoretical than empirical.[6] One cannot draw on many historical cases of conventional conflicts between nuclear-armed powers, the strategies of today's nuclear powers remain purposefully vague, and their behavior could change in a conflict. Social science theory can often shed light on policy issues with little data. The study of coercion has frequently employed this technique. For example, during the Cold War, analysts often relied on conceptual approaches to grapple with phenomena that lacked historical examples, like the effect of nuclear weapons on international politics, nuclear war termination, and inadvertent escalation.[7] In this volume, Lindsay and Gartzke's chapter on cyber warfare takes a similar approach by applying the familiar stability-instability paradox from the nuclear realm to the domain of cyber security to speculate on future threats.

Using this theoretical framework, this chapter makes five arguments about the deterrence strategies of nuclear-armed powers outside of the U.S. security umbrella. First, the fewer conventional options are available for defense, the greater the role nuclear weapons will play in a country's security strategy and the earlier their use in a conflict. Second, less capable nuclear powers will rely on a strategy of *limited nuclear options* (LNOs) to deter or to stop conventional attacks. Such a strategy envisions forcing an attacker to back down by threatening or carrying out limited but painful strikes, while at the same time raising the risk that nuclear escalation will get out of hand. Third, more capable nuclear powers will adopt more ambitious deterrence strategies that aim to defeat an attacker militarily rather than scaring it off. Some will pursue a *counterconventional* strategy: using nuclear weapons to stymie a conventional attack. Others will pursue the more bold strategy of *flexible response*: using nuclear weapons to deny an attacker's war aims anywhere on the escalation ladder, including strikes on an adversary's nuclear forces.

Fourth, in the long term, if nuclear powers confront increasing conventional threats, they will pursue greater nuclear weapons capabilities as a way to increase their options for escalation. In the grave circumstance wherein the conventional military balance begins to become increasingly unfavorable, nuclear powers will need to rely more on nuclear weapons to compensate. Quantitative and qualitative improvements in a nuclear arsenal enable a nuclear power to hold more and different targets at risk. A better command and control system allows greater flexibility in planning. More importantly, with

[6] For examples of security studies research that focuses on generating rather than testing theoretical frameworks, see Michael C. Desch, "War and Strong States, Peace and Weak States?," *International Organization* 50 (Spring 1996): 237–68; Stephen Van Evera, "Hypotheses on Nationalism and War," *International Security* 18 (Spring 1994): 5–39; Jasen J. Castillo, "Nuclear Terrorism: Why Deterrence Still Matters," *Current History* 102 (December 2003): 426–31.

[7] Thomas C. Schelling, *Arms and Influence* (New Haven, CT: Yale University Press, 1966); Robert Jervis, *The Meaning of the Nuclear Revolution: Statecraft and the Prospect for Armageddon* (Ithaca, NY: Cornell University Press, 1989); George H. Quester, "War Termination and Nuclear Targeting Strategy," in *Strategic Nuclear Targeting*, ed. Desmond Ball and Jeffrey Richelson (Ithaca, NY: Cornell University Press, 1986): 285–306; Barry R. Posen, *Inadvertent Escalation: Conventional Wars and Nuclear Risks* (Ithaca, NY: Cornell University Press, 1990).

better nuclear weapons capabilities and more options for escalation, a state will improve the credibility of its threat to use nuclear weapons first in conventional conflict. In the eyes of a potential attacker, the more options a nuclear-armed power possesses for escalation, the more likely it could use them in a war. Fifth, during conventional conflicts with these states, nuclear escalation could erupt along multiple pathways. Not only could the prospect of losing a conventional war persuade a nuclear power to deliberately use nuclear weapons, but the potential for inadvertent as well as accidental escalation will increase with the intensity and duration of a conflict.

This chapter builds on well-known theories of nuclear deterrence and engages several of the major themes of this volume. Echoing Austin Long's argument about the central role intelligence plays in deterrence, analysts can use the theoretical framework to deduce indicators that could help guide collection efforts aimed at understanding a country's nuclear strategy. Both this chapter and Tristan Volpe's share a concern about how a country credibly communicates its nuclear weapons capabilities. Like several essays (Downes, Fraiman, Greenhill, and Haun), this chapter examines the coercive strategies of the weak or asymmetric coercion. The discussion here also reinforces Todd Sechser's warnings about the overreach of the strong, especially in terms of pathways to nuclear escalation in a conventional conflict.

Nuclear Weapon States outside the U.S. Security Umbrella

Only a small part of the policy and scholarly literature on nuclear weapons focuses on the strategies nuclear powers outside the U.S. security umbrella might pursue for deterrence and defense.[8] Recently, analysts have turned their attention to the prospects for stability of a world with multiple nuclear weapons states.[9] At the moment, five such countries live outside the U.S. security

---

[8] Notable exceptions include Vipin Narang, *Nuclear Strategy in the Modern Era: Regional Powers and International Conflict* (Princeton, NJ: Princeton University Press, 2014); Vipin Narang, "What Does It Take to Deter? Regional Power, Nuclear Postures and International Conflict," *Journal of Conflict Resolution* 57 (June 2013): 478–508; Vipin Narang, "Posturing for Peace? Pakistan's Nuclear Postures and South Asian Stability," *International Security* 34 (Winter 2009–10): 38–78; Caitlin Talmadge, "Assessing the Risk of Chinese Nuclear Escalation in a Conventional War with the United States," *International Security* 41 (Spring 2017) : 50-92. Fiona S. Cunningham and M. Taylor Fravel, "Assuring Assured Retaliation: China's Nuclear Posture and U.S.-China Strategic Stability," *International Security* 40 (Fall 2015): 7–50; M. Taylor Fravel and Evan S. Medeiros, "China's Search for Assured Retaliation: The Evolution of Chinese Nuclear Strategy and Force Structure," *International Security* 35 (Fall 2010): 48–87; Jeffrey Lewis, *The Minimum Means of Reprisal: China's Search for Security in the Nuclear Age* (Cambridge, MA: MIT Press, 2007).

[9] See Brad Roberts, *The Case for U.S. Nuclear Weapons in the 21st Century* (Palo Alto, CA: Stanford University Press, 2016); Keir A. Lieber and Daryl G. Press, "The New Era of Counterforce: Technological Change and the Future of Nuclear Deterrence," *International Security* 41 (Spring 2017): 9-49; Keir A. Lieber and Daryl G. Press, "The End of MAD? The Nuclear Dimension of U.S. Primacy," *International Security* 30 (Spring 2006): 7–44; Keir A. Lieber and Daryl G. Press, "The Nukes We Need: Preserving the American Deterrent," *Foreign Affairs* 88 (November–December 2009): 39–51; T. V. Paul, Patrick Morgan, and James J. Wirtz, eds., *Complex Deterrence: Strategy in a Global Age* (Chicago: University of Chicago Press, 2009).

umbrella: Russia, China, India, Pakistan, and North Korea. These states do not seem eager to follow the U.S. lead to create a world of zero nuclear weapons.[10] Currently, Iran appears intent on joining the ranks of these regional nuclear powers but still lacks nuclear weapons capabilities.

These nuclear weapon states share three characteristics relevant to their national security. Most important, they do not live under the safety of the U.S. nuclear umbrella. They cannot depend on U.S. security guarantees, either as formal alliances, such as NATO provides for the United Kingdom and France, or informal commitments, like the historically close ties between the United States and Israel. In addition, they focus more on local security concerns than on projecting military power outside of their region, as the United States routinely does. They might challenge U.S. ability to command the commons, but they cannot usurp it. Third, these nuclear powers face a mixture of conventional and nuclear threats to their security: Russia plans against NATO; India and Pakistan continue to arm against one another; China and India compete for security; and both China and North Korea modernize their respective militaries to counter the U.S. military presence in East Asia.

Fourth, most nuclear-armed states not aligned with the United States will deter nuclear attacks against their cities and other value targets using a strategy of assured retaliation. The possibility of conventional conflict with nuclear-armed opponents means these powers need a survivable retaliatory capability to deter a nuclear attack. States will want an adversary to feel confident that any nuclear attack will result in retaliation. Assured retaliation rests on the following logic: The most credible threat to deter nuclear attacks against a country's population and economic centers is the promise and capability to do the same in return. For this reason, states strive to build nuclear forces capable of surviving a first strike to deliver a costly second strike in retaliation. An assured destruction strategy requires holding hostage what an adversary values most: its cities and the population centers of its allies. With the right delivery vehicles, nuclear forces can cause great damage to an opponent's value targets. A strategy of assured retaliation draws upon the original insight of the nuclear revolution: sometimes the threat of one nuclear weapon reaching its intended target can deter an attacker.[11] Nuclear-armed powers could threaten an attacker's homeland or something else it values, like allies, nearby forces, key ports, or important resources. Survivable forces, of any size, represent the critical element of an assured retaliation strategy.

---

[10] For discussions of this move to "Global Zero," see Matthew Kroenig, "Nuclear Zero? Why Not Nuclear Infinity," *Wall Street Journal*, July 30, 2011; Barry M. Blechman, "Crawling toward Nuclear Zero," *Nonproliferation Review* 18 (2011): 597–600; Nancy W. Gallagher, "International Security on the Road to Nuclear Zero," *Nonproliferation Review* 18 (2011): 431–44.

[11] See also the two essays by Bernard Brodie, "War in the Atomic Age" and "Implications for the Military Policy," in *The Absolute Weapon*, ed. Bernard Brodie (New York: Harcourt, Brace, 1946), 21–110; Kenneth N. Waltz, "Nuclear Myths and Political Realities," *American Political Science Review* 84 (September 1990): 731–45.

Even if the United States puts these nuclear powers in its crosshairs, they can improve the survivability of their arsenals in four ways. First, all of them possess an arsenal of mobile missiles capable of delivering some kind of retaliatory strike. Mobile missiles present an attacker with the same problem they face with submarines, but on land: tracking forces across great expanses make them hard to find. The U.S. experience hunting SCUD missiles during both wars with Iraq supports this view.[12] Second, they could rely on different basing schemes to hide their nuclear forces every day and during a crisis. These could range from underground facilities to previously unknown above-ground bases.[13] Third, to complicate an attacker's planning, nuclear powers could also disperse their nuclear forces in a crisis. Tracking mobile missiles once they leave their garrisons could prove tricky for even the United States.[14] Fourth, nuclear powers could rely on several tactics to thwart an opponent's missile defenses, including nuclear detonations to blind defense radars and saturation attacks with conventional missiles.

Nuclear Strategies to Deter or to Halt Conventional Attacks

How could a nuclear power deter conventional attacks? If deterrence fails, how would it use nuclear weapons to stop a conventional attack? Anticipating what kinds of deterrence strategies these nuclear powers could pursue today remains an important puzzle for U.S. policymakers to solve, as they consider current and future defense planning needs. Although each of these countries publishes official documents on nuclear weapons policy, these declarations fall short in describing the means and ends of specific nuclear strategies. This ambiguity probably reflects a desire to create uncertainty. If these countries drew explicit "redlines"—the conditions under which they would use nuclear weapons—then aggressors might engage in salami tactics, coming right up to drawn lines or stepping slightly over them. Think tanks in these countries write about nuclear strategy, but they often advocate particular strategies rather than describe official policy. Similarly, the absence of a clearly articulated strategy could also reflect debate within a regional nuclear power's security establishment about what kind of nuclear use policies they should follow. On the question of their nuclear strategy, then, states frequently appear like the proverbial black box, with scholars

---

[12] William Rosenau, *Special Operations Forces and Elusive Ground Targets: Lessons from Vietnam and the Persian Gulf War*, MR-1408 (Santa Monica, CA: RAND, 2001). For a more optimistic view using Cold War evidence, see Austin Long and Brendan Rittenhouse Green, "Stalking the Secure Second Strike: Intelligence, Counterforce, and Nuclear Strategy," *Journal of Strategic Studies* 38 (October 2015): 38–73.

[13] See Roger C. Molander and Peter A. Wilson, "On Dealing with the Prospect of Nuclear Chaos," *Washington Quarterly* 17 (1994): 19–39.

[14] Li Bin, "Tracking Chinese Strategic Mobile Missiles," *Science and Global Security* 15 (2007): 1–30.

disagreeing about the strategic intentions of these states.[15] Simply put, analysts lack good data on the specific deterrence strategies of these nuclear powers.

To get past the problem of limited data, this chapter presents a framework for understanding the potential deterrence strategies of nuclear powers outside the U.S. security umbrella. The framework explains the strategic choices of nuclear weapon states by examining the capabilities available to them and the external military threats they face. It builds on realist theories of international politics to generate a set of expectations about how and the conditions under which nuclear powers might try to deter or to defeat conventional attacks.[16]

My framework builds on some of the existing work on the subject. Vipin Narang, for instance, has presented strong evidence for how and why threats of nuclear first use have deterred conventional aggression.[17] He has also outlined a set of deterrence strategies regional powers could adopt. Using a different approach, Taylor Fravel and Evan Meideros offer an explanation for China's current nuclear strategy.[18] This chapter builds on these contributions by outlining a range of strategies these powers could select to deter both conventional attacks and by unpacking what nuclear use would look like if deterrence fails. My framework takes their work a step further by describing the logically available first-use strategies, what they would entail operationally, and who could adopt them.

Like other research in the realist tradition, my framework offers hypotheses connecting the potential causal effects of a regional power's security situation to its nuclear strategies.[19] Without reliable information about how regional nuclear powers craft national security policy, examining how military threats could influence their choices seems like a reasonable first cut to understand what strategies they might adopt. My framework rests on five assumptions familiar to realist theories of international politics: (1) states inhabit an anarchic international system where no central authority exists to guarantee their safety; (2) their primary interest is survival; (3) they remain uncertain about

---

[15] During the Cold War, analysts could not agree on the specific features of Soviet nuclear strategy. A similar lack of consensus exists about China's nuclear strategy. For examples from the Soviet case, see William T. Lee and Richard F. Staar, "Soviet Military Policy since World War II," *International Security* 12 (Winter 1987–88): 190–202; Michael K. MccGwire, *Military Objectives in Soviet Foreign Policy* (Washington, DC: Brookings Institution Press, 1987). For the debate on China, see Fravel and Medeiros, "China's Search for Assured Retaliation"; Marc Schneider, "The Nuclear Forces and Doctrine of the People's Republic of China," *Comparative Strategy* 28 (2009): 244–70.

[16] My baseline framework draws on Kenneth N. Waltz, *Theory of International Politics* (New York: McGraw Hill, 1979); John J. Mearsheimer, *The Tragedy of Great Power Politics* (New York: Norton, 2001); Charles L. Glaser, *Rational Theory of International Politics: The Logic of Competition and Cooperation* (Princeton, NJ: Princeton University Press, 2010).

[17] This results from unpacking what he calls "asymmetric postures." See Narang, "What Does It Take to Deter?" This section also draws on Jasen J. Castillo and Roger Molander, *Flexible Response Revisited: Assessing Pakistan's Potential Nuclear Strategies*, PM-2383 (Santa Monica, CA: RAND, October 2007).

[18] Fravel and Medeiros, "China's Search for Assured Retaliation," 48–87.

[19] For a similar approach applied to the relationship between security competition and nationalism, see Barry R. Posen, "Nationalism and the Mass Army," *International Security* 18 (Fall 1993): 80–124.

the intentions of their neighbors; (4) they possess capabilities to harm one another; and (5) they behave strategically, weighing the costs and benefits of their actions. Under these conditions, states inhabit a self-help world where they must provide for their own security and, as a consequence, worry about their relative military power.[20] In this competitive international system, states imitate and innovate successful strategies. As a result, one should expect nuclear powers to tailor U.S. and Soviet Cold War deterrence strategies to fit their own security circumstances.[21]

The framework, in short, simplifies a complicated problem with minimal data by asking how rational states could rely on nuclear weapons to counter security threats. By no means does the framework aim to explain all the variables influencing the strategic choices of nuclear powers. There are too many possibilities to list and too few data on each of them. Nor does the framework argue that all states behave rationally. It instead provides a baseline for analysis. After understanding how rational states might determine nuclear deterrence strategies, one can vary the framework's assumptions as well as add variables to create alternative hypotheses. However, to manage this difficult puzzle, one should start by examining how a state's security environment could drive its nuclear strategies.

Based on these assumptions, the chapter argues that the most important variables determining the choice of strategies to deter or to stop conventional attacks are the conventional military threats nuclear powers confront and the nuclear weapons capabilities they possess to meet these dangers. The greater the conventional threat a nuclear power faces, the more costly the strategy it will pursue to deter these threats. Similarly, the greater a nuclear power's capabilities, the more strategic options open for it to pursue.

The Degree of the Conventional Military Threat

The destructive effects produced by nuclear weapons, in terms of blast, fire, and prompt radiation, offer countries a formidable capability to protect their national interests. Specifically, nuclear weapons help states offset the military threats posed by an opponent's conventional forces. Nuclear powers face a *high degree of conventional threat* if they lack any credible conventional

---

[20] These assumptions come from Mearsheimer, *The Tragedy of Great Power Politics*, 30–32. Arguably Scott Sagan's "security model" represents a realist framework of nuclear decision-making, but it focuses on the motives for acquiring nuclear weapons rather than how to use them. See Sagan, "Why Do States Build Nuclear Weapons?," 54–86.

[21] On systemic pressures to emulate successful practices see Waltz, *Theory of International Politics*, 127–28; João Resende-Santos, "Anarchy and the Emulation of Military Systems: Military Organizations and Technology in South America, 1870–1930," *Security Studies* 5 (Spring 1996): 193–260. On innovation see Mearsheimer, *Tragedy of Great Power Politics*, 140, 166–67; Stephen P. Rosen, *Winning the Next War: Innovation and the Modern Military* (Ithaca, NY: Cornell University Press, 1991); Barry R. Posen, *Sources of Military Doctrine: France, Britain, and Germany between the World Wars* (Ithaca, NY: Cornell University Press, 1991).

options to deter or defend against attacks by a likely opponent. Under these circumstances, a net assessment comparing the two opposing forces suggests a country would lose a conventional conflict quickly. A *low degree of conventional threat* means a nuclear power possesses some conventional options to deter and defend against the military missions an adversary might attempt. Indications of conventional threat include the factors normally part of a country's net assessment of its security situation: the balance of forces both in terms of quantity and quality, geography, terrain, and the types of military missions an adversary might undertake with its conventional capabilities, and an opponent's strategy.[22]

Nuclear Weapons Capabilities

The second variable, nuclear weapons capabilities, defines the strategic options available to a country. All other factors being equal, the greater a state's nuclear weapons capabilities, the more ambitious the deterrence strategy it can pursue. These nuclear weapons capabilities include the number of warheads, its command and control, early warning systems, and the accuracy of its delivery systems. Based on these characteristics, differentiation among three types of nuclear powers is made. These categories represent a rough approximation of the quantity and quality of nuclear forces countries could possess once they decide to join the exclusive club of nuclear weapons states. Table 14.1 summarizes these defining features of nuclear powers.

New nuclear powers possess arsenals with fewer than twenty weapons deployed with a rudimentary command and control system. Because they have recently made the decision to acquire nuclear weapons, new nuclear powers field few operational weapons with limited delivery capabilities. Because of crude command and control systems, new regional powers will likely focus on safeguarding their few weapons rather than deploying them for multiple uses in a crisis or a conflict.[23] They will lack the technologies and standard operating procedures to mirror the day-to-day and generated deployment practices of other nuclear powers. Currently, North Korea stands alone as a new regional power, but should Iran develop nuclear weapons it could eventually fall into this category. New nuclear powers will face incentives to move up in the ranks of regional powers by acquiring larger arsenals if for no other reason than

---

[22] On assessing the level of conventional threat, see John J. Mearsheimer, *Conventional Deterrence* (Ithaca, NY: Cornell University Press, 1983); John J. Mearsheimer, "Why the Soviets Can't Win Quickly in Central Europe," *International Security* 7 (Summer 1982): 3–39; Charles L. Glaser and Chaim Kaufmann, "What Is the Offense-Defense Balance and How Can We Measure It?," *International Security* 22 (Spring 1998): 51; Stephen D. Biddle, *Military Power: Explaining Victory and Defeat in Modern Battle* (Princeton, NJ: Princeton University Press, 2004), 28–51.

[23] Jordan Seng, "Less Is More: Command and Control Advantages of Minor Nuclear States," *Security Studies* 6 (Summer 1997): 73–74.

TABLE 14.1 Regional Nuclear Powers: Capabilities and Threats

	FUTURE IRAN	NORTH KOREA	PAKISTAN	CHINA	INDIA	RUSSIA
Type of Regional Power	New	New	Minor	Minor	Minor	Major
Nuclear Capabilities (Deployed)	None	<10	150–200	180–240	80–100	~2,000 going to 1,550
Conventional Threat	High	High	High	Low	Low	High moving to low
	U.S. intervention;	U.S./ROK invasion;	Indian invasion across LOC and IB;	U.S. intervention in Taiwan crisis;	conflict with China/Pakistan;	conflict with NATO/China;
	few conventional options	conventional options	few conventional options	conventional options exist	conventional options exist	conventional options exist

NOTE: *ROK* Republic of Korea (South Korea); *LOC* Line of Control; *IB* International Border

improving the odds of survivability. However, it is possible that some states could conclude they never need reach beyond the capabilities of new nuclear powers.[24]

Minor nuclear powers, like China, India, and Pakistan, deploy arsenals with several dozen to several hundred warheads, improved command and control systems, and a variety of delivery systems. They have made the decision to enlarge and to improve their arsenal for security reasons but also potentially for reasons of international prestige and domestic political gains as well. Minor powers will possess command and control systems that improve their capacity to adopt different force postures for every day and during a crisis. Similarly, they will field multiple delivery systems, improving the survivability of their forces.

Major nuclear powers maintain arsenals nearly in parity with the world's most formidable nuclear-armed country, the United States. The key feature of a major power is its willingness to deploy arsenals of warheads and delivery vehicles that keep pace with the largest nuclear-armed state. In addition to the size of the arsenal, major powers will field nuclear forces with the greatest accuracy and range among nuclear-armed powers. They will also invest in the reconnaissance, surveillance, and target acquisition technologies, like satellites, that allow them to hold an adversary's nuclear forces at risk of strike. At the moment only Russia possesses a nuclear weapons arsenal with a comparable number of warheads. Russia can compete with the United States in terms of numbers but suffers from vulnerabilities in its early warning systems, problems with new delivery systems, and weaknesses in its command and control systems.[25]

The Search for Greater Nuclear Weapons Capabilities over Time

What do nuclear powers do if their security situation gets worse in the long term? According to the framework, if a country faces a persistent and worsening military threat, it will seek out a larger and more sophisticated nuclear arsenal. The pursuit of an improved arsenal will happen for two reasons. First, and most obviously, if the conventional balance worsens, a nuclear power will pursue greater nuclear weapons capabilities to compensate. This line of reasoning assumes, of course, that a country decides conventional options are not enough to safeguard its security. Recent Russian improvements in its nuclear arsenal seem to fit this pattern. Second, a country will modernize its nuclear forces to counter improvements in the nuclear capabilities of its likely adversaries. Modernization helps offset any coercive advantage a potential opponent might possess because of superior nuclear weapons capabilities.

---

[24] Arguably South Africa made such a decision, and Iran could do so as well. See Peter Liberman, "The Rise and Fall of the South African Bomb," *International Security* 26 (Fall 2001): 45–86.

[25] Pavel Podvig, "Instrumental Influences: Russia and the 2010 Nuclear Posture Review," *Nonproliferation Review* 18 (2011): 39–50.

In either case, investing in an improved nuclear arsenal allows a country to pursue a more ambitious range of deterrence strategies. Greater numbers of warheads and delivery vehicles increase its ability to hold more adversary targets at risk. Similarly, nuclear forces of high quality improve its chances of holding an opponent's military targets hostage. Although security fears might motivate a minor regional power, for example, to achieve the capabilities of a major nuclear power, it could still face domestic challenges to accomplishing this ambition, not least of which is the financial costs of such an investment.

A Range of Nuclear Weapons Strategies to Deter Conventional Attacks

Not only do nuclear weapons provide states with the means to deter nuclear attacks, but they also serve as instruments to deter and to stop conventional aggression. The threat posed by conventional militaries is, after all, one of the reasons countries acquire nuclear weapons in the first place. Countries could counter conventional attacks either by threatening or using nuclear weapons first in a conflict. Threatening the first use of nuclear weapons could represent the best course of action for a regime with few conventional options for defense and worried that defeat on the battlefield could endanger its survival. This danger is even greater if a country finds itself in a conflict with the United States. Although the United States struggles with postconflict operations, it excels at major combat operations and favors regime takedown as a war-ending strategy. An imbalance in military capabilities as well as stakes will therefore increase the chances that nuclear powers will threaten deliberate nuclear escalation as a means to safeguard their survival.[26]

The threat of a massive nuclear attack—or massive retaliation—as the initial response to conventional aggression, however, is not a credible threat when an opponent can respond in kind. Mutual vulnerability, in other words, undermines the credibility of nuclear threats to deter conventional attack.[27] The challenge for nuclear powers, then, entails finding first-use strategies that avoid triggering an all-out nuclear war. To steer clear of such an exchange, nuclear first use requires restraint.[28] Nuclear powers could threaten or conduct restrained attacks while at the same time keeping an attacker's value targets—cities or the cities of allies—hostage for future strikes. Such strikes would turn back an attacker for three reasons: because they impose a small but costly punishment; because they raise the risk of even larger punishment through

---

[26] Forrest E. Morgan et al., *Dangerous Thresholds: Managing Escalation in the 21st Century* (Santa Monica, CA: RAND, 2008), 7–45.

[27] For just a few examples of this problem, see Thomas C. Schelling, *The Strategy of Conflict* (Cambridge, MA: Harvard University Press, 1961), 187–203; Schelling, *Arms and Influence*, 92–125; Bernard Brodie, *Escalation and the Nuclear Option* (Princeton, NJ: Princeton University Press, 1966).

[28] Andrew L. Ross, "On the Origins of Limited War Theory," in *On Limited Nuclear War in the 21st Century*, ed. Jeffrey A. Larsen and Kerry M. Kartchner (Palo Alto, CA: Stanford University Press, 2013), 21–48.

TABLE 14.2 Nuclear Strategies to Deter or Stop Conventional Attack

	WHAT STRATEGY ATTEMPTS	WHO COULD DO IT
Flexible Response	Deny attacker war aims through LNOs, counterconventional strikes, and if necessary counterforce strikes	Russia
Counter conventional	Stymie attacker's strategy by striking conventional forces	Pakistan
Limited Nuclear Options: Early	Brandish or limited attacks to impose costs and signal willingness to run risks of uncontrollable escalation	North Korea Future Iran
Limited Nuclear Options as Last Resort	Brandish or limited attacks to impose costs and signal willingness to run risks of uncontrollable escalation	China India

uncontrollable escalation; or because they thwart an opponent's conventional military strategy.

With these logics in mind, four possible nuclear first-use strategies that nuclear powers can choose to deter conventional attacks can be deduced (see Table 14.2).[29] These strategies represent the best possible nuclear options for states facing a desperate situation: defeat on a conventional battlefield resulting in regime change.[30] Each strategy comes with its own set of advantages and disadvantages. Moreover, NATO explored and adopted some of these strategies during the Cold War. Modern nuclear powers therefore will likely possess some knowledge of these previous strategies and could adapt them to their own circumstances.[31] Discussion begins at the bottom of the escalation, and the strategies from the least to the most ambitious and escalatory are outlined in turn.

Late Use of Limited Nuclear Options

The first strategy is the *late use of limited nuclear options*. This strategy calls for limited nuclear actions, including brandishing nuclear weapons or small strikes, to deter a conventional attack from continuing. According to the strategy, a country reaches for these LNOs after exhausting all conventional alternatives. The strategy allows states to signal their resolve to risk further nuclear escalation if a conventional conflict does not end.

---

[29] Robert Powell, "The Theoretical Foundations of Strategic Nuclear Deterrence," *Political Science Quarterly* 100 (Spring 1985): 75–96.

[30] The chapter does not consider what some have called "catalytic strategies." These are strategies that aim to draw in the intervention of outside powers, usually the United States, to stop a conflict. As the reasoning goes, the United States or other countries will prevent escalation out of fear that a nuclear conflict looks imminent. I exclude this possibility because it seems to leave too much to chance for a nuclear power.

[31] A good account of this period is Fred Kaplan, *The Wizards of Armageddon* (Palo Alto, CA: Stanford University Press, 1983).

Limited nuclear use could begin with demonstrations: alerts, tests, and warning shots that inflict no damage.[32] These "shots across the bow" could steadily increase in violence with limited strikes against advancing forces and eventually graduate to small attacks on an adversary's cities. The strategy works by gradually punishing the attacker and by raising the possibility that events could get out of hand. Put another way, LNOs not only impose costs piecemeal but also communicate the increasing and shared risk of an uncontrollable all-out exchange between a regional power and its conventionally superior opponent.[33]

During the Cold War, for example, analysts argued that NATO could turn back a Soviet invasion of West Germany with a nuclear warning shot.[34] French nuclear doctrine during this period also called for using tactical nuclear weapons for the purpose of demonstration strikes.[35] Statements by the former head of its Strategic Plans Division, Gen. Khalid Kidwai, suggest Pakistan once followed a strategy calling for limited attacks to demonstrate resolve.[36]

A significant downside of employing this strategy concerns communication. An opponent might not understand the signal a regional power intends to send or, worse yet, might see it as a precursor to a larger attack. This possibility increases if a regional power needs to employ multiple rounds of signals. What appears limited and restrained to one side could look like the beginning of something more threatening.[37]

Another key danger associated with this strategy is that countries might conclude nuclear weapons are unnecessary to deter or to defend against nuclear attacks until they are staring defeat in the face. As such, their use could come under great stress with little or no prior planning. Under duress, the pressure to send an intense and less restrained signal could backfire. What looks limited could seem like the unraveling of a country on the verge of defeat. While this might force an attacker to back off, it could also prompt the opponent into trying to disarm a country of its nuclear forces.

According to the framework, China and India will pursue a strategy of late LNOs. Both countries possess an array of capabilities that give them options other than nuclear escalation to fend off a conventional attack. That is, China

---

[32] Alerts represent one form of brandishing of nuclear weapons that could serve as a limited option. Scott D. Sagan, "Nuclear Alerts and Crisis Management," *International Security* 9 (Spring 1985): 99–139.

[33] Robert Jervis, "Why Nuclear Superiority Doesn't Matter," *Political Science Quarterly* 94 (Winter 1979–80): 617–32; Schelling, *Arms and Influence*, 92–125.

[34] For a representative statement, see Bernard Gwertzman, "Haig Cites a Standing NATO Plan Envisioning a Warning A-Blast," *New York Times*, November 5, 1981; "Presidential News Conference," Ronald Reagan Presidential Library and Museum, November 10, 1981, http://www.reagan.utexas.edu/archives/speeches/1981/111081d.htm; "War and Peace in the Nuclear Age; At the Brink; Interview with Thomas Schelling, 1986," WGBH Media Library and Archives, March 4, 1986, http://openvault.wgbh.org/catalog/V_5293F77426B84C68A360BD6283ACF4FC. On the logic of demonstrations see Morton Halperin, *Limited War in the Nuclear Age* (New York: John Wiley and Sons, 1963), 58.

[35] David S. Yost, "France's New Nuclear Doctrine," *International Affairs* 82 (July 2006): 701–21.

[36] Scott D. Sagan, "The Evolution of Pakistani and Indian Nuclear Doctrine," in *Inside Nuclear South Asia*, ed. Scott D. Sagan (Palo Alto, CA: Stanford University Press, 2009), 234.

[37] Ross, "On the Origins of Limited War Theory," 36–42.

and India do not have to rely primarily on nuclear weapons for security. Their conventional capabilities provide a credible, first-line defense. In the Straits of Taiwan, China continues to improve the balance of power against the United States.[38] Similarly, Indian conventional capabilities still appear a fair match against the Chinese military and have increased their superiority over Pakistan's armed forces.[39] These capabilities enable them to rely on nuclear weapons only after exhausting all other conventional options.

Early Use of Limited Nuclear Options

A second strategy for deterring conventional aggression is the *early use of limited nuclear options.* As the label indicates, a nuclear power would employ the same limited options in the first strategy but carry them out at the beginning of a conventional conflict. This early use strategy comes with many of the same advantages and disadvantages. With the military balance unfavorable, a country must reach for nuclear weapons first because events on the battlefield will likely turn against it. Based on its deteriorating conventional military capabilities, it is hypothesized that North Korea would pursue an early signaling strategy.[40] As a new nuclear power, North Korea would lack enough warheads to conduct multiple rounds of signaling while retaining enough forces in reserve to hold hostage an attacker's value targets—perhaps South Korean or Japanese cities. This might seem a terrible strategy, but it represents the best option given the balance of conventional forces and a regime's desire for survival.[41]

Counterconventional Strikes

Counterconventional strikes represent a third strategy to deter or defeat conventional attacks. This strategy calls for using nuclear weapons to improve the balance of power on the battlefield. These strikes would attempt to deny an opponent the capability to win a conventional war.[42] The possibility of this type of strike would also complicate an attacker strategy. Large formations of armed forces, for example, could prove tempting targets for such strikes. A defender could also strike the follow-on echelons of an attacker's forces, staging areas, command and control centers, and fuel depots. Nuclear attacks

---

38 Eric Heginbotham et al., *U.S.-China Military Scorecard: Forces, Geography, and the Evolving Balance of Power, 1996–2017* (Santa Monica, CA: RAND, 2015), http://www.rand.org/content/dam/rand/pubs/research_reports/RR300/RR392/RAND_RR392.pdf.

39 Dinshaw Mistry, "Tempering Optimism about Nuclear Deterrence in South Asia," *Security Studies* 18 (2009): 148–82; Sumit Ganguly, "War, Nuclear Weapons, and Crisis Stability in South Asia," *Security Studies* 17 (2008): 164–84. On Cold Start, see Walter C. Ladwig III, "A Cold Start for Hot Wars? The Indian Army's New Limited War Doctrine," *International Security* 32 (Winter 2007–2008): 158–90.

40 Institute for Strategic Studies, *The Military Balance 2016* (London: IISS, 2016), 211–306.

41 Keir A. Lieber and Daryl A. Press, "The Next Korean War: Conflict with North Korea Could Go Nuclear but Washington Could Reduce the Risk," *Foreign Affairs*, April 1, 2013, http://www.foreignaffairs.com/articles/139091/keir-a-lieber-and-daryl-g-press/the-next-korean-war.

42 For a good overview of this kind of thinking, see Michael Legge, *Theater Nuclear Weapons and the NATO Strategy of Flexible Response*, R-2964-FF (Santa Monica, CA: RAND, 1983).

on the battlefield would come early in an effort to stymie an attack. Several coordinated blows would shock an opponent while also destroying the assets an attacker needs to prevail.[43] If successful, the aggressor finds it has no other choice but to halt the attack or risk further escalation, which could prove too difficult to control.[44]

It is reasonable to hypothesize that Pakistan is the only regional nuclear power moving toward a counterconventional strategy today. This move reflects Pakistan's concern over the military balance with India.[45] Although some analysts believe Pakistan can still successfully defend itself in a conventional clash with India, the long-term trends suggest the military situation will continue to deteriorate in the future.[46] The shared terrain also does not favor Pakistan. As one report observed, "Pakistan is very vulnerable to a major Indian attack using conventional forces. It has little strategic depth and many key cities like Lahore are within 100 miles of the border. The terrain is not optimal—much of it is desert—but India has already demonstrated that it can operate across it."[47] Although the Indian military's Cold Start doctrine might remain an aspiration and never come to fruition, India has embarked on a modernization program that includes conventional options for dealing with terrorist incursions from Pakistan as well as deterring a more militarily powerful China.[48] As a minor nuclear power, Pakistan possesses the capability to adopt this strategy. Some analysts point to the recent development of the Hatf-9 short-range ballistic missile as evidence for this move toward a counterconventional strategy.[49]

The counterconventional strategy also comes with its own difficulties. A regional power would need enough warheads to cover the required battlefield targets while still maintaining a reserve to hold an attacker's value targets hostage. Counterconventional strikes would require a greater amount of predelegation than the signaling strategy. Battlefield commanders would need the flexibility to carry out strikes in the changing local conditions. Nuclear attacks against advancing conventional forces would need to occur early in a conflict to strike staging grounds and prepositioned equipment. And battlefield nuclear

---

[43] Peter Feaver and Stephen D. Biddle, eds., *Battlefield Nuclear Weapons: Issues and Options*, (Cambridge, MA: CSIA Occasional Paper, 1989), 97–146.

[44] Thomas Schelling, "Nuclear Strategy in Europe," *World Politics* 14 (April 1962): 421–33; John J. Mearsheimer, "Nuclear Weapons and Deterrence in Europe," *International Security* 9 (Winter 1984–85): 19–46.

[45] Narang, *Nuclear Strategy in the Modern Age*, 55–93.

[46] On reasons for optimism, see S. Paul Kapur, "India and Pakistan's Unstable Peace: Why Nuclear South Asia Is Not Like Cold War Europe," *International Security* 30 (Fall 2005): 138–39. On India's military modernization, see Sunil Dasgupta, "The Fate of India's Strategic Restraint," *Current History*, (April 2012), 129–34.

[47] Anthony Cordesman, "The Conventional Military Balance in India, Pakistan, and South Asia," CSIS, December 28, 2001, 3, https://csis-prod.s3.amazonaws.com/s3fs-public/legacy_files/files/media/csis/pubs/asia_sa_conv_mb%5B1%5D.pdf.

[48] Evan Braden Montgomery, "Competitive Strategies against Continental Powers: The Geopolitics of Sino-Indian-American Relations," *Journal of Strategic Studies* 36 (2013): 76–100.

[49] Feroz Hassan Khan, "Minimum Deterrence: Pakistan's Dilemma," in *Small Nuclear Forces*, ed. Malcolm Chalmers, Andrew Somerville, and Andrea Berger (London: RUSI, 2011), 65–80.

strikes might appear limited to a nuclear power conducting them but seem highly escalatory to an opponent.

Flexible Response

The final possible strategy to deter conventional attacks is *flexible response*, the most ambitious of the four strategies available to nuclear powers. Flexible response envisions employing first the limited options called for by the signaling strategies and, should they fail to deter, moving up the ladder of violence to the battlefield nuclear attacks envisioned by counterconventional strategy.[50] At each level of increasing violence, a nuclear power would put the onus on an attacker to risk further escalation. The key to success lies in obtaining escalation dominance: the condition whereby a nuclear power forces an opponent to back down because the costs and risk of further escalation outweigh the benefits.[51]

A country could threaten even greater levels of violence because it possesses the ability to conduct disarming strikes on an opponent's nuclear forces. Put another way, a regional power could limit the damage done to its cities and industrial centers by striking its adversary's nuclear forces. Although the United States pursued a flexible response strategy for most of the Cold War, its boldest form was the *countervailing doctrine* articulated during the Carter administration and later enthusiastically embraced by its succeeding administration. It called for limited options and counterconventional strikes and for a variety of attacks at higher levels of violence to achieve escalation dominance. These included counterforce attacks against Soviet nuclear forces as well as against its leadership.[52]

Flexible response shares all the same dangers as the other strategies. In addition, it requires exquisite command and control to conduct several rounds of ambitious strikes, while also assessing battle damage in a timely fashion. At some point, crisis stability also becomes a concern: both sides would begin to worry about preemptive attacks on their nuclear forces as a way to limit damage. In addition, the strategy requires advanced counterforce capabilities. The basic requirements would include extremely accurate weapons, sophisticated sensors for target acquisition and battlefield management, multiple means of penetrating an opponent's air defenses, and nuclear weapons of varying yields.

According to the framework, which country could adopt a strategy of flexible response today? Given the poor state of its conventional forces, but its nevertheless impressive capabilities as a major nuclear power, it is hypothesized

[50] The core logic of escalation dominance is explained in Herman Kahn in several of his works, including *On Escalation: Metaphors and Scenarios* (New York: Praeger, 1965), 289–91, and *Thinking about the Unthinkable in the 1980s* (New York: Touchstone, 1985). Also see Matthew Kroenig, "Nuclear Superiority and the Balance of Resolve: Explaining Nuclear Crisis Outcomes," *International Organization* 67 (January 2013): 141–71.

[51] Morgan et al., *Dangerous Thresholds*, 15.

[52] Scott D. Sagan, *Moving Targets: Nuclear Strategy and National Security* (Princeton, NJ: Princeton University Press, 1990), 58–97.

that Russia pursues flexible response. Although its officials do not articulate a coherent strategy, Russia's capabilities and recent actions point to flexible response. Russia has poured resources into improving the survivability of its nuclear forces.[53] In terms of rhetoric, Russian officials claim to worry about NATO intervention into what its leaders consider its periphery. To that end, Russian military exercises focus on this possibility. These scenarios tend to end with Russia using nuclear weapons first and forcing an opponent to back down out of fear that the costs and risks of escalating are not worth the gamble.[54] Put another way, escalation dominance is a central aim of Russian nuclear strategy.[55] In an irony of history, Russia appears to have adopted the NATO script for dealing with conventional inferiority.

Implications for U.S. Power Projection Capabilities

The first-cut analysis presented here should caution U.S. policymakers as they plan for the projection of military power in general and the use of force against nuclear powers outside the U.S. security umbrella in particular. Nuclear escalation is an inherent danger present in any fight against these countries. Some pathways to nuclear escalation are deliberate, as the preceding analysis argues, while other routes to escalation are less deliberate but equally worrisome. Specifically, conventional conflicts between the United States and regional nuclear-armed opponents are likely to escalate for four broad reasons.

First, the imbalance of forces and stakes will motivate nuclear powers to deliberately threaten and, if necessary, carry out the first use of nuclear weapons if they begin to lose a conventional war. This imbalance in capabilities seems inherent in any conflict between the United States and these nuclear powers.[56] U.S. forces have demonstrated their conventional prowess on numerous occasions. They command the commons and have earned an impressive record on land, especially in terms of major combat operations. Of course, some countries would perform better than others in a conventional fight with the United

---

[53] Diane Barnes, "Experts See Russian Strides on Nuclear-Forces Update," *NTI Global Security Newswire*, March 6, 2014, http://www.nti.org/gsn/article/experts-see-russian-strides-nuclear-force-updates.

[54] Nikolas K. Gvosdev, "Russia Flexes Its Nuclear Muscles," *National Interest*, November 14, 2013, http://nationalinterest.org/commentary/russia-flexes-its-nuclear-muscles-9399.

[55] Olga Oliker, "Russia's Nuclear Doctrine: What We Know, What We Don't, and What That Means," CSIS, May 2016, https://csis-prod.s3.amazonaws.com/s3fs-public/publication/160504_Oliker_RussiasNuclearDoctrine_Web.pdf; Forrest E. Morgan, "Dancing with the Bear: Managing Escalation in a Conflict with Russia," *IFRI Proliferation Papers* no. 40 (2012): 1–47; James Quinlivan and Olga Oliker, *Nuclear Deterrence in Europe: Russia's Approach to a New Security Environment and Implications for the United States*, MG-1075-AF (Santa Monica, CA: RAND, 2011); Roger N. McDermott, "Russia's Conventional Military Weakness and Substrategic Nuclear Policy," U.S. Army Foreign Military Studies Office, 2011, http://fmso.leavenworth.army.mil/Collaboration/international/McDermott/Russia-NuclearPolicy.pdf.

[56] Morgan et al., *Dangerous Thresholds*, 7–45.

States. Nevertheless, the United States still represents a formidable opponent. Better to face it with nuclear weapons than without them.[57]

Similarly, in almost every case, the stakes will favor the defending nuclear power. To take two examples, Chinese leaders see Taiwan as part of their homeland, and the North Korean regime worries about its survival. Such regimes also know that the United States has employed regime change in the recent past. A nuclear-armed opponent of the United States would perceive itself fighting not for gain but to prevent a significant loss.[58] This asymmetry of stakes will motivate them to take great risks.

U.S. policymakers argue that counterforce capabilities will allow its forces to compensate for the imbalance of stakes.[59] They put great stock in U.S. conventional counterforce capabilities. A range of conventional precision-strike capabilities increases the U.S. ability to disarm an opponent without resort to nuclear weapons. Theater and national missile defenses provide the United States with a way to mop up any ragged retaliatory strike. These ingredients seem to create the perfect recipe for at least damage limitation, if not an outright splendid first strike.

The danger, however, is that these same capabilities will create instability in a crisis. A nuclear power will know the United States brings these capabilities to a conflict. It will worry about the survivability of its forces, especially as a conflict continues. At some point it will find itself facing the decision to use its nuclear forces or lose them. This decision might include not only rational calculation but also more emotional impulses to inflict revenge with weapons that could disappear. After all, Schelling points out in *Arms in Influence* that irrational behavior makes nuclear escalation more likely.

In addition to crisis instability, a conventional confrontation with U.S. forces could prompt inadvertent escalation. A conflict might start with both sides believing it will remain limited, but events on the battlefield could alter these perceptions.[60] As U.S. forces tear down a nuclear power's air defenses and begin to destroy command and control networks, the line between conventional and nuclear operations becomes blurred. What the United States sees as normal conventional operations could look like the precursor to strikes against a regional power's nuclear forces.[61] These efforts to blind an opponent's command and control could inadvertently transform a conventional war into a nuclear war. The possibility of inadvertent escalation is a danger some analysts

---

[57] Barry R. Posen, "Command of the Commons: The Military Foundations of U.S. Hegemony," *International Security* 28 (Summer 2003): 5–46. Of course, these advantages are not permanent; see Andrew Krepinveich, "The Pentagon's Wasting Assets: The Eroding Foundations of American Power," *Foreign Affairs* 88 (July/August 2009): 18–33

[58] Daniel Kahneman and Amos Tversky, "Prospect Theory: An Analysis of Decision under Risk," *Econometrica* 47 (March 1979): 263–91.

[59] See David Ochmanek and Lowell Schwartz, *The Challenge of Nuclear-Armed Regional Adversaries* (Santa Monica, CA: RAND, 2008), 31–56.

[60] Avery Goldstein, "China's Real and Present Danger: Now Is the Time for Washington to Worry," *Foreign Affairs* 92 (September–October 2013): 136–44.

[61] Posen, *Inadvertent Escalation*, 1–27.

have highlighted in the U.S. concept of Air-Sea Battle, a doctrine for countering China's growing anti-access, area-denial capabilities.[62]

To make matters worse, accidental or unauthorized use could emerge as another pathway to escalation. Nuclear opponents of the United States will likely undertake some kind of pre-delegation of use authority to carry out their first-use strategies. While this increases the chance of successfully conducting such a strategy, it also risks unintentional nuclear use through an error or an overzealous battlefield commander. This possibility should worry U.S. military planners and create doubts in their minds about controlling escalation in a conventional conflict with nuclear powers.

Summary

This chapter offered a framework for understanding the deterrence strategies of nuclear powers outside the U.S. security umbrella. Incomplete evidence exists about these strategies, and what analysts know could change in the future as threat environments improve or worsen. New nuclear weapons states could also emerge. Based on a few simple assumptions, the framework argues that two variables shape a country's choice of deterrence strategy: the level of military threat it faces and its military capabilities. Future work could vary the framework's assumptions and test them against emerging evidence. Realists understand states are not unitary, rational actors interested only in survival. These assumptions instead allow us to create a baseline for a first-cut analysis, setting aside domestic politics for a moment to focus on the external forces all countries grapple with to find security.

If one relaxes the framework's assumptions, then the dangers highlighted herein would look far worse than described. For example, many nuclear powers harbor revisionist aims that could put them in conflict with the United States or its allies. China's recent clashes with Japan over disputed territory represent one possibility. The dispute over Kashmir continues to fuel the security competition between India and Pakistan. What drives North Korean behavior remains a mystery. Furthermore, troubled civil-military relations could cause these countries to pursue nuclear strategies more ambitious than the level of external threat they face. Nuclear-armed states whose military possesses complete control over nuclear strategy could adopt dangerous offensive doctrines for reasons having little to do with strategic circumstances.[63]

This framework should also caution U.S. policymakers about their ability to project military power against nuclear-armed adversaries. During the Cold War, the United States and its NATO allies faced the Soviet Union from

---

[62] Joshua Rovner, "AirSea Battle and Escalation Risks," *Policy Brief*, no. 12, University of California Institute on Global Conflict and Cooperation, (January 2012).

[63] An argument made in Scott D. Sagan, "The Perils of Proliferation: Organization Theory, Deterrence Theory, and the Spread of Nuclear Weapons," *International Security* 18 (Spring 1994): 66–107.

a position of conventional weakness. They compensated for this disparity by relying on threats to use nuclear weapons first in a conflict. Today the tables are turned: the United States possesses conventional superiority and could face adversaries willing to threaten nuclear escalation to deter an attack. There are multiple pathways to escalation, and it remains unclear whether the United States could control a nuclear war once it starts, even with disarming conventional strikes and missile defenses. U.S. planners should ask what happens if they are wrong about optimistic assessments of finding, tracking, and destroying all of a nuclear-armed opponent's nuclear forces.[64] More fundamentally, it is not clear there is much worth fighting for that the United States should run these risks. The prospect of uncontrollable escalation should give U.S. defense planners pause. Scholars and policymakers need to consider alternative strategies for protecting U.S. interests and allies under these circumstances. Part of this effort should include returning to the subject of limited war and exploring the conditions under which conventional conflicts can take place without provoking nuclear escalation.

---

[64] Retired U.S. Air Force General Walter Sharp made this argument with great confidence when discussing North Korea in a radio interview last spring. See "North Korea's Threats," WBUR Boston Public Radio, April 2, 2013, available at http://onpoint.wbur.org/2013/04/02/north-koreas-threats.

CHAPTER 15

Threatening Proliferation

The Goldilocks Principle of Bargaining with Nuclear Latency

TRISTAN VOLPE

IN 1975, THE U.S. intelligence community observed that a handful of allies had attempted to compel concessions from Washington by dialing up the threat of nuclear proliferation.[1] At various times, Australia, West Germany, Italy, and South Korea demanded enhanced military assistance and defense commitments from U.S. officials, while Japan bargained for the territorial reversion of Okinawa. Each ally tried to convince the United States that compliance would be rewarded with a pledge of nuclear restraint, while noncompliance might increase the risk of proliferation. In an assessment of these episodes, the Central Intelligence Agency determined that "future nuclear politics will almost certainly include states which will exploit their threshold positions, as much or more than their actual capabilities . . . . Such cases are likely to become more common."[2] The 1975 estimate proved prescient. Over the next four decades, Pakistan, North Korea, Egypt, Libya, Iran, and Saudi Arabia threatened to proliferate if the United States failed to comply with a range of demands.

This chapter explains how a challenger can leverage its latent capacity to produce nuclear weapons to extract coercive benefits from a stronger target such as the United States. Unlike the traditional forms of economic or military punishment assessed throughout this volume, nuclear latency gives a nation the capacity to move, or threaten to move, closer to the bomb if the

[1] For a full articulation of the argument developed in this chapter, see Tristan A. Volpe, "Atomic Leverage: Compellence with Nuclear Latency," *Security Studies* 26 (2017): 517–47.

[2] U.S. Central Intelligence Agency, "Managing Nuclear Proliferation: The Politics of Limited Choice," research study, December 1975, National Security Archive (hereafter NSA), Washington, DC. I thank Austin Carson for bringing this document to my attention.

target does not modify its behavior.[3] Since nuclear weapons are the great strategic equalizers among nations, a proliferation threat puts pressure on other countries to forestall an adverse shift in the balance of power before it is too late.[4] Adversaries fear a loss in relative military power. With only a few nuclear weapons, a weak state can undercut the conventional capabilities of a superior rival by creating an entirely new strategic calculus.[5] Within an alliance, protégé proliferation increases the risk of entrapping a patron in a local conflict and restricts freedom of action.[6] Rather than endure these costs and risks, the target may decide to concede to the challenger's demands, provided the proliferation threat is backed with an assurance to foreswear nuclear weapons.

Countries bargain with nuclear latency in this way for two reasons. The most obvious is when external pressure or technical problems force a determined proliferator to cut a nuclear deal with the international community. Diplomacy is a tactical response in the evolution of a nuclear weapons program designed to ward off conflict, alleviate economic sanctions, or protect the underlying nuclear infrastructure. Even when the proliferator is targeted with the threat of punishment, compellence provides the strategic logic to transform a besieged nuclear program from a liability into a means of leverage. For instance, a former spokesman for Iran's nuclear negotiation team claimed that the revelation of covert nuclear activities led them to pursue a strategy in 2003 of "turning threats unto opportunities," by seeking to "obtain maximum concessions from their foreign counterparts in return for cooperation."[7] The related second motive for coming to the bargaining table is that nuclear latency is an alluring means to extract political and material benefits. To be sure, countries do not invest in expensive nuclear projects "simply to accumulate negotiating chips," and some are undoubtedly driven to acquire nuclear weapons.[8] But governments pursue multiple objectives over the life span of a nuclear program.[9] Japan and North Korea developed plutonium production capabilities to achieve different objectives, but each government nonetheless integrated nuclear latency into a coercive campaign designed to get the United States to change its behavior.[10]

---

[3] For the classic definition of nuclear latency, see George H. Quester, "Some Conceptual Problems in Nuclear Proliferation," *American Political Science Review* 66 (1972): 490–97.

[4] Jack S. Levy, "Declining Power and the Preventive Motivation for War," *World Politics* 40 (1987): 82–107.

[5] Michael C. Horowitz, *The Diffusion of Military Power* (Princeton, NJ: Princeton University Press, 2010), 106.

[6] Francis J. Gavin, "Strategies of Inhibition: US Grand Strategy, the Nuclear Revolution, and Nonproliferation," *International Security* 40 (2015): 9–46.

[7] Seyyed Mousavian, *The Iranian Nuclear Crisis: A Memoir* (Washington, DC: Carnegie Endowment for International Peace, 2012), 99–100.

[8] Victor Cha, *The Impossible State: North Korea, Past and Future* (New York: Ecco, 2012), 300.

[9] Scott Sagan draws this conclusion in his assessment of why states acquire nuclear weapons: "Why Do States Build Nuclear Weapons? Three Models in Search of a Bomb," *International Security* 21 (1996): 54–86.

[10] See Chapter 1 by Art and Greenhill in this volume.

When will a country be in the strongest position with its nuclear program to extract concessions from the United States? The central argument developed in this chapter is that allies and adversaries alike must surmount a dilemma to use nuclear technology as an effective bargaining chip. The more a challenger threatens to proliferate, the harder it becomes to reassure others that compliance will be rewarded with nuclear restraint. Since each technical step toward the bomb raises the costs of making a convincing nonproliferation promise, a state enters what this chapter refers to as a "Goldilocks zone" when it first acquires the ability to produce fissile material with enrichment and/or reprocessing (ENR) technology. Subsequent increases in the latent capacity to produce nuclear weapons generate diminishing returns at the bargaining table because the state must go to greater lengths to signal its benign intentions, and nuclear programs exhibit considerable path dependency as they mature over time. Contrary to the conventional wisdom about power in world politics, more nuclear technology does not automatically translate into an effective tool of coercive diplomacy.

This argument about the coercive benefits of nuclear latency connects with two general themes in this volume. First, coercive diplomacy is believed to be quite hard, and strong actors often struggle to translate overwhelming power projection capabilities into successful compellence campaigns.[11] This chapter suggests that latent forms of power may provide weaker nations with a unique yet effective tool of compellence because they can threaten to undercut the capabilities of a stronger target while offering an opportunity to prevent this power transition with a credible commitment of restraint. Second, once a challenger has enough latency to generate a credible threat, reassurances become essential for successful compellence. As Robert Art and Kelly M. Greenhill note in their chapter, however, little empirical work has been done on these types of promises, especially in the nonproliferation context.[12] In line with the chapters by Todd Sechser and Phil Haun to explain the ability and willingness of powerful challengers to assure targets, this chapter explores the conditions under which a weaker nation will be in an optimal position to bind itself to a believable nonproliferation promise after threatening the United States.

The chapter also contributes to a vibrant research agenda in the nuclear literature that challenges standard interpretations about the spread and impact of nuclear weapons. Scholars of proliferation have long focused on explaining the factors that drive nations to acquire or forgo nuclear weapons. But the possession of nuclear weapons "is not a binary variable with states either having a fully-fledged arsenal or nothing at all. It spans a continuum" from countries at various stages of nuclear latency (analyzed in this chapter), to new nuclear weapons states with limited resources attempting to deter conventionally

[11] See the chapters in this volume by Art and Greenhill, Sechser, Haun, Downes, Fraiman, and Drezner.
[12] See also Jeffrey W. Knopf, "Varieties of Assurance," *Journal of Strategic Studies* 35 (2012): 379.

superior adversaries (analyzed by Castillo in this volume).[13] In an extension of recent work by Mark Bell, Vipin Narang, and Jasen Castillo about the distinct nuclear choices that regional powers make, this chapter starts to answer Scott Sagan's call to explore "how reaching various thresholds in nuclear power technology" can be leveraged by latent nuclear nations to achieve foreign policy objectives.[14]

The Logic of Bargaining with Nuclear Technology

How does a country translate its raw technical ability to produce nuclear weapons into a means of compellence? When does nuclear technology confer the strongest advantage on a challenger? This section lays out the logic and practice of using nuclear technology as a bargaining chip in three steps. The first draws from the crisis bargaining literature to identify when nuclear technology might be most effective as a tool of compellence. The second builds on this foundation to identify a Goldilocks zone, where the country can most easily commit itself to a nonproliferation promise after making a credible threat to produce nuclear weapons. The final step establishes technical signposts to identify ex ante whether a country has too little, too much, or just the right amount of nuclear technology before it enters into negotiations with the United States.

The literature on coercive diplomacy offers a valuable starting point to build a theory of bargaining with nuclear technology. Effectiveness is measured by "how closely and quickly the target conforms to one's stipulated wishes" and depends on the credibility of the challenger's threats and assurances.[15] The challenger threatens to inflict punishment that will result in a net loss for the target but also provides an assurance not to punish if the target complies. The target is most likely to comply when it calculates that the threatened costs of punishment outweigh the costs of fulfilling the demand and is confident the challenger will not initiate punishment after the target capitulates.

But how do nuclear capabilities make threats and assurances more or less credible? Nuclear weapons create a trade-off between the credibility of deterrent and compellent threats. The ability to inflict severe and rapid punishment with nuclear forces should make the practice of deterrence more effective.[16] The challenge is how to make such threats credible. Given the risk

---

[13] Austin Long, "Proliferation and Strategic Stability in the Middle East," in *Strategic Stability: Contending Interpretations*, ed. Elbridge A. Colby and Michael S. Gerson (Carlisle, PA: U.S. Army War College Press, 2013), 387.

[14] Scott D. Sagan, "Nuclear Latency and Nuclear Proliferation," in *Forecasting Nuclear Proliferation in the 21st Century: vol. 1, The Role of Theory*, ed. William Potter and Gaukhar Mukhatzhanova (Palo Alto, CA: Stanford Security Studies, 2010), 81; see also Mark Bell, "Beyond Emboldenment: How Acquiring Nuclear Weapons Can Change Foreign Policy," *International Security* 40 (2015): 87–119; Vipin Narang, *Nuclear Strategy in the Modern Era: Regional Powers and International Conflict* (Princeton, NJ: Princeton University Press, 2014); Castillo in this volume.

[15] Robert J. Art, "To What Ends Military Power?," *International Security* 4 (1980): 8.

[16] Charles L. Glaser, *Analyzing Strategic Nuclear Policy* (Princeton, NJ: Princeton University Press, 1990).

of escalation to full nuclear war, states with nuclear arsenals can manipulate risk to signal resolve and deter aggression during a crisis. These options prove difficult to employ if the strategy is coercive diplomacy. The last clear chance to avoid catastrophe rests with the challenger, and it is harder to make believable threats with nuclear weapons unless the demands involve core national interests. Nuclear forces may be excellent for deterrence, but the "credibility of use" issue renders them less effective as a means of compellence.[17]

Nuclear technology bypasses this threat credibility problem to reverse the traditional wisdom. Since the operation of nuclear weapons production facilities can be joined with diplomatic campaigns, a nuclear program provides a more passive form of compellent punishment relative to actual military power, the raw use of force, or trade embargoes. When a challenger moves closer to the bomb, the last clear chance to avoid disaster rests with the target. In essence, the proliferation threat rigs the situation to force the target to react. To avoid costly reactions, the challenger must convince the target that compliance will be rewarded with nuclear restraint. Challengers with the technical capacity to produce nuclear weapons can make credible threats to proliferate but must also be willing to offer a convincing assurance.

How much nuclear technology is ideal for issuing credible threats and assurances? The standard view is that power endows a state with the means to threaten punishment, so targets should capitulate in the face of overwhelming military capabilities.[18] If *more power is better*, then proliferation threats should become increasingly effective the closer a state moves toward the bomb. However, Thomas Schelling emphasizes that the threat must be backed up with "a convincing, self-binding, promise" to exercise restraint once the target capitulates; otherwise a severe threat is bound to create resistance.[19] This implies that *less power is more advantageous* when using a nuclear program as a bargaining chip. The closer a state moves toward a nuclear weapons capability, the harder it becomes to issue a believable promise not to proliferate once the target complies.

The central claim of this chapter is that there is an optimal amount of nuclear technology—a Goldilocks zone—where the challenger gains the strongest advantage at the bargaining table. If the effectiveness of coercive diplomacy rests on the interaction of credible threats and assurances, then the challenger must solve a dilemma to use nuclear technology as an instrument of compellence. The proliferation threat should put enough pressure on the United States to comply, but not so much that the challenger must pay high

[17] Art and Greenhill in this volume; Todd S. Sechser and Matthew Fuhrmann, "Crisis Bargaining and Nuclear Blackmail," *International Organization* 67 (2013): 173–95.

[18] Daryl G. Press, "The Credibility of Power: Assessing Threats during the 'Appeasement' Crises of the 1930s," *International Security* 29 (2004): 136–69. But Todd Sechser uncovers an important wrinkle in this logic: power projection capabilities can create a commitment problem for strong states when they make compellent threats; weaker states resist because they fear the challenger will use its overwhelming military advantage to make more threats in the future. See Todd Sechser, "Goliath's Curse: Coercive Threats and Asymmetric Power," *International Organization*, 64 (2010): 627–60.

[19] Thomas C. Schelling, *Strategy of Conflict* (Cambridge, MA: Harvard University Press, 1960), 43; Thomas C. Schelling, *Arms and Influence* (New Haven, CT: Yale University Press, 1966), 76.

costs to make a believable promise of nuclear restraint. A country is most able to make such a mix of threats and assurances when its nuclear program first acquires the ability to produce fissile material. The threat of proliferation is potent enough at this stage that both adversaries and allies will be able to exert considerable pressure on Washington to comply with a wide range of demands. But at the same time, the costs of cutting a deal are not prohibitively high.

The threat to proliferate is not believable when the nuclear program is below this Goldilocks zone of technical capacity to produce nuclear weapons. The country must have some nuclear capabilities in place to follow through on the threat within a short period of time. Otherwise any leader could conjure up a nuclear weapons program out of thin air with the hope of gaining leverage over the United States. On the other hand, if the country builds too much capacity to produce nuclear weapons, then it becomes costly to convince the target that compliance will result in indefinite nuclear restraint. To be sure, a nation with an advanced nuclear program could always send costly signals about its motives and take steps away from the bomb to assuage the target. The problem is that the domestic political costs of reversing course tend to increase because nuclear programs exhibit considerable path dependency and generate lock-in effects over time. As a result, the leadership may become less willing to constrain its nuclear program the more it matures into an actual weapons capability, or it might end up returning home as a Pyrrhic victor if the costs paid to cut a deal outweigh the concessions extracted at the bargaining table.[20]

When exactly does a nuclear program have too little, too much, and just the right amount of nuclear technology? What are the observable signposts that demarcate the lower and upper boundaries of the Goldilocks zone?

The concept of nuclear latency measures how quickly a state could develop a nuclear weapon and provides a useful way to ground the Goldilocks analogy in the actual process of proliferation. A country's latent timeline to the bomb shrinks as it passes through four technical milestones arrayed along a continuum in Table 15.1. The first is simply to initiate a nuclear program. The government must invest significant resources just to begin indigenous research and development on the nuclear fuel cycle. The second step is to acquire the sensitive ENR technology needed to produce the fissile material for a nuclear weapon. The enrichment route uses isotope separation techniques, such as gas centrifuges or gaseous diffusion, to increase the proportion of fissile uranium. The plutonium pathway uses a nuclear reactor to produce and a chemical-reprocessing facility to separate out plutonium from spent waste fuel. The third step scales up this ENR technology to produce enough highly enriched uranium (HEU) or plutonium for a nuclear weapon. The final phase assembles this fissile material into an operational nuclear weapon.

[20] On how bargaining costs can lead to successful yet suboptimal and Pyrrhic compellence outcomes, see Lawrence Freedman, "Strategic Coercion," in *Strategic Coercion: Concepts and Cases*, ed. Lawrence Freedman (Oxford: Oxford University Press, 1998), 30.

TABLE 15.1 Technical Milestones of Nuclear Proliferation

STEP 1: INITIATE	STEP 2: CHOKEPOINT	STEP 3: FISSILE MATERIAL	STEP 4: WEAPONIZE
Initiate nuclear program; R&D on ENR technology and nuclear fuel cycle	Operate uranium enrichment facility or nuclear reactor with reprocessing capability	Produce significant quantity (SQ) of fissile material or the ability to produce an SQ quickly	Turn fissile material into a first-generation fission weapon

TABLE 15.2 The Goldilocks Zone in Practice

	NUCLEAR PROGRAM'S TRAJECTORY		
	TOO LITTLE	JUST RIGHT (SWEET SPOT)	TOO MUCH
Technical Signposts:	Emerging ambition for ENR capability, but limited ability to import and/or indigenously develop the technology	Capability and speed of progress put the nuclear program on the cusp of being able to produce fissile material with either a uranium enrichment facility or nuclear reactor and plutonium separation facility	Operational fissile material production capability for either military weapon or civilian energy program
Example Cases:	South Korea 1975 Japan 1957 Saudi Arabia 2015	North Korea 1991–94 Japan 1965–75 Libya 2003	Japan after 1975 North Korea after 2006 Iran after 2006

The boundaries of the three zones in Table 15.2 are based on the challenger's level of nuclear latency and relative speed of progress toward the next technical hurdle in the proliferation chain. The *sweet spot* is the range of nuclear programs that are on a trajectory (capability plus development speed) to produce fissile material. On the low end are countries, such as Libya in 2003, that had all the requisite pieces for a uranium gas centrifuge program on hand but ran into problems as they tried to scale up operations. Libya was in the sweet spot because it possessed a worrisome baseline level of nuclear latency, even though the program was not on a rapid vector to solve the enrichment puzzle. On the high end, a country such as North Korea in the early 1990s had a more looming capacity to produce fissile material. By being on the cusp of surmounting a major red line in U.S. nonproliferation policy, the challenger can generate a credible proliferation threat, while also offering a verifiable assurance before path dependency makes it difficult to trade away an operational ENR facility.[21]

A challenger's nuclear trajectory is stalled out in the *too little* zone when it lacks the capability and potential to master ENR technology within a reasonable amount of time. Both the uranium and the plutonium pathways present numerous science and engineering challenges, especially for less-developed countries unable to procure nuclear facilities, assistance, or material from foreign suppliers. Since it can often take at least a decade to develop enrichment or reprocessing technology, the United States or other targets do not face a credible threat of proliferation and can focus on preventing the country from making further technical progress.[22] Observable signposts for this stage range from countries with no nuclear infrastructure at all (e.g., Saudi Arabia in 2015) to nations with more advanced scientific capabilities that still remained far away from bringing an ENR facility online (e.g., Japan in 1957) or were suddenly cut off from importing sensitive technology (e.g., South Korea in 1975).

The ability to produce enough fissile material for a single nuclear weapon in a short time is a traditional firebreak separating just the right amount from *too much* nuclear technology. A rapid breakout capacity allows a country to take few risks and incur low costs if it decides to produce nuclear weapons. Such a state has the capability to present the United States with a nuclear fait accompli, so Washington will push for stringent arms control requirements before complying with demands. A nuclear program moves into this final zone before the bomb by either producing significant quantities of plutonium or HEU, or building up enough enrichment capacity to produce a bomb's worth of HEU on short order (less than a year).

Since the Goldilocks principle identifies a state's nuclear trajectory as the key causal variable driving the outcome of negotiations, these signposts provide a rubric for selecting cases along the entire continuum of technical development. To be clear, the research objective is to use case studies to expand and probe the plausibility of the sweet spot logic. Saudi Arabia in 2015 is a good candidate for examining the weak hand provided by *too little* nuclear technology. Iran's nuclear program after 2006 demonstrates the challenges created by developing *too much* capacity to produce nuclear weapons, even though the Iranians managed to reach a deal in 2015. North Korea in 1994 and Japan in the 1960s underscore how bringing *just the right* amount of technology to the bargaining table confers the strongest advantage on the challenger. Although a full test of the theory is beyond the scope of this chapter, the Goldilocks principle appears valid despite variation in regime type, relationship with

---

[21] Daniel Altman and Nicholas L. Miller, "Red Lines in Nuclear Nonproliferation," *Nonproliferation Review* (forthcoming).

[22] On technical development timelines, see Michael D. Zentner, G. L. Coles, and R. J. Talbert, "Nuclear Proliferation Technology Trends Analysis," *Pacific Northwest National Laboratory Report* (September 2005).

the United States, compellent demands, and root motives for coming to the bargaining table.

Too Little: Saudi Arabia Tries to Play the Long Game

If a country wants to compel concessions from the United States by raising the prospect of proliferation, it needs the ability to follow through on this threat within a short period of time. Otherwise the United States will find it difficult to distinguish a bluff from a genuine threat and is likely to rebuff the challenger's demands.

During the summer of 2015, for instance, Saudi Arabia attempted to take advantage of a persistent fear in Washington that Iran's nuclear program would spark an atomic arms race in the Middle East. U.S. Secretary of Defense Robert Gates underscored this worry in a speech on August 5. Secretary Gates said that the Iran deal "will provoke other countries in the region to pursue equivalent nuclear capabilities, almost certainly Saudi Arabia."[23] High-ranking Saudi officials fueled this concern with ominous statements. In May 2015 the former Saudi director of general intelligence Prince Turki al-Faisal threatened to match Iran's nuclear program: "Whatever the Iranians have, we will have too."[24] The Saudi ambassador to the United Kingdom, Prince Mohammed bin Nawaf, underscored this threat in June, claiming, "All options are on the table" as the kingdom confronted Iran.[25]

The threats were designed to put pressure on Washington. This compellence strategy was on display in May 2015 as high-level Saudi officials prepared for a summit at the White House and Camp David. In preparation, the Saudis demanded a formal "defense treaty with the United States pledging to defend them if they came under external attack."[26] Despite a massive bilateral arms transfer from the United States in 2011, valued at $60 billion, the Saudis also wanted more advanced conventional weapon systems, such as the F-35 advanced fighter jet, to give them a qualitative edge over the Iranians. These demands came on the heels of Prince Turki's threat to match Iranian enrichment capabilities.

The key weakness was that the kingdom lacked the technical means to follow through on the threat. Saudi Arabia had several small research centers but no indigenous ability to produce the fissile material that goes into a nuclear weapon. Moreover, the kingdom did not have any nuclear reactors or ability

---

[23] Reid Wilson, "Robert Gates: We Have a Flawed Iran Deal. Make the Best of It," *Morning Consult*, August 5, 2015.
[24] David E. Sanger, "Saudi Arabia Promises to Match Iran in Nuclear Capability," *New York Times*, May 13, 2015.
[25] Nawaf Obaid, "Saudi Arabia Is Preparing Itself in Case Iran Develops Nuclear Weapons," *Telegraph*, June 29, 2015.
[26] Helene Cooper, "Saudi Arabia Says King Won't Attend Meetings in U.S.," *New York Times*, May 10, 2015.

to separate plutonium from the spent fuel.[27] The Saudis faced an even longer timeline if they wanted to emulate Iran by developing an indigenous uranium enrichment capacity. Most technical experts estimated it would take the kingdom about a decade to design and build a viable gas centrifuge program.[28]

Some in Washington worried that the Saudis could get around these indigenous limitations by calling in a favor to Pakistan, since the kingdom allegedly financed Islamabad's nuclear weapons program.[29] Yet Pakistan faced strong nonproliferation incentives that ruled out the transfer of nuclear weapons, technology, or material to Saudi Arabia. Islamabad wanted to prove that it was a responsible nuclear power with no tolerance for the illicit nuclear supply networks made famous by A. Q. Khan. The Pakistanis also aspired to join the elite group of nuclear suppliers that pledged not to export sensitive nuclear technology to the Middle East.

Perhaps the Saudis were banking on the more distant worry about how Pakistan's calculus might evolve in the years ahead, especially if the country failed to gain membership in the Nuclear Supplier Group. A former Pakistani official suggested in September 2015 that Islamabad should offer "civilian nuclear cooperation to developing countries, including Islamic countries [e.g., Saudi Arabia]," by setting up legal procurement channels outside of the Nuclear Suppliers Group.[30] This was a more nuanced and credible threat than the standard concern in Washington that Pakistan might secretly transfer nuclear weapons or fissile material to pay off its debt to the kingdom. Instead, Islamabad would establish itself as an aboveboard supplier of nuclear technology to countries such as Saudi Arabia that cannot purchase sensitive technology from members of the Nuclear Suppliers Group.

Whatever the true nature of the old Saudi-Pakistan connection, it did not help Riyadh jump-start an enrichment program or acquire a cache of fissile material. Even if the Saudis managed to develop enrichment technology over the next decade, this long-term threat did not give them leverage when they demanded enhanced alliance commitments from the Americans.

Moreover, the absence of concrete capabilities on the ground made it hard for U.S. officials to determine the true nature of nuclear intent in Riyadh. Although the King Abdullah City for Atomic and Renewable Energy laid out an ambitious nuclear energy plan, the only progress made in realizing this vision by the summer of 2015 was a slew of exploratory agreements signed with the leading suppliers of nuclear technology. In contrast to the steps taken by the United Arab Emirates to begin construction on a large nuclear reactor project, Saudi Arabia was not urgently moving to operationalize its aspirations for

---

[27] Colin H. Kahl, Melissa G. Dalton, and Matthew Irvine, *Atomic Kingdom: If Iran Builds the Bomb, Will Saudi Arabia Be Next?* (Washington, DC: Center for New American Security, 2013).
[28] Olli Heinonen and Simon Henderson, "Nuclear Kingdom: Saudi Arabia's Atomic Ambitions," *Washington Institute for Near East Policy Watch*, March 27, 2014.
[29] For a refutation of this concern, see Mark Fitzpatrick, "Saudi Arabia, Pakistan and the Nuclear Rumour Mill," *Survival* 57 (2015): 105–8.
[30] Munir Akram, "India-Pakistan: Hyphenated," *Dawn*, September 13, 2015.

nuclear energy. Without clear indicators that the kingdom was serious about developing its capacity to produce nuclear energy, let alone enrich uranium, U.S. officials refused to shoulder the political costs and regional security risks of fulfilling the kingdom's requests for advanced conventional weapons and a formal defense treaty.

The White House ended up making only marginal changes to its alliance posture toward Saudi Arabia. After the May 2015 Camp David summit, President Barack Obama reassured the Saudis that the U.S. commitment to Gulf security was "ironclad," but he "stopped short of offering a formal defense pact" and instead issued "a carefully worded pledge that was far less robust than the mutual defense treaty" the Saudis had sought.[31] Concrete deliverables focused on helping the Saudis and other Gulf nations build up their own defenses against Iran, such as U.S. assistance with a regional ballistic missile defense program, joint military training exercises, and increased collaboration on maritime security in the Persian Gulf. The Saudi proliferation threat had almost no impact on U.S. behavior because this package of military assistance was decided well in advance of the summit meeting. Instead of extracting concessions, Saudi Arabia made it more difficult to procure civilian nuclear technology for peaceful purposes by signaling intent to follow in Iran's footsteps down the road.[32]

Too Much: Nuclear Buildup in Iran and North Korea

If nuclear bluffs are counterproductive, then perhaps a country should move closer to the bomb to extract the most concessions possible from Washington. On initial consideration, it seems as though being on the threshold of acquiring nuclear weapons should put the burden on the United States to cut a deal before it is too late. Once the country either produces large amounts of fissile material or builds up enough enrichment capacity to produce a bomb's worth of HEU on short order, Washington may offer a much bigger payout in a final effort to inhibit proliferation. But Schelling asserts, "The compellent threat has to be one that can be stopped or reversed when the enemy complies, or else there is no inducement."[33] In other words, the country needs to make a credible commitment of nuclear restraint.

The problem is that it becomes increasingly expensive and suboptimal for a challenger with an advanced nuclear program to offer such an assurance, for two reasons: the technical requirements of costly signaling go up in line with the level of nuclear latency, and these assurance costs may start to outweigh the concessions gained from coercive diplomacy. Iran's track record of

---

[31] Julie H. Davis and David E. Sanger, "Obama Pledges More Military Aid to Reassure Persian Gulf Allies on Iran Deal," *New York Times*, May 14, 2015.
[32] Michael R. Gordon, "John Kerry Wins Gulf States' Cautious Support for Iran Deal," *New York Times*, August 3, 2015.
[33] Schelling, *Arms and Influence*, 76.

diplomacy from 2009 to 2015 provides a clean example of both logics at play. First, in October 2009, U.S. and Iranian teams met in Geneva to negotiate a confidence-building measure. At the time, Iran had about 1,500 kilograms of low-enriched uranium (LEU), along with the centrifuge capacity to enrich this stock into enough HEU for a single nuclear weapon. The Americans proposed a trade: if Iran shipped most of the LEU stock out of the country (about 1,200 kilograms), the United States would help it secure a fuel contract for a research reactor in Tehran. In addition to increasing Iran's breakout timeline, exporting the LEU would be a costly signal that the regime genuinely intended to negotiate further constraints over the nuclear program. The talks broke down when Iran eventually rejected this fuel swap proposal.

After Geneva, the Iranians embarked on a defiant seven-month buildup in the quantity and disposition of enriched uranium, perhaps in an attempt to put themselves in a better bargaining position. By April 2010, the United States had put together a multilateral coalition to sanction Iran, so the Iranians attempted to revive the old deal in a last-ditch effort to stave off economic punishment. But Iran now had close to 2,300 kilograms of LEU, so removing 1,200 kilograms under the terms of the 2009 deal would still leave them with enough material to produce HEU for an atomic weapon.[34] The Iranians had diluted the value of their nonproliferation promise and refused to update the proposal to correct for their technical progress. Instead of strengthening Iran's hand at the bargaining table, the buildup increased the requirements of cutting a deal and catalyzed harsh multilateral sanctions.

Second, Iran managed to reach a deal at an even more advanced stage of nuclear latency in July 2015 but appeared to return home with a Pyrrhic victory. As the Iran deal indicates, a bargain can be reached even after the challenger's nuclear program moves past the sweet spot. But in order for that deal to be optimal, the benefits reaped from coercion must outweigh the heavy assurance costs paid by the challenger to issue a credible promise. Following this logic, one interpretation of the 2015 Iran deal that aligns with the Goldilocks principle is that the regime in Tehran paid high costs in return for marginal concessions. In an effort to alleviate sanctions, Iran solved the commitment problem with strong costly signals that included giving up enough nuclear latency to move back into the sweet spot, but the final outcome was far from ideal. Alternatively, perhaps the deal was optimal for Iran because the regime reaped major benefits, most notably a pathway to normalize the enrichment program, albeit at a high cost. The validity of these competing interpretations rests on a determination of how valuable the July 2015 deal was for the Iranian leadership. As Austin Long argues in this volume, intelligence collection and assessment of the challenger's objectives thereby play a crucial yet underappreciated role in estimating the relative success or failure of compellent threats.

---

[34] For details, see "Iran's Proposed LEU Deal: Skeptical but Awaiting Clarification," *Institute for Science and International Security Report*, May 17, 2010.

Beyond the reassurance costs of cutting a deal, however, is the high domestic political price some leaders must pay to trade away the nuclear program. Consider North Korean behavior during the Six Party Talks. After North Korea produced large amounts of plutonium and tested a nuclear device in October 2006, U.S. officials offered a viable plan in February 2007 for the DPRK to earn phased rewards by verifiably disabling much of its nuclear infrastructure. The Kim regime fulfilled some of the initial requirements but seemed to eventually decide that the deal was no longer valuable and refused to disable its nuclear program further. It seems plausible that the North Koreans always wanted a nuclear deterrent, so diplomacy was a clever ruse to extract side benefits that ended up forcing them to reveal their true intentions. But there is a more nuanced interpretation of the case. Perhaps the Kim regime wanted to cut a deal during the Six Party Talks, but an influential cadre of regime elites may have become steadily vested in the success of the nuclear program over its many decades of development. Given the model of regime survival in Pyongyang, the leadership would find it hard and risky to trade away this valuable commodity.[35]

The nub of the issue is that a nuclear program tends to lock in and entrap a government into a specific course of action over time.[36] This is because nuclear technology exhibits considerable path dependency: each technical step the nuclear program takes toward the bomb makes it more difficult for the government to reverse later on as new bureaucratic and domestic barriers emerge.[37] The path-dependent nature of nuclear technology means the leadership will become reluctant to trade away the nuclear program as it matures, even if it entered negotiations with the United States in good faith and would rather cut a deal. The government could implement the terms laid out by the United States, just as the North Koreans had the option to live up to the February 2007 agreement. But since the nuclear program generates increasing returns over time as a valuable commodity within the country, the leadership finds that it cannot incur the domestic political costs required to trade away this asset.

Just Right: Japan and North Korea Cut Deals in the Sweet Spot

A country's nuclear program generates the most leverage when it brings just the right amount of nuclear technology to the bargaining table. The leadership

[35] Daniel Byman and Jennifer Lind, "Pyongyang's Survival Strategy," *International Security* 35 (2010): 64.
[36] Paul Pierson, *Politics in Time: History, Institutions, and Social Analysis* (Princeton, NJ: Princeton University Press, 2004), 17–18; William Walker, *Nuclear Entrapment: THORP and the Politics of Commitment* (London: Institute for Public Policy Research, 1999).
[37] Robin Cowan, "Nuclear Power Reactors: A Study in Technological Lock-in," *Journal of Economic History* 50 (1990): 541–67.

needs to have enough capability to back up its threats, while also retaining the political flexibility to assure the United States that compliance will be rewarded with nuclear restraint. This delicate mix of threats and assurances is easiest to pull off when the nuclear program enters the Goldilocks zone by acquiring the initial ability to enrich uranium or reprocess plutonium. The key advantage of being in this fissile material sweet spot is that leadership can lock the emerging nuclear program into a benign or civilian course rather than having to pay the high costs required to reverse a mature weapons complex away from the bomb. Brief case studies of North Korean and Japanese nuclear diplomacy show that the Goldilocks effect remains constant despite variation in regime type and relationship with the United States.

North Korea entered the fissile material sweet spot in 1991, when construction on a reprocessing plant at the Yongbyon nuclear complex neared completion. After the United States opened a diplomatic channel to resolve the nuclear issue, it soon became apparent that the North Koreans were "setting the stage to negotiate with the United States on a package that would secure the greatest benefits on the easiest terms possible."[38] North Korea manipulated the plutonium program on several occasions to increase pressure on Washington. In the most striking instance, North Korea announced that it would begin to separate plutonium because Washington had no intention of complying with Pyongyang's demands.[39] North Korean officials then started a ticking clock by highlighting a crucial qualification: it would take about two months to completely unload all the spent reactor fuel, leaving "ample time for the United States and North Korea to strike a deal."[40] The explicit nature of these brinksmanship tactics indicates that Pyongyang may have recognized the leverage provided by being in the Goldilocks zone.

The ultimatums did end up revealing Washington's bottom line as U.S. officials considered a preventive strike against North Korea in the summer of 1994.[41] Before the situation could escalate out of control, the unexpected visit of former U.S. president Jimmy Carter provided Kim Il-sung an off-ramp to reach a deal. After diplomacy resumed, the United States agreed to buy out North Korea's plutonium program with a package that consisted of $50 million in energy assistance each year, $4 billion in modern nuclear reactor technology, economic and political normalization, and a negative security assurance. In return, North Korea agreed to freeze operations at the Yongbyon complex, seal the reprocessing facility for eventual dismantlement, ship all spent reactor fuel out of the country, halt construction of two large reactors, and remain a party to the Non-Proliferation Treaty (NPT). The final Agreed Framework

38 Joel S. Wit, Daniel B. Poneman, and Robert L. Gallucci, *Going Critical: The First North Korean Nuclear Crisis* (Washington, DC: Brookings Institution Press, 2005), 37.
39 Scott Snyder, *Negotiating on the Edge: North Korean Negotiating Behavior* (Washington, DC: U.S. Institute of Peace Press, 1999), 81–85.
40 Wit et al., *Going Critical*, 175.
41 Ibid., 181.

signed by North Korea and the United States on October 21, 1994, formalized the bargain.

North Korea was able to strike a low-cost and high-reward bargain with the United States because the nuclear program was in the Goldilocks zone, whereas diplomacy a decade later, during the Six Party Talks, yielded diminishing returns from the increased level of nuclear technology. In 1994 the United States paid North Korea to freeze operations at Yongbyon, with the expectation that Pyongyang would disable the plutonium facility down the road. From the North Korean perspective, it seemed as though the benefits of the Agreed Framework far outweighed the costs of cutting a deal. North Korea had not left the Goldilocks zone by producing large amounts of plutonium, so the deal focused on shutting down the reprocessing facility. This was a modest price to pay. Pyongyang avoided military attack and reaped badly needed energy assistance without having to make the tough decision to give up the nuclear option. By contrast, the production of plutonium and test of a nuclear device in 2006 forced the North Koreans to contemplate giving up their entire nuclear infrastructure in order to cut a grand bargain with the United States.

In contrast to North Korea, Japan faced strong incentives not to proliferate during the 1960s as its nuclear energy program glided into the Goldilocks zone. A report from the U.S. intelligence community in 1965 pointed out that while Japan had the technical capacity to quickly "create a deliverable nuclear *force*, probably comparable to any in the world," the government in Tokyo was unlikely to exercise this option.[42] But Prime Minister Sato Eisaku was under domestic duress to resolve the territorial status of Western Pacific islands captured by U.S. forces during the Second World War. Successive premiers before Sato were unable to convince Washington to return the islands in 1951 and 1957 because an important U.S. military base sat on Okinawa, and Japan lacked the leverage needed to strike such a bargain with the United States.[43] Sato turned to Japan's burgeoning civil nuclear industry to help him succeed where his predecessors had failed.

Since public threats would have damaged the alliance and Japan's economy, Sato drummed up uncertainty about Japan's nuclear intentions during private consultations with top U.S. officials. In 1965 the premier mentioned that China's nuclear test made it "only common sense for Japan to have nuclear weapons," and in 1969 he told a room of stunned U.S. diplomats that his nonnuclear pledge to the Japanese public was "nonsense."[44] Although he employed

---

[42] U.S. Department of State, "Background Paper on Factors Which Could Influence National Decisions concerning Acquisition of Nuclear Weapons," background paper, December 12, 1964, NSA #NP01079, 10, emphasis in original.

[43] Walter LaFeber, *The Clash: U.S.-Japanese Relations throughout History* (New York: Norton, 1998), 298–320.

[44] U.S. Department of State, "Current U.S.-Japanese and World Problems [Part 2]," memorandum of conversation, January 12, 1965, NSA #JU00437; U.S. Embassy in Japan, "Ambassador Johnson's Farewell Call on Prime Minister Sato," cable, January 14, 1969, NSA #JU01039.

much more deft and subtle tactics than the North Koreans did, the basic logic of coercive diplomacy was similar. Over the course of multiple meetings, Sato and his cabinet sold a bargain. If the Americans agreed to return the Pacific islands to the Japanese, the renewed strength of the alliance would obviate any need for Japan to go its own way and field an independent nuclear deterrent. The executive branch of the U.S. government reached the same conclusion. As one report forecast, a failed Okinawa bargain might "constitute a turning point" in the alliance by stimulating a "Japanese decision to plot a more independent military course" that would "entail serious consideration of nuclear arms development."[45] By January 1969 Washington had coalesced around the core deal proposed by Sato: Okinawa should be returned on favorable terms to ensure a nonnuclear Japan.

When it came to offering the United States a convincing nonproliferation promise in return, Sato benefited from the fact that Japan's nuclear program was in the Goldilocks zone. Japan was on a rapid trajectory to operate the complete nuclear fuel cycle by the late 1970s but had not begun reprocessing plutonium from the reactor complex. This was a prime opportunity for the government to further lock the nuclear program into the civil energy pathway by joining the new NPT. If Japan signed onto the vanguard of the NPT to "limit the proliferation of nuclear weapons world-wide," the U.S. government believed that "its involvement would tend to commit Japan more firmly to a non-nuclear role."[46] Even deep skeptics of the NPT, most notably President Richard Nixon and National Security Adviser Henry Kissinger, regarded Japan's participation in the regime to be an essential exception. The Japanese refused to sign the NPT until Sato got the terms he wanted over the reversion of Okinawa in November 1969.

Japan saw little need for nuclear weapons, but like several other U.S. allies at the time, it figured it could play on Washington's opposition to nuclear proliferation as an opportunity to extract concessions. Once Sato linked uncertainty over Japan's nuclear intentions to the reversion of Okinawa, the Japanese leadership used the emerging civil nuclear energy program to wring concessions out of the Americans before reaffirming their role in the NPT. Yet this episode was nearly five decades ago. Since then, Japan has built up one of the most advanced civil nuclear programs in the world. The Japanese could perhaps use this high level of nuclear technology to pressure China over outstanding territorial disputes in the East China Sea, but walking back on historic nonproliferation commitments to make an explicit threat would incur serious international and domestic costs. Tokyo is therefore unlikely to play the nuclear

[45] U.S. Department of Defense, "Response to NSSM 9: Review of the International Situation as of January 20, 1969, Volume V—Noncommunist Far East–Japan," United States: Secret Report, January 20, 1969, NSA #JA00036, 28.

[46] U.S. Department of State, "Japan's Prospects in the Nuclear Weapons Field: Proposed US Courses of Action," memorandum, June 15, 1965, NSA #JU00485, 14.

card in this way unless some sort of high-stakes conflict arises that cannot be resolved through normal diplomatic channels.

Next Steps for Research and Policy

This chapter has demonstrated the plausibility of the Goldilocks principle in theory and in several important cases of compellence. Further research on the topic should expand upon three themes that run throughout this volume. The first is the issue of endogeneity and selection effects in observed episodes of compellence. If a challenger is determined to acquire nuclear weapons, it may build up its nuclear latency to achieve this goal, come to the bargaining table to avoid being punished by the United States, and then refuse to trade away its nuclear options. Since coercive diplomacy is a ruse by the determined proliferator, there is no credibility problem to solve. To deal with this confounding logic, a full test of the Goldilocks principle should specify how often states use advanced nuclear programs as a bargaining chip rather than just selecting out of compellence situations in the first place to sprint toward the bomb.

The related second issue is the role that intelligence plays for the target as it attempts to estimate the challenger's goals, threats, and assurances. Intelligence monitoring can "help determine the magnitude, pace, and capabilities" of a challenger's nuclear program by focusing on measures of nuclear latency.[47] But the challenger's goals and intentions may be "far more difficult to discern than capabilities," as the "focus of intelligence efforts will be on gauging strategic intention; the desire to acquire a nuclear weapon in the first place.[48] In line with Long's call in this volume to treat intelligence as a variable rather than an assumption, a complete explanation should theorize how the target goes about assessing the challenger's capabilities and motives during the compellence process.

Third, to build upon the contributions of Sechser and Haun in this volume, additional work should explore whether the United States can credibly promise to uphold its end of the nonproliferation bargain. Successful nuclear diplomacy "requires not only a sharp sword, but also the ability to sheathe it."[49] If a challenger takes irrevocable steps away from the bomb, then the strength of this commitment may create disincentives for the United States to continue paying concessions. While the sweet spot remains the same for adversaries and allies, the perceived credibility of U.S. assurances differs when viewed from Tokyo or Pyongyang.

---

47 Robert D. Blackwill and Ashton B. Carter, "The Role of Intelligence," in *New Nuclear Nations*, ed. Robert D. Blackwill and Albert Carnesale (New York: Council on Foreign Relations Press, 1993), 218.
48 Wyn Bowen, Robert Dover, and Michael Goodman, "Intelligence and Nuclear Proliferation: An Introduction to the Special Issue," *Intelligence and National Security* 29 (2014): 319.
49 Sechser, "Goliath's Curse," 655.

What does the Goldilocks principle mean for U.S. nonproliferation policy?[50] Foremost, a premature proliferation threat provides the United States with an opportunity to probe whether modest deliverables could convince the country to forgo developing sensitive nuclear technology. As Saudi Arabia found out, Washington will reject expensive demands if the country does not have any real nuclear capabilities to trade away. But U.S. officials can then counter with a cheaper package designed to keep the potential proliferator from ever moving into the Goldilocks zone. This raises a moral hazard for the United States: an ally with no real desire for uranium enrichment could inaugurate work on a fuel enrichment plant, inflate its demands, and then bargain down to a realistic package of reassurance deliverables. The Saudis, for instance, seemed to know that the formal defense pact they requested was impossible since the treaty would need to be ratified by Congress.[51] So perhaps the Saudi gambit was designed to accomplish modest objectives, such as boosting the value and quality of U.S. military hardware provided under another arms deal or bringing Washington closer as Riyadh waded into regional confrontations with Tehran.

The risk of complying with demands at such an early stage is that the United States wastes resources buying out false nuclear ambitions. As the Goldilocks principle makes clear, however, the ally does not have a strong hand to push for expensive concessions. So long as the demands are reasonable, the premature threat creates an opening for the United States to purchase a durable promise to forgo further development of sensitive nuclear technology. Once a state surmounts the technical barriers to enriching uranium or reprocessing plutonium, U.S. options to stop or delay proliferation become limited and expensive. Complying with a country's demands in exchange for a binding nonproliferation promise may be the least worst option, as well as the final chance to cut a deal on the cheap.

In the final analysis, there are several reasons to be optimistic about the future of proliferation diplomacy. Beyond Iran, there are no contemporary U.S. adversaries that have decided to develop nuclear latency in lieu of the nuclear deterrent strategies analyzed by Castillo in this volume. If the focus shifts toward U.S. allies, then it is important to avoid conflating capability and intent to play the nuclear card.[52] In East Asia, the subtle threats made by Sato are considered anathema to the current governments in Tokyo and Seoul. Both

[50] For a comprehensive assessment, see Tristan A. Volpe, "Atomic Inducements: the Case for "Buying Out" Nuclear Latency, *Nonproliferation Review* 23 (2016): 481–493.
[51] Laura Rozen, "US Works to Assure Gulf Allies," *Al-Monitor*, May 11, 2015.
[52] Unfortunately, the rapid cooling of U.S.-German relations amid Russian revanchism in early 2017 led some in Berlin to propose the need for an indigenous German or European nuclear deterrent. But the sudden emergence of this nuclear debate in Berlin did not appear to be part of a concerted effort by the German government to extract concessions from Washington. See Ulrich Kühn and Tristan Volpe, "Keine Atombombe, Bitte: Why Germany Should Not Go Nuclear," *Foreign Affairs* 96 (July/August 2017): 103–112.

alliances with the United States have matured into healthy relationships, while the political leaders of each country have become steadily locked into civil nuclear energy programs. As a result, Japan and South Korea have the capability but no intent to threaten proliferation, despite the occasional cheap talk to the contrary about nuclear hedging from hard-line politicians in each country. In the Middle East, the Saudis and other anxious nations have clear intent but lack the capabilities needed to pressure Washington. U.S. officials may be able to limit the spread of nuclear technology in this volatile region by buying out these threats over the coming years.

CONCLUSION

KELLY M. GREENHILL AND PETER KRAUSE

Coercion is not new. Indeed, the ancient military historian Thucydides included detailed descriptions of nearly a dozen incidents of deterrence and compellence in his *History of the Peloponnesian War*.[1] However, 2,500 years on, is it still the case that "the strong do what they can and the weak suffer what they must," as the powerful Athenians say to their weaker Melian counterparts in the text's most widely recognized passage? Was it in fact ever truly thus?[2] What features of coercive bargaining are enduring, and in what ways, if any, is coercion in the twenty-first century different or even unique? Having analyzed modern coercion in nearly all its forms—intrastate, interstate, nonstate, and transnational; dyadic and triadic; military and nonmilitary—the contributions to this volume provide some definitive, some tentative, and some surprising answers to these questions.

This chapter highlights the key findings of this volume, focusing on the major lessons learned, providing a synthetic analysis of the chapters as a whole, and identifying what there is yet to learn about the causes, dynamics, effects, and outcomes of coercion. The chapter is divided into four sections. The first is devoted to a discussion of perennial concepts and theories of coercion, classics that remain relevant and valuable in the contemporary era. The second section focuses on evolutionary and revolutionary shifts in our understanding of coercion theory, which grow out of the contributions to this volume and related developments in the literature that focus on previously understudied actors, tools and mechanisms. The third section probes some of the policy implications of the volume's findings, and the final section tackles unanswered questions and future avenues for research on the power to hurt.

---

[1] Richard Ned Lebow, "Thucydides and Deterrence," *Security Studies* 16, no. 2 (2007): 163–88.

[2] Thucydides, *History of the Peloponnesian War*, trans. Richard Crawley, *Internet Classics Archive*, 5.84–116, http://classics.mit.edu/Thucydides/pelopwar.html.

The Continued Relevance of Classic Concepts

From Art and Greenhill's analytical review at the beginning of this book to Castillo's discussions of the sustained significance of nuclear weapons at the end, classic concepts of coercion remain relevant for analyzing the actors, tools, and objectives in play today. Such evergreen concepts include, but are not limited to, credibility of threats and promises, escalation dominance, the stability-instability paradox, crisis instability, and the role of (re)assurance in increasing the probability of coercive success.

Analyzing asymmetric coercion, coercing regime change, coercion by insurgent movements, and migration-driven coercion, respectively, Sechser, Haun, Downes, Krause, and Greenhill all argue that credibility remains essential to success. As Sechser and Krause both demonstrate, coercers that can credibly promise not to make more demands in the future will be more likely to succeed today. It is easier to coerce if one can reassure one's target that backing down today will not lead to more violence and aggression tomorrow. Downes identifies a particular version of this dynamic, as coercive regime change is more likely to work if a coercer can credibly threaten to deploy its superior forces *and* credibly assure the targeted leader that he or she will enjoy safe egress from power. Haun correspondingly observes that coercion may fail if coercers cannot credibly commit to offer concessions in the future in response to target cooperation.

Relatedly, and consistent with Art and Greenhill's initial observations, Krause, Sechser, Volpe, and Crawford all find that (re)assurances greatly enhance coercive success, but also highlight the potential difficulties of providing them. Volpe notes that the more potential nuclear weapons states threaten to proliferate, the harder it becomes to reassure others that compliance will be rewarded with nuclear restraint. Nevertheless there are a number of mechanisms available to solve these credibility problems, creating bargaining sweet spots that can offer attractive (or at least acceptable) outcomes to both coercer and target.

In the context of states already in possession of nuclear weapons, Castillo cautions that inadvertent escalation and crisis instability remain real and present dangers, even in a world without dueling superpowers. He asserts that in most coercive bargaining scenarios with regional nuclear powers, the regional actor will have more at stake than the United States and therefore will be more likely to risk nuclear escalation to avoid losing. In the absence of elusive near perfect counterforce capabilities, controlling nuclear escalation is but a remote possibility, a proposition with profound theoretical and policy implications.

Greenhill likewise demonstrates that escalation dominance does not require nuclear weapons. Coercive engineered migration can give those who utilize it the ability to swamp target states with (massive) unwanted flows of migrants and refugees should the coercer's demands not be met. In such cases, sanctions or war initiated by the target may be too costly or slow-acting, thus providing even relatively weak state and nonstate coercers with an escalation trump card should they possess the ability to control and/or manipulate cross-border population flows.

Finally, one of the most interesting findings of Lindsay and Gartzke's study is the existence of a cyber stability-instability paradox. Although they posit that large-scale cyber war is unlikely, they predict the world will see a great deal of provocative friction in the form of cyber espionage and crime, in part because states are constrained in their ability to escalate. This dynamic has already played out. In 2016, the United States struggled to figure out how to best respond to Russia's cyber-focused attempts to interfere with the presidential election campaign without triggering a shooting war.

Lessons from New Approaches to Coercion

Although key concepts from existing studies of conventional coercion remain valid and applicable to new circumstances, the chapters in this volume also generate a number of powerful new lessons that emerge from the authors' foci on asymmetric power dynamics and previously understudied tools, actors, and coercive mechanisms. While space constraints preclude an exhaustive accounting of these concepts, key propositions are outlined in some detail below.

Selection Effects Necessitate a Reconsideration of How One Thinks about Success Rates

Understanding the efficacy of coercion is intimately tied to assessments of its success and failure. However, the authors in this volume provide conclusive evidence that a reconsideration of how one handles such assessments is in order. In particular, the fact that coercers select the targets and objectives of coercion can skew our understanding of its efficacy because coercers are prone to choosing pliant targets and goals that are more likely to be achieved. As Sechser illustrates, coercion is a process of bargaining whereby the coercer's decision regarding the size of its demands is just as important to the outcome as the target's decision to accept or reject those demands. The coercer must strike a balance between competing interests, namely, its desire for larger concessions and the risk of triggering (and losing) a war. This leads to two unexpected outcomes: coercion by powerful actors is more likely to fail, and coercion against resolved actors is more likely to be successful. This is not because power is suboptimal for coercers or because will is disadvantageous for targets. Rather, powerful coercers make larger demands, and coercers facing resolved targets make smaller ones.

The specter of selection effects arises again in Downes's chapter when he shows that threats for regime change—perhaps the largest demand a coercer can make—succeed about 80 percent of the time, outstripping success rates for most types of coercion. However, he demonstrates that such threats are so likely to succeed because they tend to be issued *only* when the circumstances are highly favorable to the coercer.[3] The United States, for example, used threats to oust numerous foreign leaders in the Caribbean and Central America in the first two decades of the twentieth century. These countries, however, were located close to the United States and were completely overmatched in terms of military power. The United States would not issue corresponding threats of regime change in, for instance, significantly more powerful and far-flung states such as Russia or Iran today, even though the U.S. would clearly desire such an outcome.

Without an understanding of the role of selection effects in determining observed outcomes, one runs the risk of misreading the record on all aspects of coercive effectiveness. To adjust for such effects, one needs to take into account when and why actors opt for coercion in the first place. Markowitz provides one answer to this multifaceted question, explaining that states employ coercion for scarce resources (rather than relying purely on markets) the more autocratic and economically dependent on resource rents they are. Rather than taking the existence of coercion for granted, studies that identify and adjust for coercion's causes will provide far more conclusive analysis of its effects.

Power Is an Important but Complicated Variable in Coercion

A bedrock principle of coercion studies, and of international relations theory more generally, is that the powerful are more likely to succeed than are their weaker counterparts. However, chapters in this volume offer numerous examples of how the weak can resist the demands of and triumph over their stronger counterparts. Contributions herein also illustrate the need to reevaluate notions of who is defined as powerful in the first place. Greenhill and Castillo illustrate how relatively weak actors can employ, for example, coercive tools, migration, and nuclear weapons to coerce or resist powerful rivals. Greenhill explains how even nonstate actors can employ threats to unleash or manipulate migration flows to effectively pressure strong states concerned about demographic shifts and/or threats to political stability. Castillo analyzes the classic tool of early coercion studies—nuclear weapons—to argue that they provide weak states with the means to protect themselves against stronger adversaries. Straight from the U.S. and NATO Cold War playbook, countries at a disadvantage in conventional capabilities, such as aircraft, tanks, and personnel, can threaten the first use of nuclear weapons and the uncertainty of escalation to resist coercion and survive. Lindsay and Gartzke's argument about

[3] Elsewhere, Greenhill notes that that same may be true of coercive engineered migration, where success rates are also quite high (around 74 percent of the time coercers get at least some of what they seek). For success rates for all documented cases through mid-2016, see Greenhill, "Migration as a Weapon in Theory and in Practice," *Military Review* 96, no. 6 (November/December 2016): 23–36; and, for cases through the end of 2006, see again Greenhill, *Weapons of Mass Migration*.

cyber capabilities suggests similar dynamics may hold in this relatively new domain of coercion, as some countries clearly recognize.

On the flip side of the equation, Sechser argues that powerful states are emboldened to issue expansive demands with greater potential payoffs, but that those demands also carry a higher likelihood of failure. Haun takes this claim a step further, recognizing that coercion of the weak by the strong should generally succeed, as a rational strong state should not incur the costs of a coercive strategy if the weak state is expected to resist. In practice, however, Haun finds that asymmetric coercion by the most powerful country in the international system, the United States, often fails because it continues to impose sanctions or conduct military operations even after weak targets make concessions, thus providing targets no incentive to modify their behavior amid an invariable U.S. strategy of containment.

As Fraiman demonstrates, moreover, local knowledge and geographic advantages can enable even very weak states to undertake coercion with more precision and greater success than their more powerful counterparts. Such domestic advantages facilitate effective trilateral coercion. As is discussed further below, such singular advantages raise important questions about how one construes the meaning of power more generally. As such, the findings of this volume support the proposition that even in the realm of forceful persuasion, power can be issue-, context-, and behavior-specific.[4]

Even in cases of coercion where more power makes success more likely, absolute measurements of power held by unitary actors are often not the best metric for predicting success. As Krause demonstrates, an insurgent movement with prodigious amounts of personnel and weapons may be likely to fail because of extensive internal fragmentation. In contrast, a movement with fewer collective resources (and thus conventionally measured as weaker) may actually be a more effective coercer if it is dominated by a hegemonic organization that directs its strategy and ensures its credibility. In this case, the key to coercion success is the internal balance of power rather than the external sum of it.

New Tools and Dynamics Require New Theories and Approaches

Nowhere is the need for new assessments of coercion more clear than with new tools that are rapidly proliferating—cyber, drones, and smart sanctions—or long-standing tools that have renewed relevance in light of burgeoning security concerns related to climate change, insurgencies, and irregular migration and refugee flows. Lindsay and Gartzke provide in-depth typologies of cyber coercion that establish a systematic foundation (where none previously existed) from which to construct and test theories. One such theory is

[4] See, for instance, Walter Carlsneas, Thomas Risse, and Beth Simmons, eds., *Handbook of International Relations* (London: Sage, 2002), 222.

the stability-instability paradox of rampant cyber frictions but very few attacks of any consequence. Even this foundational concept requires revision in the cyber context, however, as actors have the option of disconnecting from networks and so from the threat of cyber harm, an option that is not available to them with nuclear weapons.

Drones and smart sanctions have become favored foreign policy tools of the United States in recent years, yet little is known about their effectiveness as coercive instruments. As Walsh and Drezner show, "new" doesn't necessarily mean "better." Walsh explains that, in addition to the nonexistent threat to attacking personnel, drone strikes are attractive because they are one of the most selective forms of violence due to their powerful cameras and guided missiles. Contrary to popular belief, however, he argues that they have proven far more effective as a tool of brute force and degradation than of coercion.[5]

Similarly, smart sanctions on targeted groups of elite individuals and institutions have proven to be more politically palatable for the coercer, due in part to these sanctions' more "selective" imposition of economic costs. Drezner argues that there is as yet no systematic evidence that smart sanctions are better tools of coercion than their comprehensive counterparts, however. Indeed, traditional sanctions may actually prove superior against democracies and/or when pursuing regime change due to the greater costs they impose on targets. In both cases, these favored tools of foreign policy appear to be better at reducing domestic political costs than achieving international policy objectives.

Resource wars are likewise nothing new. However, focus on them has become more prominent with recent competition in the South China Sea, as well as the melting of the Arctic and development of deep-sea drilling technologies, which together have opened up massive energy resources in one of the last unclaimed territories on earth. Markowitz provides a foundational and parsimonious theory that uses states' internal economic structures to explain variation in their decision to employ coercion to gain control of these resources and pursue exclusionary or open foreign policies.

As Crawford illustrates, diplomatic isolation is a coercive strategy with significant historical precedent. Coercive diplomacy that isolates a state—that is, reduces and weakens its ties to potential supporters—increases the costs it will be likely to endure if force is used against it. Crawford demonstrates that isolating a target state diplomatically is one of the most important things coercers can do to make their threats to use force more credible. In recent decades, the heavy focus in coercion theory on the manipulation of "audience costs" to generate credibility has obscured this fundamental aspect of power politics.

Fraiman shows that coercive isolation is even more widespread than Crawford suggests, as it is crucial for defeating the violent nonstate actors who have proliferated across the globe in recent years. The "transitive compellence"

---

[5] See also Audrey Kurth Cronin, "Why Drones Fail: When Tactics Drive Strategy," *Foreign Affairs* 92 (2013): 44–54.

strategy she describes is essentially an attempt by a coercer to isolate the violent nonstate actor (VNSA) from its base state host, thus making the VSNA's containment or expulsion more likely. Fraiman argues that this trilateral brand of coercion is both more common and more effective than is generally recognized, as many base states, even failed and failing ones, are in fact both capable and willing to effectively coerce VNSAs residing within their territory if properly incentivized.

The protests across the Arab world since 2011 have sparked renewed interest in nonmilitary coercion, yet Greenhill's study of coercive engineered migration is one of the first to examine its mechanisms and effectiveness. Such strategies not only provide new uses for old concepts like escalation dominance, but they also introduce new dynamics involving restraint, cohesion, and mass movement that existing frameworks—like the bureaucratic states on which they were built—fail to adequately understand and engage.

Previously Invisible Influences: Inclusion of Intelligence and Multiple Coercer Objectives Provides Powerful Insights

The use and effectiveness of every type of coercion—whether involving nuclear weapons, insurgency, cyber, drones, sanctions, migration, or diplomatic isolation—hinge on information concerning capabilities, intentions, and behavior. Yet intelligence as a variable rarely features in theories and analyses of coercion. Long aims to change this by demonstrating that successful coercion requires knowledge of the capabilities, will, and credibility of the coercer and target; identification of the best assets to target and discovery of their location; understanding of the past, present, and future behavior of the target to adjust strategy and assess effectiveness; and sometimes the ability of the coercer to issue and carry out threats covertly. Each of these factors requires quality intelligence and the organizations to generate it. Perfect knowledge in all of these areas is improbable, but success without intelligence in any of them is impossible.

Even a brief survey of the chapters in this volume reveals the necessity of bringing intelligence back in. Sechser shows that information matters: actors in coercive diplomacy aim to act strategically but can act only on what they know. Coercers and targets try to assess one another's power, resolve, and values, and the less they know about these three things, the greater the chances of error and the lower the chances of coercive success. Information—and, by extension, intelligence—can be decisive.

Fraiman demonstrates empirically that intelligence about targets of coercion is essential, as the more capable but less knowledgeable Turkey failed to coerce the PKK directly, but the less capable but more knowledgeable Kurdistan Regional Government did so effectively. Lindsay and Gartzke argue that no domain has greater potential for covert action than cyber due to its multiple entry points and lack of human delivery, which makes intelligence even more important to identifying, coercing, and responding to attackers and targets.

The inclusion of intelligence as an explanatory variable should generate more powerful and accurate analyses of all types of coercion.

The chapters in this volume make clear that coercers pursue multiple objectives that are often in tension with one another, whether those objectives are containment and policy change, survival and victory, or limiting death and degrading an adversary. Haun explains that strategies of containment and coercion can work at cross-purposes, as the former makes the latter more likely to fail. Economic sanctions and air power can be used to punish a target state's economy and attrit its military forces. In order for coercion to succeed, however, the threat of force must be accompanied by the credible promise to remove the threat once the target complies with demands. Krause reveals that insurgent organizations' desire for regime change is often at odds with their desire to survive, and it is only when these objectives complement each other that concerted, coercive efforts toward the former will be undertaken. Conversely, states may aim to both decrease attacks and prevent an enemy's political success in their counterinsurgency and counterterrorism strategies, but these objectives are best achieved by creating precisely opposite types of insurgent movement structures. Walsh provides evidence for this tension in counterterrorism strategy, as drone strikes appear to weaken insurgent organizations but inspire more attacks by them.[6]

Earlier studies of coercion tended to focus on singular objectives, but the contributions to this volume dramatically demonstrate that recognizing the tension between multiple objectives and how actors prioritize among them (or fail to do so) is key to understanding the dynamics and effectiveness of coercion.

Policy Implications and Prescriptions

Even a cursory perusal of contemporary newspaper headlines makes clear the continued prevalence and policy significance of coercion in international politics. To wit, as ongoing U.S.-led compellent bombing campaigns against ISIS continue (and ISIS in turn has threatened to flood Europe with still more refugees), China has threatened to use force to defend newly constructed "fait accompli" islets in the resource-rich South China Sea; parties to the recently penned Iran nuclear deal have threatened "snap-back" sanctions if Tehran fails to uphold its end of the bargain; terrorist attacks on three continents on a single day sparked fears of transnational cooperation and shared objectives across violent insurgent groups; and so on. In short, active coercion can be found on every continent, by both states and nonstate actors against other states and nonstate actors. There is moreover little reason to believe this state of affairs will change anytime soon, especially as both power dynamics and the capacity

[6] However, see Patrick B. Johnston and Aroop K. Sarbahi, "The Impact of US Drone Strikes on Terrorism in Pakistan," *International Studies Quarterly*, January 2016, online.

to credibly threaten to engage in violence and inflict pain grow more complex and more diffuse. So what lessons do the chapters in this volume offer regarding current and looming issues of international conflict, peace, and security?

Coercion Is an Iterative Bargaining Process

Using brute force to get what one wants may be appealing, but it can also be counterproductive. Coercion can sometimes succeed even against highly resolved targets; however, as Sechser illustrates, it is far more likely to do so if a coercer is willing to downgrade the magnitude of its demands. Drawing on empirical case study data, Haun echoes this conclusion, stressing that because coercion is a multistage negotiation, albeit one involving credible threats to inflict costs, strong actors must offer weak actors reasons to cooperate. Coercers must be willing to reduce or remove coercive instruments once a target complies with demands or targets will have few or no incentives to comply. Coercers must also be open to the prospect of relinquishing some of their objectives in order to end crises and reach settlements.

Moreover, concessions should not necessarily be viewed as a sign of weakness. Contrary to the claims of some skeptics in Washington and beyond, in coercive diplomacy, acquiescence does not necessarily damage a target's reputation. This is not because reputations do not matter; indeed, they matter a great deal. But their primary effect may be to push coercers into courses of action that yield no reputational inferences, as, for instance, Volpe's findings regarding potential proliferators illustrates.

Skeptics and opponents of the 2015 Iran nuclear deal should keep these lessons in mind. Specifically, the alternatives to which skeptics should compare the deal are not the outlines of a deal in which Iran would have made unlimited and unconditional concessions but rather the outlines of a deal to which the Iranians (or any target) would realistically agree. Downes's findings regarding recent failed exercises in foreign-imposed regime change point to the same conclusion. As U.S. Secretary of State John Foster Dulles put it at the height of the Cold War, "the ability to get to the verge without getting into the war is the necessary art" in the realm of coercion. This is not to suggest that brute force can never work, only that such uses of force are distinct from coercion—a point made by Schelling decades ago, yet seemingly frequently forgotten.

Invest in Intelligence and Pay Greater Attention to the Critical Role of Information

Information plays a starring role in coercive bargaining. Coercers and targets base their decisions on assumptions about the adversary's capabilities and resolve, but uncertainty can complicate these calculations. In reality it can be difficult to know the other side's military strength, willingness to fight, and values. Outcomes therefore depend not simply on the actors' military capabilities and resolve but also on their ability to learn (or communicate) this information to their relevant counterparts. Moreover, as Crawford and others show, a target's own perception of its vulnerability to coercion—that is, whether due to (relative) capabilities, geography, expectation of future costs and risks, or dependence on allies—can also play an instrumental role. Successful coercion requires knowledge of the capabilities, will, and credibility of *both* the coercer and the target.

Each of these factors requires quality intelligence and robust organizations to generate it, as Long deftly illustrates. Thus actors likely to engage in coercion—and/or be subjected to it—should invest in intelligence, play close attention to signals and information provided by both friends and adversaries, and further hone their abilities to distinguish between signal and noise.

From a more strategic perspective, heightened appreciation of the intelligence foundations of coercion could (and should) lead to more systematic evaluation of the need for certain kinds of intelligence (such as financial intelligence) that might otherwise be needlessly neglected. It could also help generate a more informed dialogue with intelligence professionals about the trade-offs in using and/or revealing certain intelligence capabilities for coercion.

Do Not Underestimate "Weak" Actors

Policymakers should be cautious about relying on relative capabilities as a measure of what is possible or probable in the realm of coercion. A failure to take weak actors seriously can undermine prospects for coercive success, make third-party coercion more difficult and complex than it need be, and heighten the risks and dangers of escalation. A number of chapters in this volume make clear that weak actors find myriad ways to help level the playing field, heightening their ability to successfully coerce (e.g., Greenhill) or resist (e.g., Castillo) actors much more powerful than themselves. As Drezner argues, strong actors should not delude themselves into believing that smart sanctions against weak actors will necessarily be effective, as it appears some in the West do vis-à-vis the mixed bag of sanctions designed to punish the Russian Federation for its behavior in eastern Ukraine. Sanctions work when the coercer is able to impose real, serious, and sustained costs on the target, and weak states, already accustomed to relative deprivation, may in fact be far less vulnerable than their more powerful compatriots. In cases where the pain is felt by the relative few—who, in the case of Russia, may have taken preemptive countermeasures—success may be still less likely.

On the flip side, as Fraiman shows, even weak states can act effectively against violent nonstate actors in their territory; here again capabilities may be less important than knowledge and the will to act. Thus, from a policy perspective, relying on aggregate measures of state capacity can lead to an underestimation of actual capacity to effectively coerce. States under threat from VNSAs have a wider array of policy options than they may recognize. Moreover, by engaging in transitive coercion, external coercers can outsource to host states many of the indirect costs and negative externalities associated with coercion.

Coercers can also indirectly exploit the unique geographic and context-specific knowledge that base states possess in the execution of this triadic instrument of persuasion, something the United States and other states should bear in mind as they select their strategies, targets, and partners in their fight against terrorist safe havens.

Beware of Foreign-Imposed Regime Change

While deposing dictators and replacing illiberal regimes may be inherently appealing, leaders should think twice, or thrice, before undertaking foreign-imposed regime change. As Downes makes clear, U.S. demands for leaders to step down in the late twentieth and early twenty-first centuries have been decidedly less successful than in earlier periods, for three reasons. First, the United States is choosing targets that are farther away and have greater capability to resist. Second, personalist dictators of the sort that U.S. policymakers have sought to oust in recent years are frequently more worried about internal threats to their rule, which causes them to discount the credibility of external threats. Third, such leaders also tend to have execrable human rights records, which reduces the attractiveness of their fleeing into exile, owing to the increased likelihood that in "retirement" they will be prosecuted for their crimes by the International Criminal Court or other judicial bodies. In other words, the likelihood of forceful threats successfully ousting foreign leaders is declining at a time when leaders of powerful liberal regimes have concomitantly become more willing to issue such threats. Liberal leaders should not delude themselves into believing that the likes of Syria's Bashar al-Assad or North Korea's Kim Jong-un will leave office peacefully in response to such threats. Leaders should thus resist issuing such threats unless they are truly willing to wage a potentially costly war to obtain regime change.

Moreover, as Greenhill argues, while targets of coercive engineered migration may find regime change attractive as a strategy to forestall future coercion, such enterprises can be costly and the outcomes uncertain, as recent experiences in Iraq, Afghanistan, and Libya make abundantly and tragically clear. Overthrowing a tyrant does not necessarily beget liberal democracy or mean an end to engineered outflows. Even in the best-case scenario, the overthrow of a sitting dictator and an increase in economic development may actually increase emigration from that state, at least in the short run. This is what many in the U.S. government fear will happen when the end of the Castro era finally comes to Cuba and, likewise, the end of al-Assad epoch in Syria and the Kim dynasty in North Korea, to cite just a few.

Recognize the Utility and Efficacy of Nonmilitary Coercive Instruments

Nonmilitary tools of persuasion—including but not limited to diplomatic isolation (Crawford), economic sanctions (Drezner, Haun), and forced migration

(Greenhill)—can be strikingly effective when skillfully deployed and selectively targeted, either alone or in conjunction with their more traditional counterparts. In some cases, they can be cheaper and less potentially escalatory than conventional force-based alternatives, while in others, they provide weak actors with unique and potentially quite consequential methods of making up for a relative paucity of military strength.

Sometimes nonmilitary tools have virtues other than their coercive power that favor their use. Drezner points out, for instance, that smart sanctions are no more (and often are less) effective at coercion than comprehensive sanctions, but they appear to solve several political problems for sender countries. Because smart sanctions are billed as minimizing humanitarian and human rights concerns, they receive only muted criticism from global civil society. Because they do not impede significant trade flows, smart sanctions can be imposed indefinitely at minimal cost. They clearly solve the political problem of "doing something" in the face of target state misbehavior, which is nontrivial as it can help ensure the survival of the sender regime to fight another day on this or other issues. They do not solve the policy problem of coercing the target state into changing its policies, however. When smart sanctions do work, which is to say, achieve their goals, they work because they impose significant costs on the target state's economy. It would behoove policymakers and scholars to look beyond the targeted sanctions framework to examine the conditions under which different kinds of economic statecraft should be deployed.

Avoid Fetishizing New Coercive Instruments

While new tools may have many virtues, they are not superweapons. As Walsh points out, for instance, drones are not a counterinsurgency panacea. Even though drones result in fewer U.S. casualties and offer selective targeting options—at least in some contexts—they may not be a particularly effective instrument of coercion for three reasons.[7] First, the United States may use them in places where it cannot or does not want to escalate beyond prevailing levels of competition or conflict. Second, fragmented insurgencies make reliable targeting more difficult. Third, drones require a permissive air environment, which is not something upon which coercers can rely.

The experience of drone use in Pakistan suggests that while drones seem to promise a cheap and easy solution to counterinsurgency dilemmas, the picture is more complex than advocates tend to acknowledge. While U.S. drone strikes have killed many militants, it is not obvious that these strikes have significantly weakened the targeted groups, which often have considerable bases of local support that enable them to survive attacks. Such attacks have also led these groups to change their behavior, in particular by increasing terrorist and

[7] Although drone pilots suffer an array of mental health issues not generally associated with manned missions.

other violent attacks within Pakistan (and beyond), an undesirable outcome that complicates U.S.-Pakistani relations.

Drones need to be more tightly integrated with other foreign policy instruments. Relying solely or primarily on drone strikes is unlikely to produce an effective counterinsurgency policy for the reasons discussed earlier. Everyone would agree with this in principle. In practice, though, there is evidence that drones have become (perhaps too much of) a centerpiece of campaigns in Pakistan and Yemen. Some suggest that the CIA devotes too much attention and too many personnel and other resources to drone strikes (John Brennan seemed to suggest this during his confirmation hearings for CIA director, for example).

This suggests that drone strikes (and strikes from manned aircraft) may have at best modest effects on ISIS. ISIS is a large and well-organized movement that has considerable capacity to ride out strikes from the air. It can also respond in ways that harm the United States, such as terrorism in Iraq, killing (Western) hostages, and sponsoring or inspiring attacks in Europe or the United States.

While this too is a controversial claim, Lindsay and Gartzke suggest there is less to fear from coercive cyber attacks than some have suggested. They contend that as long as it remains desirable to connect to the Internet tomorrow, there will be only limited harm via the Internet today. Specifically, they posit that a cyber Pearl Harbor is quite unlikely because future coercion requires states to remain plugged in, and states can respond militarily to cyber attacks, thus making large-scale aggression less attractive and less likely. On the other hand, however, these same constraints combine to make small-scale cyber aggression relatively appealing and thus more likely. This might imply a curvature to the utility of cyber coercion. Powerful, highly capable countries are vulnerable to cyber harm but can deter through other military instruments. Poor states are not vulnerable. It may be the prosperous small or digitally developing who are in trouble, since they cannot credibly deter and have high dependence on the Internet.

Choose Tools and Objectives Carefully

When evaluating success and failure, it is imperative to keep in mind that such assessments are contingent on how, when, and exactly what one is measuring and how one privileges competing imperatives. As Haun and Krause both dramatically show, objectives may cut against each other, meaning success and failure unavoidably go hand in hand. As Haun illustrates, coercing Iraq to cooperate with WMD inspections materially assisted the U.S. containment strategy while simultaneously eliminating Iraq's incentive to continue to cooperate with inspectors. Coercion failure was thus the price of containment success rather than a strategic mistake or foreign policy failure.

Similarly, as Krause makes clear with the case of Eritrea, organizational and strategic imperatives can cut in different directions, and short-term intragroup coercive successes may undermine long-term political objectives (and vice versa). If a state wants to prevent violent attacks, it should try to push for a hegemonic movement enemy. If a state wants to prevent the strategic progress of a movement, it should push for a fragmented movement enemy. In either case, unity means little, although you would not know it from the large number of state campaigns pushing for movements and insurgencies to unite. Current thinking among scholars and policymakers often addresses counterinsurgency and counterterrorism strategy without appreciating these dual objectives and the inherent tension in their achievement.

Tools and objectives of coercion must be selected carefully. Asking targets to commit political suicide or endanger their own security is likely to fail. As Crawford, Haun, and other authors show, demanding that a target relinquish a resource or cease an activity it relies upon for its security is likely to be counterproductive. For instance, as Crawford makes clear, despite its power as a nonmilitary instrument of persuasion, coercive isolation can be counterproductive if the goal is to make the target give up a resource or activity that it uses for security. Because allies are a source of security, weakening the target's alliance relationships may cause it to rely even more on the proscribed activity or resource. This lesson is broadly generalizable to both military and nonmilitary tools and is germane to cases from the Arctic Great Game outlined by Markowitz to exercises in transitive compellence elucidated by Fraiman.

While these lessons are not exhaustive, they represent an actionable selection of the collective policy-relevant insights proffered by the chapters in this volume. Taken together, these observations make clear that coercion in the twenty-first century remains a difficult and complicated proposition. Nevertheless, it is also clear that there are a variety of concrete steps actors can take to increase the likelihood of reaching successful bargaining outcomes short of full-scale conflict. These include taking into account the critical importance of the magnitude of demands; taking steps to enhance the credibility of both threats and promises (sticks and carrots); investing in intelligence; carefully evaluating relative stakes and concomitant resolve before issuing threats or demands based largely on assessments of relative capabilities; exploiting the often underappreciated virtues of new and nonmilitary instruments of persuasion while also remaining circumspect about their shortcomings; and keeping in mind the often self-sabotaging nature of conflicting objectives.

A Roadmap for Future Research

Every chapter in this volume represents a forward-looking first or second step in a research program rather than a retrospective final summation. As such, it is natural that this volume has raised as many questions as it has answered. We conclude by identifying next steps for future research to address these questions and reshape how academics and policymakers understand coercion in the twenty-first century.

New Actors, New Tools, and New Dynamics of Coercion

The authors in this volume examined new actors, new tools, and new dynamics of coercion, but there is still much to be learned. New tools and dynamics can and should be analyzed with different types of actors as coercers and targets. For example, Greenhill suggests that nonstate actors can conduct coercive engineered migration. ISIS, which has forcibly and strategically generated more than two million refugees, would make an apt jumping-off point for such analysis.[8] Fraiman provided initial evidence that one form of Crawford's coercive isolation can work against nonstate actors, and cases like the 1975 Algiers Accord—in which Iraq signed a deal with Iran that cut the latter's support for the Iraqi Kurds and coerced the insurgents to back down—provide fertile ground for an analysis of this dynamic on a grand scale.

On the flip side, Krause's theory of a coercer's internal power structure should be analyzed with state coercers whose campaigns would plausibly be impacted by the degree of internal division they suffer. In fact, this is precisely what Castillo suggests when he argues that unitary actor assumptions allow us to create a baseline for a first-cut analysis that should subsequently be relaxed. He argues that the concentration of power in a regime may make regional nuclear powers and the threat of first use and escalation even more dangerous. In any case, Castillo's study makes clear that nascent nuclear powers are understudied and undertheorized, leaving extensive gaps in nuclear coercion that need to be filled.

Drezner similarly observes that greater attention needs to be paid to the burgeoning work on politics in authoritarian countries. As Susan Allen finds, the overwhelming majority of sanctions' targets are nondemocratic polities, and the general assumption behind recent sanctions scholarship is that authoritarian leaders are better able to resist economic pressure than democratic states.[9] Clearly, however, authoritarian leaders have domestic constraints that affect their behavior in international crises.[10] Different types of authoritarian countries have different kinds of domestic constraints. A greater theoretical and empirical focus on authoritarian politics would inform both the theory and the practice of economic statecraft—and, in the process, illuminate the inner workings of nondemocratic governments.

---

[8] Sarah Kenyon Lischer, "Security and Displacement in Iraq: Responding to the Forced Migration Crisis," *International Security* 33, no. 2 (Fall 2008): 95–119.

[9] Susan Allen, "The Domestic Political Costs of Economic Sanctions," *Journal of Conflict Resolution* 52 (2008): 916–44.

[10] Jessica Weeks, "Autocratic Audience Costs: Regime Type and Signaling Resolve," *International Organization* 62 (2008): 35–64; Abel Escribà-Folch, "Economic Growth and Potential Punishment under Dictatorship," *Kyklos* 60 (2007): 187–210.

Further and Broader Testing

Contributions to this volume presented new theories and typologies, but further research, data collection, and testing are necessary to corroborate their explanatory power and identify their scope conditions. Haun's theory of asymmetric coercion requires historical analysis of variation in state choice between coercion and containment strategies, especially how successful coercion has been with and without containment (and vice versa), and why states opt to prioritize one or the other. This analysis can hopefully include identification of the point at which a state will believe it has nothing to gain from working with or giving into coercion from another state in any capacity—as seems to be the case with Israel and Iran—while others are able to make a deal in one area while still being coercive rivals in others—as with the United States and Iran on the July 2015 nuclear agreement.

Downes's argument about coercive regime change raises questions about the role of the International Criminal Court and the rise in international prosecution for war crimes in the unwillingness of leaders to step down or go into exile. In addition to addressing these issues, more analysis of the role of regime type is needed, especially personalist dictatorships that face greater domestic threats and are therefore less likely to step down. Markowitz's economic theory of foreign policy and coercion also requires quantitative and qualitative analysis to determine the extent to which it explains variation in resource competition across time and space.

The theories proffered by Fraiman, Krause, and Lindsay and Gartzke all need to be tested on a larger number of cases, although the necessary data to undertake these tests must first be acquired. Information on the foreign and domestic costs of suppressing violent nonstate actors, the strength of armed groups within insurgent movements over time, and curvature of vulnerability to cyber coercion is currently in short supply. A serious data collection effort in each area would therefore represent a significant contribution in and of itself, while also providing the empirical basis to determine how well and how far these authors' theories travel.

Coercion should be analyzed in a broader context. Many of the counterintuitive takeaways in this volume—such as multiple authors' demonstrating that strong states fail more often at coercion—are based on examining coercion (or narrow aspects of it) in a vacuum. If Sechser and Haun expanded their research from analyzing "coercive success" to "policy success"—meaning the extent to which each actor was better or worse off from the encounter—they would likely reach very different conclusions. In fact, Sechser admits that it is the high likelihood of winning the broader encounter via war that makes it more likely strong states will fail in their coercive threats, while Haun concludes that states fail at coercion because they continue to pursue a policy of containment that they value more highly.

This is doubly important for the selection effects–based findings of Downes, Haun, and Sechser (and possibly Greenhill).[11] When a state has to decide to

[11] See chapter 1 of Greenhill, *Weapons of Mass Migration*, for a discussion of potential selection effects-driven biases.

initiate coercion and explicitly set the demand, Downes reveals that it is not a huge surprise that coercers seem to be more successful than one would expect. After all, states have an interest in initiating only coercive campaigns they can win, as Haun points out. (The same might be said of non-state actors as well.) Nonetheless, powerful new insights would be gained from assessments of coercion in which the dependent variable was not achievement of a coercer's publicly stated demand but rather the shift in developments toward or away from its maximally desired objective. This way, assessments of success and failure are not tied to the public, strategic setting of demands (per Sechser and Downes), and one can better identify the impact of coercion and its true value for policy.

This advice can be expanded to analyze the outcome of situations in which both sides are trying to coerce the other. Returning to the Libya case, coercion of Libya by European states with smart sanctions was countered by coercion of Europe via migration by Libya, which was countered by military coercion by Europe, with wins and losses by both sides along the way and in the final analysis. Such coercion is therefore both cross-domain and cross-national, providing ample opportunity for weighing the impact of various coercive tools and dynamics when the context is broadened.

It is ultimately unsurprising that analysis of these new actors, tools, and dynamics of coercion opened rather than closed a Pandora's box. After all, while the findings of classic studies of coercion have thus far been more powerful, the subject matter—nuclear weapons rather than cyber weapons, drones, smart sanctions, migration, and insurgency; states rather than non-state actors; a single coercer, target, tool, and objective rather than many—was far less complex. Today these new types of coercion are not just less studied; they are also more common. Policymakers and the general public are delivering or experiencing sanctions, drone strikes, and the possibility of becoming a refugee from insurgencies every day. The authors and editors hope this volume provides a broad and deep foundation for research in these and other areas of coercion studies for many generations to come.

INDEX